The Russian Legal Practitioner

The author

WILLIAM E. BUTLER, M.A., J.D., LL.M., PH.D., LL.D., is The John Edward Fowler Distinguished Professor of Law at the Dickinson School of Law, Pennsylvania State University and Emeritus Professor of Comparative Law at University College London; Foreign Member of the National Academy of Sciences of Ukraine, the Russian Academy of Natural Sciences, and the Russian Academy of Legal Sciences. His standard treatise *Russian Law* is now in its third edition (2009) and he has published widely on all the legal systems of the Commonwealth of Independent States.

He advises international organizations, governments, and leading companies and financial institutions who invest or do business in those countries with particular reference to the interface between domestic law and practice with international investment transactions. His experience extends to banking, securities, project finance, the creation and operation of companies of all types, commercial agreements, licensing, technology transfer, privatization, finance and other leasing, concessions, economic zones, shipping, aircraft, oil and gas, nuclear power, electric power, and environmental protection.

For more than three decades he has advised on and given formal legal opinions with respect to all aspects of Russian and Soviet Law before English, American, Australia, French, and Swedish courts and tribunals and in international arbitrations, and has prepared expert opinions and reports for the Office of the Legal Advisor, United States Department of State, the United States Department of Justice, the Department of Health and Social Security of the United Kingdom, the Department for International Development (DFID) of the United Kingdom, the United Nations Office on Drugs and Crime, and for international organizations, banks, large corporations, and industry associations.

He has acted as Of Counsel to Cole Corette & Abrutyn (1988-92) and Clifford Chance (1992-94) and as Partner and Head of the CIS London Group and the Almaty and Tashkent offices of White & Case (1994-96). From 1997-2001 he was a co-founder and Senior Partner in the PwC (later Landwell) CIS International Law Firm in Moscow, and in 2002 co-founded Phoenix Law Associates CIS, a Russian law firm located in Moscow.

He is admitted to the Bar of the District of Columbia (1967) and the Bar of the Supreme Court of the United States (1970), and has been licensed by the respective Ministry of Justice in Uzbekistan (1996) and the Russian Federation (1997).

The Russian Legal Practitioner

William E. Butler

eleven
international publishing

Published, sold and distributed by Eleven International Publishing
P.O. Box 85576
2508 CG The Hague
The Netherlands
Tel.: +31 70 33 070 33
Fax: +31 70 33 070 30
Website: www.elevenpub.com

International Specialized Book Services
920 NE 58th Avenue, Suite 300
Portland, OR 97213-3786, USA
Tel: 1-800-944-6190 (toll-free)
Fax: +1 503 280-8832
orders@isbs.com
www.isbs.com

Eleven International Publishing is an imprint of Boom uitgevers Den Haag.

ISBN 978-94-90947-18-7

Printed in The Netherlands.

Preface

The reference in the title of this volume to the "legal practitioner" has been carefully chosen. It is sufficiently opaque in the English and Russian languages to give ample room to maneuver around the terminological difficulties encountered in both tongues when attempting to describe and explain the rights, duties, and legal status of those legal professionals who have acted or act on behalf of clients in legal matters in the Anglo-American and Russian legal traditions. The difficulties have been unexpectedly compounded by the ambiguities of Russian legislation regulating the Advokatura and the involvement of foreign jurists in offering legal assistance and legal services in Russia.

To fully appreciate the nuances of the issues involved, I am abandoning several decades of referring in my English-language learned writings to the "advocate", anglicizing the Russian term "advokat" (адвокат). Throughout this work, I shall refer to the "advokat" as a transliteration of the Russian term. The reason is simple enough: Russian legislation places a particular spin on the term which the English-language version does not satisfy. For the same reasons I rigorously avoid referring to the "advokat" as a "lawyer", or a "barrister", or a "solicitor", or an "attorney", or an "attorney-at-law".

With reference to the term "Advokatura", I continue my practice of using this Russian expression rather than rendering it, as many have done, as "Bar". It is most emphatically not the "Bar" in the Anglo-American understanding of that term, as I believe most foreign observers have long appreciated.

I have been "practicing" Soviet and post-Soviet law since 1968, when I gave my first professional legal opinion while a Research Associate in Law at the Harvard Law School. Although during the Soviet period such opinions were infrequent and mostly dealt with shipping, criminal, and family law matters, oddly enough the initial opinion related to a commercial investment opportunity – a foreshadowing of what was to come.

❖

Ruble figures are quoted throughout from original sources. A current approximate US dollar exchange rate would be 30 rubles to one dollar.

My gratitude to Consultant Plus in the Russian Federation for making available a personal database used to prepare this volume. Only there can an integrated text of the enactments be found which offers ready annotated access to the prior versions at every stage of amendment together with cross references to relevant subordinate normative legal acts.

status juris: 1 April 2011

Contents

Preface V

Abbreviations XI

Introduction **13**
Statistical Reporting on the Advokatura 16
Statistical Profile of the Advokatura 18
  Number of Advokats 18
  Termination of Status of Advokat 18
  Advokat Formations 19
  Employment of Advokats 19
  Applications, Complaints, and Communications against Advokats 19
  Violations of Independence of Advokats 20
  Qualifications Examinations 21
  Disciplinary Proceedings 21

Background and Context

On the History of Legal Representation in Russia **25**
Precursors of the Russian Legal Profession 30
Formation of the Russian Advokatura: 1864-1917 33
The Soviet Advokatura: 1918-1991 41
The Secret Advokatura 45
Post-Stalin Reforms of the Advokatura 47
The Post-Soviet Advokatura in Russia: 1991-2002 49

Commentary on the Federal Law of the Russian Federation "on Advokat Activity and the Advokatura in the Russian Federation"

Chapter 1 General Provisions **53**
Article 1 Advokat Activity 53
Article 2 Advokat 61
Article 3 The Advokatura and the State 75

Article 4 Legislation on Advokat Activity and the Advokatura 84
Article 5 Use of Terms Applied in Present Federal Law 86

Chapter 2 Rights and Duties of Advokat 89
Article 6 Powers of Advokat 89
Article 7 Duties of Advokat 100
Article 8 Advokat Secrecy 105

Chapter 3 Status of Advokat 113
Article 9 Acquisition of Status of Advokat 113
Article 10 Admittance to Qualifications Examination 119
Article 11 Qualifications Examination 122
Article 12 Conferment of Status of Advokat 124
Article 13 Oath of Advokat 125
Article 14 Registers of Advokats 126
Article 15 Inclusion of Information Concerning Advokat in Regional Register 127
Article 16 Suspension of Status of Advokat 131
Article 17 Termination of Status of Advokat 135
Article 18 Guarantees of Independence of Advokat 142
Article 19 Insurance of Risk of Responsibility of Advokat 145

Chapter 4 Organization of Advokat Activity and the Advokatura 147
Article 20 Forms of Advokat Formations 147
Article 21 Advokat Cabinet 149
Article 22 College of Advokats 153
Article 23 Advokat Bureau 164
Article 24 Legal Consultation Office 170
Article 25 Agreement on Rendering Legal Assistance 174
Article 26 Rendering of Legal Assistance to Citizens of Russian Federation Free of Charge 182
Article 27 Aide of Advokat 186
Article 28 Apprentice of Advokat 187
Article 29 Chamber of Advokats of Subject of Russian Federation 188
Article 30 Assembly (or Conference) of Advokats 194
Article 31 Council of Chamber of Advokats 199
Article 32 Internal Audit Commission 208
Article 33 Qualifications Commission 210
Article 34 Property of Chamber of Advokats 216
Article 35 Federal Chamber of Advokats of Russian Federation 218
Article 36 All-Russian Congress of Advokats 221
Article 37 Council of Federal Chamber of Advokats 226

Article 38 Property of Federal Chamber of Advokats 233
Article 39 Social Associations of Advokats 234

Chapter 5 Concluding and Transitional Provisions **237**
Article 40 Preservation of Status of Advokat 237
Article 41 Conducting Constitutive Meetings (or Conferences) of Advokats 239
Article 42 Conducting First All-Russian Congress of Advokats 240
Article 43 Bringing Organizational-Legal Forms of Colleges of Advokats Formed Before Entry of Present Federal Law into Force into Conformity with Present Federal Law 241
Article 44 Ensuring the Rendering of Legal Assistance Free of Charge to Citizens of Russian Federation and also Legal Assistance by Assignment 245
Article 45 Entry into Force of Present Federal Law 246

The Jurisconsult in Russia **251**
Historical Origins 251
Contemporary Status and Regulation of the Jurisconsult 254
Status of Jurisconsult 255
Functions of Jurisconsult 256
Methods Assistance 258
State Legal Bureaus 258

The Foreign Legal Practitioner in Russia **263**
Historical Background 263
Foreign Advokats in Russia 264
Foreign Jurists in Russia 266

Annex 1: Code of Ethics (31 January 2003, as amended) 267
Annex 2: Statute on Keeping the Register of Advokats of Foreign States Effectuating Advokat Activity on the Territory of the Russian Federation (19 September 2003) 287

Bibliography (with annotations) **293**

Index **303**

Abbreviations

БНА ФОИВ	Бюллетень нормативных актов Федеральных органов исполнительной власти [Bulletin of Normative Acts of Federal Agencies of Executive Power]
Бюллетень ВС РФ	Бюллетень Верховного Суда Российской Федерации [Bulletin of Supreme Court of Russian Federation]
CAdV	Code of the Russian Federation on Administrative Violations
CIS	Commonwealth of Independent States
NEP	New Economic Policy
ПСЗ	Полное собрание законов Российской империи [Complete Collected Laws of the Russian Empire]
РСФСР	Российская Советская Федеративная Социалистическая Республика [Russian Soviet Federated Socialist Republic]
САПП РФ	Собрание актов Президента и Правительства Российской Федерации [Collection of Acts of the President and Government of the Russian Federation]
СЗ РФ	Собрание законодательства Российской Федерации [Collection of Legislation of the Russian Federation]
СУ РСФСР	Собрание узаконений и распоряжений РСФСР [Collection of Legislation and Regulations of the RSFSR]

Introduction

"Legal representation" and a "legal representative" can be understood in several senses in the Russian legal system and most others. In their most basic sense, these may be an individual appearing on behalf of himself or others in a legal proceeding or simply in a legal matter (adoption, on behalf of a minor, etc.). A person may act as a legal representative by operation of law, upon request or appointment, or by being retained to provide representation services. In Muscovy (and in all likelihood, also in Kievan Rus, although specific evidence has not been discovered yet) the surviving documents indicate that such representation was known and practiced not later than the fourteenth century.

In the course of time individuals emerged who were learned in what the law provided and experienced in how the Muscovite administrative system operated. Whether these were people of cunning and purchasable, or of ability and integrity, cannot be determined with certainty. Whatever the practices were, they would need to be measured against the mores of the time. Human nature suggests both, although the surviving image in Russian folklore, anecdote, and song is not, as a rule, positive. The legal learning that existed was presumably self-taught by reading the manuscripts and studying with others who engaged in such activities; there were no formal institutions for the study of law. Universities did not exist until the Russian Academy of Sciences was established in 1724 to, under its initial mandate, both instruct and undertake research.

The terminology that evolved in the Russian language for the representative (отрешник, пособник, стряпчий, ходатай, поверенный) and the calques from foreign tongues (адвокат, юрисконсульт, юрист) give in their earlier versions the impression of the classic legal representative – a person merely acting for another – whereas the later terminology suggests a person retained and remunerated as a professional or quasi-professional to provide legal services for his principal or employer. If that be the case, the legal professional emerges in Russia during the eighteenth century onwards as an autonomous figure whose role(s) were partly dependent upon the configuration of the judicial system and the extent to which elements of adversariality were encouraged within that system.

But Russia may be unique – and certainly is unusual – in the sudden flowering that the legal profession experienced during its so-called "Golden Age" (1864-1917). This occurred under monarchical autocracy, the profession surviving in its rudiments over seven decades of Soviet authoritarianism, to emerge from 1992 into a constitutional system formally committed to a rule-of-law State. Not without reason will

Russian advokats consider that their presence in the nineteenth century contributed to the dismantling of an oppressive Imperial regime and that now they have a second opportunity to contribute to the creation of a rule-of-law State in the aftermath of the Soviet debacle.

I originally began this book in 2002 shortly after the Federal Law on Advokat Activity and the Advokatura entered into force on 1 July of that year. I was then diverted by the need to prepare the second edition of *Russian Law* (2003), but also considered it useful to observe how the profession would mature after achieving the first post-Soviet legislation to regulate its activities. This volume reflects in some measure the results of the maturation process.

It benefits from over two decades in Russian legal practice as a jurisconsult, licensed in the Russian Federation (where at the relevant time an LL.M. in Russian Law offered at the Academy University of Law, Institute of State and Law, Russian Academy of Sciences, would ensure certification) and Uzbekistan (where a formal course of continuing legal education and oral examinations were required), together with considerable time in Kazakhstan, Kyrgyzstan, Tadzhikistan, Turkmenistan, Ukraine and additional work from the other former Soviet union republics.

Russians in my experience and perception react to their own legal system and legal culture in almost schizophrenic fashion. On one hand, they demonize their law and their system ("What Russian law?!") in the media, literature,[1] memoirs,[2] and in an often appealing caustic, sardonic, and exaggerated humor to such an extent that foreigners routinely take at face value what they hear in this connection. And there is enough corruption in Russia for Russians to suspect that every person and every institution is corrupt, also not without elements of humor. These form part of the background chatter with respect to the legal system.

At the same time, Russians can be quick to litigate and as technically precocious in construing the fine points of legislation or a legal document as anyone else on this planet. Whether the legal system is a reflection or a cause I cannot be certain, but there are elements of formality and bureaucratic procedure endemic to centuries of Russian legal behavior that do separate them in degree from other legal cultures. Whatever their skepticism of the law and legal system, they feel "undressed" without an exceptionally large morass of subordinate legal acts to tell them what to do and how to do it. Likewise a matter of degree, but nonetheless perceptible. The market

1 V. V. Kapnist, Ябеда: комедия в пяти действиях [Chicaner: A Comedy in Five Acts] (Spb., 1798). See S. Kucherov for examples of the literary treatment of *striapchie* drawn from N. V. Gogol and M. E. Saltykov-Shchedrin. S. Kucherov, *Courts, Lawyers and Trials Under the Last Three Tsars* (1953), pp. 111-113. As is routinely done in English literature with respect to English law. See E. F. J. Tucker, *Intruder into Eden: Representations of The Common Lawyer in English Literature: 1350-1750* (1984).

2 See, for example, A. V. Lokhvitskii, «О наших ходатаях по делам» [On Our Solicitors], Русское слово [Russian Word], no. 2 (February 1860), pp. 43-46; P. A. Potekhin, «Отрывки из воспоминаний адвоката» [Extracts from the Recollections of an Advokat], Право [Law], no. 47 (1900), pp. 2213ff.

principle "All is permitted unless expressly prohibited" has taken root in post-Soviet society only tentatively; in my view Russians are not truly comfortable with this principle.

Unlike any other western legal culture known to me, though, Russians also extol the qualities of distinguished legal practitioners of the past and present. Even a Russian schoolchild will know the name of A. F. Koni (1844-1927), for example, the distinguished trial lawyer and legal scholar of the late nineteenth century. The courtroom pleadings of nineteenth century Russian *and later Soviet* advokats are published routinely as literature for the layman and enjoy large sales.[3] Collected biographies of Russian legal practitioners intended for the layman have been repeatedly published in the Soviet and post-Soviet periods. These are not manifestations of "hero-worship" in my perception. They are a remarkable token of respect for the contributions and rhetorical skills that this component of the legal profession has made (alas, jurisconsults have not been so singled out).

Whatever the public perception of the lawyer, moreover, the study of law has been one of the great motors of change in Russian higher education. The number of law faculties and law schools has literally exploded exponentially. In Imperial Russia by 1913 there were about 6,000 sworn attorneys, up from single numbers ca. 1865, that is, in nearly half a century. In post-Soviet Russia the numbers of advokats now exceed 66,000, having risen from a few thousand in the Russian Federation in 1991. So rapid has been the expansion that serious concerns have been expressed about the quality of Russian legal education in the lower echelons of institutions.[4] But on a *per capita* basis Russia remains "under-lawyered" in comparison with the developed industrial world.

This is the case even when one takes into account the neglected, overlooked, yet most numerous component of the Russian legal profession – the half million or more jurisconsults. Sometimes called, inappropriately, "unregulated" lawyers,[5] the jurisconsults have, as a rule, the most diversified legal experience except in criminal matters, where the advokats dominate. The foreign legal practitioner in Russia, almost invariably associated with a foreign law firm having a Russian office or other presence, is assimilated willy nilly to the jurisconsult unless the foreigner chooses to acquire the status of advokat in Russia.

In this volume we explore the legal regime of both components of the Russian legal profession – the advokat and the jurisconsult. The role of the Advokatura and the advokat is examined through the prism of the 2002 Law on the Advokatura and

3 See, for example, M. M. Vydria (ed.), Судебные речи известных русских юристов [Forensic Speeches of Noted Russian Jurists: Collection] (3d ed.; 1958). 872 p. 100,000 ptd.

4 See V. A. Tomsinov, «Преступление под названием "Юридический факультет"» [Crime Under the Name of "Law Faculty"], Закон [Law], no. 3 (2009), pp. 41-49.

5 See D. Shabelnikov, The Legal Profession in the Russian Federation (October 2008), a background report prepared for the Organization for Security and Cooperation in Europe.

Advokat Activity in the Russian Federation in the form of article-by-article commentary. References to statistical data are drawn from a vast variety of sources, including the websites of the Federal Chamber of Advokats, chambers of advokats in individual subjects of the Russian Federation, and secondary reports. Special attention is given where appropriate to the legal regime regulating foreign lawyers in Russia.

One should not draw lines between segments of the legal profession too sharply. The requirements of Russian law relating to contracts for legal services, for example, elaborated in the Federal Law on the Advokatura, are applicable to legal services generally, including contracts concluded by foreign law firms in Russia when the choice of law is Russian law. Russian advokats move in and out of foreign law firms and are often retained to assist clients of foreign law firms in matters of litigation. Foreign lawyers in Russia normally consider themselves to be bound by their own professional bar rules and regulations, whether they are "regulated" in Russia or not. Although Russian jurisconsults are not, strictly speaking, bound by the Code of Professional Ethics of an Advokat, some provisions of that Code of Ethics are of sufficient generality that all jurists would be regarded as obliged to conform to the principles set out therein.

It should be borne in mind that whatever examinations, apprenticeships, or other special training may be required by the Advokatura, or the Russian judiciary, or the notariat, the fundamental qualification for falling into the category of Russian jurist is a higher legal education from an accredited institution. This diploma confers the status of "jurist", perhaps with an additional specialization. The status of "jurist" is the prerequisite for acquiring the status of "jurisconsult", or "advokat", or judge, and so on. This is a "regulated" status. In drawing comparisons between the organization of the Russian legal profession and those of the Romano-Germanic and Anglo-American legal families, these elements must be kept in view.

STATISTICAL REPORTING ON THE ADVOKATURA

Before turning to the history of legal representation in Russia and to the 2002 Federal Law on the Advokatura, a statistical profile of the contemporary Advokatura will be helpful. Some of these statistics will recur again below in connection with individual points being addressed. They are based primarily upon submissions made by advokat formations to their respective chambers of advokats, which in turn submit reports to the Federal Chamber of Advokats. Forms are circulated for this purpose at regular intervals, and certain figures also are released by the territorial justice agencies. One example is the form circulated to advokat formations in the City of Moscow to collect "Information on the Employment of Advokats, Disciplinary Practice, and Violations of the Rights of Advokats" confirmed by the Council of the Moscow City Chamber on 22 October 2009, and a request for completed forms to be submitted before 15 January 2010.

The detail of the form must be a reflection of the types of record-keeping and statistical reporting expected of each advokat formation. While reporting compliance may not be 100% (and there are complaints from time to time about this), the percentage level of participation is over 90% and in some instances plainly cannot be less than 100% if the advokat formation is to continue to operate.

The Form is addressed to the 'executives of the management organs of advokat formation" and is divided into three sections. Section I requires "Information on the Participation of Advokats as Defenders in a Criminal Proceeding by Assignment of Agencies of Inquiry, Agencies of Preliminary Investigation, or Court". The total number of advokats in the advokat formation must be broken down into those in colleges of advokats, branches (and the number of branches), advokat bureaus, and advokat cabinets. Next should be specified the number of advokats assigned as defenders in a criminal proceeding; next the amount of payment in rubles received for such work during the reporting period, and finally the amount of indebtedness owed for performing the assigned work. The last sum is to be itemized by categories of debtor-departments: federal courts (including military and specialized), justices of the peace, agencies of inquiry and investigation of the Ministry of Internal Affairs, of the Investigative Committee attached to the Procuracy, and of other departments endowed with the right to perform inquiry and investigative functions. This data in years past enabled the advokats to campaign successfully for accelerating the payment of arrears, which in some areas had reached astronomical proportions.

Section II requires "Information on Rendering by Advokats of Legal Assistance to Citizens of the Russian Federation Free of Charge". First the form requests the number of advokats who did render such free of charge legal services, distinguished between those who did so "on a permanent basis" and those who provided "one-off" services. Next should be indicated the number of assignments to render legal assistance: (a) oral and written consultations; (b) drawing up legal documents; (c) acting as a representative in a civil proceeding; (d) acting as a representative in a civil execution proceeding; (e) acting as a representative in State agencies or other agencies and organizations. There follows an indication of the number of plaintiff indigent citizens who received legal assistance: (a) for the recovery of alimony; (b) compensation of harm for loss of breadwinner; (c) compensation for personal injury at work; (d) veterans of the Second World War; (e) citizens applying for pensions; (f) citizens who suffered from political repression; (g) minors in prevention institutions; (h) minors facing placement in juvenile institutions; (i) aged and disabled citizens in inpatient social servicing institutions; (j) persons suffering from mental distress; (k) military servicemen; (k) persons whose place of residence is unknown who are defendants in civil proceedings; and (l) others.

Section III seeks "Information on Violations of the Professional Rights of Advokats". These violations are subdivided into infringements on advokat secrecy (further subdivided into illegal interrogations of an advokat as a witness; illegal searches in the dwelling or office of an advokat; illegal operational-search measures with respect to an advokat; and others) and interference in advokat activity or obstructing such activity (failure to issue or seizure of employment certificate; refusal to admit to participate in procedural actions; refusal of meeting with client; refusal to issue documents necessary for the defense; unsubstantiated detention of an advokat; force against an advokat not involving any injury; and others.

Separately, information is asked on the number of advokats killed in the performance of their duties, as distinct from similar number of advokats injured or members of their family injured and damage to the property of advokats. Next to be reported are the number of criminal cases instituted against advokats with regard to their professional activity, or referred to a court, those deemed by a court to be not substantiated, and the termination of criminal cases. Then follows the number of complaints filed by advokats against a violation of their professional rights at the procuracy, executive of an investigative agency, or court and the number of complaints respectively satisfied by each institution or official. Guidelines are offered to avoid double counting by reason of branches of advokat formations in various subjects of the Russian Federation.

Statistical Profile of the Advokatura

The figures below come from a variety of sources, but especially the Federal Chamber of Advokats. Some will be understated by reason of reporting patterns and errors; others will be as close to absolutely correct as is humanly possible.

Number of Advokats

As of 1 January 2011 there were more than 66,000 advokats in regional registers of the 83 subjects of the Russian Federation, of whom about 2,500 were on suspended status. The number of advokats is increasing net by about 1,300 per year in the Russian Federation as a whole. In 2009 the greatest increases were recorded in Moscow City, Moscow Region, Riazan Region, and the Republic Bashkortostan. In comparison with 2008, the numbers of advokats decreased in eleven subjects of the Russian Federation. About 55% of advokats are men, and about 45% are women.

Termination of Status of Advokat

During the calendar year 2009, the status of 2,031 advokats was terminated. Of these 63% (1,281) did so by personal request. Death of the advokat was the reason in 144 instances. 28 (1.3%) were terminated by reason of being convicted for the commission of an intentional crime. 81 (4%) lost the status of advokat for the failure to perform or improper performance of professional duties in respect of a client. 78 (3.8%) violated the professional ethics of an advokat; and 233 (11.5%) had their status of advokat terminated for the failure to perform or improper performance of decisions adopted by organs of the chamber of advokats – probably failure to pay monthly contributions to expenses in most cases.

Advokat Formations

On 1 January 2010 there were 18,746 advokat formations recorded in the respective registers of the chamber of advokats. These broke down as follows into the four types of advokat formations that may exist under Russian law: colleges of advokats: 2,342; advokat bureaus: 344; advokat cabinets: 15,978; and legal consultation offices: 82.

The number of advokats on 1 January 2010 practicing within each advokat formation were as follows: colleges of advokats: 44,483 (69.7%); advokat bureaus: 2,798 (4.4%); advokat cabinets: 15,978 (25.1%); and legal consultation offices: 481 (0.8%).

Employment of Advokats

During the calendar year 2009, 38,562 advokats were assigned to act as defenders in a criminal proceeding by agencies of inquiry or preliminary investigation or a court. This was seven more than in the preceding year. The budget appropriations to remunerate this work amount to 2,735 billion rubles, or on a monthly average per advokat the sum of 5,093 rubles.

Legal assistance was rendered free of charge to citizens by 26,792 advokats, including under contracts with State legal bureaus: on a permanent basis, 20 advokats; and one-off legal assistance to a specific person, 2,028 advokats. Indigent citizens (195,189) received free legal assistance from advokats in 2009 with respect to the following matters:

- plaintiffs in first instance proceedings in courts for the recovery of alimony (33,339); death of breadwinner compensation cases (4,042); compensation for work-related injury: 4,810);
- veterans of the Second World War: 30,348;
- persons seeking the assignment of a pension: 13,432;
- minor in prevention institutions: 3,355;
- minors to be placed in prevention institutions: 5,651;
- citizens in inpatient social servicing institutions: 2,554;
- persons suffering mental distress: 2,755;
- military servicemen: 2,293;
- defendants in a civil proceeding whose place of residence is unknown: 22,919;
- other citizens in accordance with legislation of subjects of the Russian Federation: 66,238.

Applications, Complaints, and Communications against Advokats

Clients, courts, State officials and agencies, and social organizations may exercise their right to file formal complaints and other communications against what they consider to be the improper performance or failure to act of individual advokats or advokat formations.

The Federal Chamber of Advokats itself received 499 instances of recourse to it against the failure of advokats to perform their professional duties or improper performance. Of those received, 150 (30.1%) were resolved in the Federal Chamber through the giving of explanations, referral of matters to a federal agency of State power or similar agency of a subject of the Russian Federation. Some issues were submitted for consideration of the Council of the Federal Chamber of Advokats.

Many of these recourses were from the chamber of advokats themselves, some jointly with others. The majority of recourses (349) were referred to chambers of advokats of subjects of the Federation or State agencies on the grounds that the questions raised were within their competence. Others were referred to the Federal Chamber of State agencies and social organizations, including from the Administration of the President of the Russian Federation, justice agencies, the State Duma and the Soviet of the Federation, legislative agencies of subjects of the Russian Federation, and social organizations. Law enforcement agencies (13) and courts (11 special rulings and letters) were the source of a number of complaints.

The administrations of the Ministry of Justice of Russian in the subjects of the Federation received 1,440 complaints against the actions or failure to act of advokats, including 578 from courts and law enforcement agencies. Of this total, 912 were, after consideration, referred to the chambers of advokats for resolution in substance.

The chambers of advokats in the subjects of the Federation received 9,926 complaints and submissions with respect to actions or the failure to act by advokats.

Violations of Independence of Advokats

For the calendar year 2009, chambers of advokats in 53 subjects of the Russian Federation recorded a total of 1,010 violations of the professional rights of advokats. No violations were reported in 30 subjects of the Federation. The figure for 2009 is almost five times as many as for 2008, which may reflect a higher incidence of such events or greater emphasis upon reporting them.

In subjects of the Russian Federation which submitted reports for both 2008 and 2009, significant increases in violations occurred in the Republic Bashkortostan (from 6 to 43), Republic Tatarstan (from 0 to 4), Altai Territory (from 3 to 62), Khabarovsk Territory (from 1 to 19), Moscow Region (from 23 to 125), Nizhnii Novgorod Region (from 11 to 57), Rostov Region (from 38 to 74), Sverdlovsk Region (from 5 to 142), Ulianovsk Region (from 1 to 48), and St. Petersburg (from 11 to 43).

A third of the violations (399) consisted of refusals to issue documents needed for the defense of a person, especially in Moscow Region (78), Altai Territory (55), Rostov Region (50), and Sverdlovsk Region (45). The next most frequent violation was the illegal interrogation of advokats as witnesses, which happened 149 times in 2009 as compared with 47 in 2008.

Operational-search measures were taken against advokats in 2009 on 27 occasions and illegal searches of advokat premises occurred on 20 occasions.

Obstruction of advokat activity in the form of seizing and holding for an extended period documents needed for the defense from an advokat occurred 41 times. In 95 instances advokats were refused the possibility to meet with their client, especially in Sverdlovsk (30), Moscow Region (11), and Tambov Region (6). Advokats were obstructed in performing procedural actions in 117 instances.

The number of occasions on which harm was caused to the property of advokats or their families increased from two in 2008 to ten in 2009.

When violations of the aforesaid type occur, advokats, advokat formations, and chambers of advokats have the right themselves to complain, appeal, or make representations against the illegal actions of law enforcement agencies. In 2009, 631 complaints were made, including 232 to the procuracy, 185 to the executive of investigative agencies, and 214 to the courts. Of these, 203 in total were satisfied, including 69 by the procurators, 57 by the executives of investigative agencies, and 77 by the courts.

Advokats regard the failure of the State to make timely payments for legal assistance rendered under assignment by law enforcement agencies and courts to be a violation of their professional rights and independence. Representations are made especially to the Judicial Department attached to the Supreme Court of the Russian Federation about the arrears and the failure to index the amounts due for inflation. The refusal of indexation to advokats was made by the Judicial Department on the grounds that salaries of judges were not indexed. In fact, although the arrears remain substantial, they significantly decreased in 2009 as compared with 2008.

Qualifications Examinations

In the calendar year 2009, 5,997 applicants took the qualifications examination to acquire the status of advokat. Of these, 4,135 passed, or 68.9%. In some chambers of advokats (Bashkortostan, Kabardino-Balkaria, Stavropol, Voronezh, Rostov, Samara, and Tiumen) the pass rate exceeded 80%. In the Chechen Republic and North Ossetia Republic the pass rate was 100%. The pass rate was less than 50% in Marii-El, Chuvash, Altai, Irkutsk, Kemerovo, Novosibirsk, Penza, Tambov, and Tver chambers of advokats.

Disciplinary Proceedings

The presidents of chambers of advokats initiated disciplinary proceedings in 2009 with respect to 4,912 advokats, a slight increase over the 4,760 in 2008. Of this total, proceedings were terminated in 2,099 cases, and advokats were subjected to disciplinary sanctions in 2,813 cases. Of these, 338 advokats were disciplined for the improper performance of their duties as defender in a criminal proceeding at the assignment of agencies of inquiry or preliminary investigation or a court; 11 were deprived of the status of advokat.

420 advokats were disciplined for actions incompatible with the professional ethics of an advokat, broken down as follows: failure or improper performance of duties to a client (81); violation of the Code of Professional Ethics of an Advokat (78); failure to perform decisions of the organs of a chamber of advokats (233); and entry into legal force of a court judgment convicting an advokat of an intentional crime (28).

Territorial justice agencies sent 190 recommendations to the chambers of advokats about terminating the status of advokat. These recommendations were considered by the chambers of advokats, and 64 advokats were disciplined, including 26 deprived of the status of advokat. In addition, the territorial justice agencies forwarded 307 complaints by citizens, agencies, and organizations to the chambers of advokats for consideration. Of these, 71 advokats were disciplined, including ten deprived of the status of advokat.

Those advokats deprived of the status of advokat appealed the decision to a court in 109 instances. The courts found in their favor with respect to 18 decisions, usually on the grounds that the disciplinary sanction was incommensurate with the offense committed. Most courts, however, did not consider it appropriate to examine the advisability of the disciplinary sanction imposed and confined themselves to determining whether the procedures for a disciplinary proceeding had been complied with as established by the Code of Professional Ethics.

Territorial justice agencies sent two applications to a court requesting that the status of advokat be terminated with respect to three advokats. These requests were granted by the court.

Background and Context

On the History of Legal Representation in Russia

Legal representation, that is, the right and/or practice to have another individual appear to speak on one's behalf and to act in one's interest in a court of law, has a venerable history in Muscovy and Imperial Russia. Whether individuals who acted in this capacity with frequency or routinely may collectively be described as a legal profession or even the antecedents of the legal profession is more problematic, although not to be dismissed completely.

The periodization of the history of the legal profession in Russia has concentrated upon the Advokatura and its precursors to the detriment of the jurisconsult. A standard approach identifies four periods: (1) the pre-Advokatura times prior to the judicial reforms of 1864; (2) the classical Russian Advokatura (1864-1917); (3) the Soviet Advokatura (1917-1991); and (4) the modern Russian Advokatura (post-1991).[1]

The surviving documents from Kievan Rus do not mention the institute of representation in any form. The presupposition is that personal appearance in court was expected and required.[2]

The "pre-Advokatura" period in its early stages is the history of legal representation as such rather than the emergence of a group of professionals specializing in such representation. The Novgorod Judicial Charter made provision in several places for a "representative" (ответшик) to act on behalf of a party. There were no limitations on who could so act. In the Kaiser translation:

> 5. And at court [there should be no more than] two men. If someone selects someone [else to represent him in court], then he must allow him [his representative] to conduct the case. …
> 15. If a representative from some plaintiff presents himself at court, and

1 See A. V. Klevtsov, «Периодизация истории российской адвокатуры» [Periodization of the History of the Russian Advokatura], Адвокатская Палата [Advokat Chamber], no. 6 (2006), p. 4; also see A. V. Vorobev, A. V. Poliakov, and Iu. V. Tikhonravov, Теория адвокатуры [Theory of the Advokatura] (2002), pp. 444-447. Among the weaknesses of this periodization are not merely overlooking the jurisconsult and minimizing gradations in the role of the *striapchii*, but also linking the history of the institution to changes in political regime rather than, for example, the legislation on the legal profession.

2 See T. M. Shamba and V. N. Kokin, Адвокатура в Российской Федерации [Advokatura in the Russian Federation] (3d ed.; 2010), p. 26.

> the complainant will not have kissed the cross [to be faithful] to this charter, then the complainant is to kiss the cross alone, and the defendant in his place answers [the charge]; but [if] he does not kiss the cross, then he loses [the case].
> 18. If they summon a boyar or man of middling means or merchant to his land, or to [his] wife's land, then he [himself] is to answer [them] or send a representative in his place and in [his] wife's [place], [and] kiss the cross on that.
> 19. And the representative [whom the defendant nominated] and a character witness are to kiss the cross at the hearing.....
> 32. If a representative be in someone's place [and he] received a postponement, but before [the expiration] of that postponement the replacement died, then at the [expiration of the] postponement the litigant himself must appear [in court] or [he must nominate] some other representative [to appear in his place]; if he himself does not appear or if he does not nominate another representative [to appear in court in his place], then he loses the case.[3]

The text of the Novgorod Judicial Charter is incomplete, dates from about the 1470s, and incorporates elements reflecting the Muscovy presence in that principality. The extent to which these factors corrupt a pure Novgorodian account of legal representation can only be the subject of speculation. It is noteworthy, though, that these texts are believed to record the existence of customary practices rather than to newly create and introduce the concept of representation.

Legal representation under the Pskov Judicial Charter (point 58) was permitted in a more limited way to women, children, monks, nuns, or any person who is old or deaf; they might have a "helper" (пособник).[4] Officials were excluded from acting as a representative in order to avoid undue influence upon the court.

---

3 See Daniel H. Kaiser (transl. & ed.), *The Laws of Rus' – Tenth to Fifteenth Centuries* (1992), pp. 79, 81, 84. I have modified the translation of point 15, as the translation plainly contains a typing error there.

4 Kaiser, *The Laws of Rus' – Tenth to Fifteenth Centuries* (1992), p. 97. The Pskov Judicial Charter is believed to date from 1397 to 1467 and to incorporate norms from a variety of sources, among them the Russkaia Pravda, decrees of the veche, a form of popular assembly, princely charters of Alexander (1327-1330) and Constantine (1404-1417), decisions of the ruling council, and rules of customary law. See R. Hellie, in ibid., p. xxiii. In describing this period, modern Russian historians of the advokatura use the term poverennyi (attorney) to describe the type of representation available. It should be noted that the original sources do not use that word and its aptness is subject to doubt.

Vladimirskii-Budanov doubted that "hired attorneys" were possible in this period: "this is evident from the fact that the Pskov Judicial Charter (point 71) prohibited the same attorney from conducting two cases on the same day".[5]

The possibility of the plaintiff or defendant not appearing in court was provided for by the 1497 Sudebnik (Article 36),[6] in which event they might send a representative to replace them. In the 1550 version of the Sudebnik (Article 13) the parties might have representatives in the form of *striapchie* and *poruchniki* in the event of a judicial duel. Whether these should be likened to legal representatives or to "seconds" is not clear,[7] nor do the materials definitively disclose whether persons acting in these capacities were "retained" or "hired" for these roles.[8] By the end of the sixteenth century the judicial duel had disappeared from Muscovite legal proceedings and the passages of the 1550 Sudebnik were eliminated or revised accordingly.[9]

The 1649 Sobornoe ulozhenie (Chapter 10, points 108 and 109) reinforced the right of a party to be represented by another under specified circumstances:

> But if a plaintiff or defendant becomes incapacitated prior to that continuance date, and because of illness he is unable to come to the chancellery by any means: he shall send on the appointed date someone whom he trusts in his stead to pursue the suit or the defense. If someone fails to send someone in this stead on that mutually agreed date to pursue the suit or defense: direct the verdict against him in that case for that reason [point 108]...
> If that plaintiff on the appointed date or after the date proceeds to send in his stead for the trial his son, or kinsman, or anyone else; and he him-

5 M. F. Vladimirskii-Budanov, Очерки истории русского права [Survey of the History of Russian Law] (6th ed.; Spb.-Kiev, 1909), p. 616. Also see Iu. G. Alekseev, Псковская Судная грамота и ее время. Развитие феодальных отношений на Руси XIV-XV вв. [Pskov Judicial Charter and Its Time: Development of Feudal Relations in Rus XIV-XV Centuries] (1980).

6 See the translation by Horace W. Dewey, *Muscovite Judicial Texts 1488-1556* (1966), p. 15. The text is suitably vague, referring merely to "someone" to act as the substitute in order to request a postponement.

7 For a translation of the 1550 Sudebnik, see Dewey, *Muscovite Judicial Texts 1488-1556* (1966), pp. 49-50. Dewey translates the term *striapchii* as "backer" or "second". Ibid., p. 93.

8 O. I. Chistiakov (ed.), Российское законодательство X-XX веков [Russian Legislation X-XX Centuries] (1985), II, pp. 58, 99. A legacy of the Soviet era is that the Commentary to these articles makes no reference whatsoever to their implications for legal representation in Russia. For the assumption that these officials were remunerated for their services and constituted "hired attorneys", see A. G. Kucherena], Адвокатура в условиях судебно-правовой реформы в России [Advokatura in Conditions of Judicial and Legal Reform in Russia] (2009), p. 10. Also see S. Kucherov, *Courts, Lawyers and Trials Under the Last Three Tsars* (1953), p. 109: "Subsequent codes – the *Sudebniki* of Ivan III and Ivan IV, as well as the *Ulozheniye Tsarya Alekseya Mikhailovicha*– speak of hired representatives in court as of a well-established institution" (pp. 107-108).

9 See A. S. Smykalin, Русское законодательство конца XVI -- начала XVII века [Russian Legislation at the End of the Sixteenth and Early Seventeenth Centuries] (2005), p. 61.The 1589 Sudebnik had eliminated reference to the judicial duel and, accordingly, to the *striapchie* in this connection.

> self at that time is unable to go to trial because of illness or for any other reason: order that person whom he sends to trial in his stead to pursue the suit in his stead.[10]

Whether such representatives were retained or hired is not disclosed by the texts of the legislation. In short, the institute of representation was established by Muscovite legislation, but the extent to which such representation could be said to constitute the embryo of an organized legal profession is obscure.[11]

The *striapchii*, *poruchnik*,[12] "helper", and others described as representatives throughout the medieval period of Rus and Muscovy in various forms of documents are not discrete classifications. Of the terms that endured into the Enlightenment, the *striapchii* is best known in a variety of meanings. Pushkarev confirms that in Muscovite legal documents the *striapchii* was an aide, second, or representative of litigants and later came in the eighteenth and nineteenth centuries to designate persons who acted as "private solicitors" in the commercial courts. However, during the seventeenth century the *striapchie* collectively comprised a group and rank of men in service numbering perhaps as many as 800.[13] In the hierarchy of ranks they followed the *stol'niki*.[14] Some usages appear to confirm that the *striapchii* undertook to represent litigants before courts, whether remunerated or not; it is the mixing or confusion of roles that remains in doubt (i.e., did they act in the interests of the litigant represented or actually operate as court officials on behalf of the "State"). The term "poverennyi" (attorney) traces back to the 1690s, but without specific juridical usage.[15]

The term "advokat" dates from the Petrine period, ca. 1713.[16] In the "Concise Depiction of Trials or Judicial Litigation of 1715", Chapter 5 of which was entitled "On

10 R. Hellie (transl. & ed.), *The Muscovite Law Code (Ulozhenie) of 1649* (1988), I, p. 38.

11 Nonetheless, modern Russian advokats suggest that these legislative enactments indicate that the "institute of hired attorneys" existed. See Kucherena, Адвокатура в условиях судебно-правовой реформы в России [Advokatura in Conditions of Judicial and Legal Reform in Russia] (2009), p. 10.

12 The term *poruchnik* suggests an individual acting more as a second, or a guarantor, than a representative, although representation functions are implicit in those roles. The term is used in the 1497 Sudebnik.

13 See M. T. Poe, *The Russian Elite in the Seventeenth Century: A Quantitative Analysis of the "Duma Ranks" 1613-1713* (2004).

14 S. G. Pushkarev (comp.), *Dictionary of Russian Historical Terms from the Eleventh Century to 1917* (1970), p. 150. See the various examples of usage given in V. B. Krysko (ed.), Словарь русского языка XI-XVII вв. [Dictionary of the Russian Language XI-XVII Centuries] (2008), XXVIII, p. 203. In its legal usage the *striapchii* is equated to the *khodatai*; the term is traced in written sources to the 1497 Sudebnik. Poe places the striapchii just after the zhiltsy and two beneath the Dvoriane Moskovskie and stol'niki with the category of "Sub-Duma" court ranks. See Poe, *The Russian Elite in the Seventeenth Century: A Quantitative Analysis of the "Duma Ranks" 1613-1713* (2004), II, p. 24.

15 G. A. Bogatova (ed.), Словарь русского языка XI-XVII вв. [Dictionary of the Russian Language XI-XVII Centuries] (1989), XXV, p. 148.

16 Iu. S. Sorokin (ed.), Словарь русского языка XVIII века [Dictionary of the Russian Language XVIII Century] (1984), I, p. 25. The term "advokat" was initially introduced in Russian to describe a western European institution.

Advokats and Empowered Persons", litigants who were unable to appear in person in court were allowed to use advokats and other persons.[17] Although this is the first legislative use of the term "advokat", the advokat in this instance was a representative and did not differ in status from the terms used for a "representative" in earlier Russian legislation.[18] That is, the advokat replaced or substituted for the plaintiff or defendant and did not appear side by side with him to defend his interests.

Pursuant to an Edict of 5 November 1723, civil cases were prepared for hearing not by the *striapchii*, but by State officials. The parties need merely submit their requests, documents, and evidence, after which the court considered the matter. Procedural periods for considering cases were not established by legislation, which gave officials the opportunity to delay consideration arbitrarily without informing the parties as to where the case stood. This became an occasion for bribery and for seeking the assistance of others to determine at what stage the proceeding was.

Whether such views were just or otherwise, modern Russian advokats see the role of the *striapchii* becoming one in which his formal role was to collect and draw up documents, to confuse matters, to drag out and delay consideration of the case; individuals retained the services of the *striapchii* precisely to this end and evaluated the quality of services rendered against these criteria.[19] A modern critique recites that the "principal distinctive feature of the status of the *striapchii* lies in the fact that he was not linked either by control on the part of a professional corporation or by self-control in complying with professional standards. The *striapchii* was in principle unable to be in an estate and his essence was contrary to being organized in any way and to social solidarity".[20]

Perhaps reflecting his Scottish legal education, the first Russian professor of law in the Russian Empire, S. E. Desnitskii (c. 1740-1789),[21] used the term "advokat" in

17 This document may have been composed and published as early as 1712 but assuredly appeared as a separate book in March 1715. A month later it was published in a single volume together with the Military Statute, with which it is often confused. Some believe that Ernst Friedrich Krompen prepared the first draft, which may explain the introduction of the European term. Peter the Great is believed to personally have edited and added to the draft.

18 See O. I. Chistiakov, in A. G. Mankov (ed.), Российское законодательство X-XX веков [Russian Legislation X-XX Centuries] (1986), IV, pp. 404-405.

19 See Kucherena, Адвокатура в условиях судебно-правовой реформы в России [Advokatura in Conditions of Judicial and Legal Reform in Russia] (2009), p. 11. The qualities of the *striapchie* figured in European perceptions at the time of their own legal personnel: "[Jurists] ... were regarded as a boon to the rich, who could pay for their services and so prolong legal proceedings indefinitely, but as a bane to the poor, who could often afford to be represented only by half-trained but glib impostors, falsely claiming to be learned jurists. As a class jurists were seen as unscrupulous and bad Christians ... and there were many popular stories of how St Peter waited in vain at the gate of heaven for a jurist to appear". P. Stein, *Roman Law in European History* (1999), p. 92.

20 A. V. Vorobev, A. V. Poliakov, and Iu. V. Tikhomirov, Теория адвокатуры [Theory of the Advokatura] (2002), p. 59.

21 See the biographical account in V. A. Tomsinov, Российские правоведы XVIII-XX веков [Russian Jurists of the XVIII-XX Centuries] (2007), I, pp. 131-156.

his concept of the "general-advokat". In his conception the "general advokat" would be a State prosecutor or plaintiff who would in the civil and criminal courts by his presence determine that "everything in detail may be judged according to the decrees" and perform certain pre- and post-conviction functions.[22]

On 7 November 1775 Empress Catherine II elaborated a reform of State territorial-administrative division introduced by Peter the Great in 1708 and divided Russia into forty *guberniia*.[23] Pursuant to the reform the *striapchii* became an aide to the procurator and the protector of treasury interests.[24] However, these *guberniia striapchie* could not bring suit in court other than with the prior approval of the *namestnik* governing body, having presented their evidence to that body first. These roles were enhanced in further administrative-territorial reforms introduced in 1785. In the Charter on the Rights, Freedoms, and Privileges of the Well-Born Russian Nobility, dated 21 April 1785, the *striapchii* was assigned the function of overseeing that the Assembly of the Nobility did not impose requirements in violation of legislation (point 49) and of defending the Assembly of the Nobility in court (point 56). The same tasks were placed on the *striapchii* serving towns under the Charter on the Rights and Benefits for the Towns of the Russian Empire, also issued on 21 April 1785 (points 37, 44, 45) and was included in the unpromulgated State Charter to the State Peasants (points 14, 21).[25]

Who might be appointed to act as *striapchii* is not indicated. There were no requirements of age, education, moral qualities, or experience. Whether graduates of the Law Faculty at Moscow University entered service as a *striapchii* remains to be investigated.

PRECURSORS OF THE RUSSIAN LEGAL PROFESSION

In the western provinces of the Russian Empire the situation was rather different. The Lithuanian Statute of 1529 made reference (in the English translation) to the "advocate", providing that "On matters concerning estates, damages, [or] violence, no foreigner may speak as an advocate concerning that [matter] neither before us, the sovereign, nor in a land trial, but only one who is landed in the Grand Principality".[26]

22 For a translation of the Desnitskii proposal, see P. Dukes, *Russia Under Catherine the Great* (1978), I, pp. 52-53.

23 ПСЗ, XX (1st ser.), No. 14,392, pp. 229-304.

24 In his summary account of this enactment Dukes calls the *striapchii* an "attorney". See Dukes, *Russia Under Catherine the Great* (1978), I, p. 144.

25 See D. Griffiths and G. E. Munro (transl. & eds.), *Catherine II's Charters of 1785 to the Nobility and the Towns* (1991). See the references under Provincial Solicitor and Solicitor. These usages of the term *striapchii* contrast sharply with the usage in point 92(16) of the Charter on the nobility, where reference is made to the hierarchy of ranks.

26 See Karl von Loewe, *The Lithuanian Statute of 1529* (1976), p. 63. The Cyrillic texts form the basis of von Loewe's translation; the word translated as "advocate" in the original was "procurator",

The principle of legal representation of one person in place of another was replicated in the 1529 Lithuanian Statute, subject to certain documentary formalities, in much the same version as the 1497 and 1550 Sudebniks.

A form of advokatura existed in the nine guberniia (six Belorussian and Lithuanian and three Ukrainian) of Russia comprising the Western Territory which became part of the Empire in the late eighteenth century as a result of the Partition of Poland. The advokatura was organized and operated under the Lithuanian Statute and the Polish constitutions of 1726 and 1764 and was attached to the guberniia and lower (uezd and city) courts, including canon law courts.

A Report confirmed by the Emperor on 14 December 1797 of the Ruling Senate on the situation in the Lithuanian province observed that abuses were occurring by people who had knowledge of the laws and rights of litigants and who stirred up litigation, increasing the caseload of the courts. To redress the situation it was decided to increase the requirements for becoming an "advokat" in the province. An advokat should be a noble, have his own estate villages in, at least, the province, know the laws, comply with his oath, and be of good character. Those who acted as a *striapchii* might be excluded from this status if he appeared in court while intoxicated or neglecting a case by reason of drunkenness or discovered to be gambling.[27]

Young people who wished to become advokats were called "applicants" (pupils) and prepared to be given the title of advokat by studying with experienced advokats called "patrons". The patrons assumed responsibility for their pupils before the court and law and could be accompanied by the pupils in court. In certain instances the patrons could actually send their pupils to act in court in place of themselves but under their responsibility.

By an Edict of 25 June 1840, the operation of Russian civil and procedural legislation was extended to the Western Territory and the advokats there were replaced by the attorney (*poverennyi*) common throughout the Russian Empire.

Russian legislation also made provision for certain categories of the clergy and military, merchants, and others accused of a crime, that is, individuals whose rank or title attached them to a particular department of the State, to be represented by

defined in the glossary as the "representative of a litigant in court" (p. 194). The versions of the Lithuanian Statute of 1566 and 1588 contained similar norms. See I. N. Kuznetsov and V. A. Shelkoplias, История государства и права Беларуси [History of State and Law of Belarus] (Minsk, 2004), pp. 48-60. A recent Russian translation used the expression "entrusted person" (доверенное лицо) rather than "advokat" to translate "procurator", noting that this term and institution was a new phenomenon in Lithuanian law. The usage of the term gives grounds "... to speak about the 'procurator' as a specialist actually hired and highly-paid, that is, an advokat in the contemporary understanding". But the term "advokat" in the early sixteenth century meant a "governor-general" in court cases in the Grand Principality of Lithuania "as in the countries of Europe at that time". See S. Lazutka, I. Valikonyte, and E. Gudavicius, Первый Литовский статут (1529 г.) [First Lithuanian Statute (1529)] (Vilnius, 2004), pp. 283, 378.

27 Summarized in Kucherena, Адвокатура в условиях судебно-правовой реформы в России [Advokatura in Conditions of Judicial and Legal Reform in Russia] (2009), p. 12.

"deputies" from those departments. Landowners might be deputies of their peasants. Interrogations and investigative actions were to be carried out in the presence of these deputies except for (1) initial investigative actions; (2) investigation of an incident on the basis of "hot pursuit". These deputies were subdivided into the categories of "permanent" and "temporary".

The permanent deputies were individuals from the clergy, petty bourgeoisie, and merchants assigned to this task. The others were temporarily assigned to a particular investigation only. The permanent deputies were summoned to duty on the basis of a writ issued by the investigators; temporary deputies were assigned by the leadership of the departments to which they were affiliated. If for any reason an investigator arrived to perform his duties and there was no deputy, the local head of the *volost* or the *starshina* was summoned to remain until the investigation was completed or the deputy arrived.

The rights and duties of permanent and temporary deputies were regulated by legislation. They watched over the correctness and completeness of the investigation and by their signature so certified. If they disagreed with any action or failure to act by the investigator, they might set out their own view, which was attached to the file of the case. Deputies might be present as well during civil matters. They were, in substance and concept, acting more in the role of a verifier of the investigation than a defender of the person under investigation.

On 14 May 1832 the institute of the sworn *striapchii* was introduced by legislation in the commercial courts first established in St. Petersburg and Moscow and later in Odessa, Warsaw, and elsewhere. The sworn *striapchii* duly registered enjoyed a monopoly on the right of audience in the commercial courts in cases between private individuals. The list of persons who might engage in practice in the commercial courts included those who submitted attestations, service lists, or other evidence of their rank and behavior. It was left to the commercial court at its discretion to include the applicant on the list or to decline to do so orally without giving reasons. A person admitted to the ranks of the sworn *striapchii* took an oath. The courts were instructed to admit a sufficient number of sworn *striapchie* so that litigants could make a choice readily among possible individuals; however, the institute was so devised that the *striapchii* was dependent entirely upon the judge. A *striapchii* could be excluded from the list without reasons given. Nonetheless, despite the limitations and restrictions, the sworn *striapchii* was remunerated by the principal in the case on the basis of a contract.

There also existed the so-called "underground" or "street" advokatura composed of individuals who were well acquainted with the court system and officials and sought to influence the course or outcome of cases through the manipulation of legal technicalities or other forms of influence. They literally often gave their "consultations" to clients in pubs and were in the public mind during the eighteenth and nineteenth centuries associated with false accusations. As a rule, they had no formal legal education or knowledge of the law. Rather than prohibit their activities, the State sought to regulate them in rudimentary form. Under a Law of 15 October 1809, all persons in Moscow and St. Petersburg acting as *striapchie* were required to register with the police at the Address Office and to leave their internal passport or residence permit; they were thereupon issued with a residence document that served simultaneously as a residence permit and a certificate of approval to engage in their professional activity.[28]

Most of these "solicitors" remained unregulated; their presence and their activities were cited as being among the factors that led to the introduction of the judicial reforms in 1864.

Formation of the Russian Advokatura: 1864-1917

Few contest the characterization of the years 1864 to 1917 as the "Golden Age" of the Russian legal profession. The issues are rather: why and how did the Golden Age come to pass? Was it the immediate and spontaneous consequence of the enactment of legislation on judicial reform and the establishment of the Advokatura? Or was it part of the culmination of decades of increasing legal professionalization within the Russian State: that is, was it not the result rather than the commencement of legal modernization processes at work in Russian society. The case is compelling that the latter offers a better explanation.[29]

Although the point has been well made that in some measure, at least, the westernization processes instituted by Tsar Aleksei Mikhailovich and accelerated by Peter the Great represented in the field of law the development of a western legal consciousness in Russia,[30] there were Russian sources of strength to draw upon, not least the elements of a Russian legal consciousness already in place. Although Peter the Great identified "legality" (законность) with his commands expressed in legislation, hardly surprising given his view of autocracy and the fact that his realm was at war for most of his reign, the emphasis upon compliance with the written (and now printed) text represented a dramatic change for most Russians, symbolically

28 Russian doctrinal writings disagree as to whether the registration requirement extended only to solicitors in commercial cases (ходатай по делам) or to all *striapchie* in the communities concerned.

29 Most modern Russian historians of the Advokatura accept the "spontaneity" approach, as did S. Kucherov, *Courts, Lawyers and Trials Under the Last Three Tsars* (1953). For the contrary view which emphasized the lengthy gestation period during which the forces of legal modernization gathered momentum, see R. S. Wortman, *The Development of a Russian Legal Consciousness* (1976); and reviews thereof in *The American Journal of Legal History*, XXI (1977), pp. 342-346 (H. J. Berman); *Journal of Modern History* (March 1978), pp. 178-183 (Marc Szeftel); *The Slavonic and East European Review*, LVII (1979), pp. 296-297 (W. E. Butler).

30 See H. J. Berman, *The American Journal of Legal History*, XXI (1977), p. 344.

embodied in the zertsalo whose presence was required throughout the country in Russian courts.[31]

Although the teaching of law was initially left in the hands of foreign jurists appointed to the Academy of Sciences and Moscow University, young Russians sent to Scotland for study and research in law returned to take up appointments at Moscow University and enrich the discipline of law with publications influenced by the thinking of Adam Smith and his followers.[32] Moot courts were introduced into Russian legal education by Ivan Tretiakov and S. E. Desnitskii at Moscow University. The earliest Russian doctrinal writings in law included a translation of volume one of William Blackstone's *Commentaries* at the specific behest of Catherine II . The celebrated Nakaz of Catherine the Great, widely translated and disseminated throughout Europe and America, secured for Russia an eminent place in the cause of Enlightenment law reform.[33] The utilitarian thought of Jeremy Bentham was influential in Russia by virtue of his visit there in 1786 and continuing contacts with circles close to the court of Catherine II and Alexander I . Catherine II experimented with courts of equity and introduced reorganizations of the Russian administrative structure that had implications for the legal profession.

The ministerial reforms introduced by Alexander I in 1802 led to the formation of a single body of officials possessing specialized training in law, appointed more on the basis of ability and education than ancestral lineage and rank, and sharing a commitment to justice and even to the rule of law. They gradually replaced an elder generation comprising an "isolated caste without a sense of its own importance or dignity", as Wortman so aptly expressed the position. The ministerial reforms were followed by a substantial initiative headed by Mikhail Speranskii , partly under Bentham 's influence, to codify Russian law. The early efforts fell victim to the Francophobia that attended Napoleon 's invasion of Russia. After the Congress of Vienna in 1815 there was a specific rejection of a role for Jeremy Bentham[34] and a turn to the historical roots of Russian experience influenced by the writings of Friedrich Carl von Savigny. Alexander I returned to the task of codification late in his reign and rehabilitated Speranskii from exile. His successor, Nicholas I, resolved to complete

31 See "On the Formation of a Russian Legal Consciousness: The Zertsalo", in W. E. Butler, *Russia and the Law of Nations in Historical Perspective* (2009), pp. 91-101.

32 Among those who influenced the choice of Glasgow was Théodore Tronchin, a Geneva physician close to Voltaire and the French royal family, whose son studied at Glasgow. Desnitskii and Tretiakov took Adam Smith's courses in ethics and jurisprudence and studied civil law with John Millar. "Both became dedicated Smithians who devoted their subsequent careers to propagating and adapting his ethics and jurisprudence for Russian purposes". See N. Phillipson, *Adam Smith: An Enlightened Life* (2010), p. 170.

33 See W. E. Butler and V. A. Tomsinov, *The Nakaz of Catherine the Great: Collected Texts* (2010).

34 See J. Bentham, *Papers Relative to Codification and Public Instruction: Including Correspondence with The Russian Emperor, and Divers Constituted Authorities in the American United States* (1817).

the task with despatch and took resolute measures to form a team that could bring the project to completion.

The ministerial reforms were followed quickly by an expansion of the three universities within the Russian Empire (Moscow, Vilnius, Dorpat) and the establishment of universities, or institutions which soon became universities, in St. Petersburg, Kazan, and Kharkov. Law was taught from the outset at all of these.

In 1828 Speranskii and M. A. Balugianskii were invited within the Second Section of His Imperial Majesty's Personal Chancellery to form a group of able young Russians to assist with the systematization of law underway and to continue their studies in law as advanced postgraduates. The scheme included a period abroad at German universities. Upon their return several were appointed to chairs at Russian universities.

By 1833 Russia had achieved the nucleus of a trained professoriate in law, a considerable number of law graduates appointed to civil service positions, an impressive expansion of higher legal education, and a systematization and codification of legislation unrivalled elsewhere in the world. By the 1840s the legal staffs of Russian administrative and judicial agencies were manned primarily by law graduates. As these individuals rose in seniority and position, they encouraged the introduction of an independent judiciary, trial by jury, and adversarial legal procedures. By the early 1860s they succeeded in overcoming the reluctance of the ministers and the suspicion of the Tsar. The outcome was emancipation of the serfs in 1861 and the introduction of the judicial reforms of 20 November 1864. There occurred, in Wortman's expression, "an emancipation of legal expertise" essential in an industrializing, modernizing social system and increasingly complex and extended State administrative structure.

The innovations of 1864 should not be idealized or exaggerated. Those reforms introduced the "sworn attorney" (присяжный поверенный) into the Russian legal system, who operated together with the sworn *striapchii* in the commercial courts, the private attorney later introduced, the jurisconsult, and junior attorneys whose role will be addressed below.

The sworn attorney and the advokatura with which he was associated represented the highest echelon of the Russian legal practitioner. The Statute on Sworn Attorneys was first published for discussion and comment on 30 September 1862. More than 400 comments were submitted from throughout the realm; these were published in six volumes. A commission made up of thirty officials from the State Chancellery, Ministry of Justice, Ministry of Internal Affairs, Ruling Senate, *guberniia* judicial institutions, and others considered all the comments, summarized them, and then incorporated them as appropriate into a draft Statute which in turn was to be inserted into the Digest of Laws of the Russian Empire.

The judicial reforms entered into force on 17 April 1866. On that day the newly-created courts were solemnly opened and 27 sworn attorneys admitted to practice, among them such future luminaries as Anatolii Fedorovich Koni (1844-1927),[35] Dmitrii Vasilevich Stasov (1824-1906) and Konstantin Konstantinovich Arsenev (1837-1919).[36] By 1913 the number of sworn attorneys had reached about 6,000. Some became household names even down to the present day: Vladimir Danilovich Spasovich (1829-1907),[37] Aleksandr Ivanovich Urusov (1843-1900),[38] Petr Akimovich Aleksandrov (1838-1893), Sergei Arkadevich Andreevskii (1847-1919),[39] Fedor Nikiforovich Plevako (1842-1908/09),[40] Aleksandr Iakovlevich Passover (1840-1910), Nikolai Platonovich Karabchevskii (1851-1925),[41] among them.

The structure and organization of the Advokatura established in 1864 has been discussed at length in Russian and western legal scholarship.[42] We dwell here merely on certain salient features which help better understand the contemporary Advokatura.

The qualifications required to be a sworn attorney were sufficiently high to elevate those admitted to their ranks immediately to the elite of legal professionals. Candidates were expected to have a diploma from a university or other institution of higher education in law or to have passed the examinations in law as an external student and have worked for not less than five years in a judicial department in posts enabling practical skills in judicial proceedings to have been acquired; or aides to sworn attorneys who were training to become fully-fledged advokats for not less than five years. The Ministry of Justice, pursuant to the Statute on the Introduction of the Judicial Statutes into Operation, exercised its power to waive the educational requirement during the first five years of the existence of the Advokatura in favor of those who had stipulated minimums of legal or judicial experience. Among the initial candidates for admission were a doctor of legal sciences, a former sworn *striapchii* in the commercial court, and judges or other officials from State institutions.

---

35 The literature by and about Koni is massive. A useful anthology is I.V. Potapchuk (comp.), А. Ф. Кони: Избранные труды и речи [A. F. Koni: Selected Works and Speeches] (Tula, 2000).

36 Potapchuk (comp.), К. К. Арсеньев: Заметки о русской адвокатуре [K. K. Arsenev: Notes on the Russian Advokatura] (Tula, 2001).

37 Potapchuk (comp.), В. Д. Спасович: Избранные труды и речи [V. D. Spasovich: Selected Works and Speeches] (Tula, 2000).

38 Potapchuk (comp.), А. И. Урусов: Первосоздатель русской судебной защиты [A. I. Urusov: Creator of Russian Judicial Defense] (Tula, 2001).

39 Potapchuk (comp.), С. А. Андреевский: Избранные труды и речи [S. A. Andreevskii: Selected Works and Speeches] (Tula, 2000).

40 Potapchuk (comp.), Ф. П. Плевако: Избранные речи [F. P. Plevako: Selected Speeches] (Tula, 2000).

41 Potapchuk (comp.), Н. П. Карабчевский: Около правосудия: Статьи, речи, очерки [N. P. Karabchevckii: About Justice: Articles, Speeches, Essays] (Tula, 2001).

42 The best work in both its English version and later Russian translation is Eugene Huskey, *Russian Lawyers and the Soviet State: The Origins and Development of the Soviet Bar, 1917-1939* (1986), pp. 11-33. Also see E. Vaskovskii, Организация адвокатуры [Organization of the Advokatura] (Spb., 1893); Kucherov, *Courts, Lawyers and Trials Under the Last Three Tsars* (1953); Wortman, *Development of Russian Legal Consciousness* (1976); I. Gessen and M. Gernet, История русской адвокатуры [History of the Russian Advokatura] (1914-1916) in three volumes; N. V. Cherkasova, Формирование и развитие адвокатуры в России: 60-80 годы XIX в. [Formation and Development of the Advokatura in Russia: 1860-1880s] (1987).

Excluded from membership in the Advokatura were persons under the age of 25, foreigners, persons declared to be insolvent or debtors, persons in government service or holding elective office, persons deprived of or limited in status under court judgments, including clergy, persons under investigation for crimes or with prior convictions, persons of poor moral character, and those prohibited from acting on behalf of another or expelled from the ranks of sworn attorneys. In 1889 limitations were introduced on the admission of sworn and private attorneys who were not of the Christian faith, such admissions being not otherwise than with the authorization of the Minister of Justice.[43]

The Russian Advokatura was decentralized, self-governing, and, within the confines of legislation, self-regulating. By the end of the Imperial period, associations of sworn attorneys had been formed in all fourteen judicial districts of the Russian Empire in a loose relationship with the courts in each judicial district known as "chambers of justice". Each was responsible for its own admissions. An applicant filed a request to be admitted to the council of sworn attorneys specifying the necessary information and appending the documents confirming his education, work experience, and other data. The council, having considered the materials submitted and taken under advisement all information which it deemed to be necessary, adopted a decree to either accept or to reject the applicant. If the applicant was accepted, an oath was administered according to the profession of faith of the applicant. Then the applicant was entered on the list of sworn attorneys and a certificate issued to him. It was routine to publish admissions in the local media. The candidacy was then confirmed (or not) by the Minister of Justice, whose decision, if negative, might be appealed to the Ruling Senate.

In addition to accepting new members, the council of sworn attorneys in each district decided disciplinary cases and adopted decisions on other issues of common concern to the advokats. The actions of the council were reviewed at general meetings of the sworn attorneys, which also elected the council. The chambers of justice had the power to overturn decisions of the councils, but in practice this was uncommon.

Sworn attorneys had the right to accept criminal and civil cases in all courts of the district of the judicial chamber in which they were registered. At the request of his client, the sworn attorney might also operate outside of his district, in which event he was subject to the council of sworn attorneys of that court where the case was being heard. In criminal cases the sworn attorney was either retained by the client or appointed by the chairman of the court. An appointment could not be declined without justifiable reasons. Civil cases were accepted under a power of attorney issued by the

43 A. P. Galoganov, Российская адвокатура: история и современность [Russian Advokatura: History and Modern Times] (2003), p. 18. "In 1889 the Government limited the entry of Jews into the colleges of advokats, and they might thus practice only as an aide to a private attorney or *striapchii*". M. Iu. Barshchevskii, Организация и деятельность адвокатуры в России [Organization and Activity of the Advokatura in Russia] (1997), p. 12.

client, or a declaration filed by the litigant in a court, or by appointment of the council of sworn attorneys at the request of a litigant, or by appointment of the chairman of a court. The client had the right to indicate whether he was retaining the sworn attorney to conduct the case to the very end or only to carry on certain actions. A client might have several sworn attorneys acting for him if he so wished. Payment for legal services was agreed by the parties in written form. If agreement was not reached or disagreements arose of the amount, payment was made on the basis of a fee schedule.

There were a number of limitations on the sworn attorney, none of which are surprising. A sworn attorney could not act in court for his parents, spouse, children, brothers, sisters, uncles, and other kin. Nor could he act for both parties in a case, nor change sides. He was prohibited from purchasing or otherwise acquiring the rights of his clients with regard to their litigation either in his own name or under the pretext of acquiring them for other persons; all such transaction would be deemed to be invalid and the attorney subjected to disciplinary responsibility.

The sworn attorney was required not to divulge the secrets of his client not only during the case proceedings, but also upon their completion. Every sworn attorney was required to maintain a list of cases assigned to him and to submit this list to the council upon request.

For infractions a sworn attorney was subject, depending upon the offense, to criminal, civil, and disciplinary responsibility. The last was administered by the council of sworn attorneys or, in the absence thereof, by the local court. Four categories of disciplinary sanction existed: (1) warning; (2) reprimand; (3) prohibition to perform duties of a sworn attorney for a period determined by the council, but not more than one year; and (4) expulsion as a sworn attorney. Russian legislation required that certain procedures be complied with in disciplinary proceedings, including the submission of explanations by the person concerned, his appearance at the session of the council, the presence of a quorum at the council session, and the possibility to appeal against the decree of the council.

A council of sworn attorneys was formed when at least twenty such attorneys had been admitted in a judicial district and they petitioned for recognition. The council was elected annually by the general meeting and was required to report on the previous year's activities to the general meeting.

As time passed, the numbers of aides to advokats, or junior attorneys, eligible to become fully-fledged advokats increased markedly. Having registered with a sworn attorney, some practiced on their own while undergoing their apprenticeship or pupilage. In the later years of the Advokatura, about two-thirds of sworn attorneys admitted had served as aides to advokats and the balance were former judges or civil servants.[44]

44 See Huskey, *Russian Lawyers and the Soviet State*, p. 14.

The underground attorney continued to exist and flourish until the Russian revolutions of 1917.[45] Many who had engaged in this profession prior to 1864 were simply unable to meet the high qualifications imposed to become a sworn attorney, and others who might have done so were unwilling to assume the other duties that accompanied being a sworn attorney or the extent of supervision imposed by the organs of the Advokatura. In effect, anyone who wanted to become an underground attorney in Russia could do so unless he fell into the category of a person who was prohibited by law from acting in this capacity. An Explanation of the Ruling Senate elucidated which persons could not act in criminal proceedings as a defender: (1) notaries, except for defending close members of their families; (2) persons deprived of all rights of status or all special rights and privileges by judgment of a court; (3) persons who were prohibited from petitioning with regard to a court judgment, excommunicated from church, expelled from service by a court or from a religious department for moral offenses; (4) persons expelled as sworn attorneys; (5) persons excluded from being private attorneys by order of the Minister of Justice or by a judicial ruling; (6) persons removed from the ranks of private attorneys by *uezd* congresses; (7) private or sworn attorneys prohibited from engaging in professional activity as a disciplinary sanction; (8) and persons interrogated at a preliminary investigation as a witness if they were summoned to court by the opposing side. To these eight categories should be added persons who were prohibited from being attorneys in criminal cases in justice of the peace courts: (1) secretaries of justice of the peace congress or bailiffs; (2) clerks of a justice of the peace who considered the case; and (3) local justice of the peace and deputies of a procurator in the justice of the peace institutions of the judicial district concerned.

The underground attorney flourished primarily in the rural areas of Russia where there were few sworn or private attorneys.

Once the opportunity presented itself, many underground attorneys became private attorneys under the Rules on Persons Having the Right to be Attorneys with Regard to Court Cases, confirmed on 25 May 1874 in the form of amendments to the 1864 judicial reform legislation. Under the 1874 Rules persons who had received special certificates for the right to petition with regard to other cases could act as attorneys in both the general and in the justice of the peace courts. The forms of the certificates were established by the Ministry of Justice. The certificates were issued by the conferences of justice of the peace, district courts, and chambers of justice and gave the right to petition only in that court by which they were issued except for instances when an attorney who had accepted a case for proceedings in a justice of the

45 Huskey notes that a "few private law firms were formed in the aftermath ..." of the 1864 Judicial Reform by *striapchie* in an effort to compete with the sworn attorneys. He considers it likely that these firms were disbanded when the private attorney was brought under State regulation in 1874. Huskey, *Russian Lawyers and Soviet State*, p. 16, n. 17.

peace court, district, or chamber of justice at the wish of the litigants or the person on trial submitted a petition with regard to this same case to the cassational departments of the Ruling Senate.

Those who wished to be a private attorney filed a request at the respective court, appending the necessary documents certifying his identity and affirming that there were no impediments to his becoming a private attorney. If it subsequently determined that there were such impediments, the certificate was withdrawn and this person was subject to criminal prosecution. If the court refused to issue a certificate, the refusal might be appealed to the superior judicial instance.

The court which issued a certificate informed the Minister of Justice thereof and published the names of private attorneys in the local media.

The courts exercised disciplinary responsibility over the persons to whom they issued certificates. The sanctions for "incorrect and reprehensible actions" by private attorneys were: (1) a warning or caution; (2) reprimand; (3) prohibition to perform the duties of a private attorney for a period exceeding one year; and (4) exclusion from the rank of private attorneys.

The 1874 Rules also granted the right to persons who had no certificate (that is, were not private attorneys) to act in cases before justices of the peace, but not more than three cases during the year within the justice of the peace district. Individuals acting in this capacity were asked by the justice of the peace whether they had acted during the year in another's case in the justice of the peace district, and if so, how many times. False testimony would engage criminal responsibility.

The market had its own impact on the private attorney as time passed. Gradually the private attorney gravitated towards those areas where there were few sworn attorneys, primarily in the provinces and away from the principal urban centers where the courts were located. By 1914 the cities of Moscow, Petersburg, Kiev, and Warsaw had about fifty percent of all sworn attorneys but only 11.2% of the private attorneys. Over half the private attorneys were in smaller provincial towns, whereas only 6.2% of the sworn attorneys were to be found there. Competition between the two segments of the legal profession was most intense in the district courts, where they were more or less evenly represented.[46]

The superimposition of the Advokatura upon the previously existing components of the legal profession – jurisconsult, sworn *striapchii* in commercial courts, private attorney, and underground attorney – apparently had no perceptible impact upon the last. Indeed, all the jurists of these categories together were not of sufficient number to satisfy the requirements for legal services in Russia.

46 M. Gernet (ed.), История русской адвокатуры [History of the Russian Advokatura] (1916), II, pp. 3-5, 57.

THE SOVIET ADVOKATURA: 1918-1991

The periodization of the development of the Soviet Advokatura is traditionally seen to fall into the following periods: (1) 1917-1922; (2) 1922-1939; (3) 1939-1961; and (4) 1961-1991.[47] A more nuanced analysis of the first two periods suggests a different breakdown: (1) 1917-1921; (2) 1922-1927); (3) 1928-1932; (4) 1933-1939 – and a caution against over-simplification:

> ...[A] reperiodization of Soviet legal development ... shows that the shift toward the stability of law began as early as 1932 and not, as widely believed, in 1936, the year that witnessed both the enactment of the Stalin Constitution and the launching of the Great Purges. In general, the periods of early Soviet legal development ... swing back and forth from legal nihilism to legal revival. But they do not respect the divisions between the years of Leninist and Stalinist rule. The picture of Soviet legal development ... illustrates that the juxtaposition of a benign legal system under Lenin with a harsh and repressive Stalinist legal order is unjustified.[48]

Indeed, the continued existence of a group of professional people in the Soviet Union who might be retained on a fee basis by individual citizens is surprising to many, who may be forgiven for thinking that the provision of legal services either might be monopolized by the State or abolished in the inquisitorial tradition of Muscovite Russia. The initial reaction of the Bolsheviks to the Advokatura in Soviet Russia was antipathetic; it was dissolved on 24 November 1917 in Decree No. 1 "On Courts". The Petrograd and later the Moscow Advokaturas refused to recognize the legality of the dissolution and continued to function for nearly a year.[49]

Lenin himself had been a trainee advokat in the Imperial era. Expelled from his law studies at Kazan University, he completed them externally at St. Petersburg University, was admitted to legal practice, and actually appeared in court in several cases before devoting himself wholly to the revolutionary movement. He took a dim view in some of this writings about aspects of the Russian legal profession, but was never

---

47 See D. P. Baranov and M. B. Smolenskii, Адвокатское право [Advokat Law] (3d ed.; 2009), p. 59.

48 Huskey, *Russian Lawyers and Soviet State*, p. 8.

49 There was nothing new in this: "... the English revolution provoked aspirations for a new kind of legal order, startlingly similar to those expressed in the newly independent American states, in Paris in 1791-3, and for that matter, in Petrograd and Moscow following the Bolshevik seizure of power ...". Revolutionary aspirations with respect to law in England, France, and the United States had an "uncanny resemblance" to the "legal ideals of the Bolsheviks in Petrograd in 1917 ... Revolutionaries everywhere seem to have been attracted by the same utopian notion that one could have a law-abiding society without specialist lawyers". See M. Burrage, *Revolution and the Making of the Contemporary Legal Profession* (2006), pp. 414, 580.

opposed to the legal profession in principle. It was Lenin who personally inserted clauses on defenders in the early draft enactments on criminal procedure.

Decree No. 1 "On Courts" opened to every citizen who enjoyed civil rights the right to act as defense counsel.[50] Under this proviso many sworn attorneys from the Tsarist era continued to practice their profession. Although the right was retained in Decree No. 2 "On Courts", adopted 15 February 1918, Lenin modified the draft to allow "colleges" of individuals to be formed and attached to local soviets; college members might act for remuneration either as prosecutors or as defense counsel.[51] The link between prosecution and defense proved to be incompatible and was abolished in May 1918. There followed a period of constant reorganization of the provision of legal services during the next four years. For the most part the regulation of advokats was left to local soviets. Initially a fee system operated on the basis of a schedule fixed by councils within the colleges of defenders; then the colleges were reorganized and defense counsel became salaried employees just as judges and prosecutors. Into this new scheme of colleges passed many members of the Tsarist advokatura in November 1918 when they resolved to liquidate their former organizations.

In 1920 a dramatic new experiment was tried. Local soviets were obliged to confirm twice-yearly lists of individuals who were capable of acting as defenders in court; they were paid per diem from State funds. Individuals on the list found themselves pressed into the role of defender whether they wished to act or not. The system proved unworkable, and in the majority of instances defenders were appointed from officials of local justice agencies attached to the respective local soviets.

The transition to the NEP brought a fully-fledged Statute on the Advokatura, adopted 26 May 1922[52] which determined the general features of the advokatura and the functions of colleges of defenders. Under the Statute, colleges of defenders for civil and criminal cases were formed and attached to *guberniia* justice sections. This was followed on 5 July 1922 by the Statute of the College of Defenders.[53] The college of defenders, attached in each *guberniia* to the *guberniia* courts, was a social organization. There was no minimum educational requirement for membership in a college of defenders.

The college was headed by a presidium whose members were elected by the general meeting. The presidium had broad powers to admit and expel members, consider disciplinary matters, and organize legal consultation offices. College members were

50 СУ РСФСР (1917-18), no. 4, item 50.

51 СУ РСФСР (1918), no. 26, item 240.

52 СУ РСФСР (1922), no. 36, item 425. Although entitled as though it were a separate and individual Statute, the enactment was in fact an amendment to Articles 43 to 49 of the Statute on People's Courts of 21 October 1920. This technique of statute-formation replicated practices from the Imperial era.

53 On 7 June 1923 the Statute on the College of Defenders was incorporated into the Statute on Court Organization as a separate chapter by decree of the All-Russian Central Executive Committee.

confirmed by the Presidium of the guberniia executive committee, but new members could now be admitted by the College itself with subsequent notification of the committee. Members were precluded from holding simultaneously posts in State institutions and enterprises except for elective offices and law teaching positions (that is, they were distinct from jurisconsults). Defenders were at liberty to negotiate their fees with the client except with workers of State and private enterprises or employees of soviet institutions and enterprises, for whom fees were regulated by the People's Commissariat of Justice. Indigents were exempted from legal fees by court decree. The defenders then paid a stipulated percentage of their remuneration to the College to cover overhead expenses. Defenders did not enjoy a monopoly position. Close relatives of an accused or a victim and authorized representatives of certain State and social organizations also might appear in court as a defender. Other individuals, however, required the special authorization of the court.

The influence of sworn attorneys from the *ancien régime* in local advokaturas troubled many local Party organizations. Should communists be allowed to join? The Central Committee of the Party on 2 November 1922 counseled affirmatively in a Circular to all regional and provincial Party organizations; otherwise, the Committee said, the colleges would be taken over by elements hostile to Soviet power. But limitations were imposed. A communist was required to have the advance approval of a senior Party organization before joining the College; communist advokats must not accept cases, especially civil cases, involving the defense of bourgeois interests in disputes against workers or State enterprises nor in criminal cases defend clearly counter-revolutionary or other impure elements.[54]

Throughout much of the NEP period advokats worked as private practitioners, the fee arrangements being attenuated by legal consultation centers at factories or public places where workers might obtain legal advice free of charge. During the era of forced collectivization in 1929-1931, advokats in most places found themselves pressured to merge into voluntary "collectives" of advokats. The arrangements varied from locality to locality; as a rule, clients contracted for services with a collective and fees were paid to the collective. Advokats were then remunerated on the basis of quantity and quality of work performed.[55]

Greater central guidance over the legal profession ensued with the creation of a "Legal Defense Section" within the RSFSR People's Commissariat of Justice by legislation of 20 July 1930. On 27 February 1932 the RSFSR People's Commissariat of Justice adopted a Statute on Collectives of Members of Colleges of Defenders, confirming that the notion of collectives in this domain was on the whole regarded as a positive

54 The Circular was reproduced in the Еженедельник советской юстиции [Weekly of Soviet Justice], no. 1 (1923), p. 24; signed by V. M. Molotov.

55 On this period see Huskey, *Russian Lawyers and the Soviet State*; J. N. Hazard, *Settling Disputes in Soviet Society* (1960), pp. 247-300.

development. The collectives worked under the direct guidance of the presidium of colleges of advocates, whereas the colleges received their "general policy guidance and supervision" from the territorial, regional, and higher courts. The collectives admitted new members, subject to final approval by the colleges. Clients selected their own defenders from those available; fees varied depending on the qualifications, socio-legal work, and work-load of the advokat but were levied at rates worked out by the presidium of the college and confirmed by the court.[56]

The 1932 Statute was enacted at a time when the need for a legal profession at all was being seriously questioned by the Pashukanis school.[57] The importance of defense counsel was staunchly defended. The ranks of advokats were not unaffected by the Stalinist purges, their numbers in Moscow in 1935 being reduced by 10% presumably for this reason. In November 1936 a Section for Legal Defense attached to the USSR People's Commissariat of Justice was formed and a campaign undertaken to increase the numbers of advokats, especially by recruiting new members from among the working people. A second purge in 1938 was carried out to enhance the authority of the Communist Party within the Advokatura, with considerable ultimate success.

Following the adoption of the 1936 USSR Constitution, the system of court organization was remodeled and for the first time all-union legislation on the advokatura was approved on 16 August 1939, by the USSR Council of People's Commissars.[58] In all there were about 8,000 advokats for a population of 191 million persons.

The 1939 Statute established an organizational scheme for the advokatura which endured in its essentials until 2002. The advokatura was divided into regional, territory, and republic colleges, general guidance over them being charged to the People's Commissariat of Justice of the USSR in its capacity as a union republic people's commissariat – that is, it had counterparts in each of the union republics of the Soviet Union. Direct guidance was placed in the hands of an elected presidium in each college. The transition was commenced towards preferring the admission of advokats who had a higher or secondary education, although some individuals who had worked at least three years as a judge, procurator, investigator, or jurisconsult might be accepted without these educational qualifications. The collective character of the Advokatura was stressed. Only members of a college might engage in advokat activities, and only through a legal consultation office, to whom payment for services must be made by the client, rather than individually to the advokat.

56 See M. V. Kozhevnikov, История советского суда 1917-1956 годы [History of the Soviet Court 1917-1956] (1957), p. 237.

57 The Statute is one reason why Huskey argues that the return to "stability of laws" is already in evidence by 1932. He contends that the 1936 USSR Constitution should "... properly be regarded as the culmination" of the movement toward stability of laws rather than a protracted first phase. Huskey, *Russian Lawyers and Soviet State*, pp. 180-181.

58 СП СССР (1939), no. 49, item 394.

These changes, it was suggested, led advokat entities to resemble production units which operated under the one-man management of the head of the legal consultation office who in turn was subordinate to the presidium of the college of advokats. To be sure, the legal consultation office was modeled upon prerevolutionary Russian versions, but the Stalinist control mechanisms discouraged any display of initiative. Except in remote rural areas, where there was no other choice, the private practice of law disappeared, and jurisconsults were no longer permitted to be members of a college of advokats. There was strong informal pressure upon advokats to join the Communist Party, which over time, as a rule, some 60% or more did in order to advance their careers.

The People's Commissariat of Justice of the USSR issued instructions establishing binding fees for advokat services in Order No. 85 of 2 October 1939; administered the elections to the presidium of colleges of advokats by Order No. 98 of 26 October 1939, and exercised control over admission to a college of advokats by Order No. 65 of 22 April 1941. These policies endured throughout the Stalinist era.

The Secret Advokatura

Whatever Stalin may have known from Soviet intelligence sources about progress in the United States in developing an atomic bomb, historians of the Advokatura suggest that President Harry S. Truman's friendly disclosure to Stalin at the Potsdam Conference in 1945 that the United States had created an atomic bomb triggered a series of events that also affected the Soviet legal profession. Stalin is said to have made immediate urgent inquiries of his own security and scientific personnel and by 20 August 1945 to have created the "atomic industry" as a new branch of Soviet economic administration. The scientific research institutes and State enterprises merged into or created within this branch of industry were mostly located outside existing population centers on territories closed to outsiders. Phantom cities were formed one after the other without names and undisclosed on Soviet maps. Postal addresses took the form of fictitious designations: Arzamas-16, Penza-19, Tomsk-7, and so on. Nearly a decade later some of the "science cities" were given real names without indicating what kind of urban centers they were.

The closed cities rapidly grew in population, ranging from 50,000 to 100,000 persons, and naturally required the full range of urban services that any other city would require. This meant legal infrastructure – courts, procuracy, notariat, registries for acts of civil status, law enforcement, and advokats.

By an Edict of 27 June 1947 the Presidium of the Supreme Soviet of the USSR created a special Advokatura in the so-called "closed territories",[59] each territory having

59 The Edict remains unpublished, and was not included in the Собрание действующего законодательства СССР [Collection of Legislation in Force of the Union of Soviet Socialist Republics].

its own courts, procuracy, police, notariat, and Advokatura. These legal institutions had no special powers in comparison with those outside the closed territories. The designation "special" (abbreviated) was applied to them. Everything relating to their very existence was classified, including the affiliation of individuals with these closed territories, their passport stamp, the judgment of any court in the said territories, including when and where it was proclaimed. The provision of the 1936 USSR Constitution allowing justice to be administered by, *inter alia*, "special" courts was construed to encompass military tribunals, transport and camp courts, and these courts on closed territories.

The lines of administration essential to organize these infrastructures appeared within the relevant ministries. The Ministry of Internal Affairs, the Ministry of Justice, and the Procuracy of the USSR formed special administrations within each of their structures. The judicial system created sub-units to handle appeals from the closed territory courts up to and including the USSR Supreme Court. Because there was no all-union Advokatura, the selection of advokats to serve in the closed territories was passed to the chairmen of the special courts that had been formed there. Events moved so rapidly that advokats were already in place before the end of 1947 with "credentials" issued by the local courts. Advokats were present in seven closed cities and later at so-called "special-regime" objects in Moscow, Leningrad, Kaliningrad (near Moscow), the Far East, Kazakhstan (Baikonur), Kyrgyzia, Ukraine, and elsewhere.

Security considerations imposed unusual constraints upon advokat activity. Cases could be conducted only in special courts, which meant that the advokats were often underemployed. The crime rate was much lower in closed territories than elsewhere in the country. The special courts in closed territories had nothing in common with the "special boards" or "troikas" that carried out the Stalinist purges. The "special Advokatura engaged in ordinary advokat practice".[60]

The USSR Ministry of Justice itself began to appoint advokats at regime objects beginning on 12 November 1955. The camp and transport special courts had been abolished respectively in 1953 and 1956. When the USSR Ministry of Justice was itself abolished, the USSR Supreme Court assumed responsibility for directing the Special Advokatura. In due course the Special Advokatura was moved on to the RSFSR Ministry of Justice, and after its dissolution, to the RSFSR Supreme Court. It says something about the status of advokats that only in 1966, on the basis of a Decree of the USSR Council of Ministers, were the directors of regime enterprises required to provide the special courts and law enforcement agencies, and the advokats, with premises and their personnel with housing and medical services equal to that of the workers of the enterprises themselves.

60 N. N. Klen (ed.), Межреспубликанская коллегия адвокатов. 60 лет деятельности [Inter-Republic College of Advokats. 60 Years of Activity] (2009), p. 12.

On 24 July 1956 the first twenty-five legal consultation offices were created at regime objects and in closed territorial formations; their advokats served the special courts. The names of the legal consultation offices also were given classified names, which in 1971 were changed to classified numbers, for example Legal Consultation Office No. 9, 10, 19, 20, 25, 33, and others.

The 1979 USSR Law on the Advokatura permitted the creation of inter-territorial advokaturas. In 1982 at the initiative of the Minister of Justice of the USSR, V. I. Terebilov, the Inter-Republic College of Advokats was formed on the base of 134 legal consultation offices located in these regime areas. During this period, responsibility for the work of the special advokatura was placed on various agencies, including the USSR Ministry of Justice, the Supreme Court of the USSR, the RSFSR Ministry of Justice, and the RSFSR Supreme Court.[61]

Post-Stalin Reforms of the Advokatura

Changes commenced with the accession to power of N. S. Khrushchev. In an address to the Supreme Soviet of the USSR in 1957 Khrushchev called upon advokats "to assist strengthening socialist legality and the administration of justice". The 1958 Fundamental Principles of Criminal Procedure of the USSR and Union Republics gave advokats great possibilities to take part at earlier stages in certain categories of criminal cases or with certain categories of persons under investigation (Article 22).

The "decentralization" of legislation in the form of sets of "all-union fundamental principles" and "union republic codes" extended to the Advokatura. The 1958 Fundamental Principles of Court Organization of the USSR and Union Republics returned responsibility for the Advokatura to the union republics. The 1939 USSR Statute was replaced in the union republics between 1961 and 1963 by union republic statutes – in the case of the RSFSR by the Statute on the Advokatura of 25 July 1962.[62] Looking back, some saw in this Statute the first attempt since the 1917 October Revolution to return to the Advokatura "its former independence".[63]

In continuation of the reforms of the 1960s, the RSFSR Ministry of Justice confirmed an Instruction on the Procedure for the Payment of Legal Assistance Rendered

61 For names and biographies of some of the early advokats who practiced in these areas, see Klen (ed.), Межреспубликанская коллегия адвокатов. 60 лет деятельности [Inter-Republic College of Advokats. 60 Years of Activity] (2009).

62 Ведомости Верховного Совета РСФСР (1962), no. 29, item 450; transl in H. J. Berman and J. B. Quigley, Jr., *Basic Laws on the Structure of the Soviet State* (1968). See L. M. Friedman and Z. L. Zile, "Soviet Legal Profession: Recent Developments in Law and Practice", *Wisconsin Law Review* (1964), pp. 32-77; K. F. Gutsenko, "New Legislation in the Union Republics with Respect to the Legal Profession", *Soviet Law and Government*, I, no. 2 (1962), pp. 57-64.

63 Kucherna, Адвокатура в условиях судебно-правовой реформы в России [Advokatura in Conditions of Judicial and Legal Reform in Russia] (2009), p. 38. Also see D. D. Barry and H. J. Berman, "The Soviet Legal Profession", *Harvard Law Review*, LXXXII (1968), pp. 1-41.

by Advokats to Citizens, Enterprises, Institutions, State Farms, Collective Farms, and Other Organizations.[64]

Although the economic reforms of the mid-1960s chiefly enhanced the role and numbers of jurisconsults in the national economy, they also affected advokats. The joint decree of the Central Committee of the Communist Party of the Soviet Union and USSR Council of Ministers "On the Improvement of Legal Work in the National Economy" made provision for advokats to provide legal services at those enterprises which did not have jurisconsults permanently on staff. On 8 December 1972 the USSR Ministry of Justice confirmed a Standard Contract "On Rendering Legal Services at Enterprises, Institutes, and Other Organizations (Except Collective Farms) by Legal Consultations Offices attached to Colleges of Advokats", and a year later confirmed a separate standard contract for advokats to provide legal services to collective farms. Russian advokats who viewed their role as being primarily one of advocacy in court did not greet this expansion of function positively; for them it was an additional burden of representation and a further "statization" of their role in society.[65]

Some central direction over the Advokatura, as time passed, was felt to be desirable, and in 1976 work commenced on drafting an all-union enactment. The 1977 USSR Constitution (Article 161) provided for a new pattern of regulation – USSR and union republic legislation – and elevated the college of advokats to organizations of constitutional stature for the first time in Soviet history. On 30 November 1979 the USSR Supreme Soviet adopted the Law on the Advokatura of the USSR. On the basis of that Law, the RSFSR Supreme Soviet adopted the Statute on the Advokatura of the RSFSR on 20 November 1980, which remained in force until 30 June 2002.[66]

The 1980 Statute retained essentially the same structure for the Advokatura internally but, in the eyes of many, consolidated the dependence of the Advokatura upon the USSR and RSFSR ministries of justice in ways consistent with the ideological precepts of the day. However, the Statute (and the 1979 USSR Law) did not contain a definition of "advokatura" or of "advokat activity". As the processes of perestroika advanced, the Advokatura in the Russian Federation experienced between 1986 and 1988 the "boom of cooperatives", as did so many other sectors of the Soviet economy. Legal cooperatives were formed for the provision of legal services, but most did not survive for very long.

Some changes brought by the 1980 Statute were undoubtedly positive. All advokats were required to have a higher legal education. Greater emphasis began to be placed on the adversarial dimension of accusation and defense in criminal proceedings.

---

64 СП РСФСР (1966), no. 3, item 22.

65 For all of Russian history the relationship between the jurist and the State has been a major concern and preoccupation. For a useful summary, see I. S. Iartykh, Адвокатура и власть [The Advokatura and the Authorities] (2003).

66 V. I. Sergeev, Комментарий а положению об адвокатуре [Commentary to the Statute on the Advokatura] (2001).

The right of advokats to obtain documents or copies thereof from organizations was strengthened, which made it easier for them to perform their roles with respect to the collection of evidence. But as their rights expanded under criminal procedure legislation, so too did resistance grow to their presence in investigations. In 1988 advokats appeared in court in 70% of criminal cases, but were present at only about one-third of the preliminary investigations. Statistics released by the USSR Ministry of Justice show that during the 1970s more than 70% of petitions and applications submitted by advokats of the RSFSR were rejected by investigators.[67]

Beginning in the late 1980s, a number of regional colleges of advokats combined into various social organizations for the purpose of defending the interests of the advokats as a profession and also to practice law. The aspiration of advokats to create an Advokatura truly independent from the State generated serious resistance from the Communist Party of the Soviet Union. The Ministry of Justice of the USSR, under instruction from the Central Committee of the CPSU, was directed not to permit the creation of an independent Union of Advokats of the USSR. When it became clear that the process was irreversible, by a secret decision of the Politburo adopted on 2 December 1988, No. 143, the Ministry of Justice was directed to "head the work for the creation of an Association of Advokats of the USSR ... by democratic means to allot to the organization committee advokats who properly understand the tasks of the Advokatura at the contemporary stage ...".[68]

THE POST-SOVIET ADVOKATURA IN RUSSIA: 1991-2002

The drafting of the 2002 Law on the Advokatura occupied the energies of advokats for nearly a decade and a half. Various versions were produced within and outside of Government. On 12 January 1995 the President of the Russian Federation submitted a draft federal law "On the Advokatura in the Russian Federation" to the State Duma. The draft had been prepared by the Council for Judicial Reform attached to the President of the Russian Federation and confirmed for submission on 16 December 1994. It represented a compromise between drafts originating in governmental and professional circles. But it was to be many years before a version would be acceptable to the Russian parliament.[69]

67 See M. Gofshtein, «Обзор ходатайств и заявлений адвокатов РСФСР» [Survey of Petitions and Applications of Advokats of the RSFSR], Советская юстиция [Soviet Justice], no. 21 (1989), p. 31.

68 Quoted in D. N. Kozak (ed.), Научно-практический комментарий к Федеральному закону «Об адвокатской деятельности и адвокатуре в Российской Федерации» [Scientific-Practical Commentary to Federal Law "On Advokat Activity and the Advokatura in the Russian Federation] (2003), p. 24.

69 The literature on various drafts is substantial. See, among others, M. Iu. Barshchevskii, Адвокат. адвокатская фирма, адвокатура [Advokat, Advokat Firm, Advokatura] (1995), pp. 32-67.

In 1991 an All-Union Congress of Advokats was held in the Soviet Union. The Congress created a Union of Advokats, elected the executive organs thereof, and adopted a Charter. Upon the dissolution of the Soviet Union, several associations of advokats were created within the Russian Federation: the Union of Advokats of Russia, founded in 1990, became the Federal Union of Advokats based in Moscow at the Founding Congress of 12 to 13 September 1994; the Regional Association of Russian Advokats, headquartered in Saratov, was established in 1994 and combined thirteen colleges of advokats; the Guild of Advokats of Russia, based in Moscow, was formed on 27 January 1995 and combined more than forty so-called "parallel" colleges of advokats formed during the early 1990s;[70] and the Union of Advokats of the USSR, founded in 1989, which became after the demise of the Soviet Union, the International Union (or Commonwealth) of Advokats, in Moscow, brought together advokats and their colleges on the territories of Belarus, Uzbekistan, and other CIS States and a number of Russian regions; it was formed in 1994 and re-registered in 1998.[71]

The single largest social organization uniting jurists of all profiles and callings is presently the All-Russian Social Organization "Association of Jurists of Russia", formed in 2005 by the merger of the Russian Union of Jurists and the Union of Jurists of Russia. The membership of the Association in 2011 exceeded 10,000 jurists.

The legal regime of the modern Advokatura is best seen through the 2002 federal law regulating its formation and activities. Commentary is offered on its provisions article by article below.

70 See Galoganov, Российская адвокатура: история и современность [Russian Advokatura: History and Modern Times] (2003), pp. 186-202.

71 See Iu. Lubshev, Адвокатура в России [The Advokatura in Russia] (2001). The constitutive documents of many of these organizations are collected in V. M. Anufriev and S. N. Gavrilov (comp.), Организация и деятельность адвокатуры в России [Organization and Activity of the Advokatura in Russia] (2001).

Commentary on the Federal Law of the Russian Federation "on Advokat Activity and the Advokatura in the Russian Federation"

[Federal Law of 31 May 2002, No. 63-ФЗ
as amended 28 October 2003, No. 134-ФЗ;
22 August 2004, No. 122-ФЗ; 20 December 2004, No. 163-ФЗ;
24 July 2007, No. 214-ФЗ; and 23 July 2008, No. 160-ФЗ.
СЗ РФ (2002), no. 23, item 2102; (2003), no. 44, item 4262;
(2004), no. 35, item 3607; no. 52(I), item 5267;
(2007), no. 31, item 4011; (2008), no. 30(II), item 3616]

Chapter 1 General Provisions

Article 1 Advokat Activity

1. *Qualified legal assistance rendered on a professional basis by persons who have received the status of advokat in the procedure established by the present Federal Law to natural and juridical persons (hereinafter – principals) for the purposes of the defense of their rights, freedoms, and interests, and also ensuring access to justice, shall be advokat activity.*
2. *Advokat activity shall not be entrepreneurial.*
3. *Legal assistance shall not be advokat activity rendered by:*
   workers of legal services of juridical persons (hereinafter – organizations), and also by workers of agencies of State power and agencies of local self-government;
   participants and workers of organizations rendering legal services, and also individual entrepreneurs;
   notaries, patent attorneys, except for instances when an advokat acts as a patent attorney, or other persons who by a law have been specially empowered to conduct their professional activity.
4. *The operation of the present Federal Law shall not extend also to agencies and persons who effectuate representation by virtue of a law.*

1. The fact that the Russian Federation has a Law on the Advokatura will be both novel and disturbing for the Anglo-American lawyer. The legal profession in England and the United States has struggled for much of its history, and successfully on the whole, to be self-regulating and independent of the State as a fundamental prerequisite for the protection of human freedoms. Insofar as the legal profession anywhere constitutes a form of control by citizens over the State, such a characterization understates the true role of the profession. The legal profession is also a form of legal control over the State and abuses by its officials, a role which brings into question the desirability of State regulation of the profession itself.

The requirement that advokat activity be "qualified" originates in Article 48(1) of the 1993 Russian Constitution: "1. To each shall be guaranteed the right to receive qualified legal assistance".[1] To "each" means Russian citizens, foreigners, and state-

1 Transl. in W. E. Butler, *Russian Law* (3d ed.; 2009), p. 819. All references hereinafter to the Constitution have in view this translation.

less persons, for under the 1993 Russian Constitution "all" are equal before law and court. The State guarantees the equality of rights and freedoms of man and citizen irrespective of sex, race, nationality, language, origin, property and financial position, place of residence, attitude towards religion, convictions, affiliation to social associations, and other circumstances (Article 19).

The concept of "natural person" should be understood broadly to encompass persons living or deceased, in embryo, irrespective of whether they enjoy full dispositive legal capacity or not. A "juridical person" is defined in the Civil Code of the Russian Federation as "... an organization which has solitary property in ownership, economic jurisdiction, or operative management and is liable for its obligations with such property and may in its own name acquire and effectuate property and personal nonproperty rights, bear duties, and be a plaintiff or defendant in court" (Article 48(1), Civil Code).[2]

It is nothing short of remarkable that this Article makes no mention of international organizations, foreign States, legal entities which are not juridical persons, and the like.

Throughout the present Law reference is made to "principals", rather than, for example to "clients". The advokat exercises his representation functions on the basis of a power of attorney from the principal, a document which must be presented to any court, tribunal, or other organization or person before whom the advokat is appearing or acting. The terminology of the Law reinforces this status.

The "status of advokat" is addressed in the Commentary to Article 9, below. The expression "on a professional basis" is not defined as such and lends itself to many constructions. Advokats are a part, and far from the majority, of the "legal profession" composed of "jurists". A jurist is an individual who has acquired a higher legal education or is otherwise classified as a jurist on other grounds – academicians, professors, judges, arbitrators, procurators, jurisconsults, advokats, notaries, and law enforcement officials are among the categories of "jurist" that share a common educational background and pursue a career connected with the law. "Professional" in this context suggests that advokats are rendering legal assistance in their capacity as an "advokat", their calling as an advokat, in accordance with the standards of becoming and acting as an advokat. A standard of quality is implied in the expression. This in turn implies that persons who do not meet the professional requirements of an advokat may not so act, for example, in a court proceeding in that capacity because involvement would materially violate the constitutional right to receive truly qualified professional legal assistance.[3] On the other hand, it should be observed that the 1993 Russian Constitution grants to a person accused of committing a crime the

2 Transl. in W. E. Butler, *Civil Code of the Russian Federation* (2010), pp. 19-20.
3 See the Joint Letter of the Ministry of Justice of the Russian Federation and General Procuracy of the Russian Federation of 13/18 August 1999, No. 6495-СЮ, 22-5/100-96.

right to take advantage of the "assistance of an advokat (or defender) ..." (Article 48(2), Constitution).

Russian advokats regard a number of international documents as relevant to their status, functions, rights, and duties. Some of these are international treaties which, being ratified by the Russian Federation, are an integral part of the Russian legal system. Others fall into the category of "soft law" but are nonetheless routinely cited in works on the Russian Advokatura and occasionally in Russian judicial decisions. Among the treaties are the 1966 International Covenant on Civil and Political Rights, the 1995 Convention of the Commonwealth of Independent States on the Rights and Fundamental Freedoms of Man, and the 1950 European Convention on the Protection of Human Rights and Fundamental Freedoms (enumerated in the sequence in which they were ratified by the Soviet Union or the Russian Federation). The "soft law" documents include the 1948 Universal Declaration of Human Rights, the 1990 Basic Principles on the Role of Lawyers contained in documents adopted by the Eighth United Nations Congress on the Prevention of Crime and Treatment of Offenders, 1988 Code of Conduct for Lawyers in the European Union, 1990 Standards for the Independence of the Legal Profession adopted by the International Bar Association, and the Body of Principles for the Protection of All Persons under Any Form of Detention or Imprisonment contained in United Nations General Assembly Resolution 43/173 of 9 December 1988.[4]

The reference to the defense of rights, freedoms, and interests refers both to the 1993 Russian Constitution and to the 1966 International Covenant on Civil and Political Rights, ratified by the former Soviet Union, to which the Russian Federation is a party by virtue of being the "legal continuer" of the USSR. Under Article 15(4) of the 1993 Russian Constitution, the 1966 Covenant, together with other human rights treaties to which the Russian Federation is a party, are an integral part of the legal system of the Russian Federation.[5] The same applies to the 1950 European Convention for the Protection of Human Rights and Fundamental Freedoms, as amended, to which the Russian Federation is a party.

The rights and freedoms of man and citizen according to generally-recognized principles and norms of international law are recognized and guaranteed in the Russian Federation (Article 17, Constitution), are of direct effect, and determine the sense, content, and application of laws and the activity of legislative and executive power and local self-government and are ensured by justice (Article 18, Constitution). Among the major constitutional rights and freedoms within the purview of advokats in their practice are equality before law and court (Article 19); right to life

4 Excerpts of these are reproduced in E. V. Semeniako and Iu. S. Pilipenko, Адвокатская деятельность и адвокатура [Advokat Activity and the Advokatura] (2010), pp. 17-50. They are cited from time to time in Russian judicial decisions.

5 See W. E. Butler, *The Law of Treaties of the Russian Federation and Other Members of the Commonwealth of Independent States* (2002).

(Article 20); dignity of the person (Article 21); right to freedom and personal inviolability (Article 22); right to inviolability of private life, personal and family secrecy, and defense of honor and good name, and the right to secrecy of correspondence, telephone conversations, postal, telegraph, and other communications (Article 23); inviolability of dwelling (Article 25); right to use native language and to free choice of language (Article 26); freedom of movement and choice of place of sojourn and residence (Article 26); freedom of conscience and profession of faith (Article 28); freedom of thought and speech (Article 29); freedom of association (Article 30); freedom of assembly (Article 31); right to participate in the administration of affairs (Article 32); right to have recourse personally and to send individual and collective appeals to State agencies and agencies of local self-government (Article 33); right to free use of abilities and property for entrepreneurial and other economic activity (Article 34); right of private ownership (Article 35); right to freely dispose of capability to labor and choose nature of activity and profession (Article 37); right to protection of motherhood and childhood (Article 38); right to social security (Article 39); right to housing (Article 40); right to health protection and medical assistance (Article 41); right to a favorable environment (Article 42); right to education (Article 43); freedom of literary, artistic, scientific, technical, and other types of creativity and to teach (Article 44); and, as noted above, the right to qualified legal assistance (Article 48).

Access to justice includes persons who are accused in a criminal proceeding, the victims of crimes, and those who wish to defend or exercise their rights in civil, labor, family, and other interpersonal or entrepreneurial relations.[6]

2. Advokat activity is expressly declared not to be entrepreneurial activity. Nonetheless, it is designated to be a type of economic activity and classified under point 74.11 of the All-Russian Classificator of Types of Economic Activity, confirmed by Decree of the State Committee of the Russian Federation for Standardization and Metrology of 6 November 2001, No. 545-ст.[7]

The distinction between entrepreneurial and non-entrepreneurial is disingenuous, although it has important implications for the integrity and aims of the calling of advokat. Entrepreneurial activity is associated with profit by means and methods not prohibited by legislation. While advokats expect to earn a living through their activities, principally on the basis of paid legal services, those services rendered free of charge to the client are usually reimbursed by the State according to an established scale, albeit a scale which is not particularly profitable. Contrary to the situation with ordinary entrepreneurs, the State guarantees to advokats their independence, a

6 See Information Letter of the Supreme Arbitrazh Court of the Russian Federation of 20 December 1999, No. C1-7/СМП-1341, "On the Basic Provisions Applied by the European Court for Human Rights When Defending Property Rights and Rights to Justice".

7 Unpublished, but available on Consultant Plus. From 1 January 2008 to 1 January 2011 inclusive the All-Russian Classificator OK 029-2007 was in force without repealing OK 029-2001.

special status, and a special procedure for the payment of taxes (see Article 226, Tax Code of the Russian Federation).

3. Point 3 of this Article distinguishes between activity which is advokat activity and that which is not on the basis of who provides the requisite legal assistance rather than what legal assistance or type of legal assistance is rendered. The first category of such individuals are loosely referred to as "workers of legal services of juridical persons", traditionally known as jurisconsults.

During the Soviet period, jurisconsults were the single largest component of the legal profession, numbering more than 100,000 by some estimates.[8] They consisted of jurists employed by agencies of State power and administration, local self-government, State enterprises and collective farms, and other State entities. Although during the late 1920s they met collectively as a Congress, apparently they have never otherwise organized themselves into a professional association nor sought professional recognition as a component of the overall legal profession. Economic reforms of the late 1960s led to the adoption of a Decree "On the Improvement of Legal Work in the National Economy", of 23 December 1970,[9] which required the enactment, still in force, of the General Statute on the Legal Section (or Office), Chief (or Senior) Jurisconsult, and Jurisconsult of a Ministry, Department, Executive Committee of a Soviet of People's Deputies, Enterprise, Organization, or Institution. The General Statute was confirmed by Decree of the USSR Council of Ministers of 22 June 1972, in the version of 1 December 1987, as amended 21 December 1990 and by decision of the Supreme Court of the Russian Federation of 27 December 2000, No. ГКПИ 2000-1409.[10]

Pursuant to the General Statute, a Model Statute on the Legal Service of a Federal Agency of Executive Power was confirmed by Decree of the Government of the Russian Federation of 2 April 2002, No. 207. Municipal employees, as defined by the Federal Law of 28 August 1995, No. 154-ФЗ, "On General Principles of the Organization of Local Self-Government in the Russian Federation, as amended 21 March 2002, No. 31-ФЗ,[11] do not engage in advokat activity when offering legal assistance that falls within their official duties. However, it should be noted that the municipal legislation does not necessarily link such legal assistance with the individual having a higher legal education. Individual State committees have adopted normative legal acts on jurisconsults, among them the State Customs Service, which on 23 September 1994, issued an Order confirming the General Statute on the Legal Section, Legal Group, and Jurisconsult of the Customs Agency of the Russian Agency, in force as amended

8 See D. D. Barry and H. J. Berman, "The Soviet Legal Profession", *Harvard Law Review*, LXXXII (1968), p. 18.
9 See Butler, *Russian Law* (2d ed.; 2003), pp. 125-129.
10 Бюллетень ВС РФ, no. 10 (2001).
11 СЗ РФ (1995), no. 35, item 3506; (2002), no. 12, item 1093; no. 28, item 2790.

24 December 2001. Each subdivision (legal section, legal group, and jurisconsult, operates on the basis of its own Statute confirmed at an appropriate level of the State Customs Committee system.

The right of jurisconsults to offer general legal advice, for example, to other employees is not entirely clear. During the Soviet era, jurisconsults were encouraged to allocate time so that employees of the respective enterprise could seek advice on labor, family, or other personal legal matters. On the other hand, some State agencies have cautioned against going too far: the State Customs Committee of the Russian Federation in a Letter of 19 October 1994, No. 01-13/11928, "On Informing and Advising", indicated that personnel of the legal service may not combine their duties with the direct effectuation of activity connected with the performance of customs formalization and customs control. Neither has the State Tax Service and State tax inspectorate been given the duty to advise enterprises, institutions, organizations, and citizens on taxation or other legal issues that arise in the course of their activities. Such advice only need be given when this is advisable in order to properly perform their functions.

Legal assistance provided by State employees as part of their official duties does not constitute advokat activity. The Federal Law of 27 July 2004, No. 79-ФЗ, as amended, "On State Civil Service of the Russian Federation"[12] defines a State office as those established by the Constitution of the Russian Federation or federal laws for the direct execution of powers of federal State agencies and offices established by the constitutions or charters or laws of subjects of the Russian Federation for the direct execution of powers of State agencies of subjects of the Russian Federation. A List of State offices is set out in the Register of State Offices of Federal State Employees, confirmed by Edict of the President of the Russian Federation on 31 December 2005, No. 1574, as amended.[13] There are analogous registers for State employees of subjects of the Russian Federation.

Legal assistance rendered to military servicemen also does not qualify as advocate activity. The Federal Law of 27 May 1998, No. 76-ФЗ "On the Status of Military Servicemen", as amended,[14] expressly provides that legal assistance shall be rendered free of charge by military administration agencies and military justice agencies within the limits of their functional or official duties to all military servicemen, citizens discharged from military service, and members of their families with regard to questions connected with undergoing military service (Article 22). Advokats may render legal assistance to military servicemen undergoing military service in the procedure determined by the Government of the Russian Federation. The "procedure" is laid down in the Rules for the Rendering by Advokats of Legal Assistance to Military Ser-

12 СЗ РФ (2004), no. 31, item 3215, as amended.

13 СЗ РФ (2006), no. 1, item 118, as amended .

14 СЗ РФ (1998), no. 22, item 2331, as amended.

vicemen Undergoing Military Service by Call-up with regard to Questions Connected with Undergoing Military Service, and also on Other Grounds Established by Federal Laws, confirmed by Decree of the Government of the Russian Federation No. 445, of 23 July 2005.[15] Military units may pay for the services of an advokat to a military serviceman pursuant to a civil-law contract concluded between the serviceman and the advokat under these Rules, as amended.

The Plenipotentiary for Human Rights in the Russian Federation has been granted the competence to consider appeals of applicants against a decision or action or failure to act of State agencies, agencies of local self-government, officials, and State employees if the applicant had appealed against such decision, action, or failure to act in a judicial or administrative proceeding but did not agree with the decisions taken with regard to his appeal under the Federal Constitutional Law of the Russian Federation of 26 February 1997, No. 1-ФКЗ "On the Plenipotentiary for Human Rights in the Russian Federation".[16]

It should be noted that officials who do render legal assistance are required to do so within their *vires*. To act otherwise could amount to abuse of official position.

Advokat activity does not include legal assistance rendered by participants and workers of organizations rendering legal services, nor by individual entrepreneurs. This language would appear to encompass the activities of foreign law firms in the Russian Federation, as well as of other organizations, such as auditing companies, which may offer a limited range of legal services and advice. Foreign law firms by definition do not and cannot form part of the Russian Advokatura. They have a right of audience in Russian courts only through an advokat unless provided otherwise by Russian legislation. Individual foreigners have, since 1 July 2002, in principle the right to qualify as advokats, a status previously reserved solely to Russian citizens. Most foreign law firms establish a presence either by creating a representation office or branch of the parent firm or by creating a Russian juridical person in the ownership of the foreign parent or designated partners of the foreign parent (the choice of vehicle commonly being dictated by bar regulations in the foreign jurisdiction). Law firms wholly-owned by foreign lawyers and without a foreign parent, or foreign lawyers registering as individual entrepreneurs, are uncommon, although there are individual examples.

Russian legislation does not deal consistently and comprehensively with the status of foreign lawyers. In CIS jurisdictions generally the trend has been to classify foreign lawyers working for foreign law firms as a species of jurisconsult, a plausible classification since in most CIS countries foreigners may not become advokats and they are employed by or are co-owners (as partners) of the law firms with which they

15 СЗ РФ (2005), no. 31, item 3226, as amended.

16 СЗ РФ (1997), no. 9, item 1011, as amended; transl. in W. E. Butler, *Russian Public Law* (2d ed.; 2009), pp. 111-121.

are associated. Although the citizenship discrimination has been removed in Russia, on the whole non-advokat foreign lawyers are closer to the jurisconsult than to any other component of the Russian legal profession (see the Commentary to Article 2(6), below).

Auditors may, under the Federal Law on Auditor Activity of 7 August 2001, No. 119-ФЗ, as amended,[17] offer services accompanying an audit, including tax consulting, legal consulting, as well as representation in judicial and tax agencies with regard to tax and customs disputes, working out and analyzing investment projects and drawing up business plans (Article 1).

Traditionally the notary in Russia, "the humble guardian of legality", has offered a considerable repertoire of legal advice and, indeed, is a specialist in the provision of certain types of legal documentation to clients. The Fundamental Principles of Legislation of the Russian Federation on the Notariat of 11 February 1993, No. 4462-1, as amended,[18] call upon the notary to defend the rights and legal interests of citizens and juridical persons by means of performing in the name of the Russian Federation the notarial actions provided for by legislative acts. The notary is a key component of the Russian legal profession and has a higher legal education. In addition to performing notarial actions, the notary draws up draft transaction documents, applications, and other documents, prepares copies of documents and extracts therefrom, and gives explanations on the performance of notarial actions, including their legal consequences. Subjects of the Russian Federation may (and do) enlarge the powers of notaries by granting them additional rights in their laws on the notariat. Officials of agencies of executive power who are authorized by legislation to perform notarial actions also do not engage in advokat activity; such officials are chiefly in remote and rural areas where there are no State or private notarial offices.

Under the Federal Law on Patent Attorneys of 30 December 2008,[19] patent attorneys have the right to conduct cases and matters with regard to intellectual property on behalf of applicants, right-possessors, and other interested citizens and juridical persons permanently resident (citizens) or having a location (juridical persons) in the Russian Federation or beyond the limits thereof. Patent attorneys are citizens of the Russian Federation who are at least eighteen years of age, permanently reside in Russia, have at least four years experience in the area of specialization for which they wish to be attested as a patent attorney, have full dispositive legal capacity, are not State or municipal civil servants, and have been attested and registered. Advokats may not appear before the federal agency for intellectual property unless they have

---

17 СЗ РФ (2001), no. 33(I), item 3422, as amended.

18 Ведомости СНД и ВС РФ (1993), no. 10, item 357, as amended; transl. in W. E. Butler, *Russia and The Republics: Legal Materials* (2006-; looseleaf service).

19 СЗ РФ (2009), no. 1, item 24.

been registered as patent attorneys. A foreign jurist who qualifies as a Russian advokat nonetheless could not be a patent attorney because of the citizenship requirement.

Point 3 of this Article also refers to other persons specially empowered by a law to conduct their professional activity. The classic example is the legal representative who by virtue of a law acts in all State or other institutions to defend the personal and property rights and the legal interests of persons who lack or who are limited in dispositive legal capacity or who by virtue of their physical state cannot effectuate their rights nor fulfill their duties, or who are minors. As a rule, parents, adoptive parents, trustee, or guardian act as legal representatives. The position may differ from one branch of law to another, the principal enactments being the Code of Criminal Procedure, Code of Civil Procedure, Code of Arbitrazh Procedure, CAdV, and Federal Law on an Execution Proceeding.

In practice, legal advice may be given outside State structures within the context of particular programs. Needle exchange centers operating within Harm Reduction Programs, for example, routinely advise narcotics addicts on legal provisions relevant to their situation.[20] The same is true with respect to trade unions, labor inspectorates, and the like.

ARTICLE 2 ADVOKAT

1. *A person who has received the status of advokat in the procedure established by the present Federal Law and the right to effectuate advokat activity shall be an advokat. An advokat shall be an independent professional advisor with regard to legal questions. An advokat shall not have the right to enter into labor relations as a worker, except for scholarly, teaching, and other creative activity, nor also to occupy State offices of the Russian Federation, State offices of subjects of the Russian Federation, and offices of State service and municipal offices [as amended by Federal Law of 20 December 2004].*
   An advokat shall have the right to combine advokat activity with work as an executive of an advokat formation, and also with work in elective offices in the chamber of advokats of a subject of the Russian Federation (hereinafter – chamber of advokats), Federal Chamber of Advokats of the Russian Federation (hereinafter – Federal Chamber of Advokats), and all-Russian and international social associations of advokats [added by Federal Law of 20 December 2004].
2. *In rendering legal assistance an advokat shall:*
   (1) give consultations and references with regard to legal questions both in oral and in written form;

20 See W. E. Butler, *Narcotics & HIV/AIDS in Russia: Harm Reduction Policies Under Russian Law* (2005).

(2) draw up applications, appeals, petitions, and other documents of a legal character;
(3) represent the interests of the principal in a constitutional proceeding;
(4) participate as a representative of the principal in a civil and administrative proceeding;
(5) participate as a representative or defender of the principal in a criminal proceeding and proceeding for cases concerning administrative violations;
(6) participate as a representative of the principal in the examination of cases in an arbitration court, international commercial arbitral tribunal (or court), and other agencies for the settlement of disputes;
(7) represent the interests of the principal in agencies of State power, agencies of local self-government, social associations, and other organizations;
(8) represent the interests of the principal in agencies of State power, courts, and law enforcement agencies of foreign States, international judicial organs, non-State agencies of foreign States unless established otherwise by the legislation of foreign States, charter documents of international judicial organs, and other international organizations or international treaties of the Russian Federation;
(9) participate as a representative of the principal in an execution proceeding, and also in the event of the execution of a criminal punishment;
(10) act as a representative of the principal in tax legal relations.

3. *An advokat shall have the right to render other legal assistance not prohibited by a federal law.*
4. *Only advokats may act as representatives of organizations, agencies of State power, and agencies of local self-government in a civil and administrative court proceeding and court proceeding with regard to cases concerning administrative violations, except for instances when workers on the personnel establishment of the said organizations, agencies of State power, and agencies of local self-government fulfill these functions, unless established otherwise by a federal law.*
5. *Advokats of a foreign State may render legal assistance on the territory of the Russian Federation with regard to questions of the law of the particular foreign State.*
   Advokats of foreign States shall not be permitted to render legal assistance on the territory of the Russian Federation with regard to questions connected with State secrecy of the Russian Federation.
6. *Advokats of foreign States effectuating advokat activity on the territory of the Russian Federation shall be registered by the federal agency of executive power in the domain of justice (hereinafter – federal justice agency) in a special register, the procedure for keeping which shall be determined by the empowered federal agency of executive power [as amended by Federal Law of 23 July 2008].*
   Without registration in the said register the effectuation of advokat activity by advokats of foreign States shall be prohibited on the territory of the Russian Federation.

1. The decisive moment in conferment of the "status of advokat" is taking the oath of an advokat. From that instant the individual concerned acquires the status of advokat and becomes a member of a chamber of advokats. The procedure for acquiring the status of advokat is regulated by Articles 9 to 13 of the present Law. The substance of what the status of advokat means does not vary with the "form of advokat formation" with which the advokat associates: advokat cabinet, college of advokats, advokat bureau, or legal consultation office. See the Commentary on the forms of advokat formations in Articles 21 to 24 below.

The right to effectuate advokat activity is the subject of Commentary to Article 1 above.

The present Article refers to the advokat as an independent advisor with regard to legal questions. This suggests that the central pivotal element in advokat activity is the advokat's role as the provider to the client of recommendations which the client may use when entering into, changing, or terminating particular legal relations. However, the term "advisor" substantially understates the role of the advokat, who may structure transactions, actually defend the client's interests in a judicial or arbitral proceeding, or represent the client personally in other ways, or may gather evidence in a civil, arbitrazh, or criminal proceeding, draw up documents, and the like.

The adjective "independent" in this context refers not to the profession of advokat as a whole, or to the Advokatura, but rather to the advokat's role as an "advisor". However, the status of being an independent advisor derives from the special status of the profession of advokat and requires that the advokat, in advising his client, have no conflicts of interest with another client nor accept instructions or any forms of pressure from State agencies, local self-government, political parties, social associations, or other outside sources or interests, nor interference from law enforcement agencies, including the procuracy, investigator, or agency of inquiry, nor a court or arbitral tribunal. Each advokat also must act independently of the advokat community; that is, other advokats and agencies or officials of the advokatura. While this does not preclude an advokat from seeking advice from his colleagues in the interests of his client, any advice received must be purely that and not guidance or instructions. An advokat may invite a member of a chamber of advokats to assist with a case on a formal basis.

Advokats are limited in activities which they may engage in outside advokat activity. The present Law mentions three: scientific, teaching, and "other creative" activity. This limitation also existed throughout much of the Soviet era. It is a more severe limitation than exists in many other legal systems, where the test is a conflict of interest rather than an enumeration of activities. Presumably the intention of the legislator, in a market economy context, is to reduce potential conflicts of interest and encourage the advokat to concentrate his attention and energies upon his profession. Since an advokat is precluded under this formulation from holding State office, the risks of corruption from that source are minimized.

In an Explanation adopted on 10 December 2003, the Federal Chamber of Advokats determined that the prohibition against an advokat engaging in other paid activity does not extend to apprentices of an advokat. Apprentices are hired on the basis of a labor contract concluded with an advokat formation or, in the instance of an advokat cabinet, with the advokat personally – in this last instance the advokat concerned being the employer. The Labor Code of the Russian Federation (Article 98) extends entirely to apprentices, including their right to hold a second job. Advokats are recommended to stipulate in the labor contract with apprentices that the apprenticeship is their principal place of work and any prior labor relations or employment must be confirmed as terminated in the labor book (unless this is the apprentice's first job).

The question arises whether an advokat may be an investor and hold stocks, participatory shares, or shares and derive revenues or profits from the entrepreneurial activity of others. The argument has been made that such investments should be regarded as permissible, for such a prohibition would be contrary to Article 34(1) of the 1993 Russian Constitution that each has the right to free use of his abilities and property for entrepreneurial and other activity not prohibited by a law. This argument, however, begs the question, for the same observation may be made about most any additional activities undertaken by advokats. If such investments are to be permitted for advokats, presumably the conflicts of interest test should be applied and appropriate disclosures made.

The present Law offers no definition of "scientific", or "scholarly", activity. General definitions of scientific or scientific-research activity are to be found in the Federal Law of 23 August 1996, No. 127-ФЗ, as amended, "On Science and State Scientific-Technical Policy"[21] While this would enable an advokat also to engage in activity as a nuclear scientist, in practice the reference is to scientific legal research of any species or variety. In Russia, as in most continental legal systems, one refers to "legal science".

Advokats may engage in teaching activities and commonly do so, making a substantial and, on the basic of practical experience, original contribution to the educational program at many Russian and foreign educational institutions. The types of educational institutions and regulation of the teaching profession are laid down in The Law of the Russian Federation of 10 July 1992, No. 3266-1 "On Education", as amended,[22] and in accordance with the Model Statute on an Educational Institution of Higher Vocational Education (or Higher Educational Institution), confirmed by Decree of the Government of the Russian Federation on 14 February 2008, No. 71.[23] Advokats also may lecture in educational institutions created and functioning on the basis of the Model Statute on an Educational Institution of Additional Vocational

21 СЗ РФ (1996), no. 35, item 4137, as amended.
22 СЗ РФ (1996), no. 3, item 150, as amended.
23 СЗ РФ (2008), no. 8, item 731.

Education (Increasing Qualifications) of Specialists, confirmed by Decree of the Government of the Russian Federation of 26 June 1995, No. 610, as amended.[24]

In fact, there is no prohibition against advokats performing teaching activities in any educational institution, private, State, or foreign. Moreover, the expression "teaching" is broad enough to encompass special seminars, short courses, professional training schemes, and the like. When the advokat is appropriately qualified, he also may supervise and examine magister, kandidat, and doctoral dissertations. Nor need the teaching necessarily concern the law.

"Creative activity" is a broad term, defined in legislation as the "creation of cultural valuables and the interpretation thereof". Cultural valuables are moral and aesthetic ideals, norms and models of behavior, language, dialects, national traditions and customs, folklore, historical toponyms, folk arts and crafts, works of culture and art, results and methods of scientific research of cultural activity having historical and cultural significance, buildings, installations, articles, and technologies, and others. A "creative worker" is a natural person who creates or interprets cultural valuable irrespective of whether he or she is or is not associated with various associations of creative workers. These are definitions and concepts elaborated in the Fundamental Principles of Legislation of the Russia Federation on Culture, of 9 October 1992, No. 3612-1, as amended.[25]

2. Ten forms of advokat activity are enumerated in point two of this Article. Although cast as an exhaustive enumeration, it is clear from point 3 that the enumeration is not exhaustive.

(1) So-called "consultations and references" form, in the Russian practice of law, a distinctive form of "legal product" for principals that would be difficult, as such, to market in the Anglo-American legal system outside legal aid centers. They are perhaps, numerically speaking, the most common form of advice that clients receive from advokats and consist of "legal information" in written or oral form about the existing state of legislation on a particular question. One Commentary declares: "An advokat gives consultations and references irrespective of whether a specific legal relation is present or the obtaining of information arose through the simple interest of a citizen".[26]

Whereas a reference constitutes information on particular provisions of a law, a consultation constitutes an explanation or explication of the legislation. As a rule, the advokat is expected to give both at the time the client applies for assistance; that is, as a rule independent research of the issues is not expected. Where additional

24 СЗ РФ (1995), no. 27, item 2580, as amended.

25 Ведомости СНД и ВС РФ (1992), no. 46, item 2615, as amended.

26 Grinenko, in A. V. Grinenko (ed.), Комментарий к Федеральному закону «Об адвокатской деятельности и адвокатуре в Российской Федерации [Commentary to the Federal Law "On Advokat Activity and the Advokatura in the Russian Federation] (2003), p. 25.

time is required to provide an answer, a second appointment will be scheduled or the question referred to a colleague who specializes in the particular branch of law. It is prohibited to give incomplete, unspecific, or inaccurate replies to the questions. It should be explained to the client that he may receive the information requested orally or in writing. A large portion of such advocate activity is of a routine and repetitive character and figures strongly in the approach to the legal education of a jurist.

(2) The applications, appeals, petitions, and other documents drawn up by an advokat are to be of a "legal character", which means that such documents should contain a "request (or demand) concerning the commencement, change, or termination of legal relations".[27] An *application* contains a substantiated request to initiate legal relations and must be specific, addressed to the proper addressee, and be signed by the applicant. An advokat who signs an application will attach thereto his power of attorney. In some instances the applicant must initiate proceedings personally and may not use an advokat to sign on his behalf.

An *appeal* is a document of recourse to a superior agency or official that contains a request to change, repeal, vacate, or reverse a decision or to prohibit or deem illegal the action or failure to act of the agency or official with which the appeal is lodged. The appeal is addressed not to the person who performed the particular action or adopted the particular decision concerned, but rather to the superior head or other person who in accordance with a law is empowered to repeal or vacate such action or decision or failure to act. The person to whom the appeal is addressed must have the competence to resolve the matter in substance. A second or further appeal on the same grounds may be filed with the person superior to that individual who previously turned down the appeal.

A *petition* is filed to obtain the fullest possible realization of own or represented rights to perform certain actions, adopt decisions, or refuse to do so, addressed to an agency or official having the necessary competence. The petition is considered to be something more in the nature of an official character, which means it is submitted when there are determined legal relations by a person endowed with the right to petition himself or through his representative, including an advokat, to a person empowered to resolve the issue raised in the petition in the procedure established by a law. The petition is in the nature of a request for the full realization of rights which have not been violated or were violated but may be restored to an agency or official competent to satisfy the petition or not. The fact that the petition is a request does not absolve the agency or official from the duty to settle the petition issue in accordance with a law.

Although this Article does not so stipulate, it follows that the documents concerned are prepared in written form. They must be drawn up in accordance with the canons for clerical correspondence, specify the official or agency to which they are

27 Ibid.

addressed, be designated by name, and set out their substance in clear and comprehensible form. The document must be signed. Anonymous applications, appeals, and other documents will not be considered – a long established practice in light of experience with anonymous denunciations during the Stalin era. As well as drawing up the respective documents, an advokat may oversee their proper registration in those agencies to which they have been addressed as determined by departmental acts.[28]

(3) Advokats do not have an exclusive right of audience in a constitutional court proceeding, but they may be retained by a principal to so act in accordance with the Federal Constitutional Law on the Constitutional Court of the Russian Federation, of 21 July 1994, No. 1-ФКЗ, as amended (Article 53[1]).[29] The principals may include applicants who, being agencies or natural persons, have sent a recourse to the Constitutional Court, or agencies or officials who have issued or signed an act whose constitutionality is subject to verification by the Court, or State agencies whose competence is being contested. Advokats also may advise those who appear before the Court *ex officio*, or a member of the Soviet of the Federation, or a deputy of the State Duma. Representation in each instance must be based on an appropriate power of attorney or other acceptable document. Advokats are, however, affected by Article 53(2) of the Federal Constitutional Law on the Constitutional Court of the Russian Federation which limits each party to not more than three representatives.

(4) Under the Code of Civil Procedure of the Russian Federation (Article 49), an advokat may represent a principal along with other persons who have dispositive legal capacity and have been duly empowered. Under the Code of Arbitrazh Procedure of the Russian Federation, an advokat may represent an individual entrepreneur (Article 59[3]) or an organization (Article 59[5]).

In a Decree of 16 July 2004, No. 15-П, the Constitutional Court of the Russian Federation held Article 59(5) of the Code of Arbitrazh Procedure to be unconstitutional insofar as it together with the present provision operated to exclude persons rendering legal assistance from appearing in court as representatives of an organization because they were not advokats or persons on the personnel establishment of the organization concerned.[30]

(5) In a criminal proceeding an advokat may be retained to act on behalf of the prosecution or defense. Representation for the prosecution will occur when the advokat defends the interests of the victim, civil plaintiff, or private accuser (Article 45(1), Code of Criminal Procedure). When acting for the defense, the advokat may

28 An example of such a departmental act is the Provisional Instruction on the Organization of Clerical Work in a District Court, confirmed by Order of the Judicial Department attached to the Supreme Court of the Russian Federation of 29 January 1999, No. 8, as amended by Order of 15 October 2001, No. 140.

29 СЗ РФ (1994), no. 13, item 1447, as amended; transl. in Butler, *Russian Public Law* (2d ed.; 2009), pp. 518-555.

30 СЗ РФ (2004), no. 31, item 3282.

be retained to defend the interests of a suspect or accused and render legal assistance during the proceedings with regard to a criminal case. An advokat also may be retained to defend the interests of a civil defendant in a criminal proceeding.

The Code of Criminal Procedure makes provision for an advokat to be retained by a witness summoned for questioning (Article 189[5]).[31]

The Code on Administrative Violations of the Russian Federation makes provision for an advokat to take part in an administrative proceeding from the moment under Article 25.5 an administrative protocol is drawn up. The advokat may act as defender with respect to the person accused or a representative of the victim.

The Constitutional Court of the Russian Federation in a Decree of 28 January 1997, No. 2-П, held that the provisions of the Code of Criminal Procedure then in force requiring that only an advokat could be a defender upon the presentation by him of an order of a legal consultation office was not contrary to the Russian Constitution. In this case the defendant had wished to appoint a non-advokat to represent him in the preliminary investigation, an option not contemplated by the Code of Criminal Procedure, although in this instance the proposed defender was licensed to perform legal services under a governmental decree then in force.[32]

(6) An advokat may take part as a representative of a party in an arbitration court formed in accordance with the Federal Law on Arbitration Courts in the Russian Federation of 24 July 2002, No. 102-ФЗ.[33] Although this Article expressly provides that an advokat also may participate in an international commercial arbitration tribunal or court and other agencies for the settlement of disputes, the provision is superfluous because who may participate as a representative is regulated by the Rules of each arbitral court or tribunal or other locus for alternative dispute resolution. The present Law would be relevant only if advokats were prohibited or limited in such representation. The clause is a good example of "overly-ambitious legislation"

The present Law says nothing whatsoever about the right of an advokat to act as an arbitrator either within the Russian Federation or in an international arbitration court or tribunal.

(7) Under Article 10 of the 1993 Russian Constitution, State power in the Russian Federation is divided into three branches: legislative, executive, and judicial. Commentators take the view that advokats may represent the interests of principals before any or all agencies of State power irrespective of their level,[34] including the subjects

31 СЗ РФ (2001), no. 52(I), item 4921, as amended; transl. in Butler, *Russian Criminal Law and Procedure* (2011).

32 For the Decree and four dissenting opinions, see СЗ РФ (1997), no. 7, item 871.

33 СЗ РФ (2002), no. 30, item 3019; transl. in Butler, *Russia and The Republics: Legal Materials* (2006-; looseleaf service).

34 Grinenko, in A. V. Grinenko (ed.), Комментарий к Федеральному закону «Об адвокатской деятельности и адвокатуре в Российской Федерации [Commentary to the Federal Law "On Advokat Activity and the Advokatura in the Russian Federation] (2003), p. 29.

of the Russian Federation. This right to represent does not extend to agencies of State administration (for example, ministries). An All-Russian Classificator of Agencies of State Power and Administration was confirmed by Decree of the State Committee for Standards of Russia on 30 December 1993, No. 294, as amended.[35] The federal agencies of State power are divided in the Classificator into the following classification groupings: (a) President of the Russian Federation (excluding the Security Council of the Russian Federation and the Administration of the President of the Russian Federation); (b) Federal Assembly of the Russian Federation (including the Soviet of the Federation and the State Duma); (c) executive power of the Russian Federation (including the Government of the Russian Federation, federal ministries, State committees, federal committees of Russia, federal services of Russia, federal agencies of Russia, federal supervisors of Russia, and other federal agencies of executive power such as, for example, the Administration of Affairs of the President of Russia, the Chief Administration of Special Programs of the Russian Federation); (d) judicial power of the Russian Federation (including the Constitutional Court, system of federal courts of general jurisdiction, system of arbitrazh courts, system of the Procuracy, and system of the Judicial Department attached to the Supreme Court of the Russian Federation.

Agencies of State power of subjects of the Russian Federation include agencies of representative or legislative power of subjects, agencies of executive power of subjects, agencies of judicial power of subjects, including constitutional courts and justices of the peace.

Agencies of local self-government include elective agencies of local self-government of districts, cities, districts in cities, elective agencies of local self-government of settlements, rural soviets, rural population centers, and other agencies of local self-government.

Advokats may represent social associations, the definition of which is found in the Federal Law on Social Associations of 19 May 1995, No. 82-ФЗ, as amended.[36] A social association may take the form of a social movement, social foundation, social institution, political party, or others.

"Other organizations" for the purposes of this Article include noncommercial organizations created under the Federal Law on Noncommercial Organizations of 12 January 1996, No. 7-ФЗ, as amended[37] and philanthropic organizations created under Federal Law on Philanthropic Activity and Philanthropic Organizations, of 11 August 1995, No. 135-ФЗ, as amended.[38]

35 Issued as a separate publication. Available as amended on Consultant Plus.
36 СЗ РФ (1995), no. 21, item 1930, as amended.
37 СЗ РФ (1996), no. 3, item 145, as amended; transl. in Butler, *Russia and The Republics: Legal Materials* (2006-; looseleaf service).
38 СЗ РФ (1995), no. 33, item 3340, as amended.

(8) The matters enumerated in this point of the present Article likewise are within the purview of the international court, tribunal, or country concerned. The provision, however, implies that Russian advokats are advokats of "special legal capacity"; that is, may do only that which Russian legislation expressly empowered them to do. The opposite presumption should operate when a State undertakes to regulate a profession such as the legal profession; that an advokat may undertake any representation of a client which is not contrary to professional canons of ethics.

The definition of an "international treaty of the Russian Federation" is to be found in the Federal Law on International Treaties of 15 July 1995, No. 101-ФЗ.[39] Why Russian advokats should be limited in this respect is not clear. Commentators frequently fail to understand that a treaty of the Russian Federation, in order to be such, must be in force. For example, it is alleged that "an advokat has the right to represent the interests of a principal" before the International Criminal Court formed under the Rome Statute; Russia signed the Statute on 8 September 2000, but has not ratified, however, which means that the Statute is not yet an international treaty of the Russian Federation.[40] In my view a Russian advokat should have the right to appear before the International Criminal Court if instructed by a client who is before that Court and the Statute so provides, irrespective of whether the treaty is in force for Russia or whether the Law on the Advokatura so provides. This provision of the Law on the Advokatura is inconsistent with international law, for it will be a rare international document that makes special mention of a Russian advokat with respect to the right of representation.

When the Russian Federation brought a case before the International Law of the Sea Tribunal, it was represented by foreign counsel, by jurisconsults from the Ministry of Foreign Affairs of the Russian Federation, and by legal scholars.[41]

(9) The Federal Law on an Execution Proceeding of 2 October 2007, No. 229-ФЗ[42] (Article 53) does not exclude an advokat from acting as a representative of a debtor or of the recovering party (see Commentary to Article 1 above for the right of an advokat to be the legal representative of a minor in an execution proceeding). The personal participation of a citizen in an execution proceeding does not deprive him of the right to have a representative unless the duties of the debtor may be performed only personally. The powers of the representative who is an advokat must be confirmed by a power of attorney that confers a general power to act in the execution proceeding and also specially stipulates the powers of the advokat to present and recall the document

39 СЗ РФ (1995), no. 29, item 2757, as amended; transl. in Butler, *Russia and The Republics: Legal Materials* (2006-; looseleaf service).

40 See Grinenko, in Grinenko (ed.), Комментарий к Федеральному закону «Об адвокатской деятельности и адвокатуре в Российской Федерации [Commentary to the Federal Law "On Advokat Activity and the Advokatura in the Russian Federation] (2003), p. 31.

41 "Volga" (Russian Federation v. Australia), Prompt Release, Judgment, ITLOS Reports 2002, p. 12.

42 СЗ РФ (2007), no. 41, item 4849, as amended.

of execution, transfer his powers to another person, appeal against the actions of the executing bailiff, and receive the property or money awarded by the court.

The "execution of a criminal punishment" is a fundamentally different concept from that of "execution of a judgment". In a criminal proceeding, execution of punishment is a procedural stage in the application of Section XIV of the Code of Criminal Procedure of the Russian Federation. The Rules of Internal Labor Order of Correctional Institutions (point 11)[43] provide that a convicted person has the right to receive legal assistance upon his application from advokats and other persons who have the right to render legal assistance. The number of such meetings is not limited in quantity or duration, provided they are held during non-work hours of the convicted person and between the hours of rising in the morning and retiring at night.

Minors who are serving deprivation of freedom may meet with advokats and other persons who have the right to render legal assistance during hours outside those designated for study and work. The advokat needs to present identity documents and an order of a legal consultation office or other documents certifying his right to render legal assistance. Upon the written application of relatives or representatives of the trusteeship council or parental committee, legal assistance may be refused to a minor serving deprivation of freedom.

(10) Advokats may assist taxpayers in formalizing revenue declarations and may be present during tax verifications in order to ensure that tax officials comply with legislation when performing the verification. Tax officials have the right to require of the advokat that he present identity documents and an authorization to represent the client.

3. Point 3 clarifies the misleading formulation of point 2 by stipulating that an advokat may render other types of legal assistance irrespective of whether these have been consolidated in Russian legislation or not.

Among examples of other legislation allowing an advokat to act in this respect is the Federal Law "On the Fundamental Principles of the System of Preventing Delinquency and Violations of Law by Minors", of 24 June 1999, No. 120-ФЗ, as amended.[44] Parents or legal representatives of a minor who has not reached the age of criminal responsibility but who has committed a socially dangerous act may engage the assistance of an advokat to advise on materials and documents submitted by an internal affairs or procuracy agency to a commission for cases of minors. If the minor is tried in court, the participation of an advokat is obligatory, and an advokat has the standing to file an appeal against a decision to place the minor in an instructional-educational institution of the closed-type.

43 Confirmed by Order of the Ministry of Justice of the Russian Federation, 3 November 2005, No. 205, as amended. БНА ФОИВ (2005), no. 47.

44 СЗ РФ (1999), no. 16, item 3177, as amended.

Although there is support for the right of advokats to render assistance to persons suffering from mental illness pursuant to Principles adopted by the United Nations on 17 December 1991, the legal status of the United Nations document is unclear as a matter of Russian law.

Russian Commentators enumerate as "other types of legal assistance not expressly prohibited by law" the advice of an advokat to a client with regard to tactics of defense – which an Anglo-American lawyer would regard as the very essence of a proper criminal defense. This need to underscore the precise functions of an advokat is revealing in and of itself of conceptual differences in the status of the Russian advokat and some of his foreign counterparts.

4. The formulation of this point commences with the exposition of a monopoly right of advokats, which is then subject to an exception. Only advokats may act as the representatives of organizations, agencies of State power, and agencies of local self-government in civil and administrative court proceedings or a court proceeding concerning administrative violations. However, workers (including jurists) who are on the personnel establishment (whether by labor contract, independent-work contract, or other form of relationship is not stipulated) of the said entities may fulfill such functions unless established otherwise by a federal law. Plainly the "federal law" is not the Law on the Advokatura, for that would make nonsense of the clause.

The 2002 Code of Arbitrazh Procedure (Article 59) provides in this connection that, in addition to advokats, the "executives of organizations operating within the limits of powers provided for by a federal law, other normative legal act, constitutive documents, or persons on the personnel establishment of such organizations" may act as representatives in an arbitrazh court.

5. The formulation of point 5 must be one of the unhappiest ever to appear in post-Soviet Russian legislation. It consecrates an ignorance of the legal profession generally, of comparative law, and of legal practice that is nothing less than breathtaking. The formulation "advokat of a foreign State" is subject to the following observations. First, "advokat" is a defined term under point 1 of this Article (see above). Read literally, the term must refer to a Russian advokat who is employed or retained by a foreign State. Second, the formulation assumes that foreign countries (outside the former USSR) have (a) a legal specialist called an "advokat" which is defined identically as in point 1 of this Article or is entirely analogous to the Russian advokat; and (b) that such a lawyer is "of a foreign State". Both are false assumptions. While it is commonplace to speak in the English language of a lawyer being or acting as an "advocate", this is merely a narrow descriptive function of a lawyer's activity (and not only a lawyer's) rather than a professional classification. In other legal systems where the term "advocate", or "avocat" and similar terms are used, they either do not refer to a professional classification or have in view a professional classification, which at best only loosely approximates those of a Russian advokat.

The phrase "of a foreign State" plainly suggests an advokat employed or retained by, either permanently or for an individual case, to defend the interests of a foreign State; routinely, a government legal advisor – a concept which has nothing in common with the definition of an advokat in point 1 of this Article. Construed more broadly, for example, to encompass a person who is a citizen of a foreign State and who is a lawyer in the State of his citizenship, is likewise legal nonsense. In most democratic societies the legal profession is sharply differentiated from the State, precisely in order to minimize unwelcome State interference in the legal profession and its functions. In federated jurisdictions (the United States, Canada, and others) lawyers are admitted to practice in subdivisions (provinces, states, and others) rather than the foreign State as a whole.

Moreover, citizenship is an unreliable and even unfair criterion for regulation of the profession. Many Russian citizens have studied abroad and become members of the legal profession in England or individual states of the United States. Insofar as they are Russian jurists with a Russian diploma in law, they would be, and should be, recognized as able to practice Russian law in the foreign jurisdiction where they reside and, insofar as they may be qualified in Russia as a Russian advokat, to practice as a Russian advokat in accordance with Russian legislation (including, as Russian citizens, the right to act with regard to questions connected with State secrets of the Russian Federation). They are lawyers properly qualified in two or more jurisdictions – an increasingly common phenomenon in our global legal community.

Moreover, there are foreign jurists who have a diploma or higher degree in law from Russian law faculties. It would be improper to refer only to their citizenship in order to determine their rights to take advantage of the opportunities which a qualification from a Russian educational institution makes available.

The proposition in point 5 that advokats of a foreign State should render legal assistance with regard to questions of their State shows an unfamiliarity with legal practice, comparative law, and international law. First, any lawyer, including Russian advokats, routinely meets in his practice other legal systems and legal rules of a transnational nature: public and private international law, conflicts of law issues, and others which do not neatly fall into the framework of national legal systems. Second, international commercial transactions in the widest use of that term routinely contain a choice of the applicable law of several jurisdictions with respect to various documents of the transaction. The legislator's image of how the legal profession deals with these challenges is simplistic and uninformed.

Foreign lawyers present in Russia are subject to the provisions of the Federal Law "On the Legal Status of Foreign Citizens in the Russian Federation" of 25 July 2002, No. 115-ФЗ.[45] A foreign citizen is defined as a natural person who is not a citizen of

45 СЗ РФ (2002), no. 30, item 3032, as amended; transl. in Butler, *Russia and The Republics: Legal Materials* (2006-; looseleaf service).

the Russian Federation and has evidence of being a citizen or subject of a foreign State. The Commentators believe that a stateless person also would fall within the purview of point 5 of this Article,[46] although the formulation of an "advokat of a foreign State" would literally exclude such an interpretation. Point 5 of this Article does not use the term "foreign citizen".

Foreign lawyers would be subject to restrictions on territories, organizations, and objects for which special authorization is required for entry, according to a List confirmed by Decree of the Government of the Russian Federation of 11 October 2002, No. 754, as amended.[47]

Foreign lawyers may take part in obtaining evidence on Russian territory in accordance with the Hague Convention of 18 March 1970 on Taking Evidence Abroad in Civil or Commercial Matters, to which Russia acceded on 12 February 2001,[48] and serve documents under the Hague Convention of 15 November 1965 on the Service Abroad of Judicial and Extrajudicial Documents in Civil or Commercial Matters.[49]

Foreign lawyers may not render legal assistance with regard to questions connected with State secrecy of the Russian Federation, the requirements of which are established by the Law on State Secrecy.[50] This provision is used to exclude foreign lawyers from certain matters on the principle that foreign citizenship precludes a Russian security clearance. It may, of course, operate in some instances to prevent a defendant from having an advokat of his choice.

The limitation extends to two types of cases: first, those which are in substance concerned with a State secret; second, those which involve materials or information, however incidentally, in which there is a State secret affecting the parties in litigation or the character and means of obtaining particular materials in a case.[51]

6. In accordance with point 6 of this Article a special register is maintained by the Ministry of Justice of the Russian Federation for advokats of foreign States who carry out advokat activity on the territory of the Russian Federation, the procedure for

---

46 Grinenko, in A. V. Grinenko (ed.), Комментарий к Федеральному закону «Об адвокатской деятельности и адвокатуре в Российской Федерации [Commentary to the Federal Law "On Advokat Activity and the Advokatura in the Russian Federation] (2003), p. 36.

47 СЗ РФ (2002), no. 41, item 3995, as amended.

48 Federal Law of 12 February 2001, No. 11-ФЗ. СЗ РФ (2001), no. 7, item 616.

49 Federal Law of 12 February 2001, No. 10-ФЗ. "On Accession of the Russian Federation to the Convention on the Service Abroad of Judicial and Extrajudicial Documents in Civil or Commercial Matters. СЗ РФ (2001), no. 7, item 615. See Merja Norros, *Judicial Cooperation in Civil Matters with Russia and Methods of Evaluation* (Helsinki, 2010).

50 Adopted 21 July 1993, No. 5485-1, in the version of Federal Law of 6 October 1997, No. 131-ФЗ, with changes introduced by Decree of the Constitutional Court of the Russian Federation of 27 March 1998, No. 8-П.

51 See D. Kozak (ed.), Научно-практический комментарий к Федеральному закону «Об адвокатской деятельности и адвокатуре в Российской Федерации» [Scientific-Practical Commentary to Federal Law "On Advokat Activity and the Advokatura in the Russian Federation] (2003), p. 19.

keeping which is determined by the Decree of the Government of the Russian Federation of 19 September 2003, as amended, "On the Procedure for Keeping the Register of Advokats of Foreign States Effectuating Advokat Activity on the Territory of the Russian Federation" (see the Annex, below). This register is intended neither to be permissive nor to be discriminatory in character, merely to record the individuals concerned and the correctness of the information they submit.

Article 3 The Advokatura and the State

1. *The advokatura shall be a professional community of advokats and as an institution of a civil society shall not be within the system of agencies of State power and agencies of local self-government.*
2. *The advokatura shall operate on the basis of the principles of legality, independence, self-government, corporativeness, and also the principle of the equality of advokats.*
3. *For the purposes of ensuring accessibility for the population to legal assistance and facilitating advokat activity the agencies of State power shall ensure guarantees of the independence of the advokatura, effectuate the financing of the activity of advokats rendering legal assistance to citizens of the Russian Federation free of charge in the instances provided for by legislation of the Russian Federation, and also, when necessary, allocate office premises and means of communications to advokat formations.*
4. *Social security provided for citizens by the Constitution of the Russian Federation shall be guaranteed to each advokat.*

1. It is, on the one hand, a lamentable feature of Russian history and, on the other, a considerable achievement of Russian democracy that the legislator has had to confirm the independence of the Advokatura from the system of State agencies and agencies of local self-government.

The concept of a "civil society" has been widely debated in Russian legal, philosophical, scientific, and other circles since the early 1990s. Whatever configuration for such a society is postulated, the legal profession and the rule-of-law are considered to have a vital role in forming and maintaining such a society. Many advokats see themselves as promoting the harmonious adjustment of individual and social interests in a civil society, an antidote to "power" methods of social management. The present Law is seen as an occasion where the State has "recognized" this role for the Advokatura, although whether such a role should require State recognition may itself be debated.

Although the term "Advokatura" has been used frequently in Russian and Soviet legislation, including the 1922 RSFSR Statute on the Advokatura, the 1962 RSFSR Statute on the Advokatura, the 1979 USSR Law on the Advokatura of the USSR, and the 1980 Statute on the Advokatura of the RSFSR, among others, the present Law is the first to offer a legal definition of the Advokatura. There is a considerable difference of opinion in Russian doctrinal writings as to whether the Advokatura is a public-law or a private-law institution.[52] Makarov takes the view that the Advokatura is not a social organization, but rather given a special place in the system of noncommercial organizations.[53] Others, perhaps recalling the 1980 Statute, consider the Advokatura to be a species of social organization.[54]

2. Point 2 of this Article refers to five principles which should guide the Advokatura. Of these, the first – *legality* – is commonly found in other legislative acts, including those regulating civil, criminal, and arbitrazh procedure, and the judiciary. In the context of Advokatura legislation it is defined variously by the commentaries. Some believe the principle means that the Advokatura and advokat formations must be created in strict conformity with legislation in force, including the present Law and that advokats in their activities are to strictly comply with the requirements of laws and the lawful demands of State agencies and law enforcement officials.[55] It would follow that for a violation of legislation advokats bear disciplinary, administrative, or criminal responsibility, as appropriate.

Disciplinary responsibility ensues when an advokat has committed an offense defaming the honor and dignity of an advokat or diminishing the authority of the Advokatura, failing to perform or improperly performing his professional duties to a principal, or not performing the decision of an organ of the chamber of advokats adopted within the limits of its competence (see Article 17(1), Commentary). The ultimate disciplinary sanction is having the status of advokat terminated.

An advokat who has committed an administrative offense would be brought to responsibility on the general grounds set out in the 2001 CAdV. Any such administrative proceeding would be subject to the general constitutional principle that an advokat is equal, just as any other Russian citizen, before law and court (Article 19, 1993 Russian Constitution) and to Article 18 of the present Law, stipulating that an advokat may not be subjected to any form of responsibility for opinions he may have expressed while performing advokat activities unless the advokat has committed a

---

52 These differences of view have origins in Imperial Russian doctrinal writings, where some Russian jurists regarded the advokatura as a public-law institution and the advokat as a public person. See K. K. Arsenev (1837-1919), Заметки о русской адвокатуре [Notes on the Russian Advokatura] (1875), p. 146; A. M. Palkhovskii, О праве представительства на суде [On the Right of Representation in Court] (1876), p. 215.

53 O. V. Makarov, «Организационные и правовые проблемы становления адвокатуры в Российской Федерации» [Organizational and Legal Problems of Origin of Advokatura in the Russian Federation], Адвокат [Advokat], no. 1 (2005).

54 See William Burnham, I. V. Reshetnikova, and A. D. Prishliakov, Судебная адвокатура [Judicial Advokatura] (1996), p. 10; A. A. Vlasov, Адвокат как субъект доказывания в гражданском и арбитражном процессе [Advokat as Subject of Proof in Civil and Arbitrazh Procedure] (2000), p. 6.

55 Grinenko, in A. V. Grinenko (ed.), Комментарий к Федеральному закону «Об адвокатской деятельности и адвокатуре в Российской Федерации [Commentary to the Federal Law "On Advokat Activity and the Advokatura in the Russian Federation] (2003), p. 40.

criminal act or failure to act as established by the judgment of a court that has entered into legal force.

Certain provisions of the 2001 CAdV would, by definition, not extend to advokats; for example, provisions relating to entrepreneurial activity. Others an advokat may be susceptible to committing, among them obstructing the activity of the Plenipotentiary for Human Rights in the Russian Federation (Article 17.2, CAdV), or failure to perform the instruction of a judge or court bailiff (Article 13.3, CAdV). Failure to fulfill the legal demands of a procurator, investigator, inquiry official, or official effectuating proceedings with regard to a case concerning an administrative violation (Article 17.7, CAdV) would engage the responsibility of an advokat only if the last were not acting in his professional capacity.

An advokat would be subject to criminal responsibility just as any Russian citizen, subject to the requirements of Article 18 of the present Law. The 1996 Criminal Code of the Russian Federation has potentially direct application to advokats under Chapter 31, crimes against justice: obstruction of the effectuation of justice and performance of a preliminary investigation (Article 294); threat of or forcible actions in connection with the effectuation of justice or performance or preliminary investigation (Article 296); disrespect of court (Article 297); slander with respect to judge, juror, procurator, investigator, person performing inquiry, judicial marshal, judicial bailiff (Article 298); falsification of evidence (Article 303); provocation of bribe (Article 304); bribing or coercion to give testimony or evade giving of testimony or improper translation (Article 309); divulgence of data of preliminary investigation (Article 310); and divulgence of information concerning security measures being applied to judge and participants of criminal proceeding (Article 310).[56]

The crimes set out in Chapter 31 of the 1996 Criminal Code share as an object the social relations arising in connection with ensuring the normal functioning of courts and other agencies and officials acting in criminal, civil, administrative, or other proceedings. Active resistance to the effectuation of justice is required; a failure to act is not sufficient. Direct intent is essential, except for falsification of evidence under Article 303(3) and divulgence of information under Article 311(2) of the Criminal Code. An advokat also could be prosecuted for giving a bribe under Article 291 of the Criminal Code.

Advokats need to be restrained in their remarks during trial and appeal proceedings addressed to court officials. Examples are known of advokats making exceptionally sharp remarks to a judge which constituted slander. In June 1967 the Leningrad Regional Court found a citizen guilty of homicide and sentenced him to fifteen years deprivation of freedom. In the appeal against this judgment by way of cassation the defense counsel made certain accusations against the judge, including official forgery in the form of falsification of the protocol of the judicial session; in the advokat's view,

56 See Butler, *Russian Criminal Law and Procedure* (2011).

the judge distorted the testimony of one of the witnesses as set out in the protocol. The offending phrase in the text of the appeal, "to falsify evidence thus is not only base, but stupid", became known to the judge concerned. The judge turned to the procurator, and criminal charges were brought against the advokat for slander. In the slander case the trial court found the advokat guilty and sentenced him to one year deprivation of freedom conditionally and a fine of ten thousand rubles.[57]

The 2001 Code of Criminal Procedure contains certain safeguards for advokats in order to reduce the possibility that the threat of criminal prosecution might be used to pressure them. The decision to initiate a criminal case against an advokat or to involve an advocate as an accused in a criminal proceeding instituted against other persons is taken by a procurator on the basis of the opinion of a judge of a district court (Article 448). If in the procurator's opinion the indicia of a particular crime are evident in the act of an advokat, the procurator must immediately send a recommendation to the district court. The judge verifies the materials received and gives an opinion as to whether there are the indicia of a crime in the actions or failure to act of the advokat. After this verification, the materials of the file of the case are returned to the procurator, who initiates a criminal case and refers the matter for preliminary investigation by one of the departments having investigative jurisdiction over the case (Article 151).

The principle of *independence* is said to include the rules for mutual relations within the structure of advokat formations. Russian legislation makes no provision for pressure on an individual advokat in the form of instructions, recommendations, and other types of regulations or documents emanating from the advokat community. Advokat formations and self-government organs of the Advokatura are not to interfere in the proceedings regarding an individual criminal, civil, administrative or other proceeding, nor offer advice or counsel unless requested by the advokat; even if advice is sought, it is purely recommendatory in nature. On relations between an advokat and advokat formations and organs of the Advokatura, see Articles 21-24 and 29-33 of the present Law. On guarantees of advokat independence, see Article 18 of the present Law.

The principle of *self-government* as a principle of organization and activity of advokats constitutes the aggregate of rules that ensure the autonomous regulation of relations arising in the community of advokats and the separation of advokats from agencies of State power and local self-government. Under the present Law, depending upon the numbers of chambers of advokats, the conference or meeting of advokats is the highest organ of the chamber of advokats. Self-government is exercised through the chambers and their organs. Decisions are taken by a simple majority of votes of

57 Grinenko, in A. V. Grinenko (ed.), Комментарий к Федеральному закону «Об адвокатской деятельности и адвокатуре в Российской Федерации [Commentary to the Federal Law "On Advokat Activity and the Advokatura in the Russian Federation] (2003), p. 43.

those present. The competence of a meeting or conference of advokats includes forming of council of chamber of advokats of a subject of the Russian Federation; adopting decision to terminate the powers of members of the council before time; confirming the procedure for determining the norms of representation and procedure for electing delegates to a conference; election of the internal audit commission and members of the qualifications commission from among advokats; election of delegates to the All-Russian Congress of Advocates; confirmation of reports of the executive organs; confirmation of the Reglaments of the meeting or conference of advokats, the council, and the internal audit commission.

Decisions taken by organs of the chamber of advokats are binding upon members provided they are within the competence of the respective organ (see Article 29 of the present Law). However, all executive organs of the chambers of advokats are accountable to and under the supervision of the meetings or conferences of advokats of a subject of the Russian Federation.

The qualifications commission created to administer the qualifications examinations for those who apply to become advokats and to consider appeals against the actions or failure to act of advokats also are based on the principle of self-government. Advokats comprise the majority (7 of 13) of members of the commissions. See Article 33 of the present Law on the procedure for organizing and the activities of qualifications commissions.

The Federal Chamber of Advokats is the organ of self-government which operates at the federal level. Its purpose is to represent and defend the interests of advokats in agencies of State power and agencies of local self-government, to coordinate the activity of chambers of advokats, and to ensure the high level of legal assistance rendered by advokats. Decisions of the Federal Chamber of Advokats are binding upon all chambers of advokats and organs thereof and upon all advokats. See Article 35 of the present Law.

The Federal Chamber of Advokats is accountable to the All-Russian Congress of Advokats. The Congress, reflective of the principle of self-government, forms the membership of the Council of the Federal Chamber and adopt a decision concerning the termination of the powers of its members before time; confirms the reports of the Council, including the estimate of expenses for maintenance of the Federal Chamber, elects the internal audit commission; and confirms the report concerning the results of financial-economic activity of the Council of the Federal Chamber. See Article 36 of the present Law.

The principle of *corporativeness* expresses the fact that the advokatura is organized and effectuates its activities as a voluntary union of persons united by common interests and their aim to properly defend their principals and afford access to justice. The term is deemed to apply in a special way to advokats. Persons endowed with the status of an advokat operate on a specific territory of the Russian Federation and are members of the chamber of advokats for that territory. The unity of advokats within the framework of their chamber is believed to account for the special character of relations among advokats. Such relations are built upon respect by proceeding from the priority of common values and interests. "Each advokat in mutual relations with agencies of State power and local self-government must not only render assistance to his principal, but also act as a structural cell of the advokat community, act in its interests".[58] All matters collegially discussed within advokat formations or a chamber of advokats and the Federal Chamber of Advokats must be resolved by proceeding from the standpoint of their advisability for the advokat community as a whole with maximum benefit to the advokat formation of a particular type or level. Organs of the advokat community are, between meetings or conferences, to take decisions directed towards strengthening the role of advokats in a civil society and to supervise compliance with the corporative rules of the advokat community.

The right and duty of qualifications commissions to offer an opinion as to whether to discipline advokats (the majority of members being advokats) is regarded as a manifestation of the corporativeness of the advokatura (see Article 33 of the present Law).

The principle of *equality* is expressed in the fact that those who have been endowed with the status of advokat become a full-fledged member of the advokat community. Advokats enjoy the protection of Article 19 of the 1993 Russian Constitution, under which the State guarantees equality of the rights and freedoms of man and citizen irrespective of sex, race, nationality, language, origin, property and official status, place of residence, attitude towards religion, convictions, affiliation to social associations, and other circumstances. All advokats have equal rights irrespective of how long they have worked in a legal specialty or engaged in practice as an advokat. Advokats have the right to freely and autonomously choose the form of advokat formation they prefer to conduct their professional activities within. All have an equal vote in advokat meetings or conferences.

3. Although the Advokatura is independent of agencies of State power and local self-government, it interacts with such agencies constantly and extensively. Herein lie some of the principal distinctions between the Russian advokats and their Anglo-American counterparts.

It is the legal duty of agencies of State power to make certain provision for the Advokatura, including financial, so that advokats may render legal assistance free of charge. Advokats also are commonly supplied with office space and with telephone and other communications by State and local government agencies. The Federal Law of 9 January 1998, No. 7-ФЗ "On the Judicial Department attached to the Supreme

58 Grinenko, in A. V. Grinenko (ed.), Комментарий к Федеральному закону «Об адвокатской деятельности и адвокатуре в Российской Федерации [Commentary to the Federal Law "On Advokat Activity and the Advokatura in the Russian Federation] (2003), p. 47.

Court of the Russian Federation"[59] is responsible for interaction with the advokatura on matters of ensuring that the courts are properly supplied with advokat services (Article 6[2]). Such interaction consists of the exchange of information about how many advokats are actually required to ensure the normal work of the courts. Neither the courts nor the advokatura have the right to dictate to one another the conditions on the basis of which these matters will be resolved.

The Ministry of Justice continues to play a role with respect to the advokatura at the level of subjects of the Russian Federation. Under the Statute on the Chief Administration of the Ministry of Justice of the Russian Federation for a Subject(s) of the Russian Federation,[60] a chief administration has among its principal tasks the "effectuation of control and supervision in the sphere of the advokatura and notariat" (Article 3[6]) and the power to "keep the register of advokats of a subject of the Russian Federation" (Article 6[33]), issue certificates to advokats confirming their status, take part in the qualifications commissions for advokats, make recommendations to the chamber of advokats in the respective subject of the Russian Federation that the status of advokat be terminated for a particular individual, apply to a court if the chamber of advokats fails to consider a recommendation to terminate an individual's status as an advokat, and others.

By Order of the Ministry of Justice of 15 January 2001, No. 10, a Model Agreement between the Ministry of Justice of the Russian Federation and a Subject of the Russian Federation Concerning Interaction in the Sphere of Justice was confirmed. One of the matters that falls within the purview of a Model Agreement is "questions of the organization and activity of the Advokatura".[61] The Commentators see such contracts not as a method of State control over the Advokatura, but as a requirement that the State make proper provision for Advokatura activities within the given territory.

The Advokatura has certain duties to supply information to the Ministry of Justice of the Russian Federation. An Order of the Ministry of Justice of the Russian Federation of 12 April 2001, No. 119, "On the Organization of Informing the Ministry of Justice of the Russian Federation on Processes in the Sphere of Justice in Subjects of the Russian Federation"[62] determined the substance, procedure for preparation, and procedure for submitting information to the Ministry by federal administrations for federal districts and other territorial-administrative entities. Among the information to be provided is that "in the sphere of the organization and activity of the advokatura". Such information concerns, *inter alia*, the sufficiency of advokat formations in a number of subjects of the Russian Federation and their accessibility to citizens. Migration processes, refugees, and resettled persons are part of this

59 СЗ РФ (1998), no. 2, item 223; transl. in Butler, *Russian Public Law* (2d ed.; 2009), pp. 578-586.

60 Confirmed by Order of the Ministry of Justice, 21 May 2009, No. 146, as amended. Available on Consultant Plus.

61 See Paragraph 1(4), Model Agreement. *Бюллетень Министерства юстиции РФ*, no. 2 (2001).

62 See Бюллетень Министерства юстиции РФ, no. 5 (2001).

reporting. Pursuant to a Regulation of the Minister of Justice of 20 December 2001, No. 303, "On the Practice of the Realization of the Order of the Ministry of Justice of Russia of 12 April 2001, No. 119", the information on the work of the Advokatura must contain an analysis of instances of the advokats refusing to represent in cases when assigned and facts of other violations by them of their professional duties, the reasons for and trends of such violations, and measures taken jointly with the colleges of advokats regarding such instances and the effectiveness of those measures.[63]

Advokats also serve in a personal capacity on advisory bodies of State agencies. One example is the Scientific-Consultative Council attached to the Supreme Court of the Russian Federation, confirmed by Decree of the Plenum of the Supreme Court of the RSFSR on 11 December 1968, No. 45, as amended by Decrees of the Plenum of the Supreme Court of the Russian Federation of 20 December 1983, No. 10; 21 December 1993, No. 11; 25 October 1996, No. 10; and 6 February 2007, No. 5.[64] Members of the Council participate in the study and generalization of judicial practice and may prepare drafts of recommendations and opinions for organs within the judicial system.

When legislation so provides that legal assistance must be rendered to citizens free of charge, the State must pay for the services of advokats from the State budget. For many years this was regulated by the Decree of the Council of Ministers – Government of the Russian Federation of 7 October 1993, No. 1011, "On Payment for Labor of Advokats at the Expense of the State".[65] It is presently regulated by the Decree of the Council of Ministers of 4 July 2003, No. 400 "On the Amount of Payment for Labor of an Advokat Participating as Defender in a Criminal Proceeding by Assignment of Agencies of Inquiry, Agencies of Preliminary Investigation, or a Court".[66]

Office premises provided to advokat formations were made available at controlled rents on the basis of a lease[67] until the relevant enactment was deemed not to be subject to application by an unpublished Order of the Ministry of Economic Development of the Russian Federation of 30 November 2009, No. 497.[68]

4. Advokats enjoy the protection of the Labor Code of the Russian Federation[69] and other normative legal acts regulating labor, leisure, and social security. Benefits for temporary labor disability, pregnancy and birth extend to advokats and are calculated on the basis of rules established for workers who are paid on a piece-work basis

63 See Бюллетень Министерства юстиции РФ, no. 1 (2002).
64 Available as amended on Consultant Plus.
65 САПП РФ (1993), no. 41, item 3927.
66 СЗ РФ (2003), no. 28, item 2925, as amended.
67 See the Procedure for Determining the Amount of Lease Payment for the Use of Buildings, Structures, Installations, and Individual Premises in Federal Ownership, an Annex to a Regulation of the Ministry of State Property of the Russian Federation, 30 April 1998, No. 396-p.
68 Available on Consultant Plus.
69 СЗ РФ (2002), no. 1(I), item 3, as amended; transl. in Butler, *Russia and The Republics: Legal Materials* (looseleaf service; 2006-).

if the insured events occurred before 24 July 2009.[70] After 24 July 2009 advokats were covered for temporary labor disability and maternity benefits under the Federal Law on Obligatory Social Insurance in the Event of Temporary Disability and In Connection with Maternity of 29 December 2006, No. 255-ФЗ,[71] provided that they have voluntarily made contributions in accordance with legislation. Advokats have the right to labor pensions in the procedure established by the Federal Law of 7 December 2001, No. 173-ФЗ, as amended, "On Labor Pensions in the Russian Federation".[72] Advokats fall into the category of persons who provide themselves with work and whose activity is calculated as part of general labor experience for the assignment and calculation of pensions.[73] Just as other individuals who fall into this category, advokats confirm the periods of their activity by means of a document issued by the territorial agency of the Pension Fund of the Russian Federation or territorial tax agency confirming that obligatory payments have been made.[74]

Colleges of advokats are required to submit reports as required under the Federal Law of 24 July 1998, No. 125-ФЗ, "On Obligatory Social Insurance against Accidents in Production and Vocational Illnesses"[75] and are subject to fines levied in accordance with the procedure laid down by the Tax Code of the Russian Federation for the failure to comply.[76]

Advokats do not keep labor books for themselves because they are regarded as self-employed. For pension purposes advokats demonstrate their years of service on the basis of a document issued by the territorial agency of the Pension Fund of the Russian Federation or territorial tax agency showing that contributions have been paid in. Nor do advokats who have founded advokat cabinets have the right to make entries in labor books for natural persons who they may employ. These employees prove their labor experience by references, accounting records, and other documents which give evidence of making contributions to various State funds.[77]

70 See the Decree of the Presidium of the All-Union Central Trade Union Council of 12 November 1984, No. 13-6, with changes and additions of the Presidium of the Council of the All-Russian Committee of Trade Unions as of 15 April 1992, as amended by the Letter of the Social Security Fund of the Russian Federation of 18 February 1999, No. 02-10/05-807.

71 СЗ РФ (2007), no. 1(I), item 18, as amended.

72 СЗ РФ (2001), no. 52(I), item 4920, as amended.

73 See the All-Russian Classificator of Information for Social Defense of the Population, confirmed by Decree of Gosstandart Russia of 17 December 1999, No. 545-ст.

74 See point 18, Rules for Calculation and Confirmation of Insurance Experience to Establish Labor Pensions, confirmed by Decree of the Government of the Russian Federation on 24 July 2002, No. 555, as amended. СЗ РФ (2002), no. 31, item 3110.

75 СЗ РФ (1998), no. 31, item 3803, as amended.

76 See Decree of the Federal Arbitrazh Court for the North Caucasian District, 15 March 2010, Case No. A77-688/2009.

77 See the Decision of the Federal Chamber of Advokats, 25 August 2003.

Article 4 Legislation on Advokat Activity and the Advokatura

1. *Legislation on advokat activity and the advokatura shall be based on the Constitution of the Russian Federation and shall consist of the present Federal Law, other federal laws, normative legal acts of the Government of the Russian Federation and federal agencies of executive power adopted in accordance with federal laws regulating the said activity, and also of laws and other normative legal acts of subjects of the Russian Federation adopted within the limits of powers established by the present Federal Law [renumbered by Federal Law of 20 December 2004].*
2. *The Code of Professional Ethics of an Advokat adopted in the procedure provided for by the present Federal Law shall establish rules of behavior obligatory for every advokat when effectuating advokat activity, and also the grounds and procedure for bringing advokats to responsibility [point 2 added by Federal Law of 20 December 2004].*

1. The 1993 Constitution of the Russian Federation is the foundation of legislation on advokat activity and the Advokatura and stands at the apex of Russian sources of positive law. The Constitution guarantees to each the right to receive qualified legal assistance which in the instances provided for by a law is rendered free of charge (Article 48, 1993 Russian Constitution).

The present Law constitutes the single most concentrated body of basic rules regulating the organization of the advokatura as a system of independent organs, the basic rights and duties of an advokat, the acquisition of the status of an advokat, and the procedure for organs of the advokat community to function.

Several other laws contain provisions regulating aspects of advokat and Advokatura activities. The Federal Constitutional Law on the Constitutional Court of the Russian Federation, No. 1-ФКЗ, of 21 June 1994, as amended,[78] provides that an advokat may represent parties in a constitutional court proceeding (Article 53). Major codes of law of the Russian Federation, including the Civil Code, Code of Civil Procedure, Code of Arbitrazh Procedure, CAdV, Criminal Code, Code of Criminal Procedure, Labor Code, Tax Code, and others contain provisions regulating the right of representation, including the role of advokats. The Law of the RSFSR on Court Organization of 8 July 1981, as amended,[79] continues to be in force so long as its provisions are not contrary to other federal laws. Article 16 concerns: "Legal assistance of the advokatura to citizens and organizations" and provides that advokats render legal assistance in civil and criminal cases to citizens and organizations and that the rights and duties of advokats are determined by legislation in force.

---

78 СЗ РФ (1994), no. 13, item 1447, as amended; transl. in Butler, *Russian Public Law* (2d ed.; 2009), pp. 518-555.

79 Ведомости Верховного Совета РСФСР (1981), no. 28, item 976; *СЗ РФ* (2002), no. 30, item 3033.

The subjects of the Russian Federation have, within the limits of their competence, their own legislation regulating the local Advokatura. The City of Moscow, for example, in its capacity as a city of federal significance and a subject of the Russian Federation, has a Law on the Charter Court of the City of Moscow, adopted 13 February 2002, No. 10.[80] In a proceeding before the charter court the parties may have, as their representatives, advokats, persons having a learned degree in a legal specialty, among others (Article 49). Advokats may be retained by a Moscow citizen to represent him in the consideration of recourses of citizens filed against city officials or agencies pursuant to the Law of the City of Moscow "On Recourses of Citizens" of 18 June 1997, No. 25, as amended.[81] Minors have the right to be represented by an advokat when materials are referred to the Commission on the basis of the Law of the City of Moscow "On Commissions for Cases of Minors and Defense of Their Rights" of 27 April 2001, No. 20, as amended.[82] Special provision has been made in Moscow for the provision of legal services (as part of social services) free of charge to the aged and disabled.[83]

It has been rightly observed that Article 4 says nothing about international treaties of the Russian Federation or general or customary principles of international law. Nonetheless, Article 15(4) of the 1993 Russian Constitution is applicable to the Advokatura and to the activity of advokats. If an international treaty of the Russian Federation establishes rules other than provided by legislation, the rules of the treaty are to be applied. This would include the human rights conventions to which the Russian Federation is a party, all of which contain provisions relevant to the activity of advokats. However, some Russian commentators on the legislation regulating the Advokatura confuse international treaties with other international documents that do not enjoy the stature of a treaty and are not directly binding upon the Russian Federation. Moreover, the word "advocate" or "lawyer" in a foreign or international context is sometimes confused with the Russian "advokat" in the Russian commentaries (for example, the 1907 Hague conventions). Bilateral consular conventions of the Russian Federation commonly provide for access to counsel and establish conditions that differ from those of domestic legislation.

2. The requirement that a Code of Professional Ethics of an Advokat be adopted was not included in the original version of the present Law. Soviet legal doctrine prior to the 1970s had little to say about issues of professional advokat ethics. The prevailing view was that in a socialist society there was no social base for corporative ethics. The

80 Ведомости Московской городской Думы (2002), no. 3, item 10.
81 Ведомости Московской городской Думы (1997), no. 7, item 46; (2000), no. 8, item 85.
82 Вестник Московской городской Думы (2001), no. 6, item 75.
83 See the Decree of the Government of Moscow, 11 June 1996, No. 502, "On the Territorial List of Social Services Guaranteed by the State and Provided to Aged Citizens and the Disabled by Social Security Agencies of the City of Moscow". See Вестник Мэрии Москвы, no. 16 (1996).

XXII Congress of the Communist Party of the Soviet Union in 1962 adopted a Moral Code for the Construction of Communism which purported to embrace all spheres of moral relations.[84]

However, from the 1970s onwards serious work was undertaken with respect to advokat and judicial ethics which later extended to ethical standards for teachers, military officers, journalists, scholars, medical doctors, and others. For jurists this discussion led to the inclusion in the 1980 RSFSR Statute on the Advokatura of basic requirements for an advokat. An advokat must be a model of moral purity and irreproachable behavior, was obliged to constantly improve his knowledge, raise his ideological-political level and professional skills, and to actively participate in the propaganda of law.

The present Law takes a more pragmatic approach to the issue of professional ethics, but it does require the advokat to constantly improve his knowledge, enhance his skills, and comply with the Code of Professional Ethics of an Advokat. Ethical principles are incorporated in the rules that prohibit an advokat from taking part in a case where an official to whom he is related by kinship is involved, or a case in which his interests are contrary to those of the person requiring defense, or in a case in which he has previously participated as a judge, investigator, procurator, inquiry official, witness, expert, interpreter, or eye-witness. These are all limitations which help to define the professional duty of an advokat. The oath of the advokat (Article 13 below) contains a concise conception of the duty of an advokat.

Pursuant to this Article, the Code of Professional Ethics of an Advokat was adopted by the I All-Russian Congress of Advokats on 31 January 2003 and amended at the II and III All-Russian congresses (reproduced as an Annex below).[85]

Article 5 Use of Terms Applied in Present Federal Law

The use in names of organizations and social associations of the terms "advokat activity", "advokatura", "advokat", "chamber of advokats", "advokat formation", and "legal consultation office" or word combinations incorporating these terms shall be permitted only by advokats and organizations created in the procedure established by the present Federal Law [as amended by Federal Law of 20 December 2004].

The purpose of this Article is to protect the professional exclusiveness of the advokat as a particular type of Russian jurist and the organizations which confer the status of an advokat and within which advokat activities are carried on. The prohibition extends to any organization or social association on the territory of the Russian Federa-

84 See the Программа и Устав КПСС [Program and Charter of the Communist Party of the Soviet Union] (1962), pp. 201-202.

85 Transl. in W. E. Butler, *Russian Public Law* (2d ed.; 2009), pp. 878-890.

tion, including those registered under the Federal Law on Philanthropic Activity and Philanthropic Organizations of 11 August 1995, as amended,[86] and under the Federal Law on Noncommercial Organizations of 12 January 1996, as amended[87] (bearing in mind that the Advokatura is a noncommercial organization). It is odd that the prohibition is not more categorical, to encompass all juridical persons.[88]

Moreover, the prohibition is not consistent with Article 20 of the present Law, which makes mention of the advokat cabinet, college of advocates, and advokat bureau, although these may fall under the broader notion of "word combinations".

Although the Civil Code of the Russian Federation provides (Article 54) that the name of a juridical person should contain an indication of its organizational-legal form, advokat organizations do not, in practice, usually make reference to their being a noncommercial organization. However, the term "advokat" or variant thereof does comply with Article 54, as amended, insofar as it indicates the character of the activity engaged in by the organization.[89]

Examples of instances when juridical persons have attempted to include the word "advokat" in their names, even though they did not offer legal services at all, include the name "Financial Advokat" to designate an auditing company. This is considered to be illegal.[90] Others have attempted to choose names connected with legal services but not with the Advokatura – "family advokat", "economic advokat", "alternative Advokatura", "independent advokat formation", and so on. On the other hand, objections were apparently not raised with respect to a casino being named "Advokat", or journals not associated with the Advokatura nonetheless using the name: "Russkii advokat", or simply "Advokat".

It follows that it would be improper for a natural person in the Russian Federation who has not been endowed with the status of advokat to use this term to describe himself. Although the present Law imposes no sanctions for doing so, such behavior could engage responsibility under consumer protection legislation or, depending upon the circumstances, under the Criminal Code (Article 159, swindling). Those who publish or otherwise disseminate advertisements containing the improper use of words in the present Article may be found guilty of making an advertisement known

86 СЗ РФ (1995), no. 33, item 3340, as amended; transl. in Butler, *Russian Company and Commercial Legislation* (2003), pp. 621-632.

87 СЗ РФ (1996), no. 3, item 145, as amended; transl. in Butler, *Russian Company and Commercial Legislation* (2003), pp. 601-620.

88 In fact, the Ministry of Justice had so recommended when the licensing of jurists was in force. See Section 3.1, Methods Recommendations for the Effectuation by Justice Agencies of Control Over Compliance by Licensees with Licensing Conditions and Requirements of Legislation When Rendering Paid Legal Services, an Annex to the Letter of the Minister of Justice of the Russian Federation, 6 March 1998, No. 1459-EC.

89 See Butler, *Civil Code of the Russian Federation* (2010), p. 22.

90 Grinenko, in A. V. Grinenko (ed.), Комментарий к Федеральному закону «Об адвокатской деятельности и адвокатуре в Российской Федерации [Commentary to the Federal Law "On Advokat Activity and the Advokatura in the Russian Federation] (2003), p.59.

to be false and deliberately deceiving consumers, a contravention of the Federal Law on Advertising of 13 March 2006, No. 38-ФЗ, as amended (especially Article 5[1]).[91]

These considerations underscore the observation made above (see Article 2(6), Commentary) how unfortunate the reference is to "advokats of foreign States". What the position would be of a foreign lawyer in Russia who actually is called an "advocate" in his home jurisdiction can only be the subject of speculation, for the "word combination" principle would seem to be applicable.

91 СЗ РФ (2006), no. 12, item 1232, as amended.

Chapter 2 Rights and Duties of Advokat

Article 6 Powers of Advokat

1. *The powers of an advokat participating as a representative of a principal in a constitutional, civil, and administrative proceeding, and also as a representative or defender of a principal in a criminal proceeding and proceeding with regard to cases concerning administrative violations, shall be regulated by the respective procedural legislation of the Russian Federation.*
2. *In instances provided for by a federal law, an advokat must have an order for the performance of a commission issued by the respective advokat formation. The form of the order shall be confirmed by the federal justice agency. In other instances an advokat shall represent a principal on the basis of a power of attorney. No one shall have the right to demand of an advokat and his principal the presentation of an agreement concerning the rendering of legal assistance (hereinafter – agreement) for the entry of an advokat into a matter.*
3. *An advokat shall have the right to:*
   (1) *collect information necessary for the rendering of legal assistance, including request references, character references, and other documents from agencies of State power, agencies of local self-government, and also social associations and other organizations. The said agencies and organizations shall be obliged in the procedure established by legislation to issue to an advokat the documents requested by him or certified copies thereof not later than within a month from the day of receipt of the request of the advokat [as amended by Federal Law of 20 December 2004];*
   (2) *question with their consent persons supposed to possess information relevant to the matter with regard to which the advokat is rendering legal assistance;*
   (3) *collect and submit articles and documents which may be deemed to be material and other evidence in the procedure established by legislation of the Russian Federation;*
   (4) *enlist specialists on a contractual basis to explain questions connected with the rendering of legal assistance;*
   (5) *meet without obstruction with his principal alone under conditions ensuring confidentiality (including in the period of confinement under guard thereof) without limitation of the number of meetings and the duration thereof;*

(6) fix (including with the assistance of technical means) information contained in the materials of the file of a case with regard to which the advokat is rendering legal assistance, complying in so doing with State and other secrecy protected by a law;
(7) perform other actions not contrary to legislation of the Russian Federation.

4. *An advokat shall not have the right to:*
(1) accept from a person who has had recourse to him for rendering of legal assistance a commission if it has a character known to be illegal;
(2) accept from a person who has had recourse to him for rendering legal assistance a commission in instances when he:
has an autonomous interest with regard to the subject of the agreement with the principal distinct from the interest of the particular person; participated in the case as a judge, arbitral judge or arbitrator, intermediary, procurator, investigator, inquiry official, expert, specialist, interpreter, is the victim with regard to the case or a witness, and also if he is an official within whose competence was the adoption of a decision in the interests of the particular person;
be in kinship or family relations with an official who took or is taking part in an investigation or consideration of the matter of the particular person;
render legal assistance to a principal whose interests are contrary to the interests of the particular person;
(3) take a position with regard to a case contrary to the will of the principal, except for instances when the advokat is convinced of the self-incrimination of the principal;
(4) make a public statement concerning the proof of guilt of the principal if he denies this;
(5) divulge information communicated to him by the principal in connection with the rendering of legal assistance to the last without the consent of the principal;
(6) refuse to accept a defense.

5. *Non-public cooperation of an advokat with agencies effectuating operational-search activity shall be prohibited.*

1. The Federal Chamber of Advokats of the Russian Federation approved on 22 April 2004 and published as an instructional manual for advokats a booklet entitled Меры по защите профессиональных прав адвоката [Measures for Defense of the Professional Rights of an Advokat]. The work addresses in detail all of the rights and powers set out in the present Article.[1]

Point 1 of this Article sets out the types of proceedings in which an advokat is empowered in principle to appear on behalf of a party. The drafting of point 1 follows

1 Excerpts appear in See Semeniako and Pilipenko, Адвокатская деятельность и адвокатура [Advokat Activity and the Advokatura] (2010), pp. 577-589.

Article 118(2) of the 1993 Russian Constitution, which provides that judicial power is effectuated by means of constitutional, civil, administrative, and criminal procedure.[2] Accordingly, advokats are empowered to act in these four categories of proceeding, with the distinction being clarified between an administrative proceeding and a proceeding with regard to administrative violations.

Constitutional proceedings are conducted by the Constitutional Court of the Russian Federation. Advokats with a duly issued power of attorney may appear as representatives of parties before the Court, but have no monopoly right of representation. Persons having an academic degree in a legal specialty also may act as representatives, and so too may designated officials, deputies of the State Duma or the Soviet of the Federation, and others.[3] In practice, advokats usually appear on behalf of citizens who allege a violation of their constitutional rights.

Civil proceedings are conducted in accordance with the 2002 Code of Civil Procedure of the Russian Federation, which provides that advokats, *inter alia*, may be "persons participating in a case" and have, if duly empowered, the procedural rights as representative of the civil defendant granted by the Code.[4] In an arbitrazh court the parties may be represented by an advokat or by other persons providing legal assistance, including an executive of a juridical person who is a party to the proceeding (Article 59, Code of Arbitrazh Procedure). The arbitrazh court must make a formal decision to recognize or not the powers of the persons participating in the case or their representatives, examining the documents of each person to determine whether they are duly empowered.[5]

In a Ruling of the Supreme Court of the Russian Federation of 14 June 2007, No. KAC07-227,[6] the Cassational Division of the Supreme Court considered a civil case brought to deem invalid point 13.6 of the Instruction on the Procedure for the Selection for Keeping Documents in the Archive of Federal Courts of General Jurisdiction, the Placing Thereof in Sets, Recording, and Use, confirmed by Order of the Judicial Department attached to the Supreme Court of the Russian Federation of 28 December 2005, No. 157.[7] Under point 13.6 of the Instruction persons participating in a case, representatives thereof, and other persons might familiarize with a file of a case with the written authorization of the chairman of the court or deputy thereof. The plaintiff considered that point 13.6 violated Article 6(1) of the present Law. The

2 See Butler, *Constitutional Foundations of the CIS Countries* (2000), p. 465.

3 See Article 53, Federal Constitutional Law on the Constitutional Court of the Russian Federation. C3 PФ (1994), no. 13, item 1447, as amended; transl. in W. E. Butler, *Russian Public Law* (2d ed.; 2009), p. 818-855.

4 See, in particular, Article 52, Code of Civil Procedure. C3 PФ (2002), no. 46, item 4532, as amended; transl. in Butler, *Russia and The Republics: Legal Materials* (looseleaf series; 2006-).

5 See the 2002 Code of Arbitrazh Procedure. C3 PФ (2002), no. 30, item 3012, as amended; transl. in Butler, Russia and The Republics: Legal Materials (looseleaf series; 2006-).

6 Unpublished. Available on Consultant Plus.

7 Unpublished. Available on Consultant Plus.

respondent argued that point 13.6 was not a normative legal act and did not affect the rights, freedoms, and interests of man and citizen but merely established an internal procedure for archive workers. The Cassational Division rejected these arguments and held point 13.6 to be invalid as being contrary to the present Law.

Advokats may appear in domestic arbitration courts of the Russian Federation organized in accordance with the Federal Law of 24 July 2002, No. 102-ФЗ "On Arbitration Courts in the Russian Federation".[8] Here too the power of attorney is essential for an advokat representing a party to an arbitration; if the advokat draws up the petition to sue, his power of attorney will be attached thereto (Article 23). Although the Federal Law on International Commercial Arbitration is silent on advokats, they routinely participate in international arbitrations held before the International Commercial Arbitration Court (MKAC) and the Maritime Arbitration Commission (MAK) in Moscow and in international arbitrations abroad.

The 2001 CAdV provides (Article 25.5) that the participants in cases concerning administrative violations may be a "defender and representative"; either may be an advokat. Participation may commence from the moment of drawing up the protocol concerning an administrative violation or, in the event of administrative detention, from the moment of the detention. Protocols are routinely draw up except in instances when a procurator initiates a case concerning an administrative violation (Article 28.4) or an administrative punishment is assigned without drawing up a protocol (Article 28.6). When administrative detention is applied, it will normally precede the drawing up of a protocol.

The powers of advokats in a criminal proceeding are set out in the 2002 Code of Criminal Procedure. Advokats may act on behalf of the accused, victim, civil plaintiff, or private accuser. When an advokat represents the accused or defendant, he is called a "defender". However, a defender also may be a close relative of the accused or another person whom the defendant petitions to represent him. As a rule, advokats act alone without the assistance of these persons; in justice of the peace courts, such laymen may appear instead of an advokat.

A defender participates in a criminal case: (1) from the moment of the rendering of a decree concerning the bringing of a person to responsibility as an accused, except insofar as the following instances may ensue earlier; (2) from the moment of instituting a criminal case with respect to a specific person; (3) from the moment of actual detention of a person suspected of the commission of a crime in the instances provided for (a) by Articles 91 and 92 of the Code of Criminal Procedure; (b) the application to a person in accordance with Article 100 of the Code of Criminal Procedure of measures of restraint in the form of confinement under guard; (4) from the moment of the disclosure to a person suspected of the commission of a crime of a decree

8 СЗ РФ (2002), no. 30, item 3019; transl. in W. E. Butler, *Russian Company and Commercial Legislation* (2003), pp. 859-880.

concerning the designation of forensic-psychiatric expert examination; (5) from the moment of the commencement of the effectuation of other measures of procedural coercion or other procedural actions affecting the rights and freedoms of a person suspected of the commission of a crime (Article 49, Code of Criminal Procedure).

Constitutional Court practice has influenced the formulation of Article 49(3), point (5), of the Code of Criminal Procedure. On 27 June 2000 the Constitutional Court of the Russian Federation decreed (No. 11-П) in the case of V. I. Maslov that the 1993 Constitution of the Russian Federation did not link the provision of the assistance of a defender with the formality of deeming a person to be a suspect or an accused. Consequently, the formal moment of the adoption of a procedural act by an agency of inquiry, investigation, or the procuracy is neither decisive nor essential for the provision of legal assistance. Nor does the federal legislator have the right to establish conditions of limitation on when legal assistance should be provided. The constitutional right to enjoy the assistance of a defender, including an advokat, arises from the moment when the limitation on the rights of a specific person becomes real.

A defender is retained by a suspect, accused, or the legal representative thereof or by other persons on behalf of and with the consent of the suspect or accused. Several persons may be invited to act as defenders simultaneously. At the request of the suspect or accused, the inquiry official, investigator, procurator, or a court may provide a defender. If a defender fails to appear within five days from the day of petitioning for a defender, the inquiry official, investigator, procurator, or court has the right to invite the suspect or accused to invite another defender and, should he decline to do so, to take measures for the appointment of a defender. If a suspect has been detained or is confined under guard and the appearance of a defender invited by him is not possible within 24 hours, measures must be taken by the inquiry official, investigator, or procurator to appoint a defender.

A suspect or accused has the right at any time of the proceedings to waive the assistance of a defender. The waiver must be in written form, and if made during the performance of an investigative action, a notation must be made in the protocol of the investigative action. Under instances stipulated in Articles 51 and 247 of the Code of Criminal Procedure a waiver is not binding upon the inquiry official, investigator, procurator, or court. Nor does a waiver preclude the accused or suspect from later petitioning for a defender to be admitted or provided.

A defender admitted to participate in a criminal case has the right: (1) to meet with a suspect or accused in accordance with Articles 46 and 47 of the Code of Criminal Procedure; (2) collect and submit evidence needed to render legal assistance as established by Article 86 of the Code of Criminal Procedure; (3) enlist the services of a specialist in accordance with Article 58 of the Code of Criminal Procedure; (4) be present when the accusation is presented; (5) participate in the interrogation of a suspect or accused and in investigative actions performed with the participation of the suspect or accused or upon his petition or the petition of the defender; (6) familiarize himself with the protocol of the detention, decree of the application of measures of restraint;

protocols of investigative actions performed with the participation of the accused or suspect and other documents presented or which should have been presented to the accused or suspect; (7) familiarize himself at the end of the preliminary investigation with all the materials of the criminal case and copy out from the criminal file any information in any amount or make copies at his own expense; (8) submit petitions and challenges; (9) participate in the judicial examination in the courts of first, second, and supervisory instances and in the consideration of questions connected with the execution of the judgment; (10) bring appeals against actions or failure to act and decisions of the inquiry official, investigator, procurator court and participate in their consideration by the court; (11) use other means of defense not prohibited by law.

Witnesses also may invite advokats to advise them during a proceeding, in which instance the relations between the advokat and the principal are regulated under Article 2(3) of the present Law. The right of a witness to be represented by an advokat during an interrogation arises indirectly out of Article 189 of the Code of Criminal Procedure; if present, the advokat may not put questions to the witness nor comment upon the answers. However, the advokat may at the end of the interrogation note any instances in which the rights or legal interests of the witness were violated, which must be entered in the protocol of the interrogation.

2. It follows from Article 6(2) of the present Law that an advokat represents a client on the basis of an order only when expressly established by legislation. The form of an order [ордер] was established by an Annex to the Order [приказ] of the Ministry of Justice of the Russian Federation of 8 August 2002, No. 217.[9]

An advokat acts in a civil proceeding as a representative on the basis of an order issued by his advokat formation. As for arbitrazh court proceedings, the relevant legislation is confused and confusing. The 2002 Code of Arbitrazh Procedure provides (Article 61) that the powers of an advokat to conduct a case in an arbitrazh court are certified in accordance with a federal law. The present Law also refers to "instances provided for by a federal law". No other federal law addresses the issue, as a result of which the issue remains unregulated. A power of attorney from the principal would therefore seem sufficient; judicial practice commonly also requires an order from the advokat formation.

With regard to representation in cases of administrative violations, the CAdV refers to a defender or representative of the victim, when an advokat, acting on the basis of an order issued by a legal consultation office (Article 25). Although the CAdV and the present Law entered into force at more or less the same time, the former did not take into account the full range of advokat formations permitted by the last. As

9 The form is reproduced on Consultant Plus and appears as an Annex in some of the Commentaries on the Law on the Advokatura.

regards representation in customs matters, the powers of an advokat must be confirmed by an order.

The Code of Criminal Procedure requires that an advokat present an order and his certificate of the status of advokat (Article 49). Only this Code refers to the requirement of presenting the certificate.

An order is a document of strict accountability. A standard form for an order was confirmed by the aforesaid Order No. 217. Issued in an A5 format, orders are numbered consecutively and packaged in groups of 50, 100, 150, 200, or 250 as order books with numbered foils. Advokat formations acquire order books from their chamber of advokats or may order them from a printer themselves. The heads of advokat formation must order them personally from chambers of advokats, who deliver them under signature to the advokat formation.

An order contains the following imperative requisites: consecutive order number; date of issuance of each order; full name of the advokat; advokat's registration number; name of subject of the Federation; number and date of the issuance of the advokat certificate; date of fulfillment of the assignment; essence of the assignment; full name of the client; stage of consideration of the case and/or name of the agency, institution, or organization; basis for issuing the order; full name of the advokat formation; post of the person issuing the order; signature thereof; and seal of the advokat formation or branch thereof. Without the signature and seal of the head of the advokat formation or structural subdivision thereof, the order is invalid.

The order is issued under signature of the advokat recipient on the foil of the order book. As documents of strict accountability, the order book must be kept under conditions that exclude uncontrolled use or theft. Any spoiled forms are kept at the back of the order book. When an order book is used up, it is kept for a period and then destroyed in accordance with a signed document.[10]

A power of attorney issued to an advokat for the right to represent a principal is drawn up in accordance with the Civil Code of the Russian Federation (Article 185).

The prohibition contained in the present Article against requiring an advokat and principal to produce the contract for legal services is explained by the fact that the contract falls under the umbrella of advokat secrecy. On the form and content of an agreement to render legal assistance, see the Commentary to Article 25 below.

10 See the Methods Recommendations on the Procedure for the Manufacture, Keeping, and Issuance of Orders to Advokats, confirmed by the Council of the Federal Chamber of Advokats of the Russian Federation, on 10 December 2003. The text appears in See Semeniako and Pilipenko, Адвокатская деятельность и адвокатура [Advokat Activity and the Advokatura] (2010), pp. 571-572. Also see G. B. Mirzoev and N. D. Eriashvili (eds.), Адвокатура в России [Advokatura in Russia] (4th ed.; 2011), pp. 141-145.

3. The rights of an advokat set out in point 3 of this Article operate irrespective of what type of legal assistance is rendered. The examples given of what types of information may be collected by an advokat are not exhaustive.

(1) The formulation reproduces in substantial part the provisions of Article 86(3) of the Code of Criminal Procedure of the Russian Federation, although the Code does not contain a period for the person or agency questioned to reply to the query and refers to the "defender" rather than to the advokat. Here the distinction is important because the advokat is not necessarily a defender in a criminal proceeding, but may be acting as a representative of the victim or a civil plaintiff or defendant.

(2) If the advokat is not acting as a defender in a criminal proceeding, a strict reading of Article 86(2) of the Code of Criminal Procedure does not permit the advokat to question witnesses. The question becomes whether the advokat can have access to the protocols of witness interrogations, which often the preliminary investigation agencies or the courts are in no hurry to attach to the files of the case.

(3) This provision also is derived from Article 86 of the Code of Criminal Procedure.

(4)-(7) These provisions originate in Article 53 of the Code of Criminal Procedure, where reference also is made to the defender rather than an advokat.

The Federal Chamber of Advokats of the Russian Federation has issued Methods Recommendations for the Realization of the Rights of an Advokat Provided for by Article 53(1)(2) and Article 86(3) of the Code of Criminal Procedure of the Russian Federation and Article 6(3) of the Federal Law on Advokat Activity and the Advokatura in the Russian Federation, approved on 22 April 2004, to assist advokats in exercising these rights.[11]

The Supreme Court of the Russian Federation rendered a Decision on 26 June 2007[12] which deemed to be illegal point 83 of the Rules for Internal Order of Correctional Institutions, confirmed by Order of the Ministry of Justice of the Russian Federation on 3 November 2005, No. 205,[13] because that point allowed an advokat to be refused a meeting with his principal when, for example, relatives of the inmate invited the advokat to attend rather than the principal himself on the grounds that the inmate had not applied for such a meeting. This deprived the advokat of the right to a meeting with his client and the client of his right to legal assistance.

The Constitutional Court of the Russian Federation in a Ruling of 6 March 2008, No. 428-O-П,[14] has emphasized that the provisions of the Criminal Penal Code of

11 For the text, see Semeniako and Pilipenko, Адвокатская деятельность и адвокатура [Advokat Activity and the Advokatura] (2010), pp. 573-577.

12 Бюллетень Верховного Суда РФ [Bulletin of the Supreme Court of the Russian Federation], no. 1 (2009); this decision was left without change by Ruling of the Supreme Court of 26 June 2007.

13 Бюллетень нормативных актов федеральных органов исполнительной власти [Bulletin of Normative Acts of Federal Agencies of Executive Power], no. 47 (2005).

14 Available on Consultant Plus.

the Russian Federation (Article 82) and related legislation may not be regarded as permitting the arbitrary intimate personal search of an advokat visiting a client in an institution for the deprivation of freedom unless there are sufficient factual grounds testifying to an intention by the advokat to bring in prohibited articles and without the adoption by the administration of the correctional institution of a reasoned decision to conduct the personal search and a written account of the course and outcome of the respective actions.

4. Point 4 addresses for the most part situations in which an advokat would have a conflict of interest with his client. These provisions limit the rights of an advokat, representing a boundary beyond which an advokat may not proceed even when he considers that doing so might be to his client's benefit.

(1) An advokat is prohibited from accepting an assignment from a client when it is of a nature known to be illegal. As a legal professional, the advokat must determine which assignments are legal and which may not be. The presumption of knowledge of the law extends in full to the advokat, who cannot in such a situation allege in justification of his behavior that he was unaware of legislation in force. An advokat who fails to heed this prohibition may find himself accused of complicity or of being an accessory (Article 33, Criminal Code of Russian Federation). An advokat is prohibited under this provision from advising a client orally or in writing about ways to mitigate or avoid criminal responsibility or to assist a person in realizing his criminal intent. An advokat who participates in bribing an official in a criminal proceeding (Article 291, Criminal Code) also violates this provision.

An advokat also may not take part in an assignment from a client whose performance would involve an administrative violation. Relevant provisions include administrative responsibility for the failure to perform the instructions of a judge or bailiff, procurator, investigator, inquiry official, or other official, or obstructing the legal activity of an executing bailiff.

Any assignment from a client that involves an advokat violating legislation would fall under this prohibition.

(2) This prohibition involves a conflict of interest between the advokat and his client. The provision enumerates several specific instances of such a conflict which fall into three groups: (1) when an advokat previously took part in a case in another capacity; (2) when the advokat is in kinship or family relations with officials who had or who have a relationship with the case; and (3) when the advokat renders legal assistance to a client whose interests are contrary to his own. For the purposes of this Article the term "judges" means all persons to whom the 1992 Federal Law on the Status of Judges in the Russian Federation extends.[15] Arbitrators are natural persons

15 Ведомости Съезда народных депутатов и Верховного Совета Российсклй Федерации (1992), no. 30, item 1792; as amended; transl. in W. E. Butler, *Russian Public Law* (2d ed.; 2009), pp. 421-446.

chosen by the parties or otherwise appointed to settle a dispute in an arbitral tribunal pursuant either to the Federal Law on Arbitral Courts in the Russian Federation[16] or to the 1993 Law on International Commercial Arbitration.[17] A mediator is defined in the Code of Arbitrazh Procedure (Article 135(1)(2)) as a person who facilitates the settlement of a dispute in an arbitrazh proceeding while avoiding a judicial consideration thereof.[18] The fullest enumeration of persons who fall under the definition of "procurator", "investigator" and "inquiry official" is given in the Code of Criminal Procedure of the Russian Federation (Articles 5(31), 38, and 41).[19]

A specialist, expert, and interpreter are terms widely used without necessarily being related to holding a specific office. There is no list in the present Article or elsewhere of officials within whose competence the taking of a decision in the interests of a person applying for assistance to an advokat. It would in fact be impossible to compile such a list.

The victim of a crime or other violation should not be overlooked. There are definitions of the victim in the Code on Administrative Violations of the Russian Federation (Article 25.2) and Code of Criminal Procedure (Article 42).

The prohibition against an advokat acting when he has kinship or family relations with an official who may be involved in the matter protects the independence of the advokat. However, the degree of kinship is not specified, which suggests that any degree of kinship is sufficient to engage the prohibition.

The presence of the considerations enumerated above should lead to the possibility of challenging the participation of an advokat in a civil, administrative or criminal proceeding. The relevant codes of procedure contain provisions on challenges which are not entirely consistent with the present Law.

(3) This prohibition precludes an advokat from expressing doubt with respect to the behavior of his client as a means of defending his interests either in oral or in written form. An advokat should not by gestures, words, silence, or otherwise give expression to his disagreement with his client. Any written documents emanating from the advokat, whether written in his own name or that of his client, should follow the position taken by his client relating to primary or secondary elements of the defense. An advokat may not compose "multi-tiered" documents which externally take the position of the client but are inadequately argued or weakly set out the information at the disposition of the advokat as this would indirectly be contrary to the will of the client.

16 СЗ РФ (2002), no. 30, item 3019; transl. in Butler, *Russian Public Law* (2d ed.; 2009), pp. 665-681.

17 Ведомости Съезда народных депутатов и Верховного Совета Российсклй Федерации (1993), no. 32, item 1240, as amended; transl. in Butler, *Russian Public Law* (2d ed.; 2009), pp. 651-664.

18 СЗ РФ (2002), no. 30, item 3012, as amended; transl. in Butler, *Russia and The Republics – Legal Materials* (looseleaf service; 2006-).

19 See Butler, *Russian Criminal Law and Procedure* (2011), pp. 246, 270-271, 275-276

Self-incrimination by a client gives the advokat scope to take a position independently of his client, whether the self-incrimination relates to a crime, administrative offense, or disciplinary offense. Where self-incrimination occurs, an advokat has the right to take an active position contrary to the will of his client in making petitions, addresses to the court, submission of evidence, and otherwise seek to persuade the court or investigation that his client did not commit the alleged crime or offense.

(4) The rule prohibits an advokat from making public statements concerning the guilt of his client and precludes the advokat from divulging information which might be used as a source concerning disagreements in the actions of the participants on the same side. This would enable the other side to develop forms and tactics for reacting. Such statements would also suggest extreme disagreements between the advokat and his client.

(5) An advokat may not divulge information communicated to him by a client without the latter's consent. Such divulgence is prohibited in the form of public statements or any conversations with other persons, officials, and so on or in documents drawn up in the name of the advokat or the client. It is immaterial whether the information is specially-protected by law or not (see Article 23, 1993 Russian Constitution). Such information must satisfy three conditions: (1) be communicated to the advokat personally by the client or on express behalf of the client by other persons; (2) relate to information which is provided to an advokat in connection with his assignment; and (3) there is no consent of the client to the divulgence of such information.

The formulation of this prohibition is not consistent with Article 8 of the present Law below, which treats any information connected with an advokat rendering legal assistance to his client as an advokat secret.

(6) The formulation of the word "defense" is obscure in this context. Technically, an advokat becomes a "defender" only when retained by a client to act in a criminal proceeding (Article 49, Code of Criminal Procedure) or in connection with an administrative violation (Article 25.5, CAdV). It is unlikely that the legislator used the term "defense" here in these narrower meanings. The better view is that any types of legal assistance comprise "defense" for the purposes of this Article.

5. The provisions of point 5 replicate more fully a prohibition contained in the 1995 Federal Law on Operational-Search Activity (Article 17)[20] and in the Federal Law on the Federal Security Service of 3 April 1995, No. 40-ФЗ, as amended (Article 19(4)).[21] Both enactments permit the agencies concerned to conclude contracts with individuals for the supply of useful information, and both exclude the possibility of such contracts with advokats. The prohibition set out in the present Article is more sweeping, as it precludes such assistance irrespective of whether there is a contract or not.

20 СЗ РФ (1995), no. 33, item 3349, as amended.
21 СЗ РФ (1995), no. 15, item 1269, as amended.

Article 7 Duties of Advokat

1. *An advokat shall be obliged to:*
   (1) *honorably, reasonably, and in good faith vindicate the rights and legal interests of the principal with all means not prohibited by legislation of the Russian Federation;*
   (2) *execute the requirements of a law on the obligatory participation of an advokat as a defender in a criminal proceeding upon the assignment of agencies of inquiry, agencies of preliminary investigation, or court, and also render legal assistance to citizens of the Russian Federation free of charge in instances provided for by the present Federal Law [as amended by Federal Laws of 20 December 2004 and 24 July 2007];*
   (3) *constantly improve his knowledge and raise his qualifications;*
   (4) *comply with the Code of Professional Ethics of an Advokat and execute decisions of organs of the chamber of advokats of a subject of the Russian Federation and Federal Chamber of Advokats of the Russian Federation adopted within the limits of their competence [as amended Federal Law of 20 December 2004];*
   (5) *deduct monthly at the expense of remuneration received means for the general needs of the chamber of advokats in the procedure and amounts which are determined by the meeting (or conference) of advokats of the chamber of advokats of the respective subject of the Russian Federation (hereinafter – meeting (or conference) of advokats), and also deduct means for the maintenance of the respective advokat cabinet, respective college of advokats, or respective advokat office in the procedure and amounts which have been established by the advokat formation [as amended Federal Law of 20 December 2004];*
   (6) *effectuate the insurance of the risk of his professional property responsibility.*
2. *For the failure to perform or improper performance of his professional duties an advokat shall bear responsibility provided for by the present Federal Law.*

1. The enumeration of duties of an advokat in the present Law is exhaustive. However, this is misleading. Other provisions of the present Law impose duties on an advokat, including, for example, Article 25 below which requires an advokat to conclude a written agreement with his client for the provision of legal services.

The terms "honorably", "reasonably", and "in good faith" are regarded by most Russian Commentators as categories of morality and not subject to precise characterizations of behavior. Under this approach these terms are regarded as applying generally to all specific duties of an advokat. Any violation of a specific duty is simultaneously a breach of these general standards.

While advokats enjoy the freedom of speech just as any other Russian citizens, they are cautioned about appearances in the mass media. Recommendations to Advokats with Regard to Interaction with the Mass Media, confirmed by Decision of the Council of the Federal Chamber of Advokats on 21 June 2010, provide that "advokats must speak in the mass media from the standpoint of law".[22] Advokats are recommended to refrain from radical political statements and remarks, although they may speak in defense of the interests of various social groups who seek to change legislation, administrative policy, or draw public attention to a particular issue. If the norms of a specific law are contrary to constitutional or international norms consolidating human rights, the advokat should speak from the standpoint of protecting human rights. Advokats may not use the mass media for advertising purposes.

The gloss of individual Russian Commentators on this Article varies considerably from one to another. Some emphasize precepts of personal behavior: an advokat should respect the rights, honor, and dignity of persons who have applied to him for legal assistance, clients, colleagues, and other persons. In manner and dress an advokat should behave in a business-like manner. When participating in a court or administrative proceeding, an advokat should comply with norms of procedural legislation, ensure that the law is complied with in respect of his client, and petition to eliminate any violations. When making objections to judges and other proceeding participants, the advokat should do this in the correct form and in accordance with law. When an advokat for justifiable reasons cannot be present at a designated judicial session or investigative action or intends to petition to defer the session or action, the court, investigator, and other advokats should be notified in good time and agree a new appointment. An advokat may speak with the other side in a case only in the presence of and with the consent of his client. Many would regard the foregoing as aspects of etiquette rather than duties.

(1) Often the duties of an advokat are expressed in prohibitions which the advokat must comply with. Subpoint 1(1) would mean that an advokat cannot accept a matter which is known to be illegal. Nor may an advokat take part in rendering legal assistance if he has an interest in the outcome of the case different from that of his client, or undertake other actions or assignments inconsistent with this duty.

(2) The formulation of subpoint 1(2) precludes an advokat from accepting an assignment if he previously participated in a case as a judge, arbitrator, mediator, procurator, investigator, inquiry official, expert, specialist, interpreter, victim or witness or previously was an official competent to take a decision in the interests of the client.

The question has arisen in practice whether an advokat may act in a proceeding as defender if he lacks a security clearance and State secrets are or may be involved in a case. In a case before the Constitutional Court of the Russian Federation a defendant was refused counsel of his choice on the grounds that his advokat lacked special clearance granting access to a State secret provided by the Law of the Russian Federation on State Secrecy (Article 21).[23] The Court held that the "extension of the provisions of

22 Point 2.1. See the Recommendations in Semeniako and Pilipenko, Адвокатская деятельность и адвокатура [Advokat Activity and the Advokatura] (2010), pp. 630-635.

23 Российская газета, 21 September 1993.

this Article to advokats participating as defenders in a criminal proceeding and their removal from participation in the case in connection with the lack of clearance for a State secret does not correspond to the Constitution of the Russian Federation and Articles 48 and 123(3) thereof".[24] This holding was reiterated by the same Court with respect to civil proceedings in a Ruling of 10 November 2002, No. 314-O: "Articles 21 and 21^1 of the Law of the Russian Federation 'On State Secrecy' may not be applied by courts, other agencies, and officials as grounds for removal of an advokat who is a representative of a plaintiff from participation in the consideration of a case by a court of ordinary jurisdiction by way of a civil proceeding in connection with him failing to have clearance to a State secret".[25] The same position was taken in regard to arbitrazh proceedings in a Ruling of 10 November 2002, No. 293-O.[26]

The Constitutional Court in a Decree of 25 October 2001, No. 14-П, has deemed unconstitutional provisions of the Federal Law on Confinement under Guard of Suspects and Accused in the Commission of Crimes (Article 16)[27] which regulated the constitutional right to the assistance of an advokat or a defender through the provisions of departmental normative acts. This opened the possibility to unlawful limitations upon the right to counsel and made meetings between the accused or suspect and his defender or advokat dependent upon a special authorization from the person or agency which had jurisdiction over the case.[28]

(3) Subpoint 1(3) serves as justification for continuing legal education programs within the Advokatura. An advokat is expected to have knowledge of the latest changes in legislation and relevant judicial practice. Lack of knowledge or experience cannot be referred to by an advokat as justification for mistakes.

On 30 November 2007 the Federal Chamber of Advokats of the Russian Federation confirmed the Unified Methodology for Professional Training and Retraining of Advokats and Apprentice Advokats.[29] The Unified Methodology establishes the tasks, system, types, and forms of raising the qualifications for advokats and the instruction of apprentice advokats and lays down the requirements for regional training programs. Three categories of continuing legal education are established: (1) advokats with up to one year experience; (2) advokats with more than one year of experience; and (3) apprentice advokats. Advokats with more than one year experience are required to undergo continuing legal education not less than 20 hours per year and not less than 100 hours over a five-year period. Credit towards these requirements in the form of postgraduate study is permitted. Chambers of advokats in individual sub-

24 СЗ РФ (1996), no. 15, item 1768.
25 СЗ РФ (2003), no. 6, item 549.
26 СЗ РФ (2002), no. 52(II), item 5288.
27 СЗ РФ (1995), no. 29, item 2759, as amended.
28 СЗ РФ (2001), no. 48, item 4551.
29 For the text, see Semeniako and Pilipenko, Адвокатская деятельность и адвокатура [Advokat Activity and the Advokatura] (2010), pp. 623-629.

jects of the Federation may credit subscriptions to specified periodicals towards the hourly minimums and take into account other specified types of activities (seminars, conferences, mass media appearances, teaching).

(4) In subpoint 1(4), as amended, the Code of Professional Ethics of an Advokat is written into the duties of an advokat. Compliance with the Code is linked here with decisions of the chamber of advokats because the chamber is charged with enforcing the Code of Ethics.

Advokats are specially singled out in the Federal Law of 7 August 2001 "On Counteracting the Legalization (or Laundering) of Revenues Received by Criminal Means and the Financing of Terrorism" as being required to perform certain duties.[30] These duties are elaborated in the Statute on the Procedure for the Transfer of Information to the Federal Service for Financial Monitoring by Advokats, Notaries, and Persons Effectuating Entrepreneurial Activity in the Sphere of Rendering Legal or Bookkeeping Services, confirmed by Decree of the Government of the Russian Federation on 16 February 2005, No. 82;[31] the Decree of the Government of the Russian Federation of 5 December 2005, No. 715 "On Qualifications Requirements for Special Officials Responsible for Compliance with Rules of Internal Control and Programs for the Effectuation Thereof, and also Requirements for Training and Instruction of Personnel, Identification of Clients, and Beneficiaries, for the Purposes of Counteracting the Legalization (or Laundering) of Revenues Received by Criminal Means, and Financing of Terrorism";[32] the Decree of the Government of the Russian Federation of 8 January 2003, No. 6 "On the Procedure for Confirming Rules of Internal Control in Organizations Effectuating Operations with Monetary Means or Other Property";[33] Recommendations for Working Out by Organizations Effectuating Operations with Monetary Means or Other Property Rules of Internal Control for the Purposes of Counteracting the Legalization (or Laundering) of Revenues Received by Criminal Means and Financing of Terrorism, confirmed by Regulation of the Government of the Russian Federation on 10 June 2010, No. 967-p;[34] the Recommendations with Regard to Information Includes in Reports of Personnel of an Organization Concerning an Operation (or Transaction) Subject to Obligatory Control or Unusual Operation (or Transaction) confirmed by Order of the Federal Service for Financial Monitoring of 11 August 2010 No. 213;[35] and the Agreement on Cooperation of the Federal Service for Financial Monitoring and the Federal Chamber of Advokats of the Russian Federation with Regard to Counteracting Legalization (or Laundering) of Revenues

30 СЗ РФ (2001), no. 33(I), item 3418, as amended.
31 СЗ РФ (2005), no. 8, item 659.
32 СЗ РФ (2005), no. 50, item 5302, as amended.
33 СЗ РФ (2003), no. 2, item 188, as amended.
34 СЗ РФ (2010, no. 26, item 3377.
35 Unpublished. Available on Consultant Plus.

Received by Criminal Means and Financing of Terrorism of 12 July 2007 (No. 01-1-13/11), among others.

These documents collectively set out the procedures for advokats to exercise internal control over transactions involving monetary means or other property and transactions with immoveable property, the management of money, securities, or other property of a client, the management of bank accounts or securities accounts of a client; the attraction of money for the creation of organizations or to make provision for the activities or management thereof; and the like. Certain identification information must be collected with respect to the natural or juridical persons involved in such transactions.

The Federal Chamber of Advokats has itself confirmed Recommendations for the Organization of the Performance by Advokats of Requirements of Legislation on Counteracting the Legalization (or Laundering) of Revenues Received by Criminal Means and the Financing of Terrorism on 27 September 2007.[36]

(5) The financial duties of an advokat set out generally in subpoint 1(5) link compliance with behavior which goes to the heart of the advokat's relationship with his professional colleagues.

A Ruling of the Constitutional Court of the Russian Federation of 5 February 2009, No. 277-O-O,[37] provided that the establishment by chambers of advokats of financial requirements for becoming an advokat, in particular in this case a one-off entry fee of 10,000 rubles to acquire the status of advokat in the Republic Marii-El, was not consistent with the present Law. Advokats could legitimately be required to contribute to the general needs of the chamber of advokats, but the competence of organs of the chambers of advokats did not extend to levying special charges. The Court observed that Articles 7, 25, 30, and 34 of the present Law were interlinked in this connection, and that no other financial contributions could be required except for the general needs of the Advokatura in order to acquire the status of advokat.

(6) The operation of subpoint 1(6) relating to professional risk insurance was suspended until the entry into force of a federal law regulating obligatory insurance for the professional responsibility of advokats by a Federal Law of 3 December 2007. No. 320-ФЗ[38] The suspension entered into force as from 17 December 2007 and has been successively extended.

2. Responsibility in this instance includes specific provisions of the present Law and the Code of Professional Ethics of an Advokat, which is incorporated into the present Law for these purposes. Insofar as such failure to perform or improper performance

36 Semeniako and Pilipenko, Адвокатская деятельность и адвокатура [Advokat Activity and the Advokatura] (2010), pp. 616-622.

37 Unpublished. Available on Consultant Plus.

38 СЗ РФ (2007), no. 50, item 6233.

of professional duties may engage criminal, civil, administrative, labor, disciplinary, or other forms of responsibility, this provision should not be understood to exclude that additional responsibility.

Reports of disciplinary proceedings submitted by chambers of advokats segregate behavior that falls under this provision from other types of behavior for which an advokat may be held responsible.

The Council of the Federal Chamber of Advokats of the Russian Federation has adopted "Methods Recommendations for Keeping Advokat Files"[39] in connection with the duty of an advokat to render qualified legal assistance honorably, reasonably, and in good faith. An advokat cannot perform his duties properly without the careful preparation of a case, which includes studying all the relevant materials and making appropriate notes and entries: "all materials relevant to a case must be kept by an advokat in a special file, called an advokat dossier". The present Law does not specifically require that such a dossier be kept, although the requirement is said to arise from the present provision read in conjunction with Article 8(3) below. The advokat dossier also is regarded as one of the means of protecting advokat secrecy insofar as the file may be designated as such and not be used as evidence for an accusation.

Article 8 Advokat Secrecy

1. *Any information connected with the rendering of legal assistance by an advokat to his principal shall be an advokat secret.*
2. *An advokat may not be summoned and interrogated as a witness concerning circumstances which became known to him in connection with the recourse to him for legal assistance or in connection with the rendering thereof.*
3. *The conducting of operational-search measures and investigative actions with respect to an advokat (including in dwelling and employment premises used by him in order to effectuate advokat activity) shall be permitted only on the basis of a judicial decision.*
   Information, articles, and documents received in the course of operational-search measures or investigative actions (including after the suspension or termination of the status of advokat) may be used as evidence of an accusation only in those instances when they are not part of the proceeding of the advokat with regard to cases of his principals. The said limitations shall not extend to the implements of a crime, nor to articles whose circulation is prohibited or whose turnover is limited in accordance with legislation of the Russian Federation.

39 The text is published in Semeniako and Pilipenko, Адвокатская деятельность и адвокатура [Advokat Activity and the Advokatura] (2010), pp. 636-648.

1. This provision is regarded as fundamental to the professional independence of the Advokatura and each individual advokat. The Code of Professional Ethics of an Advokat links the professional independence of an advokat to his client's trust in him (Article 5, Code), and trust depends upon the preservation of professional secrecy (Article 6(1), Code). The Federal Chamber of Advokats confirmed the Recommendations for Ensuring Advokat Secrecy and Guarantees of the Independence of Advokats When Advokats Effectuate Advokat Activity on 30 November 2009.[40]

A principal, or client, for the purposes of the present Article includes any person who has concluded an agreement with an advokat for the rendering of legal services, a person to whom legal services are being rendered on the basis of an agreement between the advokat and another person, or a person to whom legal services are being rendered by an advokat free of charge or by assignment of an agency of inquiry or preliminary investigation or a court.

Neither the present Law nor the Code of Ethics offers an exhaustive definition of "information" for the purposes of advokat secrecy.[41] The Code of Ethics offers examples: (1) the fact of recourse to an advokat, including the names of the clients; (2) all evidence and documents collected by the advokat in the court of preparing the case; (3) information received by the advokat from the client; (4) information concerning the client which became known to the advokat in the process of rendering legal assistance; (5) the substance of legal advice given to or intended for the client; (6) all advokat proceedings with regard to a case; (7) the conditions of the agreement, including remuneration, concluded between the advokat and the client; and (8) any other information connected with the rendering of legal assistance by an advokat.

There is no limit of time placed by legislation or the Code of Ethics on the preservation of advokat secrecy.

Advokat secrecy figures, perhaps somewhat bizarrely, on the List of Information of a Confidential Character confirmed by an Edict of the President of the Russian Federation on 6 March 1997, No. 188, as amended,[42] with a view to improving the procedure for the publication and entry into force of acts of the President and Government and federal agencies of executive power of the Russian Federation. The term

40 For the text, see Semeniako and Pilipenko, Адвокатская деятельность и адвокатура [Advokat Activity and the Advokatura] (2010), pp. 589-604.

41 "From the moment a citizen crossed the threshold of an advokat's office, all further events are an advokat secret. The very fact of recourse to an advokat is a professional secret. The essence of the request of a client, the content of the initial consultation – also is the subject-matter of an advokat secret. Moreover, even if the future client does not himself initially have recourse to a client, but someone of his relatives with whom subsequently no agreement to conduct a case was concluded, the general rule remains unchanged – all information received from this relative, even the very fact of his recourse, is an advokat secret". M. Iu. Barshchevskii, Адвокатская этика [Advokat Ethics] (2001), p. 136.

42 СЗ РФ (1997), no. 10, item 1127; (2005), no. 39, item 3925.

"advokat secrecy" does not appear in the Code of Criminal Procedure of the Russian Federation.

The concept of advokat secrecy extends, in the view of some commentators, to remarks about individual advokats or an individual advokat formation. It would be a violation of advokat secrecy to publish critical or evaluative remarks about advokats, or to repeat such remarks made by others, or to draw comparisons with other advokats, or to make ambiguous observations about advokats that may mislead potential clients or raise unrealistic expectations. Advertisements of advokat services which violate these precepts are to be reported to the council of advokats.

The Constitutional Court of the Russian Federation in a Ruling of 6 March 2008, No. 449-О-П,[43] has reiterated that the Tax Code of the Russian Federation cannot be regarded as placing on advokats and advokat formations a duty to provide to a tax agency any documents containing information about clients and accordingly as providing responsibility for the failure to perform such duty as a tax violation.

However, an advokat contested the constitutionality of this provision of the present Law on the grounds that even his own payment documents recording receipts from a client constituted material which a tax inspectorate should not be able to obtain. The Constitutional Court drew a distinction between materials which an advokat must provide to a tax inspectorate just as any taxpayer and those which are protected under the Tax Code (Article 82) as comprising professional, including advokat, secrecy.[44]

2. Point 2 represents a cardinal change on the concept and role of the advokat in comparison with the Soviet era, especially the early years of the Soviet period. Some argued in the 1920s that the defender should be an enthusiastic supporter of State interests in a criminal proceeding, helping the court to elicit the truth.[45] Vyshinskii argued that the advokat should be an organ of the administration of justice: "In confining his task only to the interests of the person being defended as such, irrespective of the interests of society and the State, the defender acts in contradiction with himself. As a citizen and as a Soviet citizen particularly".[46]

In post-Soviet Russia the role of the advokat has been reconceptualized. Adversariality is a key element of Russian criminal procedure (Article 15), and advokat secrecy is seen as being part of that principle. The prohibition against an advokat being a witness regarding circumstances which became known to him as part of rendering legal assistance or being retained to do so is incorporated into the Code of Ethics

43 Available on Consultant Plus.

44 Available on Consultant Plus.

45 See L. Fishman, «Об адвокатской этике» [On Advokat Ethics], Рабочий суд [Worker's Court], no. 10 (1924), p. 734.

46 A. Ia. Vyshinskii, Революционная законность и задачи советской защиты [Revolutionary Legality and the Tasks of Soviet Defense] (1934), pp. 33-34.

(Article 6(6)). There is no specific sanction or responsibility for improper divulgence of an advokat secret. The duty to observe secrecy extends even to professional colleagues of the advokat; an advokat may not disclose an advokat secret to them at any time, although this situation would not include, in the view of many Russian jurists, advokats operating under a partner contract. Even if the client dies, the consent of legal successors would need to be obtained to divulge an advokat secret. Advokats are recommended to mark all files containing an advokat secret as "confidential".[47]

A Russian advokat may not divulge information in the interests of an accused but against his wish (see Article 6(4)(5) above). Russian legal doctrine is divided as to whether an advokat may divulge the fact that his client is preparing to commit a dangerous crime which could still be prevented if this were disclosed.

A Ruling of the Constitutional Court of the Russian Federation of 6 July 2000, No. 128-O, "Re the Appeal of Citizen V. V. Parshutkin against a Violation of His Constitutional Rights and Freedoms by Article 72, paragraph two, (1), of the RSFSR Code of Criminal Procedure and Articles 15 and 16 of the RSFSR Statute on the Advokatura" confirmed that an advokat may not divulge information concerning facts which became known to him within the framework of his professional activity and the circumstances of obtaining such information.[48]

In a Ruling of 6 March 2003, No. 108-O, the Constitutional Court refused a petition to allow an advokat to be questioned who allegedly had information about the falsification of evidence by an investigator. The questions, if permitted, would have been put by the advokats of another defendant in the case. The Constitutional Court, just as the trial court, relied upon the present provision in support of its view.[49]

The Court expressly referred to the precedential value of its Ruling No. 128-O in a Ruling of 29 May 2007, No. 516-O-O: "The said decisions of the Constitutional Court of the Russian Federation retain their force, and the legal positions formulated therein relating to the constitutional-law content of the right of an accused to the assistance of an advokat (or defender) and advokat immunity are binding upon courts and other law enforcers, including when deciding in a criminal case of Citizen A. L. Goldman questions connected with ensuring rights to receive qualified legal assistance, free choice of defender, and defense of advokat secrecy".[50]

The Constitutional Court elaborated its position in a Ruling of 16 July 2009, No. 970-O-O: "The activity of an advokat assumes, *inter alia*, defense of the rights and legal interests of a suspect and an accused against possible violations of criminal procedure law on the part of agencies of inquiry and preliminary investigation. For this purpose, in particular, an advokat is present when the accusation is presented to

47 See I. L. Trunov in Trunov (ed.), Адвокатская деятельность и Адвокатура в России [Advokat Activity and the Advokatura in Russia] (2006), I, pp. 204-205.

48 СЗ РФ (2000), no. 33, item 3433.

49 СЗ РФ (2003), no. 21, item 2060.

50 Unpublished. Available on Consultant Plus.

his principal. Violations of the requirements of the criminal procedure law elicited by him in so doing must be brought in the interests of the principal to the information of the respective officials and courts, that is, such information may not be considered to be an advokat secret. Accordingly, a court has the right to put questions to an advokat relating to violations which occurred of a criminal procedure law without investigating in so doing information confidentially entrusted by the person to the advokat, and also other information concerning circumstances which became known to him in connection with his professional activity".[51]

In calendar year 2009 the Moscow Region Chamber of Advokats reported twelve instances of infringements on advokat secrecy by investigators seeking to interrogate an advokat as a witness to a crime.

3. Point 3 of the present Law seeks to distinguish between materials on the premises of an advokat (home or office) which belong to or appertain to a client and those which relate solely to the advokat himself, including in his nonprofessional capacity. Advokat premises are not immune from search and seizure operations. This situation existed in Imperial Russia before the 1917 Revolution. In those times an investigator might search the office of a sworn attorney in order to discover papers passed to the attorney by the accused or by other persons.[52] The attorney merely had the right to be present during the search.

Operational-search activities are regulated by the Federal Law on Operational-Search Activity of 12 August 1995, No. 144-ФЗ, as amended.[53] The number of State agencies authorized to engage in investigative actions is considerable in the Russian Federation. These agencies include internal affairs agencies, Federal Security Service agencies, tax agencies, State protection and border protection agencies, customs agencies, intelligence agencies, and the Ministry of Justice.

The Code of Criminal Procedure of the Russian Federation treats the issue differently and omits any reference to the employment premises of the advokat (Article 27). This would raise in principle the issue of whether the present Law or the Code of Criminal Procedure takes priority. If the Code of Criminal Procedure is to be followed (Article 7),[54] preference should be given to its provisions. Happily, the dilemma is resolved. The Constitutional Court of the Russian Federation has emphasized the

51 Ruling on Refusal to Accept for Consideration Appeals of Citizen Aleksandr Mikhailovich Gavrilov against a Violation of His Constitutional Rights by Article 56(3), Para. 3, of the Code of Criminal Procedure of the Russian Federation, 16 July 2009. Unpublished Ruling. Available on Consultant Plus.

52 See Articles 368, 368[1], 369, and 360, 1864 Statute on Criminal Procedure.

53 СЗ РФ (1995), no. 33, item 3349, as amended.

54 See W. E. Butler, *Russian Criminal Law and Procedure* (2011), pp. 250-251, 258-259.

necessity for operational-search agencies to obtain in advance a special judicial decision authorizing the search of premises of an advokat or advokat formation.[55]

The issue arose again when two advokats accused of a crime became the occasion for a search to be conducted of their advokat premises in the belief that the crime had been committed in the said premises. In the end a criminal case was not instituted against them. The two advokats appealed against the actions of the investigative agency under the present Law, arguing that the provisions of the Code of Criminal Procedure authorizing the search of premises must be read against the present Law, which was a limitation on the Code of Criminal Procedure.

Citing its Ruling No. 439-O, the Constitutional Court observed that the priority of the Code of Criminal Procedure over other federal laws was not absolute and might in particular be limited by rules, in the event of a conflict, which were later in time or *lex specialis*.[56] Moreover, the Court said, the Code does not have priority over legislative acts establishing additional guarantees for the rights and legal interests of individual categories of persons who enjoy a special status. Since advokat secrecy must be ensured and protected not only in connection with a criminal case, but also with respect to an advokat participating in a civil or administrative proceeding, the federal legislator was right to regulate the immunity of the advokat in a special law rather than branch legislation. The absence in the Code of Criminal Procedure of provisions expressly indicating the need to obtain a judicial decision as a condition for carrying out investigative activities on advokat premises may not be regarded as creating an exception to Article 8(3) of the present Law.

Advokat premises do not enjoy immunity against operational-search operations. Only certain materials are protected, which in practice may be difficult to distinguish one from the other. The implements of a crime on advokat premises, for example, do not enjoy any protection. Depending upon the crime being investigated, one may readily imagine that office computers might be regarded as implements of a crime. Narcotics, weapons, and other articles whose circulation is limited or prohibited would be subject to seizure during an operational-search operation of advokat premises.

Chambers of advokats have adopted tables of "recommended actions" to be taken by advokats if their place of work or their dwelling is subjected to a search. These actions, in recommended sequence, are: (1) demand and obtain from the persons arriving to perform the search a copy of the judicial decision authorizing the performance of this investigative action; (2) place a sign or plaque on the door indicating that a premise is an advokat's place of work; (3) specify an advokat's place of work in the agreement between the advokat formation and the client; (4) indicate in an order

55 See the Ruling of the Constitutional Court of the Russian Federation of 8 November 2005, No. 439-O. СЗ РФ (2006), no. 5, item 633.

56 Ruling No. 673-O-O, 21 October 2008. Unpublished. Available on Consultant Plus.

of the executive that all documents transferred to an advokat are under the regime of confidentiality; (5) caution the law enforcement personnel that they are searching a premise used by an advokat and that there are documents subject to protection which contain an advokat secret. If such documents are taken, an appropriate notation should be made on the protocol; (6) appeal against the actions of the agencies which conduct an illegal search; (7) inform the chamber of advokats about the search; and (8) if an advokat secret was disclosed during the search, inform the client thereof.[57]

57 These appear in Annex 1 to the Recommendations for Ensuring Advokat Secrecy and Guarantees of the Independence of Advokats When Advokats Effectuate Advokat Activity on 30 November 2009. See Semeniako and Pilipenko, Адвокатская деятельность и адвокатура [Advokat Activity and the Advokatura] (2010), pp. 598-602.

Chapter 3 Status of Advokat

Article 9 Acquisition of Status of Advokat

1. *A person who has a higher legal education received in an educational institution of higher professional education having State accreditation, or an academic degree with regard to a legal specialty shall have the right to acquire the status of advokat in the Russian Federation. The said person also must have work experience with regard to a legal specialty of not less than two years or undergo training in an advokat formation within the periods established by the present Federal Law.*
   Work experience with regard to a legal specialty shall be calculated for persons whose higher legal education is first received as higher professional education not earlier than from the moment of graduation from the respective educational institution [paragraph added by Federal Law of 20 December 2004].
2. *Persons shall not have the right to apply for the acquisition of the status of advokat and effectuate advokat activity:*
   (1) who are deemed to lack dispositive legal capacity or have limited dispositive legal capacity in the procedure established by legislation of the Russian Federation;
   (2) who have a record of conviction not cancelled or removed for the commission of an intentional crime.
3. *A decision concerning the conferment of the status of advokat shall be adopted by the qualifications commission attached to the chamber of advokats of a subject of the Russian Federation (hereinafter – qualifications commission) after the taking of the qualifications examination by the person applying to acquire the status of advokat (hereinafter also – applicant).*
4. *In the work experience with regard to a legal specialty necessary to acquire the status of advokat shall be included work:*
   (1) as judge;
   (2) in State posts requiring a higher legal education in federal agencies of State power, agencies of State power of subjects of the Russian Federation, and other State agencies;
   (3) in posts requiring a higher legal education in State agencies of the USSR, RSFSR, and Russian Federation situated on the territory of the Russian Federation which existed before the adoption of the prevailing Constitution of the Russian Federation;
   (4) in municipal posts requiring a higher legal education;

(5) in posts requiring a higher legal education in organs of the Judicial Department attached to the Supreme Court of the Russian Federation;
(6) in posts requiring a higher legal education in the legal services of organizations;
(7) in posts requiring a higher legal education in scientific-research institutions;
(8) as a teacher of legal disciplines in institutions of secondary professional, higher professional, and postgraduate professional education;
(9) as an advokat;
(10) as the aide of an advokat;
(11) as a notary.

5. *An advokat shall have the right to effectuate advokat activity throughout the entire territory of the Russian Federation without any additional authorization whatsoever.*
6. *Foreign citizens and stateless persons who have received the status of advokat in the procedure established by the present Federal Law shall be permitted to effectuate advokat activity throughout the entire territory of the Russian Federation unless provided otherwise by a federal law.*

1. The term "status of advokat" originates in the present Law. An advokat is a person who has acquired the status of advokat and the right to engage in advokat activity (Article 2 above).

The formulation of this Article speaks of a "person" without determining whether this may be a natural person and/or a juridical person, although the subsequent sense of the formulation suggests that "natural person" is intended. The term "person" would encompass citizens of the Russian Federation, including those who acquire Russian citizenship, foreign citizens, stateless persons, and individuals who have dual citizenship, one of which is Russian.

Point 1 substantially reproduces the requirements for becoming an advokat set out in the 1980 RSFSR Statute on the Advokatura with the addition that a person who has an "academic degree" may become an advokat. This means that a person whose primary diploma is in a discipline other than law but who acquires a postgraduate academic degree (kandidat or doctor of legal sciences) in law may become an advokat. In practice the LL.M. has been accepted for these purposes provided there is a first degree in law, although the legislation and the Russian classification of learned degrees is ambiguous in this respect. One commentator has written in this regard, "... one may conclude that a natural person having one of the said degrees of higher professional education has the right to apply for the acquisition of the status of advokat".[1]

A higher education must for the purposes of the present Law be received in an institution of higher vocational education having State accreditation pursuant to the Federal Law of 22 August 1996, as amended, "On Higher and Post-Graduate

1 D. P. Baranov, in I. L. Trunov (ed.), Адвокатская деятельность и Адвокатура в России [Advokat Activity and the Advokatura in Russia] (2006), I, p. 131.

Vocational Education".[2] Academic degrees and titles are conferred in accordance with the Decree of the Government of the Russian Federation of 30 January 2002, No. 74, as amended "On Confirmation of the Unified Register of Academic Degrees and Academic Titles and the Statute on the Procedure for the Awarding of Academic Degrees".[3] Only diplomas issued by the Ministry of Education and Science of the Russian Federation or other State agencies of the former Soviet Union and Russian Federation endowed with corresponding functions in the State attestation of scientific workers or diplomas issued in countries with which the Russian Federation has concluded treaties or agreements on the recognition and equivalence of diplomas are recognized for these purposes.

Work experience is linked in the Russian Federation with the moment of entering into labor relations on the basis of a labor contract, the procedure for concluding which is regulated by the Labor Code of the Russian Federation. Under the Labor Code labor relations also may arise on the basis of a labor contract that exists by reason of election to office, appointment or confirmation in post, being sent to work under a quota established by legislation, or a judicial decision concerning the conclusion of a labor contract. The Labor Code (Article 14) provides that periods with which the Code connects the arising of labor rights and duties commence from the calendar date on which they commence, provided that this date does not precede the moment of graduation from a respective educational institution.

However, the formulation of the 2004 amendment to this point has given rise to numerous disputes among applicants for the status of advokat who understand the formulation to mean that work experience obtained before receiving a second higher education should be taken into account. It would have been clearer to simply provide that the work experience is relevant after obtaining a higher legal education.

The period of work experience in an advokat formation is from one to two years pursuant to Article 28 of the present Law.

2. Point 2 determines two categories of persons who may not apply to acquire the status of advokat or engage in advokat activity.

(1) Dispositive legal capacity is defined in the Civil Code of the Russian Federation (Article 21) and the capacity of a citizen by his own actions to acquire and effectuate civil rights, create civil duties for himself, and perform them. This capacity arises in full from the age of majority or marriage, whichever first occurs. Individuals may be deemed by a court to lack dispositive legal capacity (Article 29, Civil Code) by reason of mental illness or may be limited in dispositive legal capacity (Article 30, Civil Code) as a consequence of alcoholism, narcotics addiction, and the like. The

2 СЗ РФ (1996), no. 35, item 4135, as amended.
3 СЗ РФ (2002), no. 6, item 580, as amended.

procedure for legal capacity limitations or deprivations is regulated by Chapter 31 of the Code of Civil Procedure of the Russian Federation.

(2) A record of conviction is cancelled or removed in accordance with the Criminal Code of the Russian Federation (Article 86). An intentional crime for the purposes of the present Article is one which was committed with direct or indirect intent (Article 26, Criminal Code).

3. The requirement of a qualifications examination and the power to adopt a decision conferring the status of advokat upon a successful applicant is established by point 3 of the present Article. See Article 33 of the present Law and Commentary below. On the qualifications examination, see Article 11 and Commentary below.

4. Point 4 of the present Article is not exhaustive. It sets out eleven examples of work considered to qualify as work in a legal specialty necessary to acquire the status of advokat. With certain exceptions, the enumeration is analogous to requirements set out in a Letter of the Ministry of Justice of the Russian Federation of 10 October 1995, No. 09-06-137-95, in response to queries.[4]

(1) The determination of who qualifies as a "judge" for these purposes is based on the Law on the Status of Judges in the Russian Federation. All judges in the Russian Federation enjoy a unified status, subject to certain qualifications in legal status based on federal laws or laws of subjects of the Russian Federation (e.g., military judges).[5]

(2) The Federal Law on State Civil Service of the Russian Federation of 27 July 2004, as amended,[6] determines what constitutes a State post. That determination, read against the Letter of the Ministry of Justice of 10 October 1995 (see above), means that work in procuracy agencies, internal affairs agencies, Federal Security Service, and counter-intelligence agencies for which the requisite educational qualifications are provided fall into this category.

(3) The reference is to the 1993 Russian Constitution. An exhaustive enumeration of relevant posts does not exist but is widely assumed to include posts in State agencies of the former USSR, RSFSR, and Russian Federation which provided for the performance of duties corresponding to presently existing State posts.

(4) A municipal post is defined in the Federal Law of 8 January 1998, as amended, "On the Fundamental Principles of Municipal Service in the Russian Federation".[7] Municipal posts are subdivided into elective posts and those filled on the basis of a labor contract. Legislation of subjects of the Federation routinely categorizes elective posts as category "A" and those filled by labor contract as posts "B" and "C".

4 Unpublished, but available on Consultant Plus and shown as still in force as of 1 January 2011.

5 Ведомости Съезда народных депутатов и Верховного Совета Российской Федерации (1992), no. 30, item 1792, as amended; transl. in W. E. Butler, *Russian Public Law* (2d ed.; 2009), pp. 421-446.

6 СЗ РФ (2004), no. 31, item 3215, as amended.

7 СЗ РФ (1998), no. 2, item 224, as amended.

Categories "B" and "C" comprise "municipal posts of municipal service". Municipal service is defined as "professional activity effectuated on a permanent basis in a municipal post which is not elective". For the purposes of the present Law municipal service in a category "B" or "C" post is what is intended.

(5) Under the Federal Law of 8 January 1998 "On the Judicial Department attached to the Supreme Court of the Russian Federation",[8] the said Judicial Department is a federal State agency engaged in the organizational provision of the activity of federal courts of ordinary jurisdiction, the financing of justices of the peace, organs of the Judicial Community, and others. Those who work for the Judicial Department are State employees and a higher legal education is required.

(6) The legal services of organizations includes, at a minimum, those legal services regulated by the General Statute on the Legal Section (or Bureau), Chief (or Senior) Jurisconsult, or Jurisconsult of a Ministry, Department, Executive Committee of Soviet of Deputies of Working People, Enterprise, Organization, or Institution, confirmed by the USSR Council of Ministers on 22 June 1972, as amended.[9] Persons who have a higher legal education may be appointed to the post of jurisconsult, subject to certain exceptions.

The question is whether individuals working for foreign companies or law firms in Russia meet the test of being employed by a "legal service" of an "organization". In Uzbekistan the present writer took the necessary examinations there for the provision of legal services and was licensed as a "senior jurisconsult" with the powers to head a law office. This equated the branch of a foreign law firm with an organization providing legal services. There is no such equivalent examination or attestation in the Russian Federation, and it is unclear how the Russian authorities would treat such employment.

(7) Under the Federal Law of 23 August 1996, "On Science and State Scientific-Technical Policy"[10] a scientific research organization is a species of scientific organization. A scientific organization, in turn, is a juridical person, irrespective of organizational-legal form and form of ownership, or a social association of scientific workers, engaged in basic scientific and/or scientific-technical activity, training of scientific workers, and operating in accordance with the constitutive documents of a scientific organization. Higher educational institutions may have scientific-research subdivisions.

Persons working in scientific-research organizations are subdivided into three categories: (1) scientific worker or researcher, a person who has necessary qualifications and is professionally engaged in scientific and/or scientific-technical activity;

---

8 СЗ РФ (1998), no. 2, item 223, as amended; transl. in W. E. Butler, *Russian Public Law* (2d ed.; 2009), pp. 578-586.

9 СП СССР (1972), no. 13, item 70, as amended; transl. in W. E. Butler, *The Soviet Legal System: Documentation and Legislation* (1978), pp. 311-318.

10 СЗ РФ (1996), no. 35, item 4137, as amended.

(2) specialist or technical engineer who has a secondary vocational or higher professional education and is capable of obtaining a scientific and/or scientific-technical result or the realization thereof; and (3) a scientific servicing worker who helps ensure the creation of necessary conditions for scientific and/or scientific-technical work in a scientific organization. To obtain the status of an advokat a person must engage in labor activity as a scientific worker – be classified as scientific personnel or the heads of sections, laboratories, or scientific-research institutions.

(8) The framework for higher education in the Russian Federation is set out in the Law on Education of 10 July 1992, in the version of 13 January 1996, as amended.[11] For the purposes of obtaining the status of advokat, no distinction is drawn as to the level in the system of higher education legal disciplines must be taught. Legal education is offered at secondary, university, and post-graduate levels.

(9) For work as an advokat of relevance, see Article 2 of the present Law and Commentary thereto.

(10) Pursuant to Article 27 of the present Law below, an aide to an advokat is hired under a labor contract with the advokat formation or, if working in an advokat cabinet, with the advokat himself, usually for a fixed term. Some Russian commentators believe that points 1 and 4 of the present Article are contradictory to one another insofar as they allow work as an aide to an advokat to be counted in work experience and an aide to be appointed to his position before completing his higher education. Others see no contradiction, suggesting that the work experience of an aide may be counted towards the status of advokat only after the aide completes his higher legal education. The very disagreement over this issue suggests that the text of the present Article requires adjustment in the interests of clarification.

It should be noted that the position of an apprentice to an advokat (Article 28 below) does not count towards work experience for acquiring the status of advokat. The "category of apprentice as such has merely methods significance; an apprentice is a person preparing to take the qualifications examination for conferment of the status of advokat".[12]

(11) A notary, whether private or State, is required in the Russian Federation to have a higher legal education and to have undergone an apprenticeship in a State notarial office or with a private notary for at least one year, to have passed a qualifications examination, and to have a license to engage in notarial activity. These requirements are laid down in the Fundamental Principles of Legislation of the Russian Federation on the Notariat of 11 February 1993, as amended.[13]

11 СЗ РФ (1996), no. 3, item 150, as amended.

12 See S. N. Ivanov, «О некоторых нормах законодательства об адвокатской деятельности» [On Certain Norms of Legislation on Advokat Activity], Адвокат [Advokat], no. 11 (2004).

13 Ведомости Съезда народных депутатов и Верховного Совета Российской Федерации (1993), no. 10, item 357; transl. in W. E. Butler, *Russian Public Law* (2d ed.; 2009), pp. 813-843.

Work experience as a private detective does not qualify as relevant experience towards receiving the status of advokat, notwithstanding the fact that a higher legal education is a qualification that many private detectives have.[14]

5. The territory of the Russian Federation is defined by the Law of the Russian Federation of 1 April 1993, as amended "On the State Boundary of the Russian Federation".[15] Although a literal reading of this Law would limit an advokat strictly speaking to practicing within the territory over which the Russian Federation has sovereignty, including airspace, the formulation is unusual in excluding such areas as the continental shelf and exclusive economic zone where offshore structures may be erected or areas outside the Russian Federation with respect to which there are status of forces agreements or areas where Russian forces or law enforcement personnel may serve as part of operations conducted by an international organization.

6. This provision equates foreign citizens and stateless persons who have received the status of advokat in the Russian Federation with Russian citizens who have received the said status. In fact foreign citizens are precluded from travelling to or visiting certain closed areas or territories of the Russian Federation not by a law, but by subordinate normative legal acts of the Russian Federation.

The List of territories for which a foreign citizen requires special authorization to visit was confirmed by Decree of the Government of the Russian Federation on 4 July 1992, as amended. In all there are territories where visits by foreign citizens are regulated in nineteen subjects of the Russian Federation.[16]

Article 10 Admittance to Qualifications Examination

1. *A person meeting the requirements of Article 9(1) and (2) of the present Federal Law shall have the right to have recourse to a qualifications commission of a chamber of advokats of a subject of the Russian Federation with an application concerning the conferment of the status of advokat on him [as amended by Federal Law of 20 December 2004].*
2. *An applicant in addition to the application shall submit to the qualifications commission a document certifying his identity, questionnaire containing biographical information, copy of the labor book or other document confirming work experience*

14 See the Law on Private Detective and Protection Activity in the Russian Federation of 11 March 1992, as amended. Ведомости Съезда народных депутатов и Верховного Совета Российской Федерации (1992), no. 17, item 594, as amended; transl. in W. E. Butler, *Russian Public Law* (2d ed.; 2009), pp. 964-979.

15 Ведомости Съезда народных депутатов и Верховного Совета Российской Федерации (1992), no. 17, item 594, as amended.

16 See W. E. Butler, *Russian Foreign Relations and Investment Law* (2006), p. 129.

in legal specialty, copy of document confirming higher legal education or presence of learned degree in legal specialty, and also other documents in instances provided for by legislation on advokat activity and the advokatura.

The provision of unreliable information may serve as grounds for refusal to admit the applicant to the qualifications examination.

3. *The qualifications commission shall, when necessary, organize within two months the verification of the reliability of documents and information submitted by an applicant. In so doing a qualifications commission shall have the right to have recourse to respective agencies with a query concerning verification or confirmation of the reliability of the said documents and information. The said agencies shall be obliged to inform the qualifications commission concerning the results of the verification of documents and information or confirm their reliability not later than a month from the day of receipt of the query of the qualifications commission.*
4. *After completion of the verification, the qualifications commission shall adopt a decision concerning the admittance of the applicant to the qualifications examination.*
5. *A decision concerning the refusal to admit an applicant to the qualifications examination may be adopted only on the grounds specified in the present Federal Law. A decision concerning refusal to admit to the qualifications examination may be appealed to a court.*

1. Article 10 sets out the procedure for an applicant being admitted to take the qualifications examination in order to acquire the status of advokat. Point 1 is essentially declaratory, providing that a person who meets the requirements of Article 9(1) and (2) above has the right to make application in writing for the qualifications examination.

2. Point 2 enumerates the documents which must be submitted to the qualifications commission together with the written application to sit the qualifications examination. The form of the application is appended to the 2003 Statute on the Procedure for Passing the Qualifications Examination for Conferment of the Status of Advokat. The first is a copy of an identity document, which for Russian citizens will be their internal passport and for foreign citizens their foreign passport. For stateless persons other identity documents may be produced. The second document is a questionnaire whose form and content are determined by the qualifications commission; a model questionnaire also is appended to the aforesaid 2003 Statute. The questionnaire seeks relevant biographical information from the applicant.

Third is a copy of the labor book or other document confirming work experience in a legal specialty. Under the Labor Code of the Russian Federation (Article 66), the labor book is the primary document recording the labor activity and labor experience of a Russian citizen. Each labor book contains information about the worker, job performed, transfers to other work, dismissals, grounds for termination of the labor contract, and information about awards for success in work. At the worker's request information may be entered about holding two or more jobs at the same time. The phrase "other documents" confirming labor experience in a legal specialty would include duly formalized extracts from orders of institutions or organizations.

Fourth is a copy of the document confirming that the applicant has a higher legal education or an academic degree in a legal specialty. Persons having a higher legal education must submit a diploma of the State form issued by an institution of higher education having State accreditation. An academic degree is certified by diplomas for the kandidat or doctor of legal sciences issued by the High Attestation Commission of the Ministry of Education and Science of the Russian Federation.

Under amendments introduced by Decision of the Federal Chamber of Advokats of 2 April 2010, an applicant to take the qualifications examination must give evidence that he is registered at a permanent place of residence and as a taxpayer in the subject of the Russian Federation in which he applies to take the examination.

The application to take the qualifications examination also contains a question as to whether the applicant has been admitted to take the qualifications examination in another subject of the Russian Federation within the last twelve months.

The provision of unreliable information is grounds for a refusal to admit an applicant for the qualifications examination. Unreliable information would include incorrect biographical data or information about work experience or education that is untrue. The 2003 Statute (point 1.7) enumerates five grounds for refusal to admit to the qualifications examination: (1) the applicant's communication of information that is untrue or the submission of documents not properly formalized; (2) the applicant's lack of a higher legal education from an institution having State accreditation or an academic degree of the proper specialty; (3) the lack of two years' work experience or lack of information of his having experience as an aide to an advokat for at least a year; (4) the applicant lacks or is limited in dispositive civil legal capacity; (5) the applicant has a record of criminal conviction unremoved or uncancelled. If an applicant is refused admission to the examination, he is issued at his request an extract from the protocol of the commission session containing the reasoned decision of the commission, which he may appeal to a court.

3. The Qualifications Commission has the right, but not the duty, to verify the reliability of the information submitted by an applicant for the qualifications examination. Two months are granted for this purpose from the day of submission of the application to the commission as measured by the date of registration of the documents in the organ of the commission for clerical correspondence. The information is verified by sending queries or otherwise determining the reliability of the documents. Queries may be sent to State agencies, institutions, and organizations, law enforcement agencies, and public health agencies. Queries are routinely sent to internal affairs agencies with regard to a record of convictions, to narcological dispensaries with regard to the use of narcotics or alcohol, and to mental institutions with regard to mental illnesses. Replies from these institutions may lead to enquiries with a court

to determine whether an applicant has limited dispositive legal capacity. Agencies which receive queries from a qualifications commission are expected to reply within one month from the date of receipt of the query calculated from the date of registration of the query at the respective recipient agency.

4. The qualifications commission takes a formal decision to admit or to refuse to admit an applicant to the qualifications examination based upon the results of the verification of the information contained in the application and accompanying documents. A written ballot is signed by each member of the commission. The form of the ballot is set out as Annex 3 to the Statute on the procedure for taking the qualifications examination.

5. A decision of the qualifications commission to refuse to admit an applicant to the qualifications examination may be appealed to a court in the procedure established by the Code of Civil Procedure of the Russian Federation. The appeal must be made within three months from the day when the applicant learned about the violation of his rights. The application is considered by a court within ten days with the participation of the applicant and a representative of the agency or official whose decision is being appealed.

If the court considers the suit to be substantiated, it will adopt a decision to order the respective agency or official to eliminate entirely the violations permitted. The decision is sent within three days to the respective agency or official from the day of the entry of the court decision into legal force. The court will refuse to satisfy the suit if it is established that the decision to refuse admittance to the qualifications examination was adopted in accordance with law and within the power of the respective agency or official.

Article 11 Qualifications Examination

1. *The Statute on the procedure for taking the qualifications examination and evaluation of the knowledge of applicants, and also the list of questions proposed for applicants, shall be worked out and confirmed by the council of the Federal Chamber of Advokats.*
2. *A qualifications examination shall consist of written answers to questions (or testing) and an oral conversation.*
3. *An applicant who has not passed a qualifications examination shall be admitted in a repeat procedure established by the present Federal Law to take the qualifications examination not earlier than a year later [as amended by Federal Law of 20 December 2004].*

1. The procedure for taking the qualifications examination is regulated by the Statute on the Procedure for Passing the Qualifications Examination for Conferment of the

Status of Advokat, confirmed by Decision of the Council of the Federal Chamber of Advokats of the Russian Federation on 24 April 2003, as amended 25 August 2003, 25 June 2004, and 2 April 2010. The examination consists of two parts. The first part may take the form of either written answers to questions or of "testing" in the form of answers to multiple choice and/or true/false questions. The last are commonly administered with the use of computers.

2. Once the results of Part One of the examination are available and the candidate has performed satisfactorily, he proceeds to Part Two of the examination, which consists of an oral examination given by the qualifications commission itself. The "questions" to be answered are placed on a sheet of paper, several sheets being placed upside down on the table for the candidate to select one without seeing the questions. Having chosen a sheet (or "ticket", as the Statute provides), the candidate has 45 minutes to think about the answers prior to appearing before the qualifications commission. The candidate may have with him collections of normative acts, the texts of codes, or other reference materials. All questions on the "ticket" must be answered, and once the candidate has completed his answers, including to any supplementary questions put by commission members, the qualifications commission deliberates in his absence whether to pass the candidate or not.

The qualifications examination is the equivalent of the Bar examination in the United States or in England and Wales. The questions which a candidate may be asked are public knowledge. The number of questions eligible to be placed on the sheet of paper has been reduced from 600 to approximately 445; they cover all branches of law. The formulation of each question was confirmed on 6 April 2005 by the Council of the Federal Chamber of Advokats of Russia and is reviewed periodically. Books are available to intending advokats which contain all the questions and model answers to each.[17] The questions also are placed on the website of the Federal Chamber of Advokats.[18]

The style of the questions replicates that used in Russian university examinations: "67. Juridical Person. Concept, Indicia, Types". The punctuation is correct; there is no question mark. The correct answer is for the candidate to impart as much relevant knowledge as he can recall by way of explication, or gloss, on the words. All questions are of equal weight for assessment purposes. The subject-matter covered includes professional activities and ethics, civil, criminal, company, housing, family, labor, and tax law, civil, arbitrazh, and criminal procedure, and proceedings in the Constitutional Court of the Russian Federation and the European Court of Human Rights.

17 See, for example, I. L. Trunov, Энциклопедия будущего адвоката [Encyclopedia of a Future Advokat] (2006).

18 See the List of 445 questions to be used from 1 March 2011. www.fparf.ru

3. The decision to pass or fail the candidate is taken by a simple majority of votes recorded on a written and signed ballot. The candidate is informed of the result on the same day. An unsuccessful candidate, or a candidate who fails without justifiable reasons to appear for the examination, may apply to retake the examination after one year has elapsed.

The administrative tasks of a qualifications commission are performed by a secretary, who also keeps the archive of the commission. The secretary keeps minutes of each examination, recording the date and place, surnames and initials of commission members present, requisites of identity documents submitted by the examinees, numbers of examination tickets, additional questions and answers of the examinees, and the final voting results of the commission. The protocol is signed by all commission members irrespective of how they may have voted on matters before the commission. The ballots and tests are appended to the protocol and kept for three years.

An applicant is issued within three days after taking the qualifications examination an extract from the protocol of the session of the commission containing the decision to confer or not confer the status of advokat on the applicant. A second copy of the extract is placed in the personal file of each examinee. The personal files of applicants who passed the examination are kept in the archive of the qualifications commission for 75 years and then are subject to destruction. The files of those who failed the examination are kept for three years. Information about advokats or about the work of the commission may be issued at the request of citizens and organizations, including courts, procuracy, inquiry, and investigation agencies upon the written instruction of the chairman of the qualifications commission.

Article 12 Conferment of Status of Advokat

1. *A qualifications commission shall within a three-month period from the day of filing by the applicant of an application concerning the conferment on him of the status of advokat adopt a decision concerning the conferment or refusal to confer the status of advokat on the applicant.*
   The decision of the qualifications commission concerning the conferment of the status of advokat on the applicant shall enter into force from the day of the taking of the oath by the applicant.
2. *A qualifications commission shall not have the right to refuse to an applicant who has successfully passed the qualifications examination the conferment of the status of advokat, except for instances when after passing the qualifications examination circumstances are discovered which obstruct admission to the qualifications examination. In such instances the decision concerning refusal to confer the status of advokat may be appealed to a court.*
3. *The status of advokat shall be conferred on the applicant for an indefinite period and shall not be limited by a determined age of the advokat.*

1. The formulation of point 1 is not linked with the qualifications examination because circumstances may permit a person to apply for conferment of the status of advokat without necessarily passing the qualifications examination. The results of the qualifications examination have no period of validity linked with them. This would suggest, for example, that an advokat who has passed the qualifications examination and worked as an advokat, then left the profession for a period of time, and seek to renew his status of advokat should not have to resit the qualifications examination. On this principle years may elapse between these events but not affect the results of the original examination.

The decision of the qualifications commission to confer the status of advokat is not decisive for the commencement of such status. The status of advokat runs from the moment of taking the oath of advokat.

2. The circumstances set out in point 2 of the present Article would be unusual, essentially the discovery of information that would have precluded the applicant from being admitted to the qualifications examination in the first place. Should such circumstances come to light, the qualifications commission may refuse conferment of the status of advokat. The procedures for doing this are not elaborated in the present Law. Any such refusal may be appealed to a court in accordance with the Code of Civil Procedure.

3. There is no minimum or maximum age for the status of advokat to be conferred on a person. Once conferred, the status of advokat remains in place unless and until the advokat leaves the profession or until death.

Article 13 Oath of Advokat

1. *In the procedure established by a chamber of advokats, the applicant who has successfully passed the qualifications examination shall take an oath of the following content:*

   "I solemnly swear honorably and in good faith to perform the duties of advokat, to defend the rights, freedoms, and interests of principals, being guided by the Constitution of the Russian Federation, law, and the Code of Professional Ethics of an Advokat".
2. *From the day of taking the oath an applicant shall receive the status of advokat and becomes a member of the chamber of advokats.*

1. The oath is compulsory. The moment that the applicant takes the oath marks the time from which he becomes a member of the chamber of advokats; or, more precisely, the taking of the oath marks the moment of entry into force of the decision of the qualifications commission to confer the status of advokat.

2. The swearing of the oath is a type of professional ritual. There are no regulations as to how each chamber of advokats should arrange this solemn occasion. The practice therefore varies from one college to another. Those who are classified as advokats of a foreign State are not involved in professional rituals in Russia by reason of receiving the respective certificate.

Variations in practice from one chamber of advokats to another led to amendments being adopted on 2 April 2010 by Decision of the Council of the Federal Chamber of Advokats to the 2003 Statute on the Procedure for taking the qualifications examination. The amendments recommended that the oath be taken by each newly-qualifying advokat not later than one month from the day of taking the examination so that if they had qualified in another subject of the Federation, that information could be removed from the register of advokats before taking the oath in a new subject of the Federation.

Article 14 Registers of Advokats

1. *The territorial agency of the federal agency of executive power in the domain of justice (hereinafter – territorial justice agency) shall keep the register of advokats of a subject of the Russian Federation (hereinafter –regional register).*
2. *The territorial justice agency shall annually not later than 1 February send to the chamber of advokats a copy of the regional register. The territorial justice agency shall inform the chamber of advokats of the respective subject of the Russian Federation within a 10-day period from the day of making the said changes about making changes in the regional register.*
3. *The procedure for keeping regional registers shall be determined by the federal justice agency.*

1. The territorial agency of the Federal Registration Service has been given the competence to keep the register of advokats within the respective subject of the Russian Federation. The register contains information about persons who have received the status of advokat and who have the right to effectuate advocate activity. By Order of the Ministry of Justice of the Russian Federation of 5 February 2008, No. 20 "On Confirmation of the Administrative Reglament for Performance by Territorial Agencies of the Federal Registration Service of the State Function for Keeping the Register of Advokats of a Subject of the Russian Federation and Issuance of Certificates to Advokats", as amended,[19] the procedure for establishing the initial registers of existing advokats requires the entries be made on the basis of documents provided for in Article 40(2) and (3) of the present Law (see Commentary to Article 40 below) and that the date of admitting a person to membership in a college of advokats be taken as the

19 Available on Consultant Plus.

date on which the status of advokat was confirmed. Documents received at the territorial agency of the Ministry of Justice of the Russian Federation in accordance with Article 40(3) of the present Law were retained to form the register files of advokats.

2. The register of advokats was kept initially in accordance with the "Procedure for Keeping the Register of Advocates of a Subject of the Russian Federation", confirmed by Order of the Ministry of Justice of the Russian Federation, No. 211, of 29 July 2002, and is presently set out in the Administrative Reglament of 5 February 2008.

3. The territorial justice agency has the legal duty to provide to the chamber of advokats on its territory an annual copy of the register and to notify any changes therein within 10 days of making such.

These registers are quite distinct from the register of advokats of foreign States, which are kept only at the federal level by the Ministry of Justice of the Russian Federation. There is no obligation of the Ministry to provide reports to organs of the Advokatura in the Russian Federation.

Article 15 Inclusion of Information Concerning Advokat in Regional Register

1. *A qualifications commission shall within a seven-day period from the day of adoption of the respective decision concerning the conferment of the status of advokat on an applicant inform the territorial justice agencies, which within a month's period from the day of receipt of the notification include the information concerning the advokat in the regional register and issue a respective certificate to the advokat.*
2. *The form of the certificate shall be confirmed by a federal justice agency. On the certificate shall be specified the surname, forename, and patronymic of the advokat and his registration number in the regional register. On the certificate must be a photograph of the advokat certified by the seal of the territorial justice agency.*
3. *The certificate shall be the sole document confirming the status of an advokat, except for the instance provided for by point 5 of the present Article [as amended by Federal Law of 20 December 2004].*
   A person whose status as an advokat was terminated or suspended after the adoption of the respective decision by the council of the chamber of advokats shall be obliged to surrender his certificate to the territorial agency of justice which issued the said certificate [added by Federal Law of 20 December 2004].
4. *An advokat may simultaneously be a member of a chamber of advokats only of one subject of the Russian Federation, and information concerning him shall be entered only in one regional register. An advokat shall have the right to effectuate his activity only in one advokat formation confirmed in accordance with the present Federal Law.*

5. *An advokat who has adopted a decision concerning a change of membership in the chamber of advokats of one subject of the Russian Federation to membership in the chamber of advokats of another subject of the Russian Federation shall inform by registered letter the council of the chamber of advokats of the subject of the Russian Federation (hereinafter also – council of chamber of advokats, chamber) of which he is a member [as amended by Federal Law of 20 December 2004].*
The council shall inform the territorial justice agency about the said decision of the advokat within a ten-day period from the day of receipt of the notification of the advokat. If the advokat has indebtedness with regard to deductions to the chamber of advokats the council shall have the right not to send the said notification until payment in full by the advocate of the amount of indebtedness [as amended by Federal Law of 20 December 2004].
The territorial justice agency shall exclude information about the advokat from the regional register not later than a month from the day of receipt of the notification of the council. In so doing the advokat shall be obliged to hand over his own certificate to the territorial justice agency. In place of a certificate handed over by the advokat the territorial justice agency shall issue to the advokat a document confirming the status of advokat. In this document shall be specified the date of inclusion of the information concerning the advokat in the regional register and the date of exclusion of information concerning the advokat from the regional register. An advokat shall be obliged within a month's period from the day of exclusion of the information concerning him from the regional register by registered letter to inform the council thereof of the chamber of advokats of that subject of the Russian Federation of which he intends to become a member [as amended by Federal Law of 20 December 2004].
The council of the chamber of advokats of the respective subject of the Russian Federation shall within a month from the day of receipt from the advokat of the said notice verify information concerning the advokat and render a decision concerning his acceptance as a member of the chamber of advokats. The council shall inform the territorial justice agency and the advokat about this decision within a ten-day period from the day of adoption of the decision [as amended by Federal Law of 20 December 2004].
The territorial justice agency shall within a month's period from the day of receipt of the said notice submit information concerning the advokat to the regional register and issue a new certificate to the advokat.
6. *An advocate from the day of conferment of status of advokat or entry of information concerning the advokat into the regional register after a change by him of membership in the chamber of advokats, or renewal of the status of advokat, shall be obliged to inform the council of the chamber of advokats about the form of advokat formation chosen by him within a three-months' period from the day of ensuing of the said circumstances [as amended by Federal Law of 20 December 2004].*

7. *The failure to enter information concerning an advokat in a regional register or the failure to issue a certificate to an advokat within the periods established by the present Federal Law may be appealed to a court.*
8. *The procedure for the change by an advokat of membership in a chamber of advokats of one subject of the Russian Federation to membership in a chamber of advokats of another subject of the Russian Federation shall be determined by the council of the Federal Chamber of Advokats [as amended by Federal Law of 20 December 2004].*

1. Point 1 of the present Article establishes two periods during which certain actions must be performed. The first is a seven-day period during which a qualifications commission must notify the justice agency that the status of advokat has been conferred on an advokat. The second is a period of one month during which the justice agency must (a) include information about the advokat in a register, and (b) issue a certificate to the advokat. The advokat is then notified that the respective information has been included in the register and that his certificate is ready for collection.

2. The form of the certificate is set out in Annex 2 of the Administrative Reglament for Performance by Territorial Agencies of the Federal Registration Service of the State Function for Keeping the Register of Advokats of a Subject of the Russian Federation and Issuance of Certificates to Advokats of 5 February 2008, as amended, confirmed by Order of the Ministry of Justice. The certificate contains the full name of the advokat, registration number in the register of advokats, and a certified photograph. A certificate not properly formalized or containing erasures or corrections is considered to be invalid.

3. Except for provisional documentation issued to an advokat who is in transition from one regional register to another (see point 5 below), the certificate of an advokat is the only document which certifies the status of advokat. An advokat keeps this certificate with him at all times and presents it when necessary. If an advokat's status is suspended or terminated, the certificate of an advokat must be surrendered to the territorial justice agency which issued the certificate. The very same certificate is returned to the advokat in the event of reinstatement.

4. Although an advokat may practice anywhere on the territory of the Russian Federation, he may be registered as an advokat only in one subject of the Russian Federation and may be a member of only one advokat formation. This limitation would appear to apply only within the Russian Federation and would not preclude a Russian advokat from being qualified to practice as a member of a foreign bar outside Russia, although the similarity of terminology may make such affiliation doubtful in other CIS jurisdictions.

Exceptions exist for advokats registered in the City of Moscow, Moscow Region, St. Petersburg, or Leningrad Region. Advokats who are members of any one of these four chambers of advokats may engage in advokat activity irrespective of whether they have a place of residence on those territories.

5. Advokats may and do change their jurisdiction of registration from time to time for personal and/or professional reasons. Providing that the formalities set out in point 5 are complied with, the advokat is at liberty to change membership of a chamber of advokats from one subject of the Federation to another. The decision to leave one chamber of advokats is within the discretion of the advokat concerned provided that there are no arrears in deductions owed to his chamber of advokats. Although the chamber of advokats to which an advokat wishes to transfer must adopt a decision to accept him, there appear to be no grounds on which such an application may be rejected provided that the advokat is in good standing where he previously practiced.

Such a change requires the surrender of the certificate of an advokat and the issuance of a new certificate by the territorial justice agency in the subject of the Russian Federation to which the advokat is transferring. Provisional documentation is issued to cover the transition until the respective registration is made and a new certificate issued. For all practical purposes, a change of jurisdiction within which an advokat is registered amounts to a notification procedure rather than a new admission.

However, in a Decision of the Council of the Federal Chamber of Advokats adopted 2 April 2010 it was decided to replace the Provisional Procedure for Change of Membership in a Chamber of Advokats of One Subject of the Russian Federation to Membership in the Chamber of Advokats of Another Subject of the Russian Federation, confirmed by Decision of the Council of the Federal Chamber of Advokats on 6 April 2005, with a new Procedure issued as Annex No. 1 to the Decision of 2 April 2010. The circumstances which led to the change were experience with a "few advokats" who were registered as advokats in one subject of the Federation but resided in another. This practice resulted in the advokat concerned losing his close organizational link with the chamber of advokats in his subject, or not participating in accordance with the established procedure in criminal cases upon assignment by agencies of inquiry, preliminary investigation, or a court to provide legal assistance free of charge.

Evidence of an advokat residing in one subject but engaging in activity in another subject of the Federation would include: whether an advokat has an office or dwelling premise to receive clients that is used on the basis of a lease or right of ownership, a sign or other information about the advokat, placing information somewhere that an advokat is carrying on advokat activity in a particular subject of the Federation in which he is not registered by the respective chamber of advokats, or participating in a criminal proceeding as a defender by assignment.

An advokat applying to change membership from one subject of the Federation to another may be asked to submit notarially certified documents or originals confirming his change of place of residence and a certificate of tax registration in the subject of the Federation to which he has moved.

6. Once an advokat has completed the registration formalities in his new subject of the Federation, he has a period of three months to notify the chamber of advokats about his choice of advokat formation. The same applies if the advokat has renewed his status of advokat.

7. An advokat may appeal to a court in accordance with the Code of Civil Procedure a failure to enter information about him in the regional register or to issue a certificate of an advokat to him within the periods established by the present Law. This right of appeal affects both new advokats and those transferring from one chamber of advokats to another.

8. Individual chambers of advokats have discretion to regulate the procedure for a change of membership in one chamber of advokats of one subject of the Russian Federation to another provided that such procedures are consistent with the present Law.

ARTICLE 16 SUSPENSION OF STATUS OF ADVOKAT

1. *The status of advokat shall be suspended on the following grounds [as amended by Federal Law of 20 December 2004]:*
   (1) *election of the advokat to an agency of State power or agency of local self-government for the period of work on a permanent basis;*
   (2) *inability of an advokat to perform his professional duties for more than six months;*
   (3) *call-up of an advokat to military service;*
   (4) *deeming of an advokat to be missing in the procedure established by a federal law.*
2. *In the event of the adoption by the court of a decision concerning the application to an advokat of compulsory measures of a medical character the court may consider the question of suspension of the status of the particular advokat.*
3. *Suspension of the status of an advokat shall entail suspension of the operation with respect to the particular advokat of the guarantees provided for by the present Federal Law except for guarantees provided for by Article 18(2) of the present Federal Law.*

3[1]. *A person whose status of an advokat has been suspended shall not have the right to effectuate advokat activity, and also to occupy elective offices in organs of the chamber of advokats or Federal Chamber of Advokats. A violation of the provisions of the present point shall entail termination of the status of advokat [added by Federal Law of 20 December 2004].*

4. *The council of the chamber of advokats of that subject of the Russian Federation within whose regional register information has been submitted concerning this advokat shall adopt the decision concerning suspension of an advokat.*
5. *After termination of operation of the grounds provided for by points 1 and 2 of the present Article, the status of an advokat shall be reinstated by decision of the*

council which adopted the decision concerning suspension of the status of advokat on the basis of a personal application of the advokat whose status was suspended [as amended by Federal Law of 20 December 2004].

5^{1}. *A decision of the council of the chamber of advokats concerning suspension of the status of an advokat or refusal to renew the status of an advokat may be appealed to a court [added by Federal Law of 20 December 2004].*

6. *The council of a chamber of advokats within a ten-day period from the day of adoption by it of a decision concerning the suspension or reinstatement of the status of advokat shall inform the territorial justice agency thereof in written form for the inclusion of the respective information in the regional register, and also a person whose status of an advokat was suspended or reinstated, except for the instance of suspension of the status of advokat on the grounds provided for by point 1(4) of the present Article, and advokat formation in which the said person effectuated advokat activity [as amended by Federal Law of 20 December 2004].*
The territorial justice agency shall within a 10-day period from the day of receipt of the said notice submit information concerning the suspension or reinstatement of the status of advokat in the regional register.

1. There is a certain overlap but not complete coincidence between suspension of the status of advokat in Russia and a member of a bar in the United States electing to become inactive. The concept of suspension did not exist in Soviet legislation on the Advokatura. An advokat who by reason of prolonged illness or other circumstances for which he was not at fault had to leave the college of advokats and later reapply for admission on the general grounds. Reinstatement was guaranteed only for those who had served in elective office or been called-up to active military service (Article 12, 1980 Statute on Advokatura of RSFSR).

The legislation is ambiguous with respect to who must take the initiative to decide on suspension. In the case of elective office or military service, the advokat is best placed to know the situation. Inability to perform professional duties may or may not be within the ability of the advokat to communicate, and an advokat who is legally missing is hardly in a position to take the initiative.

(1) The term "election" here could also encompass "selection", although the formulation suggests permanent work for a term of elective office. Advokats routinely take positions from time to time in State service to assist with individual projects or to secure a steady income; suspension would be an appropriate measure in at least some of these situations.

(2) Illness or recuperation from illness would be a routine example of such inability, but the legislation imposes no criteria and offers no guidance for determining this. It is open for this criterion to be construed broadly in practice, as necessary. The "inability" must be continuous rather than episodic. Some Russian Commentators apprehend that this provision is so general that abuses may arise, for example, to remove from practice an advokat no longer advantageous to the advokat formation.

(3) Under the Federal Law of 28 March 1998, as amended, "On Military Duty and Military Service",[20] Russian male citizens from 18 to 27 years of age are subject to call-up under specified circumstances for period from twelve to twenty-four months. Military service ends from the date the military serviceman is excluded from the personnel list of the military unit in which he served.

(4) The deeming of a person to be missing is a formal legal procedure carried out in accordance with the Civil Code of the Russian Federation (Article 42). Such a procedure may be instituted in court upon the application of interested persons if at his place of residence there has been no information with regard to his whereabouts for a year. The precise procedures for deeming a person to be missing are set out in the Code of Civil Procedure of the Russian Federation (Chapter 30).

2. Compulsory measures of a medical character may be assigned by a court to a person who has committed an act provided by the Special Part of the Criminal Code of the Russian Federation in a state of non-imputability, or a person who after committing a crime suffered mental distress making impossible the assignment or execution of punishment, or a person who committed a crime and suffer from mental disturbance not precluding putability.

Some will regard this provision as unusually generous to an advokat who, regardless of the circumstances, has committed a crime but nonetheless his status of advokat is not terminated. Moreover, while the court "may consider" the question of whether the status of an advokat should be suspended, the court does not take the ultimate decision. That decision rests with the chamber of advokats in the relevant subject of the Russian Federation.

3. Point 3 clarifies an issue which is not immediately apparent to an English-speaking jurist. In the Russian language and law suspension of "status" does not automatically mean that those rules which operated with respect to an advokat in the past cease to operate. Here the legislator clarifies that suspension of status entails the suspension of the operation of guarantees except those set out in Article 18(2) of the present Law. It is not the guarantees which are suspended, but their operation during the period of suspension. All the guarantees remain in place, but with one stipulated exception they are not in force.

3^1. The same logic is present in this newly-inserted point as was witnessed in point 3 above. Suspension of the status of advokat engages as a consequence not only the failure of certain guarantees to operate, but also the result that a suspended advokat may not engage in advokat activity or hold elective office in a chamber of advokats. Here an additional sanction is introduced for violation: termination of the status of advokat (see Article 17 below).

20 СЗ РФ (1998), no. 13, item 1475, as amended.

While the sanction of termination would be appropriate for an advokat who engages in advokat activity after suspension of his status, this is less obvious with respect to holding elective office. The culprit under this formulation is the person who is elected rather than those who voted for him.

The present Law is silent as to whether an advokat whose status is suspended must nonetheless continue to bear expenses for the general needs of the advokat formation to which he belongs for maintenance or whether this advokat may engage in other paid activity besides scientific, pedagogical, or other creative activity.

4. This imperative provision vests only the council of the chamber of advokats in which an advokat is registered with the power to suspend the status of advokat. Even though a court may "consider" whether an advokat should be suspended in status when applying compulsory measures of a medical character, the ultimate decision lies not with the court. One must assume that the recommendation of a court would be given considerable weight by the chamber of advokats when deciding whether to proceed with suspension or not.

5. Reinstatement in the status of advokat is taken at the initiative of the advokat whose status was suspended on condition that the grounds on which suspension was granted no longer operate. The formulation is no longer "operate" rather than no longer "exist". The council which made the initial decision to suspend the status of advokat also makes the decision to reinstate by removing the suspension. The "council" for these purposes is the same organ which took the original decision to suspend but not necessarily composed of the same individuals who served on the council when the initial decision was taken. This requirement precludes an advokat whose status was suspended from changing chambers of advokats during the suspension and seeking reinstatement from another chamber of advokats.

5^1. This added provision introduces a remedy for an advokat who disagrees with either the decision to suspend his status of advokat or a decision to refuse to reinstate him by removing the suspension. Application to a court for either purpose would be in accordance with the Code of Civil Procedure of the Russian Federation. This doubtless opens the door for a chamber of advokats to suspend or refuse reinstatement without giving grounds for this. In recent years more than one hundred advokats have availed themselves of this possibility. Some have succeeded.

6. Point 6 establishes the paper-flow once a decision has been taken by the council of advokats to suspend or reinstate the status of advokat. The territorial justice agency, the advokat himself, and the advokat formation to which the said advokat belongs(ed) are all duly notified within the stipulated period. Appropriate entries are made in the regional register.

Article 17 Termination of Status of Advokat

1. *The status of advokat shall be terminated by the council of the chamber of advokats of a subject of the Russian Federation in whose regional register information was inserted concerning the advokat on the following grounds [as amended by Federal Law of 20 December 2004]:*
   (1) *the filing by the advokat of an application concerning the termination of the status of advokat at the council of the chamber of advokats [as amended by Federal Law of 20 December 2004];*
   (2) *entry into legal force of the decision of a court concerning the deeming of an advokat to lack dispositive legal capacity or be of limited dispositive legal capacity;*
   (3) *death of an advokat or entry into legal force of the decision of a court concerning the declaration thereof to be deceased [as amended by Federal Law of 20 December 2004];*
   (4) *entry into legal force of the judgment of a court concerning the deeming of an advokat to be guilty of the commission of an intentional crime [as amended by Federal Law of 20 December 2004];*
   (5) *eliciting of circumstances provided for by Article 9(2) of the present Federal Law [added by Federal Law of 20 December 2004];*
   (6) *violation of provisions of Article 16(31) of the present Federal Law [as amended by Federal Law of 20 December 2004].*
2. *The status of an advokat may be terminated by decision of the council of the chamber of advokats of a subject of the Russian Federation in whose regional register information was entered concerning the advokat on the basis of the opinion of a qualifications commission in the event of:*
   (1) *failure to perform or improper performance by an advokat of his professional duties to the principal;*
   (2) *violation by an advokat of the Code of Professional Ethics of an Advokat;*
   (3) *failure to perform or improper performance by an advokat of decisions of organs of the chamber of advokats adopted within the limits of competence thereof;*
   (4) *establishment of the unreliability of information submitted to a qualifications commission in accordance with the requirements of Article 10(2) of the present Federal Law;*
   (5) *absence of information in the chamber of advokats for four months from the day of the ensuing of circumstances provided for by Article 15(6) of the present Federal Law concerning selection by an advokat of the form of advokat formation [point 2 added by Federal Law of 20 December 2004].*
3. *A person whose status of an advokat was terminated shall not have the right to effectuate advokat activity, and also to occupy elective offices in organs of a chamber of advokats or the Federal Chamber of Advokats. A violation of the provisions of the present point shall entail the responsibility provided by a federal law [added by Federal Law of 20 December 2004].*

4. *The council within a ten-day period from the day of its adoption shall inform in written form about the decision adopted in accordance with points 1 and 2 of the present Article the person whose status of advokat was terminated, except for the instance of termination of the status of advokat on the grounds provided for by point 1, subpoint (3) of the present Article, the respective advokat formation, and also the respective territorial justice agency, which shall make the necessary changes in the regional register [as amended by Federal Law of 20 December 2004].*
5. *The decision of the council of a chamber of advokats adopted on the grounds provided for by points 1 and 2 of the present Article may be appealed to a court [as amended by Federal Law of 20 December 2004].*
6. *The territorial justice agency possessing information concerning circumstances which are grounds for termination of the status of advokat shall send a submission concerning termination of the status of advokat to the chamber of advokats. If the council of the chamber of advokats within a three-months' period from the day of receipt of the such submission has not considered it, the territorial justice agency shall have the right to have recourse to a court with an application concerning termination of the status of advokat [as amended by Federal Law of 20 December 2004].*

1. Organs of the Advokatura, advokat formations, and individual advokats routinely receive thousands of complaints, appeals, recourses, and applications each year with respect to the quality of legal services rendered or not rendered, as the case may be. These must be addressed in an orderly fashion. Many, perhaps most, will be found to be without foundation, or addressed to the wrong organ or person, or otherwise fail to be within the jurisdiction or competence of the addressee. Others will have merit and deserve consideration by the appropriate components of the Advokatura and may lead to the disciplining of an individual advokat or the termination of his status as an advokat.

The Federal Chamber of Advokats of the Russian Federation confirmed on 6 June 2006, as amended on 2 April 2010, the Procedure for the Consideration and Settlement of Recourses to Advokat Formations and Chambers of Advokats of Subjects of the Russian Federation.[21] The Procedure sets out in elaborate detail how submissions received are to be processed and referred, or not, for further action.

The present Article establishes and distinguishes procedurally between two types of situation in which the status of advokat may be terminated. The first type involves situations in which the chamber of advokats may itself terminate the status of advokat; the second engages situations in which the chamber of advokats terminates the status of advokat on the basis of an opinion from the qualifications commission formed within the said chamber of advokats.

21 See Semeniako and Pilipenko, Адвокатская деятельность и адвокатура [Advokat Activity and the Advokatura] (2010), pp. 561-570.

The formulation of the Article has been severely criticized by Russian commentators: "... the endowing of management structures of a chamber of advokats (council and qualifications commission) with such extensive powers is absolutely incomprehensible since by reason of the imprecision of the formulations of the law any, even the most minor disciplinary offense, may be elevated to the rank of grounds for termination of the status of advokat".[22]

(1) An advokat may request that his status of advokat be terminated. In effect such a request, if granted, means that the advokat is leaving the profession. Such a request must be filed by the advokat personally and in writing. The application is filed at the council of the chamber of advokats of the subject of the Russian Federation in whose regional register the information about the advokat has been recorded.

(2) A court may determine that an advokat is limited in or lacks civil dispositive legal capacity, in which event the status of advokat is terminated from the moment such court decision enters into legal force. Pursuant to the Code of Civil Procedure of the Russian Federation (Article 209), the decision of a court concerning dispositive legal capacity enters into force upon the expiry of the period for an appeal by way of cassation, which must be filed within ten days from the day of the adoption of the decision of the court in final form.

(3) The status of advokat terminates with the death of the advokat or his being declared to be deceased by decision of a court. An advokat's death must be certified by the issuance of a death certificate by the Agency for the Registry of Acts of Civil Status (ZAGS).

A court may declare a person to be deceased pursuant to Chapter 30 of the Code of Civil Procedure of the Russian Federation. The application is filed in the court at the place of residence or location of the interested person. The application must specify for what purpose the applicant seeks to have the individual declared to be deceased and set out the circumstances on the basis of which the advokat may be believed to have died. A procurator participates in such a proceeding. The court decision serves as the basis for ZAGS to issue a death certificate.

(4) An advokat who has committed an intentional crime (as distinguished from a crime committed through negligence) is subject to having his status of advokat terminated when the judgment of the court finding the advokat guilty enters into legal force. Pursuant to the Code of Criminal Procedure (Article 390), the judgment of a court of first instance in a criminal proceeding enters into force upon the expiry of the period for appeal to an appellate instance or by way of cassation – ten full days from the day of proclamation of the judgment or from the day of handing over copies of the judgment to the convicted person confined under guard. The judgment of

22 K. V. Pitulko and V. V. Koriakovtsev, Постатейный комментарий к ФЗ «Об адвокатской деятельности и адвокатуре в РФ» [Article-by-Article Commentary to the Federal Law "On Advokat Activity and the Advokatura in the Russian Federation"] (2003), p. 68.

a court of appellate instance enters into legal force upon the expiry of the period for appeal thereof by way of cassation if the parties have not appealed against it. If the cassational instance does not vacate the judgment, it enters into legal force on the day that the cassational ruling is rendered.

(5) The present Article was amended in 2004 to make a cross-reference to Article 9(2) of the present Law and establish the consequence of termination of the status of advokat if the said advokat had, before receiving his status, been deemed to lack or be limited in civil dispositive legal capacity or had an uncancelled or unremoved record of conviction for an intentional crime.

(6) The present Article was amended in 2004 to give effect to the consequences of violating Article 16(3^1) of the present Law by engaging in advokat activity or holding elective offices in organs of a chamber of advokats after suspension of the status of advokat.

2. On the basis of the opinion of the qualifications commission, the council of a chamber of advokats of a subject of the Russian Federation may decide to terminate the status of advokat on any of the following grounds, each of which is formulated in very general terms. These approximate what in the United States would be characterized as being "disbarred" or in the United Kingdom as being "struck off". All of the possibilities enumerated below are within the discretion of the council of the chamber of advokats, which "may" exercise its powers under the circumstances described but is not required to do so.

(1) The failure of an advokat to perform or the improper performance of professional duties to a client is a basis for termination of the status of advokat. The present Law gives no guidance as to how the existence of such grounds is to be determined. Client complaints, in practice, are the principal source, but on occasion a Russian court will send copies of decisions or other materials to the chamber of advokats for action. As a rule, dissatisfied clients are not content with the outcome of the case even though the advokat may have done everything within his abilities and powers to defend his client's interests fully. In one study conducted in St. Petersburg, half of the complaints against advokats were based on the client perception that the unsatisfactory outcome of their matter was the direct fault of their advokat. In the disciplinary proceedings brought, fewer than half of such complaints were found to be justified.

In a Ruling of 3 July 2007 the Supreme Court of the Russian Federation considered an appeal filed by A. G., an advokat since 1999 in Vladimir Region, against his status of advokat being terminated from 11 August 2005 because he failed to perform a requirement to be present as defender in a criminal proceeding at a city court upon assignment of the court and to provide legal assistance free of charge. The advokat was in fact on duty to accept such an assignment and, in the view of the Court, was aware of that duty. The Supreme Court reviewed all aspects of the case and concluded that the disciplinary proceeding had been properly conducted by secret ballot in accordance with the Code of Professional Ethics of an Advokat. The appeal was rejected.[23]

(2) The Code of Professional Ethics of an Advokat was adopted by the First All-Russian Congress of Advokats on 31 January 2003 and twice amended since. By virtue of this reference, the Code becomes one of the foundation documents for assessing the professional quality and performance of an advokat in the performance of professional duties.

There are several codes of ethics which may apply to jurists in Russia, including those applicable to judges, auditors, customs officers, bailiffs in certain regions, and notaries.[24]

The Qualifications Commission of the Chamber of Advokats of the City of Moscow came to the following view in 2008 with respect to disciplinary proceedings in an individual case. This is an example of the style and nature of disciplinary proceedings which also has intrinsic interest for the conclusions reached:

> 1. The Qualifications Commission notes that under the general rule the arbitrary (without the authorization of the person presiding) leaving by an advokat from the hall of the judicial session before a break is announced in the judicial session is inadmissible and may be adjudged to be a violation by an advokat of the norms of legislation on advokat activity and the advokatura and/or the Code of Professional Ethics of an Advokat.
>
> However, the Qualifications Commission recalls that in a disciplinary opinion published for general information with respect to Advokat K of 24 September 2004 (Decision of the Council of the Chamber of Advokats of the City of Moscow, No. 61, of 7 October 2004) the legal position of the Commission was expressed that "illness" (inflammation, high temperature) is a circumstance precluding the possibility of an advokat continuing to participate in a judicial session, the expression of will of the court as to whether the advokat has the right to leave the courtroom or not **by reason of illness** having no legal significance since by virtue of the 1993 Russian Constitution (Articles 20 and 21) each has the right to life, no one should be subjected to torture, coercion, and other treatment demeaning human dignity; by virtue of Articles 18 and 56(3) of the 1993 Russian Constitution the said rights and freedoms are of direct operation, and determine the sense, content, and application of laws and are not subject to limitation even under conditions of an extraordinary situation.[25]

23 Unpublished. Available on Consultant Plus.

24 These are collected in A. G. Masleev, Кодексы профессиональной этики юриста: Сборник [Codes of Professional Ethics of a Jurist: Collection] (2008).

25 Вестник Адвокатской палаты г. Москвы [Herald of the Chamber of Advokats of the City of Moscow], no. 11-12; 13-14 (2004), pp. 9-11; no. 7, 8, 9 (2008), p. 52.

(3) Membership in the Advokatura implies that an advokat will comply with all decisions taken by organs of the Advokatura within their competence and presumably assumes that each advokat is informed in a timely manner about decisions taken. No correlative duty of Advokatura organs to communicate decisions to members of the college of advokats is precisely set out in the present Law and no time period or specific means of transmission imposed.

1. Advokat T. on 18 January 2008 passed the qualifications examination and on 30 January 2008 took the oath of an advokat. However, by June 2008 Advokat T. had failed to inform the Chamber of Advokats of the City of Moscow about her choice of advokat formation and had not paid the obligatory deductions due for the needs of the Chamber of Advokats. She was summoned by registered letter and telegram sent to her home address to appear at the personnel section of the Chamber of Advokats but failed to do so. Her indebtedness for 2008 amounted to 2,400 rubles. A disciplinary proceeding was instituted against Advokat T. on 23 June 2008 and the materials of the case referred to the Qualifications Commission.

On 30 June 2008 Advokat T. filed a written explanation which indicated that in late March 2008 she was obliged for family reasons to leave Moscow and had not expected to be away for more than two months. She wished to pay up her arrears upon her return and requested that her status of advokat be suspended until the grave family circumstances permitted her to come back. She submitted medical evidence that indicated her grandmother had suffered a stroke in March 2008 and required constant home supervision, being paralyzed and unable to speak. Advokat T. did not appear at the session of the Qualifications Commission, although duly notified. Under Article 23(3) of the Code of Professional Ethics of an Advokat, the failure of an advokat to appear at a disciplinary hearing was not grounds for postponement of the hearing.

The Qualifications Commission determined that circumstances had occurred which prevented Advokat T. from selecting the form of advokat formation, informing the Council of the Chamber of Advokats about her choice, and commencing the performance of advokat activity. On the basis of the evidence submitted, the Qualifications Commission concluded that her failure to comply was justified, as was her failure to make the monthly financial contributions required to maintain her status as advokat. Accordingly, the Qualifications Commission terminated the disciplinary proceeding for the absence in her actions and failure to act of a violation of the present Law or the decisions of organs of the Chamber of

Advokats of the City of Moscow. The Council of the Chamber concurred with this Opinion.[26]

(4) This sub-point is a cross reference to Article 10(2) above and determines the consequences of the failure to submit reliable information to the qualifications commission in the documents submitted to take the qualifications examination. The consequence can be termination of the status of advokat.

(5) A grace period is incorporated in this provision for an advokat, once granted the status of advokat, to choose the type of advokat formation he wishes to create or join. Article 15(6) gives the advokat three months to notify his choice; this provision enables an advokat who has not notified his choice within four months to have his status of advokat terminated. If in effect the period given to an advokat to make his choice is viewed as a "shopping period", the failure to culminate and notify the choice within the deadlines may lead to termination of the status of advokat.

3. Point 3 of the present Article is a mirror image of Article 16(3^1) above. While there may be cases of an advokat continuing to practice after his status of advokat has been terminated, it is less easy to imagine this person serving in elective office in a council of a chamber of advokats or the Federal Chamber of Advokats. There is no specific responsibility provided in a federal law for the violation referred to in this point.

4. Point 4 addresses the procedural formalities connected with the notification and recording of a decision taken by the council of a chamber of advokats to terminate the status of advokat. Within a ten-day period the council must notify the advokat concerned, the respective advokat formation, and the territorial justice agency. Nothing is said about the notification of a decision not to terminate, nor of the right of the advokat concerned to be present at the deliberations of the council of the chamber of advokats or the qualifications commission.

5. Appeal of a decision of the council of a chamber of advokats to a court is pursuant to the Code of Civil Procedure of the Russian Federation (Chapter 25).

6. Point 6 establishes an independent source for a disciplinary proceeding to be instituted against an advokat. How a territorial justice agency may come to possess information that should be considered by the council of a chamber of advokats is not disclosed. A likely source is a submission by an agency of inquiry, investigation, or a procurator, but presumably an ordinary citizen could also bring such information to the attention of a territorial justice agency. If the council of the chamber of advokats

26 Summarized from Вестник Адвокатской палаты г. Москвы [Herald of the Chamber of Advokats of the City of Moscow], no. 10-11 (2008), pp. 30-36.

does not consider the matter within a period of three months, the territorial justice agency may apply to a court to have the status of advokat terminated for the individual advokat concerned.

This provision in effect establishes a measure of administrative and judicial control over the Advokatura. The court is given the right to divest an advokat of his status independently of the Advokatura, which would seem to infringe upon the independence of that institution. Appeal against a judicial decision to terminate the status of advokat would lie under the Code of Civil Procedure of the Russian Federation.

ARTICLE 18 GUARANTEES OF INDEPENDENCE OF ADVOKAT

1. *Interference in advokat activity effectuated in accordance with legislation or the obstructing of this activity in any way whatsoever shall be prohibited.*
2. *An advokat may not be brought to any responsibility (including after the suspension or termination of the status of advokat) for an opinion expressed by him when effectuating advokat activity unless the guilt of an advokat in a criminal action (or failure to act) is established by the judgment of a court which has entered into legal force.*
   The said limitations shall not extend to civil-law responsibility of an advokat to a principal in accordance with the present Federal Law.
3. *Demanding and obtaining from an advokat, and also from workers of advokat formations, chambers of advokats, or the Federal Chamber of Advokats, of information connected with the rendering of legal assistance with regard to specific cases shall not be permitted.*
4. *An advokat, members of his family, and the property thereof shall be under the defense of the State. Internal affairs agencies shall be obliged to take necessary measures with regard to ensuring the safety of an advokat, members of his family, and the preservation of property belonging to them.*
5. *Criminal prosecution of an advokat shall be effectuated in compliance with the guarantees for an advokat provided for by criminal procedure legislation.*

1. The guarantees afforded to an advokat consist of professional (linked with advokat activity), personal security (protection of his person and property), and procedural (formalities linked with criminal prosecution of an advokat).

The general formulation contained in point 1 prohibits any form of interference or obstruction by any subject of law. Obstruction may be understood to encompass the intentional creation of obstacles for the performance by an advokat of his duties or exercise of his powers. Examples may be a refusal to issue information references to an advokat, or not allowing an advokat to familiarize himself with the file of a case, and so on. Interference would include any effort by third persons to pressure an advokat in their own interests. The Criminal Code of the Russian Federation contains no provisions relating to such obstruction or interference. Point 1 is accordingly of a programmatic nature.

Point 1 is consistent with the Basic Principles on the Role of Lawyers adopted by the Eighth United Nations Congress on the Prevention of Crime and the Treatment of Offenders (1990), which provide that "Governments shall ensure that lawyers (a) are able to perform all their professional functions without intimidation, hindrance, harassment, or improper interference; (b) are able to travel and consult with their clients freely both within their country and abroad; and (c) shall not suffer, or be threatened with, prosecution, or administrative, economic or other sanctions for any action taken in accordance with recognized professional duties, standards, and ethics" (point 16).

2. Point 2 of the present Law is sometimes characterized by Russian Commentators as establishing the principle of "advokat immunity". To the extent to which this term is appropriate, advokats enjoy "immunity" with respect to opinions uttered by them in their professional capacity, whether with reference to a specific case or in public discussions of the administration of justice, so long as they retain the status of advokat and thereafter as and when such status is suspended or terminated. This is in effect a lifetime grant of immunity.

The rationale for such immunity relates mostly to the domain of criminal law: the statutory and ethical requirement that an advokat defend his client in court and elsewhere by taking the line of defense dictated by his client. This approach emphasizes the "representational" role of the advokat and for these purposes treats him as the "mouthpiece" of his client. The advokat has no autonomous will of his own in this respect and consequently should not be accountable independently for any views expressed. These are the views of his client.

An advokat does bear criminal responsibility for crimes which he may personally have committed. Examples would include incitement of a client to bribe an official, or acting as an intermediary in bribery, slander, insult, arrogation, and others. Read literally, the present point would appear to no longer apply and immunity no longer exist once the advokat is convicted for a crime committed by him and the judgment has entered into legal force.

Civil responsibility of an advokat to his client is another matter. No immunity is granted with respect to the civil-law aspects of an advokat-client relationship. The view has been expressed that the responsibility of an advokat to his client should be confined to the amount of the fee received by an advokat for his work, and even a refund of the fee should not be in full unless the advokat did no work at all on the matter.[27] However, this position is not embodied in legislation, and an advokat may

27 K. V. Pitulko and V. V. Koriakovtsev, Постатейный комментарий к ФЗ «Об адвокатской деятельности и адвокатуре в РФ» [Article-by-Article Commentary to the Federal Law "On Advokat Activity and the Advokatura in the Russian Federation] (2003), p. 71.

remain responsible to his client under the general provisions regulating delictual responsibility and the provisions of the contract concluded with the client.

Point 2 is consistent with the Basic Principles on the Role of Lawyers adopted by the Eighth United Nations Congress on the Prevention of Crime and the Treatment of Offenders (1990), which provide that "Lawyers shall enjoy civil and penal immunity for relevant statements made in good faith or oral pleadings or in their professional appearances before a court, tribunal or other legal or administrative authority" (point 20). The Basic Principles continue: "Lawyers like other citizens are entitled to freedom of expression … In particular, they shall have the right to take part in public discussion of matters concerning the law, the administration of justice and the promotion and protection of human rights …" (point 23). However, the present Point is broader than the Basic Principles, not requiring good faith and creating a life-time immunity.

3. Although the prohibition against obtaining materials relating to a specific case from the sources specified in Point 3 of the present Article is intended to reinforce the concept of advokat secrecy (Article 8 above), the formulation does not protect the sources specified against a general search for information regarding cases. That loophole inevitably places at risk materials concerning specific cases.

4. Russian advokats have been killed in the performance of their duties or by reason of their involvement in civil and criminal proceedings. According to the Federal Chamber of Advokats, in the calendar years 2007 and 2008 together, six advokats were murdered and 24 were attacked and injured. In 2009 a well-known Moscow advokat was killed in the center of Moscow.

Russian legislation extends law enforcement protection to virtually all trial participants except advokats in the Federal Law of 20 April 1995 "On State Defense of Judges and Officials of Law Enforcement and Control Agencies", as amended.[28] Advokats do not figure on the List of "protected persons" (Article 2). Although some advokats carry licensed sidearms for personal protection, point 4 is programmatic.

5. The Code of Criminal Procedure of the Russian Federation (Article 447) establishes that certain formalities must be complied with if a criminal case is instituted against an advokat, or the advokat is brought as an accused and the criminal case was instituted with respect to other persons or the fact of the commission of an act containing the indicia of a crime. The formality is that with respect to an advokat the case must be instituted by the executive of the investigation agency of the Investiga-

28 СЗ РФ (1995), no. 17, item 1455, as amended.

tive Committee attached to the Procuracy of the Russian Federation for a subject of the Russian Federation (Article 448).[29]

In all other respects the constitutional guarantees extended under Russian law to other citizens in a criminal prosecution also apply to an advokat.

ARTICLE 19 INSURANCE OF RISK OF RESPONSIBILITY OF ADVOKAT

An advokat shall effectuate in accordance with a federal law the insurance of the risk of his professional property responsibility for a violation of the conditions of the agreement concluded with a principal concerning the rendering of legal assistance.

Pursuant to Article 45(1) of the present Law, the requirement to acquire obligatory professional risk insurance was to enter into force as of 1 January 2007. This date was postponed indefinitely until the entry into force of a federal law regulating obligatory insurance for the professional responsibility of advokats by Federal Law of 3 December 2007. No. 320-ФЗ[30] The suspension entered into force as from 17 December 2007 (see Commentary to Article 7(1)(6) above).

However, pursuant to Article 7(1)(6) of the present Law, an advokat may voluntarily insure the risk of professional property responsibility, in which case the insurance premiums are included among the deductions that may be made by an advokat in accordance with Article 25(7) of the present Law.

Contracts for the insurance of responsibility of this nature are concluded in accordance with the Civil Code of the Russian Federation (Article 932). Such insurance contracts may be concluded in the instances provided for by a law. Only the risk of responsibility of the insurant itself may be insured, and a contract not corresponding to this requirement is void.[31]

29 See W. E. Butler, *Russian Criminal Law and Procedure* (2011), pp. 535-539.
30 СЗ РФ (2007), no. 50, item 6233.
31 See W. E. Butler, *Civil Code of the Russian Federation* (2010), p. 299.

Chapter 4 Organization of Advokat Activity and the Advokatura

Article 20 Forms of Advokat Formations

1. *The forms of advokat formations shall be: advokat cabinet, college of advokats, advokat bureau, and legal consultation office.*
2. *An advokat shall have the right in accordance with the present Federal Law autonomously to select the form of advokat formation and place of effectuation of advokat activity. An advokat shall be obliged to inform the council of the chamber of advokats in the procedure established by the present Federal Law about the selected form of advokat formation and place of effectuation of advokat activity.*
3. *In the instances provided for by Article 24 of the present Federal Law an advokat shall effectuate advokat activity in a legal consultation office.*

1. The terms "form", "type", and "organizational-legal form" are used extensively in the Civil Code of the Russian Federation and other legislative acts in connection with juridical persons but are not defined there. The absence of a definition is the more regrettable because the terms are used in different senses and meanings.[1]

Article 50 of the Civil Code contains an exhaustive list of the organizational-legal forms of commercial juridical persons but merely an exemplary enumeration of non-commercial organizations. The exemplary enumeration is expanded in the Federal Law on Noncommercial Organizations of 12 January 1996, as amended, No. 7-ФЗ.[2] Russian legal doctrine has offered various glosses on the term "organizational-legal form". Martemianov believes that the organizational-legal form of an enterprise is the "… aggregate of property and organizational distinctions and means of forming the property base, peculiarities of interaction between the owners, entrepreneurs, and labor collective of the enterprise, their responsibility to one another and their

1 See, generally, O. V. Pospelov, Формы адвокатских образований в России [Forms of Advokat Formations in Russia] (2008).
2 СЗ РФ (1996), no. 3, item 145, as amended; transl. in Butler, *Russia and The Republics: Legal Materials* (looseleaf service; 2006-).

competitors".[3] Totev suggests that an organizational-legal form formalizes and consolidates the autonomy of an enterprise when it engages in economic activity.[4] It is an expression that, insofar as it is discussed, is done so from the standpoint of entrepreneurial and civil law.

In the context of the Advokatura, however, the concept of organizational-legal form encompasses advokat formations that have the status of a juridical person (college of advokats, advokat bureau, legal consultation office) and those that do not (advokat cabinet). Accordingly, it is suggested that the advokat formation is simply classified into different forms.[5]

The list of advokat formations in point 1 is an exhaustive one.

2. Point 2 underscores the freedom of choice reserved to an advokat with respect to the advokat formation which he prefers to create. The fact that the List is exhaustive is regarded by some as a limitation on the freedom of choice of the advokat, a limitation on his legal capacity. The better view is that the provision creates a broad spectrum of possible choices within which the advokat enjoys a preferred and privileged position compared with legal professionals who do not engage in advokat activity. Within these choices the advokat is free to choose what type of law he practices, where he does so, with whom, and to change these choices at his discretion.

The freedom and right to engage in advokat activity conceptually derive from several principles contained in the 1993 Russian Constitution: the freedom to choose the nature of one's occupation (Article 37); the freedom to join together in order to engage in professional activity (Article 30); the freedom to own, possess, use, and dispose of property alone or jointly with other persons (Article 35); and the freedom of contract to enter into civil-law and other transactions (Articles 35, 74, and 75). These are not specified or elaborated in the present Law, however.[6]

The organizational-legal forms of advokat formations, with the obvious exception of the advokat cabinet, impose no numerical quotas on those formations which are collective in nature. The minimum is two, and there is no maximum except as decided by the founders themselves or by the chamber of advokats.

The sole duty in this respect is to inform the council of the chamber of advokats in a subject of the Russian Federation about the chosen form of advokat formation and the location thereof. Pursuant to Article 15(6) of the present Law (see above), an advokat must make such notification within six months from receiving the status of

3 V. S. Martemianov, Хозяйственное право [Economic Law] (1994), I, p. 75.

4 K. Iu. Totev, «Предприятие и его организационно-правовая форма» [The Enterprise and Organizational-Legal Form Thereof], Государство и право [State and Law], no. 10 (1994), pp. 61-67.

5 A. P. Belykh, in I. L. Trunov (ed.), Адвокатская деятельность и Адвокатура в России [Advokat Activity and the Advokatura in Russia] (2006), p. 258.

6 Belykh, in Trunov, Адвокатская деятельность и Адвокатура в России [Advokat Activity and the Advokatura in Russia] (2006), p. 259.

advokat or of a change of membership in a chamber of advokats and due registration thereof in the regional register, or renewal of status of an advokat. The failure to comply with this procedure within the stipulated period is grounds for termination of the status of advokat (Article 17, present Law) — what Belykh appropriately calls an "organizational sanction" for a violation.[7]

There are certain limitations upon an advokat of relevance in this connection. Under Article 15(4) of the present Law, an advokat may engage in advokat activity only within one advokat formation. A branch of an advokat formation would not be included within the limitation because a branch remains an integral part of the advokat formation which creates it.

3. Legal consultation offices are formed by a chamber of advokats upon the recommendation of an agency of State power of a subject of the Russian Federation. In this respect the wishes of the advokats themselves are irrelevant. Only advokats sent by the chamber of advokats may work in legal consultation offices (Article 31(3), present Law). An advokat may refuse to be sent to a legal consultation office. The present Law provides no legal consequences in the event of such a refusal and requires no special reasons to be given for doing so.

ARTICLE 21 ADVOKAT CABINET

1. *An advokat who has taken a decision to effectuate advokat activity individually shall found an advokat cabinet.*
2. *An advokat shall send to the council of the chamber of advokats by registered letter a notice concerning the founding of an advokat cabinet in which information is specified concerning the advokat, location of the advokat cabinet, procedure for the effectuation of telephone, telegraph, postal, and other communications between the council of the chamber of advokats and the advokat.*
3. *An advokat cabinet shall not be a juridical person.*
4. *An advokat who has founded an advokat cabinet shall open accounts in banks in accordance with legislation, have a seal, stamp, and letterheads with the address and name of the advokat cabinet containing an indication of the subject of the Russian Federation on whose territory the advokat cabinet was founded.*
5. *Agreements concerning the rendering of legal assistance in the advokat cabinet shall be concluded between the advokat and principal and shall be registered in the documentation of the advokat cabinet.*

7 Belykh, in Trunov, Адвокатская деятельность и Адвокатура в России [Advokat Activity and the Advokatura in Russia] (2006), p. 260.

6. *An advokat shall have the right to use dwelling premises for the site of the advokat cabinet which belong to him or to members of his family by right of ownership with the consent of the last.*
7. *Dwelling premises occupied by an advokat and members of his family under a contract of rental may be used by the advokat for the site of the advokat cabinet with the consent of the landlord and all persons who have reached majority residing jointly with the advokat.*

1. The organizational-legal form of the advokat cabinet signifies a sole practitioner. The individual form of advokat activity chosen does not preclude an advokat from collaborating on a complex case with other advokats, nor does this form preclude the advokat from hiring a secretary, bookkeeper, or other personnel or from having aides and trainees. This organizational-legal form was experimented with in Russia before the enactment of the present Law within colleges of advokats.

Views differ among Russian advokats as to whether an individual or a collective approach to organizing the practice of law is preferable. Some stress the constraining effects of being in a collective environment; others stress the support available in a collective. Many believe it to be inadvisable for a young and inexperienced advokat to practice alone.

The form of the decision taken by an advokat to establish an advokat cabinet is not specified in the present Law. In practice the decision is expected to be in written form. The Council of the Chamber of Advokats of Moscow Region in a decision of 29 January 2003 "On the Procedure for Founding Advokat Cabinets in Moscow Region" indicated that within seven days after opening bank accounts an advokat must provide the Chamber of Advokats of Moscow Region with the signed written decision of the advokat to practice individually and to found an advokat cabinet. The decision must contain the date on which the decision was adopted, the full and abbreviated names of the advokat cabinet, the willingness of the advokat to keep documentation of an advokat cabinet concerning agreements to render legal assistance concluded between the advokat and the principal using the form confirmed by the Council of the Chamber of Advokats of Moscow Region together with orders in the form confirmed by the Ministry of Justice of the Russian Federation.

2. Separate from the decision to be a sole practitioner is the notification of the founding of the advokat cabinet, which must be sent by registered post to the chamber of advokats and contain information concerning the advokat himself, registration number, advokat certificate number, name of the advokat formation in which the advokat was previously a member and confirmation of the termination of membership in that formation; the location of the advokat cabinet; and the telephone, telegraph, postal, and other communications links between the Council and the advokat.

The information provided is not only used for communication purposes, but also to draw up the schedule for the advokat to participate as a defender in a criminal or civil proceeding on the basis of an assignment from an agency of inquiry, preliminary investigation, procuracy, or court.

The present Law does not define the concept of "location" of an advokat cabinet. The advokat is free to designate where the advokat cabinet is situated, and that site need not necessarily be the same place where the advokat performs his professional activity. So long as an address is indicated which enables the chamber of advokats to contact the advokat, that address will be deemed to be the location of the advokat cabinet.

3. Since an advokat cabinet is not a juridical person, the advokat himself must register with Russian tax agencies and perform the duties of a taxpayer. An advokat cabinet may not be an owner of property nor have property in economic jurisdiction or in operative management. Nor is an advokat cabinet liable for obligations of the advokat to third persons. An advokat cabinet may not acquire or exercise property rights or bear duties in its own name.

4. When opening a bank account, an advokat who has established an advokat cabinet submits to the relevant bank or credit institution his passport, certificate of an advokat, and a card with samples of signatures and imprints of the seal of the advokat cabinet in order to conclude a contract of bank account in accordance with the Civil Code of the Russian Federation (Chapter 45). Pursuant to the Letter of the Ministry of the Russian Federation for Taxes and Charges of 4 October 2004, No. 24-1-10/700, advokats who have an advokat cabinet are obliged to submit to tax agencies information concerning the opening or closure of a bank account within a ten-day period and the banks or credit institutions are required to make a similar notification to the tax agencies within a five-day period.[8]

The notice concerning the opening or closure of a bank account is drawn up according to the form confirmed by Order of the Federal Tax Service of 21 April 2009, No. MM-7-6/252.[9]

Numerous organizations in Russia will manufacture seals and stamps for organizations – in sharp contrast to the Soviet era when such items could only be obtained through the security agencies. An order will be accepted for these items from an advokat upon the presentation of the advokat certificate and a notification from the chamber of advokats concerning the founding of the advokat cabinet and appropriate evidence of tax registration.

Tax agencies register an advokat at his place of residence on the basis of information provided by the council of the chamber of advokats of a subject of the Russian Federation pursuant to Article 85(2) of the Tax Code of the Russian Federation, as

8 Available on Consultant Plus.
9 Available on Consultant Plus.

amended, which provides: "2. Chambers of advokats of subjects of the Russian Federation shall be obliged not later than the 10 of each month to notify the tax agency at the location of the chamber of advokats of the subject of the Russian Federation information concerning advokats entered in the preceding month in the register of advokats of the subject of the Russian Federation (including information concerning the form of advokat formation chosen by them) or excluded from the said register, and also the decisions adopted for this month concerning the suspension (or renewal) of the status of advokats".[10]

The advokat practicing through an advokat cabinet will thus be registered with the tax inspectorate whether he appears for this purpose or not. In practice this procedure has created difficulties for advokats because the registration does not take place until the month following their decision to open an advokat cabinet. The advokat concerned encounters difficulties in opening a bank account, ordering seals and stamps, and completing other organizational procedures which routinely require evidence of tax registration, although in many instances evidence of having the status of advokat should suffice. These difficulties may be circumvented if the advokat himself takes the notification of the chamber of advokats personally to the tax registration authorities at once and arranges for prompt tax registration.

5. The advokat who operates through an advokat cabinet acts in his own name in relations with third persons. Agreements with a principal to provide legal services are concluded directly between the advokat and the client and are registered as part of the documentation of the advokat cabinet.

6. The possibility for an advokat to use a dwelling premise in his ownership or owned by members of his family as the location of his advokat cabinet was introduced by the present Law. There is no requirement that the advokat himself must permanently reside in the premise; accordingly, any dwelling premise owned by the advokat or his family may be used for this purpose. If members of his family own the respective premise, he must have their consent to use the space for an advokat cabinet.

In the Moscow Region, pursuant to a Decision of 29 January 2003, "On the Procedure for Founding Advokat Cabinets in Moscow Region", the advokat must submit to the chamber of advokats a xeroxed copy of the document establishing the right of ownership to the dwelling premise or nondwelling premise, contract of lease, or other document confirming the right to use the premise and a document confirming the composition of the family and the residence registration in that premise.

10 СЗ РФ (1998), no. 31, item 3824, as amended; transl. W. E. Butler, *Tax Code of the Russian Federation* (2004), pp 239-241.

7. If the advokat or members of his family rent a dwelling premise, the premise also may be used for an advokat cabinet provided that the consent of the landlord and all members of the family who reside together with the advocate and who have reached majority (eighteen years of age) is obtained. In a Decision of the Chamber of Advokats of Moscow Region of 29 January 2003 "On the Procedure for Founding Advokat Cabinets in Moscow Region" it was stipulated that within 7 days after opening bank accounts an advokat must submit to the chamber of advokats the written consent of all persons (family members, landlord, persons who have reached majority and reside jointly with the advokat) to the use of the dwelling premise for accommodating the advokat cabinet.

The requirement that written consent be obtained is important because under Article 292(3) of the Civil Code, family members of the owner of a dwelling premise have the right to demand the elimination of violations of their rights to the dwelling premise by any persons, including the owner.

Although apartment premises are in practice extensively used in Russia for advokat cabinets and other advokat formations because premium office space is in short supply and exceedingly expensive, advokats are aware that these premises, especially when they have not been adapted to receive clients comfortably, are far from ideal. It is common practice for advokats who contract to provide legal services to an organization to require that the organization provide office space for them to work on site. Professional confidentiality issues may arise in these situations. In any event the chamber of advokats needs to be notified so that the advokat premise in the organization enjoys privileged protection against operational-search measures.

ARTICLE 22 COLLEGE OF ADVOKATS

1. *Two or more advokats shall have the right to found a college of advokats.*
2. *The college of advokats is a noncommercial organization based on membership and operating on the basis of a charter confirmed by the founders thereof (hereinafter also – charter) and a constitutive contract concluded by them.*
3. *Advokats, information concerning whom is inserted only in one regional register, may be founders of the college [as amended by Federal Law of 20 December 2004].*
4. *Founders shall determine in the constitutive contract the conditions for the transfer to the college of advokats of its property, conditions of participation in its activity, the procedure and conditions for admission to the college of advokats of new members, the rights and duties of the founders (or members), and the procedure and conditions for the withdrawal of founders (or members) from the composition thereof.*
5. *The charter must contain the following information:*
   (1) the name of the college of advokats;
   (2) the location of the college of advokats;
   (3) the subject and purpose of activity of the college of advokats;

(4) the sources of formation of the property of the college of advokats and orientations of the use thereof (including the presence or absence of an indivisible fund and orientations of the use thereof) [as amended by Federal Law of 20 December 2004];
(5) the procedure for the management of the college of advokats;
(6) the information concerning branches of the college of advokats;
(7) the procedure for the reorganization and liquidation of the college of advokats;
(8) the procedure for making changes in and additions to the charter;
(9) other provisions not contrary to the present Federal Law and other federal laws.

6. *Requirements of the constitutive contract and charter shall be binding upon the college of advokats itself and its founders (or members).*
7. *The founders thereof shall send by registered letter to the council of a chamber of advokats notice concerning the founding, reorganization or liquidation of the college of advokats. The notice concerning the founding or reorganization of a college of advokats must contain information concerning advokats effectuating advokat activity in the college of advokats, the location of the college of advokats, the procedure for the effectuation of telephone, telegraph, postal, and other communications between the council of the chamber of advokats and college of advokats. Notarially certified copies of the constitutive contract and charter must be appended to the notice [as amended by Federal Law of 20 December 2004].*
8. *A college of advokats shall be considered to be founded from the moment of its State registration. State registration of a college of advokats, and also making an entry in the unified State register of juridical persons concerning the termination of its activity shall be effectuated in the procedure established by a federal law concerning the State registration of juridical persons.*
9. *The college of advokats shall be a juridical person, have an autonomous balance sheet, open accounts in banks in accordance with legislation of the Russian Federation, have a seal, stamps, and letterheads with the address and name of the college of advokats containing an indication of the subject of the Russian Federation on whose territory the college of advokats is founded.*
10. *The college of advokats shall have the right to create branches throughout the entire territory of the Russian Federation, and also the territory of a foreign State if this has been provided for by legislation of the particular foreign State.*
    Notice shall be sent by registered letter concerning the creation or closure of a branch of a college of advokats to the council of the chamber of advokats of a subject of the Russian Federation on whose territory the college of advokats was founded, and also to the council of the chamber of advokats of a subject of the Russian Federation on whose territory the branch of the college of advokats was created. The notice concerning the creation of a branch of a college of advokats must contain information concerning the advokats effectuating advokat activity in the branch of the college of advokats, the location of the college of advokats and its branch, the procedure for the effectuation of telephone, telegraph, postal, and other communications between the

council of the chamber of advokats and college of advokats and branch thereof. To the notice must be appended notarially certified copies of the decision concerning the creation of a branch of the college of advokats and statute on the branch [as amended by Federal Law of 20 December 2004].

Advocates effectuating advocate activity in a branch of a college of advokats shall be members of the college of advokats which created the respective branch [as amended by Federal Law of 20 December 2004].

Information concerning advokats effectuating advokat activity in a branch of a college of advokats shall be entered in the regional register of that subject of the Russian Federation on whose territory the branch is created [as amended by Federal Law of 20 December 2004].

Information concerning advokats effectuating advokat activity in a branch of the college of advokats created on the territory of a foreign State shall be entered in the regional register of the subject of the Russian Federation on whose territory the college of advokats was founded [added by Federal Law of 20 December 2004].

11. *Property contributed by the founders of a college of advokats shall belong to it by right of ownership.*
12. *Members of a college of advokats shall not be liable for its obligations, and the college of advokats shall not be liable for the obligations of its members.*
13. *A college of advokats shall in accordance with legislation of the Russian Federation be the tax agent of advokats who are members thereof with regard to revenues received by them in connection with the effectuation of advokat activity, and also their representative with regard to settlement of accounts with principals and third persons provided for by constitutive documents of the college of advokats.*

    A college of advokats shall be obliged to notify the chamber of advokats about changes in the composition of member-advokats of the college of advokats [added by Federal Law of 20 December 2004]..
14. *A college of advokats shall bear the responsibility provided for by legislation of the Russian Federation for the failure to perform or improper performance of the duties of tax agent or representative.*
15. *Agreements concerning the rendering of legal assistance to the college of advokats shall be concluded between the advokat and principal and shall be registered in the documentation of the college of advokats.*
16. *Nothing in the provisions of the present Article may be regarded as a limitation of the independence of an advokat when performing commissions of the principal, and also his personal professional responsibility to the last.*
17. *A college of advokats may not be transformed into a commercial organization or any other noncommercial organization except for instances of transformation of the college of advokats and advokat bureau in the procedure established by Article 23 of the present Federal Law.*
18. *The rules provided for noncommercial partnerships by the Federal Law "On Noncommercial Organizations", if these rules are not contrary to the present Federal*

Law, shall apply to relations arising in connection with the founding, activity, and liquidation of the college of advokats.

1. The term "college of advokats" was used in Soviet legislation to refer to the core unit of the Advokatura. Those colleges were created by the union republics with the consent of the union republic ministry of justice throughout the entire Soviet Union.

In the present Law a college of advokats is one of the collective forms of engaging in advokat activity, being in principle a noncommercial partnership (Article 8, Federal Law on Non-Commercial Organizations) with the peculiarities established by the present Article. Two or more advokats, that is, persons who have received the status of advokat and are able to engage in advokat activity, are required to form a college of advokats. The other way to create a college of advokats would be to reorganize an advokat bureau (Article 23(11), present Law).

2. There is no time limit associated with the drafting of the constitutive contract or submission thereof. This task can be performed at the leisure of the founding advokats and reflect the deal struck between them. The charter of the college of advokats is adopted by the founders at the initial constitutive meeting of the college of advokats.

The present Law does draw a distinction between founder-advokats and member-advokats. However, nothing seems to turn on the distinction, which is purely of a temporal nature. Some advokats found a college, and others enter as members once it is founded. There is no difference in their legal status.

3. The requirement that the founders of a college of advokats be registered only in one regional register appears to be directed towards the convenience of assembling the documents necessary for founding a college rather than an attempt to limit competition.

4. The present Law sets out the minimum conditions that must be incorporated in a constitutive contract concluded between the founders of a college of advokats. These include the conditions for the transfer of property to the college by the founders, the amount of contributions by the participants, the procedure for participation in the college of advokats, the procedure for admitting new members to the college, the rights and duties of the founders or members of the college, and the procedure and conditions for founders or members to withdraw from the college. In practice the founders are likely to create a privileged status for themselves in comparison with those who join later in order to cover the formation costs of the college.

The present Law contains no special provisions on the sources of capital or property to be contributed to the college of advokats, whether it may come from outside sources, be borrowed, be invested by insurance companies or other sources that may wish to "back" a college of advokats for their own reasons.

Prior to the entry into force of the present Law, all colleges of advokats had established entry fees to be paid by individual advokats admitted to membership in the college. Although the present Law is silent on this point, the practice was carried over and is almost invariably recorded in the constitutive documents of the college.

5. The provisions set out in point 5 of the present Article whose inclusion in the charter is imperative track similar provisions in the Federal Law on Non-Commercial Organizations adapted to the situation of advokats. The highest management organ of a college of advokats is the Meeting of Advokat Members of the College, which meets at intervals stipulated by the charter. If the college of advokats is a large one, it may opt to create a "conference" to act as a management organ, which will in fact be a representative organ to which a stipulated number of advokats are elected by the membership at large.

The competence of the Meeting of Advokat Members of the College will vary from one college to another, depending upon the formulations of the charter. Typically the Meeting will (1) form the presidium and adopt decisions that terminate before time the powers of presidium members; (2) confirm the procedure for determining norms of representation and the procedure for electing delegates to a conference of the College, if one there be; (3) elect the internal audit commission and members of the qualifications commission; (4) determine the obligatory deductions from each advokat for the general needs of the College; (5) determine the entry fee for the College; (6) confirm the personnel establishment and estimates for the maintenance of the College presidium; (7) confirm the report of the internal audit commission on the financial and other economic activities of the College; (8) confirm the report of the presidium, including the use of financial resources of the College; (9) confirm the reglaments of the Meeting and/or conference and presidium; (10) determine the location of the presidium of the College; (11) confirm the personnel establishment of organs of the College; (12) establish incentives and types of responsibility for advokats; (13) consider appeals against decisions of the presidium of the College; (14) confirm the Statute on the branch of a college, as and when one is created; (15) adopt other decisions relegated to the competence of the Meeting and/or conference.

The executive organ of a college of advokats will most likely be either the chairman of the college or, in a larger college, the presidium which, in turn, will have a chairman of the presidium. In either instance the chairman will act in the name of the college without a power of attorney, that is, *ex officio*, represent the college in relations with agencies of State power, local self-government, social associations and other organizations, and natural persons; issue powers of attorney and conclude transactions in the name of the college; dispose of property of the college in accordance with the estimate and the designation of the property; direct the apparatus of the college and hire and dismiss college workers; organize the verification of appeals and other materials relating to advokats, demand written explanations from them, and submit proposals to the presidium for consideration; convene a Meeting of the college and see over the implementation of presidium decisions and decisions of the Meeting or conference. This list is exemplary and will vary from one college to another.

It is routine practice for colleges of advokats to create an internal audit commission composed of at least three members from among the advokats. This is not to be confused with a financial audit performed by an accounting firm. The remit of an internal audit commission goes far beyond financial matters to include the efficiency and quality of management. In the experience of the present writer the reports of an internal audit commission are an insightful and sometimes savage critique of the management of the day and generate a lively discussion. The members of the commission are elected by majority vote at the Meeting, and in turn elect their own chairman and deputy chairman. They operate in accordance with a Statute on the Internal Audit Commission adopted by the Meeting or conference and report annually to the membership at large. If for any reason a member of the internal audit commission cannot complete his term of office, he is replaced by an advokat appointed by the presidium or chairman of the college.

Colleges of advokats routinely create a qualifications commission whose operations are guided by the present Law and the charter.

6. The present Law provides that the requirements of the constitutive contract and the Charter are binding upon members of the college. The same applies to decisions adopted by the Meeting and/or conference and the presidium of the college. The present Law does not determine how and when these requirements and decisions are communicated to members, merely that they must be communicated.

It would be common practice in colleges of advokats for advokats to have the right to demand from the presidium a copy of the protocol (minutes) of the Meeting and/or conference or an extract therefrom.

7. Point 7 of the present Article requires colleges of advokats to notify to the relevant chamber of advokats information concerning the creation, reorganization, or liquidation of the college and to provide contact information of all relevant types. This requirement exists for all advokat formations.

8. Just as other juridical persons, the college of advokats is considered to exist from the moment of State registration in accordance with the Federal Law "On the State Registration of Juridical Persons", of 8 August 2001, No. 129-ФЗ[11] and the Decree of the Government of the Russian Federation of 17 May 2002, No. 318 "On the Empowered Federal Agency of Executive Power Effectuating the State Registration of

11 СЗ РФ (2001), no. 33(I), item 3431, as amended; transl. in Butler, *Russia and The Republics: Legal Materials* (looseleaf service; 2006-).

Juridical Persons", as amended.[12] The completion of registration will be recorded in the Unified State Register of Juridical Persons.

Under Article 12 of the Federal Law of 8 August 2001, the following documents must be submitted by a college of advokats seeking registration:

(a) an application signed by the applicant concerning State registration according to the form confirmed by the federal agency of executive power empowered by the Government of the Russian Federation. It shall be confirmed in the application that the constitutive documents submitted correspond to the requirements established by legislation of the Russian Federation for constitutive documents of a juridical person of the said organizational-legal form, that the information contained in these constitutive documents, other documents submitted for State registration and application concerning State registration, are reliable, that when creating the juridical person the procedure for the founding thereof established for juridical persons of the particular organizational-legal form has been complied with, including paying up of the charter capital (or charter fund, contributed capital, share contributions) at the moment of State registration, and in the instances established by a law the questions of the creation of the juridical person have been agreed with the respective State agency(ies) and/or agencies of local self-government [as amended by Federal Law of 23 June 2003];
(b) the decision concerning the creation of a juridical person in the form of a protocol, contract, or other document in accordance with legislation of the Russian Federation;
(c) the constitutive documents of the juridical person (originals or copies certified in a notarial procedure) [as amended by Federal Law of 23 June 2003];
(d) extract from the register of foreign juridical persons of the respective country of origin or other evidence equal in legal force of the legal status of the foreign juridical person-founder;
(e) document concerning the payment of State duty.

A college of advokats created by way of reorganization will be registered under a different procedure set out in Article 14 of the Federal Law of 8 August 2001:

(a) the application signed by the applicant concerning the State registration of each newly arising juridical person created by means of reorganization according to the form confirmed by the federal agency of execu-

12 СЗ РФ (2002), no. 20, item 1872, as amended.

tive power empowered by the Government of the Russian Federation. It shall be confirmed in the application that the constitutive documents of the juridical persons created by way of reorganization correspond to the requirements established by legislation of the Russian Federation to the constitutive documents of a juridical person of the particular organizational-legal form, that the information contained in these constitutive documents and application concerning State registration is reliable, that the act of transfer or separation balance sheet contains provisions concerning legal succession with regard to all obligations of the newly arising juridical person with respect to all of its creditors, and that all creditors of the person being reorganized have been notified in written form about the reorganization and in the instances established by a law the questions concerning the reorganization of the juridical person have been agreed with the respective State agencies and/or agencies of local self-government [as amended by Federal Law of 23 July 2008];
(b) the constitutive documents of each newly arising juridical person created by means of reorganization (originals or copies certified in a notarial procedure) [as amended by Federal Law of 23 June 2003];
(c) the decision concerning the reorganization of the juridical person;
(d) the contract concerning merger in the instances provided for by federal laws [as amended by Federal Law of 23 December 2003];
(e) the act of transfer or separation balance sheet;
(f) the document concerning payment of State duty;
(g) the document confirming the submission to the territorial agency of the Pension Fund of the Russian Federation information in accordance with Article 6(2), subpoints (1) to (8) and Article 11(2) of the Federal Law of 1 April 1996, No. 27-ФЗ "On the Individual (Personified) Record in the System of Obligatory Pension Insurance" (hereinafter – Federal Law "On the Individual (Personified) Record in the System of Obligatory Pension Insurance" [added by Federal Law of 19 July 2007].

The registering agency must provide to the applicant within not later than one day a document confirming that a college of advokats has been entered in the State register of juridical persons. A reorganization of an advokat bureau into a college of advokats is completed from the moment of State registration of the college, at which time the bureau is considered to have terminated its existence. State registration may be refused only if the documents submitted are incorrect or insufficient or the application has been submitted to the wrong registering agency.

9. Unlike the advokat cabinet, the college of advokats is a juridical person, which means that the college has an autonomous balance sheet, opens bank accounts in accordance with Russian legislation, and has a seal, stamps, and letterheads with the

name and address of the college and indicating the subject of the Russian Federation in which it has been founded. The college of advokats exercises the civil rights and duties of a juridical person, subject to the present Law and the Federal Law on Non-Commercial Organizations, in accordance with the Civil Code of the Russian Federation.

10. Point 10 of the present Law is a conceptually-flawed provision. In granting a college of advokats the right to create branches in the Russian Federation and on the territory of foreign States, this provision does nothing more than reiterate Article 55 of the Civil Code of the Russian Federation and reinforce the requirement that if a branch is to be established, this must be indicated in the charter of the college of advokats. The right to create a branch through the entire territory of the Russian Federation is understood to mean that a college of advokats may create branches either within and/or beyond the subject of the Russian Federation in which it is registered.

However, the provision goes farther and actually contemplates that a foreign State may authorize the creation of branches of a Russian college of advokats on its territory. Given the general lack of regulation of the organization of the legal profession in European and Anglo-American jurisdictions and the unlikelihood that any country will make specific provision in its legislation for a Russian college of advokats, the Russian legislator has failed to recognize and take into account one of the fundamental principles of the market economy: that which is not expressly prohibited, is permitted. The appropriate formulation here would be to say that colleges of advokats may create branches on the territory of foreign States unless prohibited from doing so by the legislation of the foreign State concerned.

The infelicity goes beyond this, however. The Russian legislator has assumed that the Russian concept of a "branch" (which is indeed not a juridical person) will be shared by the foreign State concerned – which is most unlikely. The requirements that a branch operate on the basis of a Statute and a power of attorney issued to the head of the branch are laid down by Russian legislation and unlikely to be shared by jurisdictions outside the CIS countries who do not share the legacy of Soviet law. The tax status of any such presence in a foreign State will be governed by the foreign State and not by Russian legislation.

The formulation of this provision would appear to limit advokat formations to Russian conceptions and not enable Russian advokat formations to choose other organizational-legal forms available to them under the legislation of a foreign jurisdiction. Similarly, if the advokat formation in a foreign State employed foreign jurists to engage in advokat activity as understood in Russia, it would appear that under this provision they are required to be Russian advokats, which would severely limit the competitiveness of the Russian branch on the legal services market and probably be unrealistic in most situations.

11. Property contributed to or acquired by a college of advokats is in the ownership of the college. Such property will, as a rule, consist of four basic components: (1) contributions by the founders and members to the capital of the college; (2) membership dues paid by founders and members; (3) other contributions made to the college; (4) property acquired by the college of advokats in the course of its operations. If the charter of the college so provides, a member who withdraws from the college has the right to the return of his contribution or to receive the money equivalent thereof.

If the college is liquidated, the members of the college have the right to receive that portion of their property remaining after the settlement of accounts with creditors or the value of this property within the limits of the value of property transferred by members of the non-commercial partnership to its ownership. However, the distribution of property in the event of liquidation may not exceed the actual amount of their property contributions – that is, there may be no distribution of "surplus" or "profit" unless established otherwise by federal legislation or the constitutive documents of the college of advokats.

12. In its capacity as a juridical person, the college of advokats is responsible for its obligations with the property in its ownership. The college is not responsible for obligations of the individual advokats, and the last are not responsible for obligations of the college.

The constitutive documents may make provision for other property and nonproperty rights of members of a college of advokats, for example, the right to receive financial assistance from the college in the event of need.

13. A college of advokats has the status of tax agent for its members. Tax agents under the Tax Code of the Russian Federation (Article 24) are persons on whom duties have been placed relating to the calculation, withholding from the taxpayer, and transfer to the budget system of the Russian Federation of taxes. In its capacity as a tax agent a college of advokats is obliged to calculate and in a timely manner calculate and withhold from monies to be paid to the taxpayer the respective taxes, within one month to notify the tax agency in writing about any impossibility to withhold monies and the amount of indebtedness due, to keep a record of revenues withheld and transferred to the budget system personally for each taxpayer, and to submit documents to the tax agency necessary to supervise the correctness of the calculation, withholding, and transfer of taxes to the budget.

The college of advokats also acts as the representative of its advokat members in settling accounts with a client or third persons and any other matters provided for by the charter of the college.

14. The college of advokats bears responsibility for the failure to perform or improper performance of the functions of tax agent or representative. The Tax Code (Article

123) imposes fines in the amount of 20% of the amount subject to transfer to the budget for the improper or incomplete transfer of monies due.

15. When concluding contracts with a principal, or client, for legal services, an advokat acts in his own name and not in the name of the college of advokats. Although model contracts for legal services exist based on the Civil Code of the Russian Federation (Chapter 39), the position taken in Russian legal doctrine is that a college of advokats should in no way interfere in its contractual practice with the independence of the advokat or influence his professional responsibility to his client.

Although one could imagine several reasons why the college of advokats would maintain a register of all agreements concluded by its members with clients, one overriding reason is the role of the college as tax agent for its members. The recording of agreements concluded by advokats enables the college to monitor revenues received and/or anticipated and the respective tax consequences. There are no normative legal acts which regulate the forms of recording agreements by colleges of advokats and neither the justice agencies nor the organs of advokat self-management are empowered to issue binding instructions on this matter.

16. Although the formulation of point 16 of the present Article sounds hortatory, it is intended to function as a guide to interpretation and to place the independence of the advokat as a paramount consideration when applying the present Law.

17. "Transformation" for the purposes of this provision of the present Law is a species of reorganization. The prohibition against transformation of a college of advokats into a commercial organization is understandable, as such a possibility would open opportunities for corporative abuse and enrichment incompatible with the advokat's profession.

18. The Federal Law on Noncommercial Organizations is the residual enactment to be turned to when the present Law does not address matters relating to the regulation of a college of advokats. For these purposes the college of advokats is equated to a noncommercial partnership. The present Law, for example, does not address the circumstances and procedure under which a member may be expelled: whether if by decision of the other members, there must be a simple or a qualified majority in favor, or whether there must be unanimity, or on what grounds expulsion would be justified. The Federal Law on Noncommercial Organizations also contains no requirements and offers no guidance on this issue.

It is recommended in Russian legal doctrine that these matters be addressed in the constitutive documents of the college of advokats. The legislation does not limit an expelled member in any way in his right to a share of the property in the college to which he may have contributed.

Chambers of advokats have experienced difficulties in several subjects of the Russian Federation with verifications undertaken by the Federal Registration Service in exercise of the power of the said Service to supervise the activities of noncommercial organizations. The methods and means of exercising such supervision are set out in the Federal Law on Noncommercial Organizations, as amended (Article 32(3)-(15). In a Decision of the Council of the Federal Chamber of Advokats adopted 3 April 2007 strong exception was taken to the activities of the Federal Registration Service (routinely checking against *ultra vires* activities, money laundering, and financing of terrorism and extremist activity): "The legal status and sphere of activity of chambers of advokats cardinally differs from the legal status and sphere of activity of noncommercial organizations of other forms, which has been stipulated by the adoption of the special Law on the Advokatura" (point 3).

In some instances agencies of the Federal Registration Service demanded that chambers of advokats produce constitutive documents, lists of members, samples of seal imprints, publications in the mass media, accounts, estimates of revenues and expenses, tax declarations, payment orders, cashier books, and numerous other bookkeeping materials. These demands, in the view of the Federal Chamber, were in violation of Article 32(3) of the Federal Law on Noncommercial Organizations.[13]

Article 23 Advokat Bureau

1. *Two or more advokats shall have the right to found an advokat bureau.*
2. *The rules of Article 22 of the present Federal Law, unless provided otherwise by the present Article, shall apply to relations arising in connection with the founding and activity of an advokat bureau.*
3. *Advokats who have founded an advokat bureau shall conclude a partnership contract between themselves in simple written form. Under a partnership contract the partner-advokats shall be obliged to combine their efforts in order to render legal assistance in the name of all the partners. A partnership contract shall be a document which contains confidential information and shall not be provided for State registration of an advokat bureau [as amended by Federal Law of 20 December 2004].*
4. *There shall be specified in a partnership contract:*
   (1) the period of operation of a partnership contract;
   (2) the procedure for the adoption of decisions by the partners;

13 For the text of the Decision, see Semeniako and Pilipenko, Адвокатская деятельность и адвокатура [Advokat Activity and the Advokatura] (2010), pp. 604-609. The Ministry of Justice undertook its own verifications, which resulted in similar objections addressed in a Decision of the Council of the Federal Chamber of Advokats of 30 November 2009. The text appears in ibid., pp. 609-611.

(3) the procedure for election of the managing partner and his competence;
(4) other material conditions.

5. *The conducting of the general affairs of an advokat bureau shall be effectuated by the managing partner unless established otherwise by the partnership contract. An agreement concerning the rendering of legal assistance with a principal shall be concluded by the managing partner or other partner in the name of all partners on the basis of powers of attorney issued by them. In the power of attorney shall be specified all limitations of the competence of the partner concluding the agreement and transactions with the principal and third persons. The said limitations shall be brought to the information of principals and third persons.*
6. *A partnership contract shall be terminated on the following grounds:*
   (1) expiry of the period of operation of the partnership contract;
   (2) termination or suspension of the status of an advokat who is one of the partners, unless preservation of the contract in relations between the other partners is provided for by the partnership contract;
   (3) dissolution of the partnership contract upon the demand of one of the partners unless preservation of the contract in relations between the other partners is provided for by the partnership contract.
7. *From the moment of termination of the partnership contract its participants shall bear joint and several responsibility for the failure to perform common obligations with respect to the principals and third persons.*
8. *In the event one of the partners withdraws from the partnership contract he shall be obliged to transfer to the managing partner the proceedings with regard to all cases relating to which he rendered legal assistance.*
9. *An advokat who has withdrawn from the partnership contract shall be liable to principals and third persons with regard to common obligations which arose in the period of his participation in the partnership contract.*
10. *Nothing in the provisions of the present Article may be regarded as a limitation of the independence of an advokat when performing commissions of the principal, and also his personal professional responsibility to the last.*
11. *An advokat bureau may not be transformed into a commercial organization or any other noncommercial organization, except for instances of the transformation of an advokat bureau into a college of advokats.*
12. *After termination of a partnership contract advokats shall have the right to conclude a new partnership contract. If the new partnership contract is not concluded within a month from the day of termination of the operation of the previous partnership contract, the advokat bureau shall be subject to transformation into a college of advokats or to liquidation [as amended by Federal Law of 20 December 2004].*
    From the moment of termination of a partnership contract until the moment of transformation of an advokat bureau into a college or advokats or the conclusion of a new partnership contract advokats shall not have the right to conclude agreements concerning the rendering of legal assistance.

1. During the Soviet period, the term "advokat bureau" was not used. After about 1990 that expression was used by some traditional and alternative colleges of advokats.

The advokat bureau is a collective form of advokat formation which, just as the college of advokats, requires two or more advokats for formation. Although no maximum number of advokats is prescribed by the present Law, the partnership relations mean in practice that the advokat bureau is likely to remain rather small.

2. An advokat bureau is a noncommercial organization operating in the form of a noncommercial partnership on the basis of a partnership contract concluded among the advokats. Russian legal doctrine is divided on how to understand the present point of Article 23. The rules of Article 22 are said to apply to relations arising in connection with the founding and activity of an advokat bureau unless Article 23 provides otherwise. Some read this formulation as permitting or requiring the founders of an advokat bureau to conclude a constitutive contract and adopt a charter for the bureau.[14] On this reading, the partnership contract is either the constitutive contract or additional to the requirements of Article 23, a reading perhaps reinforced by the fact that Article 22(18) equated the college of advokats to a noncommercial partnership. Others understand Article 23 to mean that only a partnership contract is required to form an advokat bureau and that contract would contain all the details necessary to create and manage the bureau.[15] The latter view is believed to be the better view.

3. The present Law requires that the partnership agreement for the creation of an advokat bureau be concluded in simple written form. This is a civil-law contract to which the general provisions of the Civil Code of the Russian Federation on the law of obligations in general and contracts in particular extend (especially Chapters 27 to 29) and Chapter 55 concerning a contract of simple partnership or joint activity to the extent it may be applicable.[16] There is, however, a crucial distinction between the partnership contract to create an advokat bureau and a contract of joint activity (or simple partnership) under Chapter 55 of the Civil Code. The simple partnership involves the partners combining their property contributions, whereas in the crea-

14 See Belykh, in Trunov, Адвокатская деятельность и Адвокатура в России [Advokat Activity and the Advokatura in Russia] (2006), p. 301.

15 See A. V. Grinenko (ed.), Адвокатура в Российской Федерации [The Advokatura in the Russian Federation] (3d ed.; 2009), p. 76.

16 The Plenum of the Supreme Arbitrazh Court has determined that a contract concerning the creation of an economic society is a contract on joint activity which falls under Chapter 55 of the Civil Code and to which the general rules regulating contracts apply. See point 6, Decree of the Plenum of the Supreme Arbitrazh Court of the Russian Federation, 18 November 2003, No. 19 "On Certain Questions of the Application of the Federal Law 'On Joint-Stock Societies'". Хозяйство и право [Economy and Law], no. 1 (2004).

tion of an advokat bureau, the advokats combine their "joint efforts" to render legal assistance.

In effect the present Law endeavors to combine the status of a noncommercial organization as a juridical person with the legal features of a contract of simple partnership and the status of an advokat.[17] The result is an organizational-legal form which is illogical from the standpoint of Russian civil law.

Point 3 does not provide that the partnership contract is not a constitutive document; however, in the case of a joint-stock society the simple partnership contract to create the society is not a constitutive document, as noted above in point 2. But where an economic society is created, there is a charter which does serve as a constitutive document. In the case of an advokat bureau, there is no charter.

The partnership agreement is a privileged document containing confidential information and is accordingly not be submitted for State registration of the advokat bureau. The bureau is subject to State registration without the agreement.

4. The Civil Code of the Russian Federation (Article 432) sets out what are regarded as the material or essential provisions of a contract. These are the provisions concerning the subject-matter of the contract, conditions which are named in a law or other legal acts as being material or necessary for contracts of the particular type, and those conditions relative to which agreement must be reached according to the statement of one of the parties.[18] Point 4 of the present Article determines the material provisions that must be incorporated or addressed in the partnership contract of an advokat bureau.

A partnership contract is a fixed-term contract. Because the term is a material condition, the partners cannot avoid fixing the term for which the contract should be in force. In the event of the failure to do so, the contract is considered to be not concluded. This requirement has important implications in practice. First, upon the expiry of the period of operation of the contract, it terminates. Second, upon the expiry of the partnership contract the partners have the right (point 12 below) to enter into a new contract. The literal interpretation of this clause suggests that the old contract may not be prolonged and that it must be followed by a new one. This perception is reinforced by point 6 below, which enumerates two instances when the partnership terminates unless the partnership contract provides otherwise; expiry of the contract does not fall into this category. If the partners cannot or do not wish to agree a new contract, the advokat bureau must be transformed into a college of advokats or liquidated. There also are issues arising out of point 9 below and the extent to which

17 See L. A. Demidova and V. I. Sergeev (eds.). Адвокатура в России [The Advokatura in Russia] (2nd ed.; 2005), p. 178.

18 Butler, *Civil Code of the Russian Federation* (2010), p. 146.

partners who have withdrawn from the partnership may remain liable to clients and third persons once the partnership contract has terminated as a whole.

5. The managing partner of an advokat bureau, it is often suggested, is, by analogy, the executive organ of the bureau. That analogy would be more persuasive in situations where the managing partner acts alone on behalf of the advokats who are members of the bureau. It is possible, however, to make provision in the partnership contract that any partner may act for the bureau or that all partners conduct the affairs of the bureau jointly. In any event, the ultimate truth of the analogy may lie in how the partnership takes decisions rather than who is designated to be the managing partner.

6. Point 6 contains a list of grounds for the termination of a partnership contract. Russian legal doctrine justly points to the infelicity of this formulation. The Civil Code of the Russian Federation makes provision for the termination of obligations (Chapter 26) and the "change and dissolution of a contract" (Chapter 29). It would be proper to speak about the termination of obligations in a partnership contract. Under Article 407 of the Civil Code, an obligation terminates entirely or partly on the grounds provided by the Civil Code, other laws, other legal acts, or the contract. This enumeration of grounds is not exhaustive. Accordingly, the formulation of point 6 of the present Article should be considered in the context of Chapter 26 of the Civil Code, and not Chapter 29.

It would follow that in addition to the grounds for termination set out in the present point, the general rules in Chapter 26 of the Civil Code for the termination of obligations are applicable. The obligations of a partnership contract terminate with the death of one of the partners unless the contract provides otherwise, and also terminate upon the liquidation of the advokat formation (Article 419, Civil Code).

As a type of civil-law contract, a partnership contract also may be changed or dissolved pursuant to Chapter 29 of the Civil Code, including in instances when an advokat withdraws from the partnership contract or when a new advokat is admitted to the partnership. The view is expressed in Russian doctrinal writings that when a partner-advokat withdraws from the partnership contract, this is accompanied by a demand for dissolution of the contract. While this is assuredly possible, it would seem equally appropriate for the withdrawing partner to request a change of the contract. The present Law does not prohibit this alternative merely by making reference to dissolution. Dissolution and change of a contract are two distinct concepts with different legal consequences. Article 450 of the Civil Code would be relevant, which means that a change or dissolution of the contract might be by agreement of the parties or by decision of a court in accordance with Article 450(2) of the Civil Code.

The easiest way to exclude termination of a partnership contract when a partner withdraws is simply to provide that the contract will remain in force with regard to the partners who do not withdraw.

7. Upon the termination of the partnership contract, the participants thereof bear joint and several responsibility for the failure to perform common obligations to a client or third persons. Articles 322 to 325 of the Civil Code contain the rules concerning a joint and several duty or responsibility. Advokats who owe a joint and several duty are exposed to a creditor, who has the right to demand performance from all the advokats or any one of them individually for all or part of the obligation owed. The grounds and extent of responsibility are determined in accordance with the general rules set out in Chapter 25 of the Civil Code. One would ordinarily anticipate that a client or third person would expect an advokat who owes the performance of an obligation to provide such performance in kind by rendering the legal services contracted for. Financial sanctions in the form of penalties or fines would in all probability have a secondary place here.

There is an assumption that one advokat's services are as good as any other's, which may not be the case. Advokats differ in their abilities, specializations, experience, and reputation. It is entirely conceivable that a client who had recourse to one advokat would not be satisfied with the legal services of other members of an advokat bureau. If the contracting advokat were unable to act, the question is open whether the client has a case for breach of contract or whether advokat services are mutually replaceable.

8. Under this provision an advokat does not take his clients with him upon leaving the advokat bureau, at least those whom he is actively serving. Russian legislation on the Advokatura does not contemplate the concept of a "client base" in the sense that western law firms do. The Commentaries are silent on such issues, apart from this imperative provision of the legislation.

9. Point 9 is consistent with the concept of partnership generally. No time limit is placed on this responsibility, which is often viewed as a major disadvantage of partnerships generally. If the withdrawing partners cannot effective limit such responsibility by contract upon withdrawal, they would be well advised to identify the precise sources of such responsibility and quantify them to the extent possible.

10. To the extent that this formulation is something more than rhetorical reinforcement of advokat independence, it offers a rule of construction which may be helpful in determining the limits and purpose of other provisions of the present Article.

11. The sole alternative open to the partners in an advokat bureau is either to conclude a new partnership contract and continue to use that form of advokat formation or to transform the advokat bureau into a college of advokats. Transformation into a commercial organization or into another advokat formation except the advokat bureau is not an option, which constitutes an exception to the general provisions of Articles

57 to 65 of the Civil Code of the Russian Federation. This would not preclude the advokats from forming an advokat cabinet, but not by way of transformation.

As a juridical person, the advokat bureau falls under the provisions of the Federal Law on Insolvency (or Bankruptcy) of 26 October 2002, No. 127-ФЗ, as amended.[19]

12. Point 12 addresses an interval of time that may arise when a partnership contract terminates and the partner(s) concerned have not otherwise entered into a new partnership contract or otherwise become part of a permissible advokat formation. This provision precludes advokats from concluding an agreement to render legal assistance but would not preclude him continuing to provide legal assistance under existing contracts.

Article 24 Legal Consultation Office

1. *If on the territory of one judicial district the total number of advokats in all advokat formations located on the territory of the particular judicial district comprises less than two per federal judge, the chamber of advokats upon the recommendation of the agency of executive power of the respective subject of the Russian Federation shall found a legal consultation office [as amended by Federal Law of 20 December 2004].*
2. *A legal consultation office shall be a noncommercial organization created in the form of an institution. Questions of the creation, reorganization, transformation, liquidation, and activity of the legal consultation office shall be regulated by the Civil Code of the Russian Federation, Federal Law "On Noncommercial Organizations", and present Federal Law.*
3. *The submission of an agency of executive power of a subject of the Russian Federation concerning the creation of a legal consultation office must include information concerning:*
   (1) the judicial district in which it is required to create a legal consultation office;
   (2) the number of judges in the particular judicial district;
   (3) the necessary number of advokats in the particular judicial district;
   (4) the material-technical and financial provision for the activity of a legal consultation office, including the premise to be granted to the legal consultation office, organizational-technical means to be transferred to the legal consultation office, and also sources of financing and amount of means allocated for the payment of labor of advokats to be sent for work in the legal consultation office [as amended by Federal Law of 20 December 2004].
4. *After agreeing with the agency of executive power of a subject of the Russian Federation the conditions provided for by point 3(4) of the present Article, the council*

19 СЗ РФ (2002), no. 43, item 4190, as amended; transl. in Butler, *Russia and The Republics: Legal Materials* (looseleaf service; 2006-).

of the chamber of advokats shall adopt a decision concerning the founding of the legal consultation office, confirm the candidacies of the advokats to be sent for work in the legal consultation office, and send by registered letter a notice concerning the founding of the legal consultation office to the agency of executive power of the subject of the Russian Federation [as amended by Federal Law of 20 December 2004].

5. *The council of a chamber of advokats shall confirm the procedure in accordance with which advokats shall be sent for work in legal consultation offices. In so doing payment to advokats effectuating professional activity in legal consultation offices of additional remuneration at the expense of means of the chamber of advokats may be provided by the council of a chamber of advokats [added by Federal Law of 20 December 2004].*

1. The term "legal consultation office" is being used today in quite a different meaning from the recent past. During the Soviet era, the legal consultation office was the principal place to which clients applied for legal services from advokats. In those times the legal consultation office was the primary organizational-legal form in which legal services were made available. All advokats were attached to a legal consultation office. The legal consultation offices were distributed more or less evenly throughout the administrative-territorial entities of the former Soviet Union.

Under the present Law a legal consultation office is formed at the initiative of a State formation (subject of the Russian Federation) to redress a perceived per capita shortage of advokats within a particular judicial district. Point 1 of the present Article uses a proportion, or ratio, of advokats per federal judge as the relevant criterion. Justices of the peace are not considered to be federal judges for this purpose and therefore are not part of the mathematical calculation of the ratio. Nor are arbitration judges or the branches of advokat formations taken into account as part of the ratio.

The procedure for the submission of a recommendation to establish a legal consultation office is established by a law of the particular subject of the Russian Federation.

The contemporary concept of the legal consultation office is among the features of the Russian Advokatura that sharply distinguishes it from European and Anglo-American models of professional regulation. Russian legislation imposes an express duty upon the Advokatura to establish, staff, and maintain at its own risk and expense a physical professional presence where there is a shortage of advokats. Such a presence must be established at the initiative and desire of the State and not the profession. The chamber of advokats refers advokats to staff the legal consultation office. Some suggest that this model is a form of consideration on the part of advokats in return for the freedom granted to choose where they prefer to work and open their offices. While they may prefer to concentrate their presence in well-populated urban areas, advokats as a profession are not allowed to neglect less populated areas and deprive people there of legal services, the more so since rural areas tend to be less prosperous and a larger percentage of the population requires legal services to be provided free of charge or at low cost.[20]

2. A legal consultation office is a noncommercial office created in the form of an institution. It follows from Article 14(1) of the Federal Law on Noncommercial Organizations that the decision of the owner (the chamber of advokats) to create an institution and the charter confirmed by the said owner are the constitutive documents of a legal consultation office. However, this is not precisely consistent with the Civil Code of the Russian Federation (Article 52) which provides that a constitutive contract and charter should be the constitutive documents of an institution. Russian jurists differ as to whether the Civil Code or the Federal Law on Noncommercial Organizations should have priority. As *lex specialis* and later in time, in this Commentator's view the Federal Law on Noncommercial Organizations should be accorded priority.

A legal consultation office is considered to be in existence from the moment of its State registration as a juridical person. The property of a legal consultation office is held by right of operative management and is transferred to it from the property held by the chamber of advokats. Because it is an institution, a legal consultation office works on the basis of an accounting document called an "estimate", which is confirmed in advance annually by the meeting or conference of advokats in the particular subject of the Russian Federation. Among other things, the estimate confirms the "property solitariness" of the institution. It goes without saying that the legal consultation office must have the other requisites of a juridical person: name, seal, location, and so on.

A legal consultation office may be reorganized and liquidated in accordance with the Civil Code, the Federal Law on Noncommercial Organizations, and the present Law. Reorganization takes the forms set out in Article 57 of the Civil Code. The Federal Law on Noncommercial Organizations (Article 17) permits an institution to be reorganized into a foundation, autonomous noncommercial organization, or economic society; the present Law contains no limitations on the reorganization of a legal consultation office.

A legal consultation office is liquidated on the basis of the Civil Code (Articles 61-64) and the Federal Law on Noncommercial Organizations (Articles 18-21). If liquidation is voluntary, the council of the chamber of advokats takes the decision. If liquidation is compulsory, only a court may take the relevant decision. If the assets of a legal consultation office are insufficient to meet the demands of creditors, under the Federal Law on Noncommercial Organizations (Article 19) suit may be brought

20 Nonetheless, severe inequalities exist with respect to the per capital access to legal services. On the situation in the Sakha (Yakutia) Republic, see A. Iu. Pripuzova, «Обеспечение доступности юридической помощи в условиях Крайнего Севера» [Ensuring Accessibility to Legal Assistance in Conditions of the Far North], Адвокат [Advokat], no. 10 (2009), pp. 82-84.

against the chamber of advokats. Any property remaining after the demands of creditors are satisfied is transferred to the owner of the legal consultation office unless provided otherwise by legislation or the constitutive documents of the institution. Liquidation is completed from the moment an appropriate entry is made in the unified State register of juridical persons.

3. Point 3 requires the agency of executive power seeking to establish a legal consultation office in its subject of the Russian Federation to submit a request that must contain the data enumerated: the judicial district where it is intended to create the legal consultation office; the number of judges in that judicial district; the number of advokats needed to staff the legal consultation office; and details of provision to be made for the physical facilities of the legal consultation office and the sources of finance. Some Russian advokats have criticized this formulation because an active role is contemplated for the subject of the Federation involved; it has been suggested that under these circumstances the legal consultation office *de facto* becomes a regional advokat formation – which implies powerful and influential by reason of its patronage and size, especially in under populated areas where the commercial presence of the advokats is likely to consist of only a few individual advokats.

Supporters of the legal consultation office model observe that its special status originates in the reasons for creating these offices: the provision of legal services in remote and inaccessible areas. Financial support for the office comes from two primary sources: the founding chamber of advokats and the budget of the respective subject of the Federation. The remuneration paid to advokats who staff legal consultation offices is determined at the meeting or conference of advokats of the subject of the Federation. Some legal consultation offices exercise their right under the Civil Code (Article 50) to engage in entrepreneurial activity directed towards achieving the purposes for which the institution was founded.

4. Point 4 determines the procedural sequence for decisions to be taken with respect to establishing a legal consultation office. First, the subject of the Russian Federation must establish that the criteria for creating a legal consultation office are present. Once that has been done and the physical and financial conditions have been agreed, the council of the chamber of advokats must find advokats who are willing to staff the office and submit their names, together with other relevant materials, to the agency of executive power of the subject of the Federation. Presumably, if the subject of the Federation disagreed with the staffing arrangements, objections might be submitted.

5. Point 5 requires the council of the chamber of advokats to confirm the procedure for sending advokats to work in a legal consultation office. Arrangements vary from one subject of the Federation to another. Under amendments adopted in 2004, the council was given discretion to effectively "top up" remuneration levels approved by the meeting or conference of advokats at its annual meeting.

Article 25 Agreement on Rendering Legal Assistance

1. *Advokat activity shall be effectuated on the basis of an agreement between the advocate and principal.*
2. *An agreement shall be a civil-law contract concluded in simple written form between the principal and the advokat(s) for the rendering of legal assistance to the principal himself or person designated by him.*
   [paragraph two lost force – by Federal Law of 20 December 2004];
   [paragraph three lost force – by Federal Law of 20 December 2004];
   Questions of the dissolution of an agreement concerning the rendering of legal assistance shall be regulated by the Civil Code of the Russian Federation with the exceptions provided for by the present Federal Law.
3. *An advokat irrespective of in what register information about him has been inserted shall have the right to conclude an agreement with a principal irrespective of the place of residence or location of the last.*
4. *Material conditions of an agreement shall be:*
   (1) indication of the advokat(s) who have accepted the commission as an attorney(ies), and also his (or their) affiliation to the advokat formation and advokat chamber;
   (2) subject-matter of the commission;
   (3) conditions of payment of remuneration by the principal for legal assistance rendered;
   (4) procedure and amount of contributory compensation for expenses of advokat(s) connected with performance of the commission;
   (5) amount and character of responsibility of advokat(s) who have accepted performance of the commission.
5. *The right of an advokat to remuneration and contributory compensation for expenses connected with performance of a commission may not be assigned to third persons without the special consent of the principal to this.*
6. *Remuneration to be paid to an advokat by the principal and/or contributory compensation of expenses to an advokat connected with the performance of a commission shall be subject to obligatory placement at the cashier of the respective advokat formation or credited to the settlement account of the advokat formation in the procedure and within the periods which have been provided for by the agreement.*
7. *At the expense of remuneration received an advokat shall effectuate professional expenses for [as amended by Federal Law of 20 December 2004]:*
   (1) common needs of the chamber of advokats in the amounts and procedure which shall be determined by the meeting (or conference) of advokats;
   (2) maintenance of respective advokat formation;
   (3) insurance of professional activity;
   (4) other expenses connected with the effectuation of advokat activity.

8. *The labor of an advokat participating as a defender in a criminal proceeding by appointment of agencies of inquiry, agencies of preliminary investigation, or court shall be paid at the expense of means of the federal budget. Expenses for these purposes shall be taken into account in a federal law on the federal budget for the next year in a respective special-purpose item of expenses [as amended by Federal Law of 24 July 2007].*
   The amount and procedure for remuneration of an advokat participating as a defender in a criminal proceeding by appointment of agencies of inquiry, agencies of preliminary investigation, or court shall be established by the Government of the Russian Federation [as amended by Federal Law of 24 July 2007].
9. *Material-technical and financial provision for rendering legal assistance in inaccessible and little-populated localities shall be an expenditure obligation of the subject of the Russian Federation.*
   The procedure for contributory compensation of expenses to an advokat who has rendered legal assistance to citizens of the Russian Federation free of charge in the procedure established by Article 26 of the present Federal Law shall be determined by laws and other normative legal acts of subjects of the Russian Federation [as amended by Federal Laws of 22 August 2004 and 20 December 2004].
10. *The amount of additional remuneration payable at the expense of means of the chamber of advokats to an advokat participating as a defender in a criminal proceeding by assignment of agencies of inquiry, agencies of preliminary investigation, or court and the procedure for the payment of remuneration for the rendering of legal assistance to citizens of the Russian Federation free of charge shall be established annually by the council of the chamber of advokats [as amended by Federal Laws of 20 December 2004 and 24 July 2007] .*

1. A distinction is sometimes drawn in the Russian language and statutory drafting between legal assistance rendered to clients by qualified jurists (юридическая помощь) and legal assistance made available through institutional channels pursuant to international "legal assistance" (правовая помощь) treaties. It is a nuance almost impossible to express in the English language.[21] The present Article and the present Law throughout refer to legal assistance in its first meaning.

The formulation of point 1 of this Article creates an imperative rule from which derogation is not permitted. The formulation also represents a considerable departure from past Russian practice insofar as the agreement is concluded between the client and the advokat himself rather than the advokat formation with which the advokat is associated. Even in an advokat bureau, where one of the partners concludes the agreement with the client in the name of the other partners, this is done not in

21 Iu. I. Stetsovskii, Советская адвокатура [Soviet Advokatura] (1989), p. 7.

the name of the bureau, but in the name of each partner advokat who has given a respective power of attorney.

2. Point 2 establishes several imperative conditions for the contract between an advokat and client. First, the agreement is a civil-law contract, which means that the agreement is regulated by the provisions of the Civil Code of the Russian Federation, especially Article 420 which provides that a "contract shall be considered to be an agreement of two or several persons concerning the establishment, change, or termination of civil rights and duties". Setting aside a certain tautological element of the formulations, the legislator offers little by way of guidance as to what is the subject-matter of the agreement, that is, what is "legal assistance"? In Russian legal doctrine the question is whether "legal assistance" is work, a service, or something else. The distinctions have doctrinal significance and tax implications. The Tax Code of the Russian Federation distinguishes sharply between the "delivery of goods", "fulfillment of work", and "rendering of services".

In its present formulation point 2 gives greater freedom of contract to advokats. The initial version of the present Law contained paragraphs two and three of point 2 (repealed on 20 December 2004) which stipulated the types of civil-law contract which advokats might conclude. The removal of that restriction gives greater, but not unlimited scope, for advokats to be creative in their contractual relations with clients.

An agreement with an advokat for legal services may concern either the client himself or another person, in which event the other person must confirm the agreement and agree to the legal services being rendered. This often happens in criminal proceedings, when the family or a relative of the client retains an advokat subject to the client subsequently consenting to this retention. Criminal procedure legislation permits an advokat to be retained to render legal services in accordance with an order of an agency of inquiry, preliminary investigation, procuracy, or court even if the client does not consent to this. Under circumstances specified in the Code of Criminal Procedure (Article 52), the client's refusal of legal services is not binding upon those agencies assigning an advokat to defend the client's rights.

The Civil Code of the Russian Federation regulates the dissolution or change of a contract in Chapter 29. Any exceptions established in the present Law represent *lex specialis.*

The Constitutional Court of the Russian Federation in a Decree of 23 January 2007, No. 1-П,[22] determined with respect to the Civil Code of the Russian Federation that the inclusion in the text of a contract concerning the compensated rendering of legal services provisions conditioning the payment of remuneration upon a positive outcome of the case for the plaintiff was contrary to the basic principles of civil

22 СЗ РФ (2007), no. 6, item 828. This outcome provoked three major dissenting opinions by individual members of the Constitutional Court.

legislation permitting the parties to determine any conditions of a contract unless those provisions were contrary to legislation (Article 1(2), Civil Code of the Russian Federation). A contract for remuneration is concluded for the performance of duties by the parties. The Civil Code in Articles 779 and 781 does not assume a situation in which the demands of the performer of services are based upon a favorable result from a court decision to be adopted in the future. The failure of the Civil Code to contemplate such an arrangement is not unconstitutional.

3. While advokats are registered within a particular subject of the Russian Federation and linked to an Advokatura within that subject, they are at liberty to accept assignments from any client, irrespective of where the client is located or resident. A client accordingly has the choice of any advokat within the Russian Federation to engage for professional services. An advokat, in turn, may represent a client anywhere in the Russian Federation or abroad.

The question arises in practice whether advokats need any other documents in order to act on behalf of a client. Some Russian courts have required advokats performing representation functions in a civil proceeding to submit a power of attorney. The judges took the view that, without a power of attorney, an advokat is merely acting as an advokat and may not be regarded as a representative of his client. This view is rejected in Russian doctrinal writings. The advokat, they stress, is not a procedural player in a proceeding. In a civil proceeding an advokat may be only a representative, and an order issued by an advokat formation empowering the advokat confirms his representation powers.

In a criminal proceeding the existence of an agreement for an advokat to defend the rights of a suspect or accused is confirmed only by an order. Individual orders must be submitted by the advokat to various agencies and courts of various instances.

Advokats are recommended when travelling outside the population center in which they ordinarily work to formalize a business trip certification of the established form. This document may be used not only to justify expenses, but also to confirm important reasons for a failure to appear by reason of travel delays, and the like.

4. The Civil Code of the Russian Federation (Article 421) provides that natural and juridical persons are at liberty to conclude contracts. Compulsion to conclude a contract is permissible only when the Civil Code or other legislation so provides, or a contractual obligation freely assumed so stipulates. Mixed contracts containing elements of various types of contract provided or not provided for in the Civil Code are permitted. An agreement for legal services may, accordingly, be concluded for a particular type of services, including representation in court, or for a complex of legal services.

The Civil Code (Article 432) stipulates that a contract is concluded when agreement regarding all the material conditions of the contract has been reached in the form required. Point 4 of the present Law sets imperative material conditions in an agreement concluded between an advokat and his client. These material provisions extend to any contract for legal services in the Russian Federation, in this Commentator's view, whether concluded by advokats or by law firms and auditing companies providing legal services to clients.[23]

In addition to the material provisions enumerated in point 4 of the present Article, an agreement for legal services must incorporate the information provided for by the Federal Law of 7 August 2001, as amended, "On Counteracting the Legalization (or Laundering) of Revenues Received by Criminal Means and the Financing of Terrorism", as amended.

The types of contract typically concluded with respect to legal services vary. This also was true in Imperial Russia, where contracts of personal hire, independent-work, and customer order were well developed.[24]

Under the modern Civil Code of the Russian Federation, a contract of commission, for example, provides that one party is obliged to perform determined legal actions in the name of and at the expense of the other party (Article 971, Civil Code). The actions involved in representation in a court would normally fall into this category. Legal assistance in the forms of consultations, provision of legal information, drafting of documents, legal analysis of contracts, and the like would fall into the category of the compensated rendering of services (Chapter 39, Civil Code). In addition, Article 783 of the Civil Code provides that the general provisions on independent-work contract are applicable to a contract for the compensated rendering of services unless this is contrary to Articles 779 to 782 of the Civil Code or the distinctive elements of the subject-matter of a contract for the compensated rendering of services. The independent-work provisions apply when the client receives some result in material form, whereas legal services involving a nonmaterial result would fall under Chapter 39 of the Civil Code.

The distinction was expressed as follows by Braginskii and Vitrianskii: "Decisive significance for demarcating the independent-work contract and contract for the rendering of services is the nature of the interest of the respective party – the customer – lying at the basis thereof. If this interest comes down to performing actions, the contract is the compensated rendering of services, and when the performance of actions is supposed with the transfer of a result, there is an independent-work contract for which the principle is immanent: 'the result crowns the matter'. Services

23 See the Information Letter of the Supreme Arbitrazh Court of the Russian Federation, 29 September 1999, No. 48 "On Certain Questions of Judicial Practice Arising When Considering Disputes Connected with Contracts for the Rendering of Legal Services", available on Consultant Plus. The Information Letter provided: "a contract for the rendering of legal services may be considered to be concluded if determined actions have been enumerated therein which the performer is obliged to perform, or a determined activity is specified which he is obliged to effectuate".

24 For a discussion of Russian doctrinal writings and Ruling Senate decision, see M. V. Kratenko, Договор об оказании юридической помощи в современном гражданском законодательстве [Contract on Rendering Legal Assistance in Contemporary Civil Legislation] (2006), p. 34.

occur primarily when the result of the actions, if there is such, is beyond the limits of the contract".[25]

These distinctions find reflection in the Tax Code of the Russian Federation. Work for the purposes of taxation is activity whose results have material expression and may be realized in order to satisfy the requirements of an organization or juridical person, whereas a service is activity whose results do not have material expression and is realized and consumed in the process of effectuating that activity.[26]

What is contractually characterized as "complex" legal assistance has no material expression and encompasses the right to apply to advokats at any time (what in Anglo-American practice is called a retainer), provide informational, analytical, and consultation legal services, representation of the interests of the client in courts or other agencies, and render other legal services. The actual extent of legal services is not stipulated and depends upon various factors affecting the legal status of the client.

5. The prohibition against an advokat assigning his right to remuneration and compensation for expenses to a third person without the client's permission is an imperative rule. Its application should be read against the Civil Code of the Russian Federation (Articles 382-390), which regulates the transfer of creditor rights to another person.

6. The requirement in point 6 that money earned by an advokat should be paid to the advokat formation or deposited to the account of the advokat formation in accordance with the agreement is imperative. Since this remuneration will, once the agreement has been performed, be paid to the advokat concerned, the remuneration is subject to taxation. Some Russian jurists suggest that the failure to comply with this requirement engages criminal responsibility under Article 198 of the Criminal Code of the Russian Federation (evasion of payment of tax or insurance contribution to State extrabudgetary funds by natural person).[27]

7. The provision with regard to professional expenses is of a general character. Those which are actually deductible for taxation purposes are determined by the Tax Code of the Russian Federation.

The provision with regard to professional insurance has been addressed above (see Commentary to Articles 7 and 19).

---

25 See M. I. Braginskii and V. V. Vitrianskii, Договорное право: Договоры о выполнении работ и оказании услуг [Law of Contract: Contracts on the Fulfillment of Work and Rendering of Services] (2002), III, p. 221.

26 See W. E. Butler (ed. & transl.), *Tax Code of the Russian Federation* (Moscow, 2004), p. 90.

27 See W. E. Butler (ed. & transl.), *Russian Criminal Law and Procedure* (2011), pp. 130-131.

8. Under the Code of Criminal Procedure of the Russian Federation (Article 50[5]), if an advokat participates in a preliminary investigation or judicial examination by appointment of an inquiry official, investigator, or court the expenses for his work are to be paid from the federal budget.

The amount paid to advokats who participate in a criminal proceeding as a defender by assignment of agencies of inquiry, agencies of preliminary investigation, of a court is determined by a Decree of the Government of the Russian Federation, No. 400, of 4 July 2003, as amended, "On the Amount of Payment for Labor of an Advokat Participating as a Defender in a Criminal Proceeding by Assignment of Agencies of Inquiry, Agencies of Preliminary Investigation, or Court".[28] An advokat receives not less than 275 nor more than 1,100 rubles per day for acting as an appointed defender; if he works at night or on a holiday or weekend, the rate is not less than 550 rubles nor more than 2,200 rubles. The complexity of the case is taken into account when determining the rate of payment.

Complexity in turn has regard to the systemic jurisdiction of the case (what level of court hears the case at first instance), the number and gravity of the crimes, the number of suspects, accused, or persons on trial, the size of the file of the case, whether the advokat has to travel to another locality, and other circumstances. There are percentage increments for advokats working in areas of the Far North or other areas with adverse climatic conditions. Payment is made to the advokat on the basis of a decree of the agency of inquiry, preliminary investigation, or court upon the application of the advokat. When a case is prolonged, the advokat may apply for payments each month for time worked. Payment is to be made to the advokat formation within 30 days from the date of receipt of the decree in accordance with the Procedure for the Settlement of Accounts for the Payment of Labor of an Advokat Participating as a Defender in a Criminal Proceeding by Assignment of Agencies of Inquiry, Agencies of Preliminary Investigation, or Court Depending on the Complexity of the Criminal Case, confirmed by Order of the Ministry of Justice and Ministry of Finances of the Russian Federation of 15 October 2007, No. 199/87н.[29]

The advokat's time is calculated in days actually worked by the advokat on the case irrespective of the length of the work during the day. The rate of 1,100 rubles (doubled if at night or on holidays or weekends) is paid per day of participation in criminal cases considered at first instance by the Supreme Court of the Russian Federation or a court with jurors, or cases relegated to the systemic jurisdiction of the supreme court of a republic, territory of regional court, court of a city of federal significance, court of an autonomous region, or area or fleet military court. The rate is 825 rubles per day (doubled if at night or on holidays or weekends) if the case involves three or more accused or persons on trial; or the case involves an accusation of three or more crimes;

28 СЗ РФ (2003), no. 28, item 2925, as amended.

29 БНА ФОИВ, no. 45 (2007).

or the size of the file of the case exceeds three volumes. The rate is 550 rubles (doubled as noted above) if the case is considered in a closed judicial session or on circuit, the suspect, accused, or person on trial cannot by reason of physical or mental defects himself exercise his right to defense, or the suspect, accused, or person on trial does not have a command of the language in which the proceeding is conducted. The lowest rate of 275 rubles (doubled as noted above) applies to other criminal cases. These rates may be increased on the basis of a reasoned decree of the agency of inquiry or preliminary investigation or court when the complexity of the case so merits.

The legality of the Order of 15 October 2007 was challenged in a suit brought to the Supreme Court of the Russian Federation on the grounds that a provision of the Procedure offered no definition of with respect to the "complexity of a case" but rather introduced the concept of "actual employment" of an advokat, a concept absent in Russian labor legislation but one enabling law enforcement agencies and courts to arbitrarily use this concept to confine remuneration to an advokat to his participation in judicial sessions. This approach was alleged to violate his right to payment for labor as an advokat, that is, to take full account of the services provided. The Supreme Court regarded his construction of the Procedure as incorrect and rejected it as being grounds for deeming a normative legal act to be invalid.[30]

The rights of an advokat are violated if the remuneration due to an advokat is not remitted or is remitted with delay to the advokat formation concerned; applications by an advokat for payment are left without satisfaction by the agencies concerned; or the agencies concerned fail to calculate the amounts of remuneration due to the advokat. Depending upon the nature of the violation, an advokat may appeal against the illegal actions of an official, file a written claim or demand for payment, or bring suit in court. In so doing the advokat may act personally or with the assistance of his advokat formation.

If a suit is filed by an advokat formation which is a juridical person, the suit is within the jurisdiction of arbitrazh courts (Article 28, Code of Arbitrazh Procedure). If the advokat sues personally, he will use the courts of ordinary jurisdiction. When arbitrazh courts are used, the defendant is the Russian Federation in the person of the Ministry of Finances or other agencies which are juridical persons and finance the activity of law enforcement agencies. By a Methods Recommendation on the Procedure for the Recovery of Indebtedness for Payment of Labor of Advokats for Participation as a Defender in a Criminal Proceeding by Assignment of Agencies of Inquiry, Agencies of Preliminary Investigation, or a Court, approved by the Council of the Federal Chamber of Advokats on 27 May 2004,[31] advokats are given the spe-

30 See Decision of the Supreme Court of the Russian Federation, 9 October 2008, No. ГКПИ08-1840. Бюллетень Верховного Суда РФ [Bulletin of the Supreme Court of the Russian Federation], no. 12 (2009). The decision was left without change by Ruling of the Supreme Court, 23 December 2008.

31 See Semeniako and Pilipenko, Адвокатская деятельность и адвокатура [Advokat Activity and the Advokatura] (2010), pp. 557-561.

cific names and coordinates of defendants, depending upon by whom the assignment to act as a defender was made.

9. Point 9 places on the individual subjects of the Russian Federation the duty to assume obligations to make provision for material and technical assistance to advokats rendering assistance in remote areas of the country or to indigent clients. The procedure for payment of compensation to advokats is relegated to each individual subject of the Federation.

In practice advokats in remote areas of Russia who accepted assignments in criminal cases were not remunerated for expenses connected with appearing in those remote localities on the grounds that the Code of Criminal Procedure of the Russian Federation (Article 131) did not treat such expenses as "procedural costs" eligible for reimbursement. In a Ruling of 5 February 2009, No. 289-O-П, the Constitutional Court determined that in its constitutional legal meaning Article 131 of the Code of Criminal Procedure assumes the inclusion of the expenses of an advokat participating in a criminal case by assignment of an inquiry official, investigator, or court connected with his appearance at the site where procedural actions are performed within the concept of procedural costs eligible for reimbursement.[32]

10. The financial burden of advokats acting as defenders in criminal proceedings by assignment is shared with the Advokatura of which they are members. The remuneration paid by the State to the respective advokat formation for the services of an advokat is regarded as a minimum level of remuneration which needs to be augmented by the Advokatura. The council of each respective chamber of advokats determines how much additional remuneration should be paid, which effectively means that each chamber of advokats shares with the State the financial burden of providing legal services in criminal cases by assignment.

Article 26 Rendering of Legal Assistance to Citizens of Russian Federation Free of Charge

1. *Legal assistance to citizens of the Russian Federation whose average individual revenue is lower than the amount of the living minimum established in a subject of the Russian Federation in accordance with federal legislation, and also citizens of the Russian Federation living alone whose revenues are lower that the said amount, shall be rendered free of charge in the following instances [as amended by Federal Law of 28 October 2003, No. 134-ФЗ. СЗ РФ (2003), no. 44, item 4262]:*

32 Available on Consultant Plus.

(1) to plaintiffs – with regard to cases considered by courts of first instance concerning the recovery of alimony, compensation of harm caused by death of breadwinner, mutilation or other impairment of health connected with labor activity;
(2) to veterans of the Great Fatherland War – with regard to questions not connected with entrepreneurial activity;
(3) to citizens of the Russian Federation – when drawing up applications concerning the assignment of pensions and benefits;
(4) to citizens of the Russian Federation who suffered political repressions – with regard to questions connected with rehabilitation.

2. *The List of documents necessary in order for citizens of the Russian Federation to obtain legal assistance free of charge, and also the procedure for the provision of the said documents, shall be determined by laws and other normative legal acts of subjects of the Russian Federation.*
3. *Legal assistance shall be rendered in all instances free of charge to minors confined in institutions of the system for the prevention of delinquency and violations of law of minors.*

1. This article enumerates the categories of indigent citizens who have the right to receive legal assistance free of charge and the types of legal assistance to be rendered on that basis. Contrary to the position taken in the 1980 RSFSR Statute on the Advokatura, the exemption of a citizen from payment for legal assistance is no longer in the discretion of the head of the legal consultation office, presidium of the college of advokats, procurator, court, or agencies of preliminary investigation. In comparison with the 1980 Statute, this Article also broadens the categories of persons who qualify for exemption by including veterans of the Second World War with regard to questions not connected with entrepreneurial activity and persons who suffered from political repressions with regard to questions connected with rehabilitation.

2. The categories of citizens enumerated in this Article are exhaustive. The living minimum revenue for citizens is established by each of the 83 subjects of the Russian Federation and may vary one from the other; as amended, point 1 of the Article presumes that each subject of the Federation has established its own minimum and that each must be in accordance with federal legislation. The List of documents needed for exemption from payment for legal assistance and the procedure for issuance of those documents also is determined by the subjects of the Federation.

In Archangel Region, for example, the List of documents required is determined by the Regional Law on Rendering Legal Assistance Free of Charge to Citizens of the Russian Federation on the Territory of Archangel Region and Nenets Autonomous National Area of 26 November 2008, No. 615-31-03, as amended.[33] The List includes

33 Ведомости Архангельского областного Собрания депутатов четвертого созыва (2008), no. 31. Available on Consultant Plus Regional Data Base.

plaintiffs at first instance in cases involving the recovery of alimony, compensation for harm caused by death of a breadwinner, mutilation or other impairment of health connected with labor activity; for veterans of the Second World War on matters not connected with entrepreneurial activity; for citizens generally, the drawing up of pension applications; and for citizens who suffered from political repressions, issues linked with rehabilitation. Minors confined in juvenile institutions are given legal assistance free of charge in all instances.

The concept of average individual revenue of a citizen is defined in the Federal Law of 24 October 1997, No. 134-ФЗ "On the Living Minimum in the Russian Federation", as amended,[34] as the aggregate amount of revenue of each member of a family or citizen living along divided by the number of all members of the family. A family is understood to be persons linked by kinship and/or affinity and reside and keep a household jointly, and the living minimum is the cost of a consumer basket plus obligatory payments and charges. The Government of the Russian Federation establishes the per capita living minimum also with regard to socio-demographic groups as a whole for the Russian Federation, as adjusted in subjects of the Russian Federation by agencies of executive power of those subjects quarterly on the basis of a consumer basket and data of the State Committee of the Russian Federation for Statistics concerning the level of consumer prices for foodstuffs, nonfoodstuffs, services, and obligatory payments.

For the Russian Federation as a whole the living minimum is calculated according to a methods instruction confirmed by a joint Decree of the Ministry of Labor and Social Development of the Russian Federation and the State Committee of the Russian Federation for Statistics of 28 April 2000, No. 36/34 "On Confirmation of the Method for Calculation of the Amount of the Living Minimum as a Whole for the Russian Federation", as amended.[35] For these purposes the population is divided into three socio-demographic groups: the able-bodied population; pensioners, and children up to fifteen years of age. If a subject of the Russian Federation does not establish a living minimum, those established by the Government of the Russian Federation are used.

Also of relevance are the Federal Law on the Procedure for Recording Revenues and Calculation of the Average Per Capita Revenue of a Family and Revenue of a Citizen Living Alone in order to Deem Them to be Indigent and Rendering to Them of State Social Assistance of 5 April 2003, No. 44-ФЗ,[36] and the Decree of the Government of the Russian Federation of 20 August 2003, No. 512, "On the List of Types of Revenues to be Taken into Account When Calculating the Average Per Capita Revenue of a Family and Revenue of a Citizen Living Alone for the Rendering of State

34 СЗ РФ (1997), no. 43, item 4904, as amended.
35 Available on Consultant Plus, as amended.
36 СЗ РФ (2003), no. 14, item 1257.

Social Assistance to Them".[37] Applications are made through the agency of social defense of the population at the place of residence or sojourn of the citizen.

3. The duty of the Russian Federation agencies of State power to finance the activity of advokats who render legal assistance to citizens of the Russian Federation free of charge in the instances provided by legislation of the Russian Federation is laid down in Article 3(3) of the present Law. The concept of legal assistance being rendered "free of charge" [*бесплатно*] should not be confused with the concept of "without payment" [*безоплатно*]. The element of being "free of charge" is applicable to the citizen qualifying for free legal assistance but does not extend to the advokat himself, whose services are not free but are subject to remuneration by the State at a level adequate for the efforts expended.

Minors confined in institutions of the system for the prevention of delinquency are eligible for legal assistance free of charge. Such institutions have been defined in the Federal Law of 24 June 1999, No. 120-ФЗ "On the Fundamental Principles of the System of Prevention of Delinquency and Violations of Law of Minors", as amended.[38] The variety of institutions is substantial (see Articles 13, 15, and 22 of the said Law) and also includes certain public health institutions for abandoned children.

The procedure for paying for the labor of an advokat rendering legal assistance when a minor is being considered for placement in a center for temporary confinement for minor offenders administered by internal affairs agencies is not determined by legislation, but an analysis of general relevant legislation suggests that the duty of payment rests with the federal budget.[39]

Decisions connected with the procedure for rendering legal assistance free of charge (distributing commissions among advokat formations, establishing additional remuneration for advokats who render such assistance, determining the amounts of such remuneration, and so on) and the procedure for the participation of advokats as defenders in a criminal proceeding upon the designation of agencies of inquiry, preliminary investigation, procuracy, or court must be adopted by chambers of advokats, pursuant to Article 44(1) of the present Law, within twenty days from the day of registration.

37 СЗ РФ (2003), no. 34, item 3374, as amended.

38 СЗ РФ (1999), no. 2, item 3177, as amended.

39 See the Survey of Legislation and Judicial Practice of the Supreme Court of the Russian Federation for the First Quarter of 2009, confirmed by Decree of the Presidium of the Supreme Court of the Russian Federation on 3 June 2009. Excerpts are published in Semeniako and Pilipenko, Адвокатская деятельность и адвокатура [Advokat Activity and the Advokatura] (2010), pp. 492-495.

Article 27 Aide of Advokat

1. *An advokat shall have the right to have aides. Persons having a higher, uncompleted higher, or secondary legal education may be aides of an advokat, except for persons specified in Article 9(2) of the present Federal Law.*
2. *An aide of an advokat shall not have the right to engage in advokat activity.*
3. *An aide of an advokat shall be obliged to keep advokat secrecy.*
4. *An aide of an advokat shall be hired on conditions of a labor contract concluded with the advokat formation, and if an advokat effectuates his activity in an advokat cabinet – with the advokat who is the employer with respect to the particular person. An advokat formation shall have the right to conclude a fixed-term labor contract with a person ensuring the activity of one advokat during the effectuation by the last of his professional activity in the particular advokat formation [as amended by Federal Law of 20 December 2004].*
5. *Social insurance of an aide of an advokat shall be effectuated by the advokat formation in which the aide works, and if the advokat effectuates his activity in an advokat cabinet – by the advokat in whose advokat cabinet the aide works.*

1. Although aides of an advokat were not provided for in the 1980 RSFSR Statute on the Advokatura, they were in fact employed in some colleges of advokats on the basis of labor contracts.[40] They were not individuals who had a higher legal education.

The sole requirement for an aide under the present Law is that he has a higher, uncompleted higher, or secondary legal education. A person who lacks or who has limited civil dispositive legal capacity or who has an unremoved or uncancelled conviction for an intentional crime may not be employed as an aide to an advokat.

2. The prohibition contained in point 2 of the present Article suggests that aides are hired to perform technical duties for an advokat: preparation of documents, typing, secretarial duties, and perhaps legal research. Their functions would appear to amount more or less to the Anglo-American concept of the paralegal.

3. Aides of an advokat are required to observe advokat secrecy, which suggests that an aide may not be interrogated as a witness with regard to circumstances that became known to him as a result of performing his employment duties. The Code of Criminal Procedure of the Russian Federation does not use the term "advokat secrecy".

40 For a critique of the shortcomings of Russian labor legislation with respect to aides and apprentices of advokats, see V. V. Arkhipov, «Закон об адвокатской деятельности и адвокатуре и трудовос законодательство» [Law on Advokat Activity and Advokatura and Labor Legislation], Адвокат [Advokat], no. 2 (2009), pp. 35-44.

Advokats are required to familiarize aides of advokats with the Code of Professional Ethics of an Advokat (Article 3) and ensure that they comply with the norms of the Code that relate to their labor duties.

4. The labor contract on the basis of which an aide of an advokat is hired is governed by the Labor Code of the Russian Federation. He accordingly is not required to pay the various contributions that an advokat must pay to the college of advokats or to the Federal College of Advokats.

The employer is the advokat formation, or the advokat who creates an advokat cabinet if he hires an aide. Nothing is said in point 4 of the present Article about the earnings of an aide. Presumably market conditions apply and the experience and skills of the aide are taken into account.

The present Law does not address payment for sick days for aides. Presumably this is dealt with by chambers of advokats themselves, who create wage funds from the deductions for the maintenance of advokats to be paid to those who become ill.

5. Social insurance for the aide of an advokat is the responsibility of the advokat formation or, in the case of an advokat who creates an advokat cabinet, of the advokat in whose cabinet the aide works.

Article 28 Apprentice of Advokat

1. *An advokat having advokat experience of not less than five years shall have the right to have apprentices. Apprentices of an advokat may be persons having a higher legal education except for persons specified in Article 9(2) of the present Federal Law. The period of apprenticeship shall be from one year up to two years.*
2. *An apprentice of an advokat shall effectuate his activity under the direction of an advokat, fulfilling his individual commissions. The apprentice of an advokat shall not have the right autonomously to engage in advokat activity.*
3. *An apprentice of an advokat shall be obliged to keep advokat secrecy.*
4. *An apprentice of an advokat shall be hired on conditions of a labor contract concluded with the advokat formation, and if an advokat effectuates his activity in an advokat cabinet – with the advokat who is the employer with respect to the particular person.*
5. *Social insurance of an apprentice of an advokat shall be effectuated by the advokat formation in which the apprentice works, and if the advokat effectuates his activity in an advokat cabinet – by the advokat in whose advokat cabinet the apprentice works.*

1. Apprentices were mentioned in the 1980 RSFSR Statute on the Advokatura (Article 11(2)). Persons who had graduated from a higher legal educational institution, had no work experience in the specialization of jurist or who had less than two years of

experience in legal work might be admitted to a College of Advokats after undergoing an apprenticeship for a period of from six months up to one year.

Under the present Law the position is regulated from the standpoint of the advokat rather than the apprentice. The apprenticeship does not necessarily lead to membership of the Advokatura; the apprentice must to become an advokat ultimately pass the necessary examinations for membership in the Advokatura. Consequently, an advokat with not less than five years experience as an advokat may have apprentices. The apprentices must have a higher legal education, may not have an unremoved or uncancelled record of conviction, and must have full dispositive civil legal capacity. The period of apprenticeship is from one year up to two years. An apprenticeship is consequently not a career in and of itself, unlike the aide of an advokat, who may serve without limitation of time imposed by legislation.

2. An apprentice to an advokat may perform assignments of the advokat having a legal nature under his supervision. Although the apprentice may not engage in advokat activity by himself, he may assist the advokat in individual cases or undertake legal research.

3. The apprentice is obliged to comply with the requirements for advokat secrecy. The same observations made with respect to aides of an advokat in this respect apply to apprentices (see Commentary to Article 27 above).

Advokats are required to familiarize apprentices of advokats with the Code of Professional Ethics of an Advokat (Article 3) and ensure that they comply with the norms of the Code that relate to their labor duties.

Advokats are required to familiarize apprentices of advokats with the Code of Professional Ethics of an Advokat (Article 3) and ensure that they comply with the norms of the Code that relate to their labor duties.

4. The hiring arrangements of an apprentice approximate those of an aide, except that since the period of apprenticeship is limited to a maximum of two years, the labor contract will doubtless be of fixed-term.

5. The arrangements for social insurance of an apprentice are the same as those for an aide of an advokat, and subject to the same qualifications made in the Commentary to Article 27 above.

Article 29 Chamber of Advokats of Subject of Russian Federation

1. *A chamber of advokats shall be a non-State, noncommercial organization based on the obligatory membership of advokats of one subject of the Russian Federation.*
2. *A chamber of advokats shall operate on the basis of general statutes for organizations of the particular type provided for by the present Federal Law.*

3. *A chamber of advokats shall have its own name containing an indication of its organizational-legal form and the subject of the Russian Federation on whose territory it is formed.*
4. *A chamber of advokats shall be created for the purpose of ensuring the rendering of qualified legal assistance, the accessibility thereof to the population throughout the entire territory of the particular subject of the Russian Federation, organization of legal assistance rendered to citizens of the Russian Federation free of charge, representation and defense of the interests of advokats in agencies of State power, agencies of local self-government, social associations, and other organizations, control over the professional activity of persons permitted to effectuate advokat activity, and compliance by advokats with the Code of Professional Ethics of an Advokat.*
5. *A chamber of advokats shall be formed by the constitutive assembly (or conference) of advokats.*
   A chamber of advokats shall be a juridical person, have an autonomous balance sheet, open settlement and other accounts in banks in accordance with legislation of the Russian Federation, and also have a seal, stamps, and letterheads with its own name containing an indication of the subject of the Russian Federation on whose territory it is formed.
6. *Advokats shall not be liable for obligations of the chamber of advokats, and a chamber of advokats shall not be liable for the obligations of advokats.*
7. *A chamber of advokats shall be subject to State registration, which shall be effectuated on the basis of a decision of the constitutive assembly (or conference) of advokats and in the procedure established by the federal law on the State registration of juridical persons.*

7[1]. *A chamber of advokats shall not be subject to reorganization. Liquidation of a chamber of advokats of a subject of the Russian Federation may be effectuated on the basis of a federal constitutional law concerning the formation within the Russian Federation of a new subject in the procedure which is established by the federal law [as amended by Federal Law 20 December 2004].*

8. *Only one chamber of advokats may be formed on the territory of a subject of the Russian Federation, which shall not have the right to form its structural subdivisions, branches, and representations on the territory of other subjects of the Russian Federation. The formation of inter-regional and other inter-territorial chambers of advokats shall not be permitted.*
9. *Decisions of organs of a chamber of advokats adopted within the limits of their competence shall be binding upon all members of the chamber of advokats.*
10. *A chamber of advokats shall not have the right to effectuate advokat activity in its own name, nor to engage in entrepreneurial activity.*

1. The present Law introduced for the first time in modern Russian history a unified regulatory scheme for the Advokatura in all subjects of the Russian Federation. The chamber of advokats is a unification of all advokats within each subject of the Federa-

tion not for the purpose of jointly rendering legal assistance, but rather to advance and protect the corporative interests of the advokats. It is a widely shared view among advokats that without this approach it would be impossible to achieve the true independence of the Advokatura.

There is a State and public interest engaged in this structure too. The Advokatura has a public responsibility to make provision for legal assistance to individual categories of the population who cannot afford to pay for it. Meeting this responsibility does not necessarily coincide with the private interests of advokats individually. The chamber of advokats acts to defend the interests collectively of its members before State and local agencies of power and self-government and non-State organizations, supervises the admission of law graduates to the profession, and ensures the advokats comply with the ethical standards of the profession.

The conceptual principle underlying the present Law is that within each subject of the Russian Federation there may and does exist only one chamber of advokats which has no structural subdivisions, branches, or representations and which may not enter into joint organizational schemes with the chambers of advokats in other subjects of the Russian Federation. The chamber of advokats within each subject of the Federation enjoys a monopoly position: all advokats must be affiliated with it and no other chamber is permitted to exist. Juridically, the chamber of advokats is a non-State, noncommercial organization which operates in accordance with the 1993 Russian Constitution, the Federal Law on Noncommercial Organizations, the present Law, and the charter of each chamber (when such has been adopted).

2. The formulation of point 2, widely repeated in doctrinal writings, is not necessarily the case.[41] Charters which do exist routinely expand upon the provisions of the present Law while remaining consistent with it.

3. In practice this provision has been widely misunderstood by Russian advokats. The Council of the Chamber of Advokats of the City of Moscow issued a Letter on 31 July 2003, No. 541, which indicated that many advokat formations had declared on their seals, letterheads, forms, and other requisites that the respective formation belonged

41 A. P. Galaganov is incorrect in writing that "Chambers of advokats operate on the basis of general provisions for organizations of the particular type, that is, each of the chambers of advokats of subjects of the Russian Federation operates not on the basis of a charter adopted by itself, but on the basis of the provisions of the" [present Federal Law]. See A. P. Galaganov, in I. L. Trunov (ed.), Адвокатская деятельность и адвокатура в России [Advokat Activity and the Advokatura in Russia] (2006), I, p. 238. The Charter of the Chamber of Advokats of Moscow Region was adopted by the Conference of Founders on 23 October 2002 and is in force as amended on 17 March 2006. Available on the Chamber website.

to the chamber of advokats of the City of Moscow or to justice agencies. They were requested to make revisions and delete any such references.[42]

4. Point 4 sets out the purposes of the activity of a chamber of advokats. The charters of individual chambers commonly add to the enumeration contained in the present Law. The Chamber of Advokats of Moscow Region, for example, specified that the purposes of the chamber included, additionally: organizing professional study according to confirmed syllabuses (point 2.1.5) and submitting proposals, having regard to the opinion of the advokat community, in the procedure established by law to legislative agencies of a subject of the Russian Federation with regard to improving legislation regulating the organization and activity of the advokatura of a subject of the Russian Federation (point 2.1.7).

The representation functions are construed extensively. Presidents of chambers of advokats may be chosen by the Federal Chamber of Advokats to be a representative of the Federal Chamber in a federal district pursuant to the Statute on the Representative of the Council – Deputy President of the Federal Chamber of Advokats in a Federal District, confirmed by the Council of the Federal Chamber on 25 August 2003. The Moscow Region Chamber of Advokats appoints under its Charter and the Statute on the Representative of the Council of the Chamber of Advokats of Moscow Region in the Judicial District a person to represent the interests of the Moscow Region Chamber of Advokats on the territory of the judicial district.

5. The current practice of founding a chamber of advokats by a conference or constitutive assembly of advokats is a considerable departure from the Soviet era. Under the 1980 RSFSR Statute on the Advokatura, colleges of advokats were formed by the Ministry of Justice jointly with respective agencies of executive power. The State no longer has a role in forming a chamber of advokats other than to register the formation thereof after the decision is adopted.

The classic elements of the legal capacity of a juridical person contained in the Civil Code of the Russian Federation are enumerated in point 5 with respect to a chamber of advokats. An advokat formation is a fully-fledged participant of civil law relations with the right to conclude transactions in its own name consistent with its charter and/or Russian legislation, to be a plaintiff or defendant in court or an arbitral tribunal, or to be an applicant before the Constitutional Court of the Russian Federation. The rights of a juridical person arise from the moment of State registration of the chamber of advokats.

Nonetheless, there are sound reasons to suppose that in fact a chamber of advokats has special legal capacity, rather than general, notwithstanding the provisions of the

42 Available on the website of the Chamber of Advokats of the City of Moscow: www.advokatrus.ru/doc/567.

present Law. It would be "... difficult to allow the possibility of some extended affiliation of property whose ordinary designation obstructs its use by a chamber of advokats since actions are required from it that are incompatible with its special legal capacity".[43] A transaction for such property, it is suggested, would be invalid under the Civil Code of the Russian Federation (Article 173). However, there is no legal limitation on the ability of a chamber of advokats to invest available monies into revenue-producing securities, although "... such investments (being speculation on the stock exchange and close in legal status to entrepreneurial activity) usually are incompatible with the nature of financing the revenues and expenses of a chamber of advokats".[44]

6. Given its legal status as a juridical person, it follows that the advokats who are members of a chamber of advokats bear no liability for obligations of the chamber, and the chamber in turn bears no liability for debts of individual advokats.

7. The State registration of a chamber of advokats is done in accordance with the Federal Law of the State Registration of Juridical Persons of 8 August 2001, as amended.[45] For registration purposes the applicant may be the president of the chamber of advokats or another person acting on the basis of a power of attorney issued by the president. The applicant certifies by his signature the application submitted to the registering agency together with identity documents. The signature must be notarially certified.

7^1. A chamber of advokats is not subject to reorganization in the forms set out in the Civil Code of the Russian Federation (Article 57). Liquidation was not originally contemplated either, but the merger of subjects of the Russian Federation required that the chambers of advokats in each undergo a change of identity in some fashion. Rather than merge the chambers of the merging subjects of the Federation, it was decided that they should be liquidated and a new chamber of advokats formed in the merged subjects of the Federation. The number of subjects of the Russian Federation has by merger decreased from 89 to 83 since the 1993 Russian Constitution entered into force. The number of chambers of advokats has been adjusted accordingly.

Nonetheless, the charters of some chambers of advokats make specific provision for the possibility of reorganization and liquidation. The Charter of the Chamber of Advokats of Moscow Region provides: "The reorganization and liquidation of the

43 See G. B. Mirzoev and N. D. Eriashvili (eds.), Адвокатура в России [The Advokatura in Russia] (4th ed.; 2011), p. 68.

44 Ibid., p. 70. It is suggested that the internal documents of a chamber of advokats should limit or prohibit such investments. The present writer has found no examples of such limitations or prohibitions in the internal documents of chambers of advokats.

45 СЗ РФ (2001), no. 33(I), item 3431, as amended; transl. in W. E. Butler, *Russian Company Law and Commercial Legislation* (2003), pp. 1-15.

Chamber shall be possible only on the conditions and in the procedure determined by legislation of the Russian Federation" (point 10.3.).

8. The present Law prohibits more than one chamber of advokats being created and registered in a subject of the Russian Federation. Perhaps this approach dictated the requirement that when subjects of the Federation merged, their respective chambers of advokats did not merge or otherwise reorganize; they were liquidated. One new chamber of advokats was created in their place in the new subject of the Federation formed by the merger.

The prohibition against multiple chambers of advokats in one subject of the Federation is explained by the nature of the powers of the chamber of advokats to form the community of advokats and the need to ensure compliance with the Code of Professional Ethics of an Advokat. The same logic is used to prevent chambers of advokats from forming subdivision, branches, or representations in other subjects of the Federation and to prohibit the creation of inter-regional or other inter-territorial chambers of advokats.

9. Since the chamber of advokats is an entity in which membership is not voluntary, but compulsory, for advokats and operates as a regulatory body, the decisions taken as part of its management functions are binding upon all members, including those whose membership is terminated or suspended, provided such decisions are within its competence. Although not specifically mentioned in the present Law in this respect, decisions of a chamber of advokats are binding also upon aides and apprentices of advokats and upon the management organs of the chamber.

Decisions of the chamber adopted by an assembly or conference of advokats are brought to the information of all members of the chamber. Advokats may request a copy of the protocol of the assembly or conference or an extract therefrom. In practice, many decisions of the assembly or conference are posted on the website of the respective chamber of advokats.

10. Since a chamber of advokats does not have the legal capacity to render legal assistance – this task being left to the advokat formations created by members of the chamber – there is an express prohibition against a chamber of advokats rendering legal assistance in its own name or in any respect whatsoever. The same prohibition extends to any entrepreneurial activity, which follows from the general federal law on noncommercial organizations. The arrangement of continuing legal education programs, the publication of journals, bulletins, and monographs, and the maintenance of websites with details of how to contact individual advokat-members of the chamber are not considered to be "entrepreneurial" for the purposes of the present Law.

The Charter of the Chamber of Advokats for Moscow Region expressly empowers that chamber to issue a monthly scientific-practical journal and bulletin (point 2.2.3.).

Article 30 Assembly (or Conference) of Advokats

1. *The assembly of advokats shall be the highest organ of a chamber of advokats of a subject of the Russian Federation. An assembly (or conference) of advokats shall be convoked not less than once a year.*
   An assembly (or conference) of advokats shall be considered to be empowered if not less than two-thirds of a chamber of advokats (or delegates of the conference) take part in its work.
2. *There shall be relegated to the competence of the assembly (or conference) of advokats:*
   (1) *forming the council of the chamber of advokats of a subject of the Russian Federation, including the election of new members of the council and termination of powers of members of the council subject to replacement, in accordance with the procedure for the renewal (or rotation) of the council provided for by Article 31(2) of the present Federal Law, adoption of decisions concerning the termination of powers of members of the council before time, and also confirmation of decisions of the council concerning termination before time of powers of members of the council whose status of advokat was terminated or suspended [as amended by Federal Law of 20 December 2004];*
   (2) *election of members of the internal audit commission and election of members of the qualifications commission from among the advokats [as amended by Federal Law of 20 December 2004];*
   (3) *election of representative(s) to the All-Russian Congress of Advokats (hereinafter – congress) [as amended by Federal Law of 20 December 2004];*
   (4) *determination of the amount of obligatory deductions of advokats for common needs of the chamber of advocates;*
   (5) *confirmation of the estimate of expenses for maintenance of the chamber of advokats;*
   (6) *confirmation of the report of the internal audit commission concerning the results of the internal audit of financial-economic activity of the chamber;*
   (7) *confirmation of reports of the council, including execution of the estimate of expenses for maintenance of the council;*
   (8) *confirmation of the reglament of the assembly (or conference) of advokats;*
   (9) *determination of the location of the council;*
   (10) *creation of special-purpose funds of chamber of advokats [as amended by Federal Law of 20 December 2004];*
   (11) *establishment of measures of incentive and responsibility of advokats in accordance with Code of Professional Ethics of an Advokat [as amended by Federal Law of 20 December 2004];*
   (12) *adoption of other decisions in accordance with the present federal law [renumbered in accordance with Federal Law of 20 December 2004].*

3. *Decisions of the assembly (or conference) of advokats shall be adopted by a simple majority of votes of advokats participating in the assembly (or delegates of the conference).*

1. Whether the members of a chamber of advokats meet as an assembly or as a conference depends upon the size of the membership of the chamber. The numerical threshold for determining whether an assembly or conference will be held is 300 advokats. The City of Moscow, Moscow Region, and St. Petersburg chambers of advokats all have well in excess of 300 advokats and accordingly convoke a conference of advokats once a year. The tenth regular annual conference of advokats of the Moscow Region, for example, was held on 28 January 2011.

The reasons for this approach are, above all, ones of technical feasibility. Even in large cities it is difficult to find and rent a premise capable of accommodating several thousand advokats. The discussion of issues from the floor is awkward and voting is cumbersome.

The quorum is either two-thirds of the advokats in a chamber or two-thirds of the delegates elected to represent their colleagues in a conference. In principle, the present Law does not differ greatly from the respective norms regulating the organization and holding of an assembly or conference of advokats set out in the 1980 RSFSR Statute on the Advokatura. This continuity is attributed to the fact that the chambers of advokats are the approximate equivalent of the territory or regional colleges of advokats from the late Soviet era when the colleges had as members all the advokats of a particular territory or region.

The present point does not specify who is responsible for convoking the annual assembly or conference. The council of the chamber of advokats does so pursuant to Article 31(2)(14) of the present Law. This represents a change from the 1980 RSFSR Statute on the Advokatura, which empowered agencies of State power to convene an assembly or conference of the colleges of advokats.

An extraordinary meeting of a chamber of advokats may be convoked at the initiative of the membership of the chamber (one-third) or at the request of a territorial justice agency. However, the last may merely "request" such a meeting, and not convoke it.

2. Point 2 of the present Law establishes the competence of the assembly or conference and in practice determines the agenda of the annual meeting. Although the formulation of point 2 refers only to the "competence" of the assembly or conference, this has been understood by some chambers of advokats to mean "exclusive

competence".[46] There is in fact no provision of the present Law which would prevent a chamber of advokats delegating competence to another of its organs.

The president of the chamber calls the assembly or conference to order. The presiding chairman and secretary of the assembly or meeting and the counting commission are elected by the advokats present. The counting commission counts the ballots prepared in advance for items on the agenda. A protocol on the vote count is signed by all members of the counting commission and passed to the person presiding to be read out and attached to the protocol of the assembly or conference. The secretary of the assembly or conference keeps the protocol or the assembly or conference.

The protocol of an assembly or conference must indicate: the time and place of holding the event, the total number of registered participants, the names of the person presiding, secretary, and members of the counting commission; the principal tenets of speeches, questions put for voting, voting results, and decisions adopted by the assembly or conference, and the signatures on the protocol of the person presiding and the secretary. If it chooses to do so, the assembly or conference may elect a presidium.

(1) This subpoint requires the assembly or conference to form the principal organ of the chamber of advokats and to confirm membership changes that may have occurred in that organ since the previous assembly or conference.

(2) On the internal audit commission, see Article 32 below and the Commentary thereto. On the qualifications commission, see Article 33 below and the Commentary thereto. The assembly or conference elects only the advokat members of the qualifications commission; other members are elected or appointed by the agencies or organizations which have representatives of the commission.

(3) The All-Russian Congress of Advokats meets every five years. Each chamber of advokats will in advance of a forthcoming Congress choose a representative(s) to be present, depending upon how many each is entitled to have based on the numerical membership of each chamber of advokats.

(4) Advokats make a number of payments each year for various purposes. The sum referred to in this sub-point is a deduction to be made for the common needs of the chamber of advokats. This varies from one chamber to another, depending upon the number of advokats and the expenses budgeted for each financial year. For the calendar year 2010, for example, the Chamber of Advokats of Moscow Region levied a monthly charge of 540 rubles, which was the same sum for the year 2009. The sum is payable each month by direct debit to the chamber of advokats. Sums payable to the Federal Chamber of Advokats are not included in this figure.

46 See, for example, the Charter of the Chamber of Advokats of Moscow Region (point 5.8). Also see Iu. A. Kostanov, in A. V. Grinenko (ed.), Комментарий к Федеральному закону «Об адвокатской деятельности и адвокатуре в Российской Федерации (постатейный) [Commentary to Federal Law "On Advokat Activity and the Advokatura in the Russian Federation" (Article-by-Article)] (2003), p. 218.

In the instance of the Moscow Region Chamber of Advokats certain advokats were exempted from making payments for the common needs of the chamber. These included advokats with forty years or more experience in the Advokatura; and advokats with poor eyesight who fell into the I or II groups of disabled persons; women ad vokats on pregnancy or birth leave; certain other advokats on medical leave for more than three months; and all advokats who were veterans of the Second World War.

(5) A composite estimate is submitted for approval by the assembly or conference. The Moscow Region Chamber of Advokats approved for the calendar year 2010 a total estimate of 34,625,113.79 rubles. This figure represented an increase over the calendar year 2009 of approximately three million rubles of actual expenditure.

(6) Confirmation of the internal audit routinely occurs early on the agenda of an assembly or conference. In the case of the Moscow Region Chamber of Advokats this item was second on the agenda of the ninth conference held in January 2010. Traditionally, the report of the internal audit commission goes far beyond accounting and bookkeeping matters, although these may be addressed in the report. Members of the commission are at liberty to discuss the quality of performance by members of the council of the chamber and/or personnel employed by the chamber of advokats. Reports can be severely critical of the efficiency and effectiveness of actual operations.

(7) Reference is made here to at least two reports and possibly others. The initial agenda item usually is the report of the council of the chamber of advokats concerning its work during the preceding year, followed by a report on the execution of the estimate of revenues and expenses for that year. Approval or confirmation of the report on estimates will include those items which were overspent during the preceding year. Note will be taken of indebtedness to the chamber of advokats reflecting contributions not paid by the end of the reporting year by individual advokats.

(8) The adoption of a Reglament to set out the procedures for conducting an assembly or conference is a legal requirement. The text is available to advokats but not, as a rule, included on websites of the chambers of advokats.

(9) The determination of the location of the council is normally an early and permanent decision. The assemblies or conferences are routinely held in a premise rented for this purpose, such as a large hotel or meeting hall. The council occupies a premise on a permanent basis. The location is the legal address of the chamber of advokats. The chamber may or may not be physically located on the territory of the subject of the Federation concerned. Both the legal address and the physical headquarters of the Chamber of Advokats of Moscow Region, for example, are in the City of Moscow.

(10) The present Law was amended in 2004 to allow chambers of advokats to create "special funds". It is common practice to establish a fund, for example, to remunerate advokats who undertake assignments to defend individuals in criminal cases at the expense of advokats who prefer not to do work of this nature and in lieu of doing so make a contribution at an agreed level to the special fund of the chamber of advokats. In the calendar year 2009 contributions were made to this special fund in the City of Moscow by 270 colleges of advokats, 180 advokat bureaus, and 1,000

advokat cabinets, The total amount of contributions was 16,900,000 rubles, and expenditures from the fund came to 15,600,000 rubles. The funds were disbursed to 95 advokat formations.

(11) The Federal Chamber of Advokats pursuant to the Statute on Measures, Grounds, and Procedure for Incentives of the Federal Chamber of Advokats of the Russian Federation, confirmed on 10 December 2003, as amended 1 December 2004, 8 October 2008, and 7 July 2009, established marks of distinction for the labor of advokats in rendering qualified legal assistance to natural and juridical persons and defending their rights and legal interests. These fall into three categories: (1) awards: the "Order for Loyalty to Advokat Duty"; the Medal "For Service in Defending the Rights and Freedoms of Citizens", first and second degree; (2) incentives: the badge "Honorary Advokat of Russia", and various certificates of honor and gratitude; and (3) other incentives, such as a commemorative medal, diploma, or letter of gratitude. Several incentives are linked to years of service. The Order requires uninterrupted service as an advokat for twenty years; the Medal, first degree, requires fifteen years of service and second degree not less than ten years. In exceptional instances the periods of service may be less. The badge is awarded to advokats who have at least thirty years of service.

Foreign jurists and legal associations are eligible to be awarded the Medal for Service in Defending the Rights and Freedoms of Citizens.

Chambers of advokats establish various kinds of rewards and incentives for advokats themselves and personnel of the chamber. The Moscow Region Chamber of Advokats, for example, appropriated on 18 November 2009 the sum of 352,000 rubles to pay bonuses to personnel of the apparatus of the Chamber of Advokats based on work results for the calendar year 2009. The Charter of the Moscow Region Chamber of Advokats authorizes recommendations to be made for State, departmental, and Federal Chamber of Advokats awards, together with awards conferred by the Chamber itself. In Moscow Region there are five categories of awards that may be conferred: an expression of gratitude; a diploma; a valuable gift; a monetary bonus; and the lapel badge: "Honored Advokat of the Moscow Region Chamber of Advokats" (point 4.5, Charter of Moscow Region Chamber of Advokats).

The disciplinary measures that may be established by a chamber of advokats, using the Moscow Region Chamber of Advokats as an example, include a comment, a warning, and termination of the status of advokat (point 4.7, Charter of Moscow Region Chamber of Advokats). These may be imposed for a disciplinary offense, which in the Charter of the Moscow Region Chamber of Advokats is defined at a "violation of a law or norms of the Code of Professional Ethics of an Advokat when performing professional activity or the failure to fulfill decisions of general meetings (or conferences) of advokats and decisions of organs of the chamber of advokats ..." (point 4.6).

(12) Other decisions include philanthropic donations by the chamber of advokats to worthy causes, increases in remuneration for advokats who undertake criminal defense work, authorizing the acquisition of property, and others.

3. Although the minimum for a quorum is two-thirds of the registered advokats in a chamber, decisions are adopted by a majority vote of those present. Neither the present Law nor charters of a chamber of advokats, insofar as they exist, require a qualified majority for any questions before an assembly or conference.

ARTICLE 31 COUNCIL OF CHAMBER OF ADVOKATS

1. *The council of a chamber of advokats shall be the collegial executive organ of the chamber of advokats.*
2. *The council shall be elected by the assembly (or conference) of advokats by secret ballot in a quantity of not more than 15 persons from the membership of the chamber of advokats and shall be subject to renewal (or rotation) once in two years by one-third. In so doing the provisions of Article 41(6) of the present Federal Law shall not apply [as amended by Federal Law of 20 December 2004].*
   In the event of regular rotation the president of the chamber of advokats shall submit for consideration of the council candidacies for members of the council for withdrawal and also candidacies of advokats for filling vacant offices of members of the council of the chamber of advokats. After confirmation by the council of the chamber of advokats candidacies submitted by the president shall be submitted for consideration of the assembly (or conference) of advokats for confirmation [added by Federal Law of 20 December 2004] .
   If the assembly (or conference) of advokats does not confirm candidacies submitted, the president of the chamber of advokats shall submit for confirmation of the assembly (or conference) of advokats new candidacies only after consideration thereof and confirmation by the council of the chamber of advokats [added by Federal Law of 20 December 2004].
3. *The council of a chamber of advokats shall:*
   (1) *elect from its composition the president of the chamber of advokats for a term of four years and upon his recommendation one or several vice presidents for a term of two years, and determine the powers of the president and vice presidents. In so doing the same person may not occupy the office of president of a chamber of advokats more than two terms in succession [as amended by Federal Law of 20 December 2004];*
   (2) *in the interval between assemblies (or conferences) of advokats adopt decisions concerning the termination before time of powers of members of the council whose status of advokat was terminated or suspended. The said decisions shall be submitted for confirmation of the next assembly (or conference) of advokats [added by Federal Law of 20 December 2004];*
   (3) *determine the norm of representation for a conference and procedure for the election of delegates [as amended by Federal Law of 20 December 2004];*
   (4) *ensure accessibility to legal assistance throughout the entire territory of the subject of the Russian Federation, including legal assistance to be rendered to*

citizens of the Russian Federation free of charge in instances provided for by the present Federal Law. For these purposes the council shall adopt decisions concerning the creation of legal consultation offices upon the recommendation of the agency of executive power of the subject of the Russian Federation and send advokats for work in legal consultation offices in the procedure established by the council of the chamber of advokats [as amended by Federal Law of 20 December 2004];

(5) determine the procedure for the rendering of legal assistance by advokats participating as defenders in a criminal proceeding by assignment of agencies of inquiry, agencies of preliminary investigation, or court, and in other instances, bring this procedure to the information of the said agencies and advokats, and control the execution thereof by advokats [as amended by Federal Laws of 20 December 2004 and 24 July 2007];

(6) determine the procedure for the payment of remuneration at the expense of means of the chamber of advokats to advokats rendering legal assistance to citizens of the Russian Federation free of charge;

(7) represent the chamber of advokats in agencies of State power, agencies of local self-government, social associations, and other organizations;

(8) facilitate the raising of the professional standard of advokats, including confirm syllabi for raising qualifications of advokats and study by apprentices of advokats, and organize professional study with regard to the said syllabi [as amended by Federal Law of 20 December 2004];

(9) consider appeals against the actions (or failure to act) of advokats, taking into account the opinions of the qualifications commission;

(10) defend the social and professional rights of advokats;

(11) facilitate the provision of advokat formations with employment premises;

(12) organize the informational provision of advokats, and also an exchange of work experience between them;

(13) effectuate methods activity [as amended by Federal Law of 20 December 2004];

(14) convoke not less than once a year an assembly (or conference) of advokats and form the agenda thereof;

(15) dispose of property of the chamber of advokats in accordance with the estimate and with the designation of the property;

(16) confirm the reglaments of the council and internal audit commission and personnel establishment of the apparatus of the chamber of advokats [added by Federal Law of 20 December 2004];

(17) determine the amount of remuneration of the president and vice-presidents, other members of the council of the chamber of advokats, and members of the internal audit and qualifications commissions within the limits of the estimate of expenses confirmed by the assembly (or conference) of advokats for the maintenance of the chamber of advokats [added by Federal Law of 20 December 2004];

(18) keep the register of advokat formations and branches thereof on the territory of the respective subject of the Russian Federation [added by Federal Law of 20 December 2004];

(19) give within the limits of its competence with regard to queries of advokats explanations on the occasion of possible actions of advokats in a complex situation concerning compliance with ethical norms on the basis of the Code of Professional Ethics of an Advokat [added by Federal Law of 20 December 2004].

4. *In the event of the failure of the council of the chamber of advokats to execute the requirements of the present Federal Law, the powers of a council may be terminated before time at an assembly (or conference) of advokats. An extraordinary assembly (or conference) of advokats shall be convoked by the council upon the demand of not less than half of the members of the chamber of advokats, upon the demand of the territorial justice agency, or by decision of the council of the Federal Chamber of Advokats [as amended by Federal Law of 20 December 2004].*

   In the event of the systematic failure by the council of the chamber of advokats to execute decisions of organs of the Federal Chamber of Advokats adopted within the limits of the competence of the said organs including in the event of the failure to pay obligatory deductions for common needs of the Federal Chamber of Advokats for more than six months, an extraordinary assembly (or conference) of advokats shall be convoked by the council of the Federal Chamber of Advokats [as amended by Federal Law of 20 December 2004].

   In the decision of the council of the Federal Chamber of Advokats must be specified the grounds for convocation of an extraordinary assembly (or conference) of advokats, the time and place of holding the assembly (or conference) of advokats, the norm of representation, and the procedure for election of delegates to the conference [added by Federal Law of 20 December 2004].

5. *Sessions of the council shall be convoked by the president of the chamber of advokats as necessary, but not less than once a month. A session shall be considered to be empowered if not less than two thirds of the members of the council are present at it.*

6. *Decisions of the council shall be adopted by a simple majority of votes of members of the council participating in the session thereof and shall be binding upon all members of the chamber of advokats.*

7. *The President of a chamber of advokats shall represent the chamber of advokats in relations with agencies of State power, agencies of local self-government, social associations, and other organizations, and also natural persons, act in the name of the chamber of advokats without a power of attorney, issue powers of attorney and conclude transactions in the name of the chamber of advokats, dispose of property of the chamber of advokats by decision of the council in accordance with the estimate and designation of the property, effectuate hiring and dismissal of workers of the apparatus of the chamber of advokats, convoke sessions of the council, and ensure the execution of decisions of the council and decisions of the assembly (or conference) of advokats.*

The President of a chamber of advokats shall institute a disciplinary proceeding with respect to an advokat(s) when there is a permissible occasion and in the procedure provided for by the Code of Professional Ethics of an Advokat [added by Federal Law of 20 December 2004].

8. *The president and vice presidents, and also other members of a council, may combine work in the council of a chamber of advokats with advokat activity, receiving in so doing remuneration for work in the council in the amount determined by the council of the chamber of advokats [as amended by Federal Law of 20 December 2004].*
9. *The council of a chamber of advokats shall not have the right to effectuate advokat activity in its own name, nor to engage in entrepreneurial activity.*

1. The council of a chamber of advokats operates in the intervals between an assembly or conference of the chamber of advokats.

2. The present Law imposes a maximum limit on the membership of the council of a chamber of advokats. There is no minimum number. The actual size of the council varies from one chamber of advokats to another. The Charter of the Moscow Region Chamber of Advokats (point 5.12) reproduces the identical language from the present sub-point, which leaves the actual number of council members open to the discretion of each annual meeting.

Candidacies for membership on the council of a chamber of advokats are initiated by the president, who obtains the confirmation of the council and then submits the names to the assembly or conference for consideration. It is unclear whether the council is required to approve the entire slate of candidacies or votes upon each candidacy individually. In the absence of a categorical indication otherwise, the assembly or conference is at liberty to do one or the other.

Candidacies rejected by the assembly or conference may not be replaced by other candidacies from the floor of the assembly or conference. The president is required to initiate other candidacies and submit these first to the council for approval and, assuming this approval is obtained, then submit the candidacies to the assembly or conference. Unless alternative candidacies have been prepared in advance, or the council is convened during the assembly or conference, a literal reading of the provision would mean that vacancies exist on the council until the following year or an extraordinary meeting.

3. The enumeration of powers of the council of a chamber of advokats falls into three categories: (1) organizational-administrative; (2) organizational-provision; and (3) representative.

(1) The present Law imposes a limit on the number of successive terms the president of the council of a chamber of advokats may serve. The limitation would not preclude an individual from standing down for a term and then running again for an additional two terms. The limitation does not extend to the vice presidents.

It is unclear whether the rotation rule applies to the president of the council.

(2) While the council has the power effectively to remove from its membership advokats whose status of advokat is suspended or terminated, there is no power to replace them with provisional appointments.

(3) The norm of representation for selecting delegates to represent advokats at the annual conference of advokats is determined well in advance and notified to every advokat who is a registered member of the chamber of advokats. For its eighth annual conference (2010), the Chamber of Advokats of the City of Moscow determined in a Decision of 24 September 2009 that one delegate per 20 advokats would be chosen and that members of the Council of Advokats, Qualifications Commission who are advokats, Internal Audit Commission, and members of the Council of the Federal Chamber of Advokats registered as advokats in the City of Moscow would all be delegates to the conference over and above the norm of representation.

The delegates were elected as follows. Advokats in colleges of advokats and advokat bureaus numbering 20 or more advokats hold elections in their respective advokat formations. At least 25% of the advokats in the respective formation must take part in these elections. Advokats in advokat cabinets, colleges of advokats, or advokat bureaus numbering less than 20 advokats take part in a general meeting organized by the council of the College of Advokats of the City of Moscow. Each advokat has one vote in these meetings, and proxy voting is not permitted. Formulas are provided to resolve representation where the numbers are less than ten or exceed ten.[47]

(4) This is among the major functions of the council of a chamber of advokats and one which distinguishes it from professional bars and law societies in other countries which do not share the Soviet legal heritage. In its Report for the calendar year 2009 the Chamber of Advokats of the City of Moscow reported that the council received 181 requests for legal assistance to be rendered free of charge. These requests were distributed to the advokat formations in Moscow and in a number of instances the work of advokats was remunerated from a special fund maintained by the Chamber for these purposes.

However, the rendering of legal services free of charge encountered a difficulty. The City of Moscow had appropriated six million rubles from its budget to be applied to these purposes, but the actual rendering of legal assistance had been virtually suspended. The reason was that the City of Moscow had raised the level of incomes which citizens needed to qualify for such assistance above the minimum living wage.

(5) The sub-point refers to the participation of advokats as defenders in criminal proceedings pursuant to Article 51 of the Code of Criminal Procedure of the Russian Federation or, less commonly, Article 50 of the Code of Civil Procedure of

47 See Protocol No. 9 to the Decision No. 119, of the Council of the Chamber of Advokats of the City of Moscow, 24 September 2009. Available at www.advokatymoscow.ru. The same meeting of the Council confirmed a Reglament for conducting the said meetings of advokats for the election of delegates.

the Russian Federation. The Russian Advokatura is the principal, but not exclusive, source for the appointment of defenders. In the City of Moscow, where 2,044 advokat formations were registered as of 1 January 2010, most of the monies appropriated by the Moscow City Chamber of Advokats to support the provision of legal services free of charge under Article 51 of the Code of Criminal Procedure went to 95 advokat formations specializing in criminal matters.

Statistics from Moscow Region for 2009 indicate that 1,688 advokats undertook work on assignment from investigative agencies, an increase of 6% over the previous year. Article 51 criminal defenses produced revenues from the federal budget of 38,479,770 rubles. With regard to civil matters, in Moscow Region 1,418 advokats, or about 30% of the registered advokats in that Region, gave advice free of charge to 21,926 citizens, in whose interests 24,073 assignments were performed. No payments were made to advokats in Moscow Region from the budget of the Government of that Region; however, the Moscow Region Chamber of Advokats paid 2,965,760 rubles from its own special fund for Article 50 legal advice in civil matters.

The existence of a special fund to which advokat formations not participating in Article 51 assignments contribute is among the principal ways in which the chambers of advokats comply with their statutory duties in this respect.

(6) The remuneration to be paid to advokats each year for rendering legal services free of charge is an agenda item routinely in all chambers of advokats. The Chamber of Advokats of Moscow Region appropriated on 27 January 2010 an additional 1,500,000 rubles for remuneration to advokats who rendered legal services free of charge which enabled the daily rates for such services to be increased.

(7) The council of a chamber of advokats finds itself acting in a representative capacity with respect to its membership in relations with State agencies in a number of respects. Chambers of advokats have negotiated with State financial agencies concerning arrears in payments to advokats for performing legal services by assignment of agencies of inquiry or preliminary investigation. Illegal searches of advokat premises or improper treatment of advokats who attempt to meet with their clients in custody have led to meetings being arranged between the council of a college of advokats and law enforcement agencies.

(8) Chambers of advokats operate a number of continuing legal education schemes for aides and apprentices of advokats, so-called "young advokats", and experienced advokats. These schemes, as a rule, figure in the annual reports submitted to the assembly or conference of a chamber of advokats. In the City of Moscow, for example, the Chamber of Advokats uses the Russian Academy of the Advokatura and the Russian Legal Academy of the Ministry of Justice of the Russian Federation for some of its programs, supplying both instructors and attendees. During the first year after receiving the status of advokat, in Moscow all advokats are required to complete a compulsory course entitled "Advokat Competence – Introduction to the Profession". The Council of Young Advokats in 2009 organized conferences and round tables on aspects of international arbitration and arbitrazh procedure.

(9) The President of the council is the initial recipient of complaints and submissions made with regard to disciplinary matters of an advokat. These he considers and decides whether to institute a disciplinary proceeding by making a referral to the qualifications commission for initial consideration. The council acts as an appellate instance from decisions of the qualifications commission with respect to disciplinary matters of advokats.

The Chamber of Advokats of the City of Moscow, for example, in 2009 received 700 complaints and submissions. The President of the Chamber instituted a disciplinary proceeding with regard to 155 of these (of which 35 were from judges) and transferred them to the qualifications commission for consideration. The proceedings were terminated in 86 of the 155 cases, primarily on the grounds that no violation of Russian legislation or the Code of Ethics had been committed. The most frequent complaints were that the rules for concluding contracts with the client had been violated, professional duties had been performed improperly, or disrespect had been displayed to the court.

(10) Chambers of advokats have become pro-active in defending the professional rights and interests of advokats and pursuing public relations campaigns to this end. The City of Moscow Chamber of Advokats, for example, prepared and published an explanation and opinion concerning the right of advokats not to be summoned as a witness by investigators or a court and materials concerning the immunity of advokats from the search and seizure of their records.

(11) Securing office space is a problem in Russia, especially in large urban centers. While advokat formations usually are successful in locating something suitable, this is not the case for legal consultation offices to which citizens apply for legal assistance rendered free of charge. The chambers of advokats will routinely negotiate with State and local authorities for accommodation that will be convenient for clients and seek rental subsidies from local government. In the City of Moscow, 65 advokat formations received rent deductions for premises supplied by the City or, in the case of commercial rentals, a subsidy that under Moscow legislation is indexed through the year 2012.

(12) Information provision takes two principal forms: a modern website maintained by each chamber of advokats in Russia; and, for the larger chambers of advokats, periodical press and monographs. The Chamber of Advokats of the City of Moscow publishes its own monthly Вестник Адвокатской палаты г. Москвы [Herald of the Chamber of Advokats of the City of Moscow] and co-sponsors the monthly professional journal Адвокат [Advokat], as well as issuing monographs on professional topics from time to time.

The principal organ of the Federal Chamber of Advokats is the Новая адвокатская газета [New Advokat Newspaper], whose print run is 3,000 copies per issue. The difficulties of establishing a printed organ in a market economy are well illustrated by the complaints of the Federal Chamber that as of 15 March 2010 many (18) chambers of advokats had not subscribed to the publication at all, only a few chambers had organized subscriptions among their constituents, and some chambers received one or two copies, but not more. In the Sakhalin, Tyva, and Saratov chambers of advokats not a single advokat subscribed, and each chamber itself only received one copy. No one subscribed in Ingushetia or Adygei at all. Single copies went to Karelia, Pskov Region, Novgorod, and Murmansk. Four subscriptions for the Amur Region, where there were 298 advokats, and so on.

(13) "Methods activity" is a broad term which encompasses a variety of measures directed towards assisting advokats master or complete certain tasks. A common manifestation of such activity is the publication of "Methods Instructions" on particular topics.

(14) See Article 31 above and Commentary.

(15) "Dispose" in this context means conclude transactions with respect to and requires that such transactions be foreseen and provided for in the annual estimate of the chamber of advokats. On 27 January 2010, for example, the Moscow Region Chamber of Advokats sought authorization from the annual conference for the council to "spend monetary means necessary for the purchase of a land plot under the building of the Chamber of Advokats of Moscow region, relegating the said expenses to the item "Miscellaneous and Unforeseen Expenses" of the budget. If the funds available under that item were insufficient, authorization was requested to use "economies arising under other items of the estimate". The authorization was granted.

(16) The reference here is to reglaments that operate as rules of procedure for the commissions concerned. The personnel establishment is incorporated in the yearly estimate for revenues and expenses of the chamber of advokats.

(17) The remuneration paid varies from one chamber of advokats to another, depending upon their size and resources. In the Moscow Region Chamber of Advokats members of the council received, in 2010, 6,500 rubles per month. Members of the qualifications commission were paid 6,500 rubles per session. For the year 2009 members of the internal audit commission were given a bonus of 5,000 rubles each.

(18) Although advokats are registered with the territorial justice agency, the advokat formations that exist on the territory of a chamber of advokats are registered with the said chamber. The numbers which they report annually may be regarded as conclusive and exhaustive, except insofar as formations may not have bothered to register. Occasional complaints suggest that such instances are not unknown, albeit infrequent.

The City of Moscow Chamber of Advokats reported that as of 1 January 2010 there were 2,044 advokat formations in the City: 412 colleges of advokats; 219 advokat bureaus, and 1,413 advokat cabinets. This was an increase of 170 over the calendar year 2008.

(19) Explanations are given as required and routinely published on the websites of chambers of advokats and/or in the printed media. Some chambers of advokats publish the explanations issued by other chambers as guidance to their own membership.

4. This subpoint was introduced by amendment in 2004 to create a reserve position for the Federal Chamber of Advokats in the event that a chamber of advokats failed to comply with its statutory obligations or decisions of the Federal Chamber of Advokats. The present Commentator is unaware of any use of the powers granted herein.

5. This sub-point sets a statutory minimum for the frequency of council meetings and establishes a quorum of two-thirds for valid business to be conducted.

6. No business before a council requires a qualified majority of votes, a policy reflective of "advokat democracy", although not necessarily typical of juridical persons.

7. The legal capacity of the president of the council of a chamber of advokats is in effect set out in sub-point 7 of the present Article. The formulation is exhaustive; nothing is said about adding additional powers for the president to exercise, although in practice decisions of the council routinely assign the president to undertake additional duties.

The Charter of the Moscow Region Council of Advokats is not untypical in placing specific and general powers additionally upon its president. The Charter (point 5.20.7.) provides that "additional powers of the President shall be determined by decision of the Council of the Chamber". The present Law does not authorize this possibility of enlarging the powers of the president and is arguably inconsistent with the special legal capacity of a chamber of advokats.

The additional powers exercised by a president of the council of a chamber of advokats include: organizing and planning the work of the council and ensuring that preparations are made for the consideration of questions at sessions of the council; presiding at council sessions; disposing of credits within the confirmed estimate; corresponding in the name of the council with State agencies, enterprises, institutions, organizations, and individual citizens; directing the work of the apparatus of the council, and exercising supervision over the execution of decisions adopted by the assembly or conference or by the council of the chamber. The president also serves *ex officio* as chairman of the qualifications commission.

The president may delegate some of his powers and duties to his vice presidents and/or other members of the council.

At least one vice president is elected by the council of a chamber of advokats from among its membership. The president recommends the candidacies for vice president. In the absence of the president, a vice president acts in his place on the basis of a power of attorney.

The present Law does not determine under what circumstances the powers of the president or vice president terminate. The Charter of the Moscow Region Chamber of Advokats enumerates seven instances in which termination occurs (points 5.21 and 5.22): by personal resignation; expiry of term of office; death; impossibility of performing the duties of the office for more than four months; termination of the status of advokat; change of membership in a chamber of advokats; and termination of membership in the council of the chamber of advokats as provided under the Charter. A vice president, in addition, loses his office when a president is re-elected, although if a re-elected president so chooses, he may nominate a vice president for a new term.

8. The officers and members of the council of a chamber of advokats are not prohibited *ex officio* from engaging in advokat activity. They are remunerated for their service on the council. In Moscow Region the remuneration of council members for the calendar year 2010 was 6,500 rubles per month. No distinction was drawn in the decision adopted by the conference of advokats of Moscow Region between officers and ordinary members of the council with respect to remuneration.

9. The formulation of sub-point 9 of the present Article replicates that of Article 29(10) above. Since the council does not enjoy separate legal personality from the chamber of advokats, the formulation seems inappropriate. At best, the council could undertake any advokat activity solely in the name of the chamber of which it is an organ, were it permitted to do so.

ARTICLE 32 INTERNAL AUDIT COMMISSION

1. *In order to effectuate control over the financial-economic activity of a chamber of advokats and its organs an internal audit commission shall be elected from among the advokats, information concerning which shall be included in the regional register of the respective subject of the Russian Federation.*
2. *The internal audit commission shall be accountable concerning the results of its activity to the assembly (or conference) of advokats.*
3. *Members of the internal audit commission may combine work in the internal audit commission with advokat activity, receiving in so doing remuneration for work on the internal audit commission in the amount determined by the council of the chamber of advokats. Members of the internal audit commission shall not have the right to occupy other elective office in a chamber of advokats [as amended by Federal Law of 20 December 2004].*

1. The internal audit commission originated in the Soviet period as an institution typically formed on the basis of legislation in State enterprises. It was a form of worker participation in and supervision over management. The institution has been retained in the post-Soviet period and is commonly found in Russian State and private juridical persons, although not, as a rule, in those with foreign investments. The Federal Law on Noncommercial Organizations makes no specific reference to the internal audit commission.

The internal audit commission is elected by the assembly or conference of advokats each year for a one-year term of office. The members must come from the chamber of advokats. The Moscow Region Chamber of Advokats elects five persons each year to the internal audit commission. The regional register of advokats includes information about the internal audit commission.

2. The internal audit commission is accountable, and reports annually, to the assembly or conference which elected it. Members of the commission are required to familiarize themselves with the documentation of the chamber of advokats reflecting the financial and economic activity of the chamber. Neither the council of the chamber nor workers in the apparatus of the chamber have the right to refuse to provide documents to members of the commission.

The internal audit commission verifies whether the expenses of the chamber of advokats for the maintenance of the apparatus of the council of the chamber of advokats, legal consultation offices, payment of remuneration to council members, internal audit commission members, and members of the qualifications commission, and additional remuneration to advokats rendering legal services free of charge or by assignment, and other expenses made by the chamber of advokats or its organs conform to the estimate. The internal audit commission is not concerned with the financial operations of advokat formations themselves except the legal consultation offices. The president of the council is responsible for ensuring that the requests made by members of the internal audit commission for materials are met.

The internal audit commission as a whole may request that an external audit be conducted by an independent auditor or accounting firm. One-third of the membership of a chamber of advokats may also insist on an external audit. The choice of external auditor is made by the chairman of the internal audit commission. The report of the internal audit commission and the opinion of an external auditor are read out at the assembly or conference of advokats and appended to the protocol of the meeting. The Charter of the Moscow Region Chamber of Advokats requires that the report of the internal audit commission be confirmed by the assembly or conference (point 6.6). Nothing is said about the consequences if the assembly or conference refuses to confirm the report.

3. Members of an internal audit commission may not hold other elective office within the chamber of advokats while serving on the commission. In many chambers of advokats they receive no remuneration whatsoever for the service on the commission, although the present Law allows remuneration to be paid to them. This is perhaps a reflection of the Soviet period, when members of such commissions did serve on a voluntary basis and the time spent on their internal audit assignments was set off against their normal work hours.

The practice in the Moscow Region Chamber of Advokats is not to pay members of the internal audit commission, but to reward them with a bonus each year for their "active activity". In the calendar year 2009 the bonus for each commission member was 5,000 rubles.

ARTICLE 33 QUALIFICATIONS COMMISSION

1. *A qualifications commission shall be created for giving qualifications examinations to persons applying for conferment of the status of advokat, and also for the consideration of appeals against the actions (or failure to act) of advokats.*
2. *A qualifications commission shall be formed for a term of two years in the quantity of 13 members of the commission according to the following norms of representation:*
   (1) from the chamber of advokats – seven advokats, including the president of the chamber of advokats of the subject of the Russian Federation. In so doing an advokat-member of the commission must have experience of advokat activity of not less than five years [as amended by Federal Law of 20 December 2004];
   (2) from the territorial justice agency – two representatives;
   (3) from the legislative (or representative) agency of State power of a subject of the Russian Federation – two representatives. In so doing the representatives may not be deputies or State or municipal employees. The procedure for the selection of the said representatives and requirements for them shall be determined by laws of subjects of the Russian Federation;
   (4) from the supreme court of the republic, territory or regional court, court of city of federal significance, court of autonomous region, and court of national autonomous area – one judge;
   (5) from an arbitrazh court of the subject of the Russian Federation – one judge;
3. *The president of the chamber of advokats shall be chairman ex officio of the qualifications commission.*
4. *A qualifications commission shall be considered to be formed and empowered to adopt decisions when there are present in its membership not less than two thirds of the number of members of the qualifications commission provided for by the present point.*
5. *Sessions of the qualifications commission shall be convoked by the chairman of the qualifications commission as necessary, but not less than four times a year. A session shall be considered to be empowered if not less than two thirds of the members of the qualifications commission are present at it.*
   Decisions adopted by a qualifications commission shall be formalized by a protocol which shall be signed by the chairman and secretary. If when voting a member of the qualifications commission has a special opinion differing from the decision adopted by the majority of votes of members of the qualifications commission present at the session, the said opinion shall be submitted in written form and attached to the protocol of the session [added by Federal Law of 20 December 2004].
6. *Decisions of the qualifications commission with regard to the question of the taking of qualifications examinations by persons applying for conferment of the status of*

advokat shall be adopted by a simple majority of votes of members of the qualifications commission participating in the session thereof by means of voting by inscribed ballots. The form of the ballot shall be confirmed by the council of the federal chamber of advokats. The ballots for voting, texts of written replies to questions (or testing) shall be attached to the protocol of the session of the qualifications commission and kept in the documentation of the chamber of advokats as stationary of strict accountability for three years. The decision of the qualifications commission shall be announced to the applicant immediately after the voting [as amended by Federal Law of 20 December 2004] .

7. *A qualifications commission shall give an opinion with regard to the results of consideration of an appeal concerning the presence or absence in the actions (or failure to act) of an advokat of a violation of the norms of the Code of Professional Ethics of the Advokat or the failure to perform or improper performance by him of his duties.*
   The opinion of the qualifications commission shall be adopted by a simple majority of votes of members of the qualifications commission participating in its session by means of voting by inscribed ballots. The form of the ballot shall be confirmed by the council of the Federal Chamber of Advokats. The advokat and the person who appealed against the actions (or failure to act) of an advokat shall have the right to an objective and just consideration of the appeal. The said persons shall have the right to involve an advokat for consideration of the appeal at his choice [as amended by Federal Law of 20 December 2004].
8. *Advokat-members of a qualifications commission may combine work on the qualifications commission with advokat activity, receiving remuneration in so doing for work on the qualifications commission in the amount determined by the council of the chamber of advokats [as amended by Federal Law of 20 December 2004].*

1. The qualifications commission of a chamber of advokats is principally concerned with two matters: (1) administering qualifications examinations to persons who wish to acquire the status of advokat; and (2) considering complaints against advokats and offering opinions and recommendations with regard to these, that is, in effect administering disciplinary proceedings.

However, the qualifications commission is not an organ of the chamber of advokats. It is rather a body attached to a chamber of advokats whose membership consists only partly of advokats. Although reports are made to the assembly or conference of advokats on certain aspects of the commission activities, the commission is not accountable to the chamber of advokats.

Under the 1980 RSFSR Statute on the Advokatura the functions of the qualifications commission were placed on the presidium of the colleges of advokats. However, in the 1990s many colleges created autonomous qualifications commissions from their own membership and removed this responsibility from the Presidium.

2. The numerical membership of a qualifications commission is established by the present Article. Advokats comprise a simple majority (seven places, including the president of the chamber of advokats *ex officio*). Accordingly, every two years each chamber of advokats must elect six advokats from among its members to serve on the commission.

(1) The formulation of the experience required to serve on the qualifications commission is of interest here. Reference is made not to the status of advokat for a period of five years, but to experience of being an advokat, which implies an advokat who is active in rendering legal services to clients.

(2) Two members of the commission are chosen by the territorial justice agency. In the instance of the Moscow Region Chamber of Advokats, these are individuals from the Chief Administration of the Federal Registration Service of Moscow Region.

(3) The legislative organ of the subject of the Russian Federation in which the chamber of advokats exists provides two representatives on the qualifications commission. In the instance of Moscow Region, the representatives come from the Moscow Regional Duma.

The subjects of the Russian Federation determine in their own legislation how the two representatives on the qualifications commission are to be selected. In the City of Moscow, for example, this determination is made under the Law of the City of Moscow of 23 October 2002, No. 52, "On Representatives of the Moscow City Duma on the Qualifications Commission attached to the Chamber of Advokats of the City of Moscow". Such representatives must be citizens of the Russian Federation who have a higher legal education and work experience in a legal specialty of not less than five years. Persons excluded by this Law from serving as representatives are enumerated: (1) deputies of legislative (or representative) agencies of State power and agencies of local self-government; (2) State and municipal employees; (3) persons deemed by a court to lack or be limited in dispositive legal capacity; (4) persons registered in neurological or psychological dispensaries; and (5) persons having an uncancelled or unremoved record of conviction for a crime. Each deputy of the Moscow City Duma may nominate a candidacy to serve on the commission. Other subjects of the Russian Federation have similar legislation.

(4) The judicial representative comes from one of the courts of ordinary jurisdiction serving the relevant subject of the Russian Federation. For the Moscow Region one judge acts from the Moscow Regional Court. It is remarked upon in Russian doctrinal writings that while a judge serves on the qualifications commission for advokats, advokats do not serve on the qualifications commissions for judges.

(5) A judge from the arbitrazh court of Moscow Region is the relevant judicial agency for these purposes.

Placing non-advokats on the qualifications commissions was not a measure greeted by widespread acclaim in advokat circles. As experience has accumulated with the practice, however, many advokats believe the mixed qualifications commissions have proved themselves and contributed to a lessening of tension between the profession and the State and judicial agencies.

3. In his *ex officio* capacity the president of the chamber of advokats is the seventh advokat member of the qualifications commission and acts as the chairman of the commission.

4. Point 4 establishes the minimum appointees necessary for the qualifications commission to be empowered to take decisions. Two-thirds of thirteen members means that a minimum of nine must be designated (some sources suggest ten members). If the agencies that have the right to place members on the qualifications commission are delayed or negligent in doing so, the commission is able to operate with at least nine members in place.

5. Point 5 addresses a different issue, namely, the minimum number of commission members who must be present for the commission to be quorate. The percentage quorum required is two-thirds, but the precise number will depend upon how many members have been appointed. Assuming that at least nine have been appointed, then six would need to be present at a meeting for the qualifications commission to be able to adopt decisions.

The chairman of the commission convokes sessions in accordance with the Reglament of the qualifications commission.

The qualifications commission must be convoked at least four times a year. In the calendar year 2009 the qualifications commission of the Moscow Region Chamber of Advokats held 22 sessions.

Decisions adopted by a qualifications commission are recorded in a protocol which is signed by the president and secretary of the commission. A "special", or dissenting, opinion may be submitted in written form by any commission member who wishes this to be recorded as an attachment to the protocol of the meeting.

6. As noted above, the qualifications commission takes in principle two kinds of decisions. In this point the basic procedures are set out for adopting decisions with regard to candidates who have taken the qualifications examination for the status of advokat. On these matters the members vote in the presence of the candidate by using a standard ballot whose form is confirmed by the council of the chamber of advokats and signing their ballot (inscribed ballot). On the ballot the commission members check either "pass" or "fail". A simple majority of the quorum present is sufficient; no abstentions are possible, but a dissenting member may write a special opinion which will be attached to the protocol of the meeting. In the event of a tie vote, the candidate is deemed to have passed. The ballots themselves are appended to the protocol, as are the written test results of each candidate. These materials are retained in the files for three years. The decision of the commission is disclosed orally

to the candidate immediately after being adopted and formal notification in writing follows shortly afterwards.

In Moscow Region during the calendar year 2009 twelve of the 22 sessions of the qualifications commission were devoted to examinations (second stage – conversations with applicants). 412 persons applied to take the qualifications examination; 264 actually appeared to sit. 79 did not complete the examination (10 the computer element; 69 the oral component). Of those who applied in 2009, 62 actually sat the examination in 2010. One-third of the applicants for the examination were aides or apprentices of advokats in the Moscow Region.

In Moscow Region the numbers of applications from aides and apprentices were twice so numerous that the receipt of applications from others was suspended. Complaints also were received about inadequate computer facilities in remote parts of the Region. Applications in Moscow Region are received in accordance with the Reglament Establishing the Procedure for Registration on the List of Candidates for Filing Documents for Admittance to the Qualifications Examination for Conferment of the Status of Advokat, confirmed by the Council of the Chamber of Advokats of Moscow Region on 15 September 2010.[48]

The examination consists of two stages: computer testing and an oral examination. On the computer each applicant must answer 50 questions chosen at random by the computer from 150. The candidate has 30 minutes to answer at least 40 of these correctly. A successful candidate then passes on to the second stage, the oral examination. The oral examinations are held on days determined by the chairman of the commission, but not less than seven times per year in Moscow Region. During the oral examination, each candidate is given a "ticket" containing four questions chosen by the commission at its discretion from among the list of questions approved by the Council of the Federal Chamber of Advokats. The questions eligible for inclusion are published in advance on the website.

A candidate appearing for the oral examination first submits identity documents and then selects an examination "ticket" from among those lying upside down on a table. He then has at least 45 minutes to reflect on the questions and prepare his replies in his head. All four questions must be answered by the candidate, and the commission may put supplementary questions from the approved list. The candidate must successfully answer all four questions. The failure to pass one question is a failure on the examination.

If the candidate fails the examination, or if the candidate fails to appear for the examination without a justifiable reason, a year must elapse before the candidate will be admitted to the examination a second time.

48 Decision of the Council of the Chamber of Advokats of Moscow Region, No. 9/23-4, 15 September 2010; available on the website of the Chamber.

7. Point 7 addresses the voting procedures of the qualifications commission in disciplinary matters, normally based upon a formal allegation in the form of a complaint or appeal that an advokat has not performed his professional duties properly or has violated the Code of Professional Ethics of an Advokat. On 1 March 2007 it was determined by Ruling of the Constitutional Court of the Russian Federation, No. 293-O-O,[49] that on 23 December 2003 a complaint had been received at the Moscow City Chamber of Advokats against an advokat requesting that the advokat be deprived of the status of advokat. On 17 September 2004 the Qualifications Commission determined that proceedings in the matter should be terminated because more than six months had elapsed since the alleged offense was committed. On 7 October 2004 the disciplinary proceeding was terminated for this reason. An appeal to a court against the termination of the disciplinary proceeding was initially rejected for failure to pay State duty and eventually the courts ruled against the appellant. The Constitutional Court eventually rejected the petition on the grounds there was no constitutional issue to be decided.

On 15 July 2008 the Constitutional Court of the Russian Federation, in Ruling No. 456-O-O, rejected the view of two advokats that a special ruling issued by a court under the Code of Criminal Procedure (Article 29[4]) in connection with a criminal proceeding prejudices their rights under the Constitution (Article 55) as a law diminishing their rights and freedoms. The Constitutional Court observed that a special ruling did not have the force of *res judicata* for the chamber of advokats to which the special ruling was referred and declined further proceedings in the case.[50]

During the calendar year 2009 the qualifications commission of the Moscow Region Chamber of Advokats devoted ten sessions to the consideration of 400 disciplinary proceedings instituted with respect to advokats on the basis of complaints or appeals files by clients, vice presidents of the chamber, justice agencies, and courts. Opinions were submitted with respect to all 400 proceedings and decisions taken by the council of the chamber.

On disciplinary matters the qualifications commission is required to offer in the form of an opinion a finding as to whether an advokat did or did not act in violation of the Code of Professional Ethics of an Advokat or did or did not perform his professional duties property. A simple majority vote is required by commission members present. Abstentions are not possible. An opinion dissenting from the majority may be appended in writing to the protocol of the session. The ballots are appended to the protocol and kept in the archive of the chamber of advokats. The results of the voting are not immediately disclosed to the parties.

49 Unpublished. Available on Consultant Plus.
50 Unpublished. Available on Consultant Plus.

8. Membership on the qualifications commission is not a full time position; indeed, six members are non-advokats employed elsewhere. The advokat members of the commission are accordingly permitted to engage in advokat activity.

In Moscow Region members of the qualifications commission were granted remuneration of 6,500 rubles per session of the commission.

Article 34 Property of Chamber of Advokats

1. *Property of a chamber of advokats shall be formed at the expense of deductions effectuated by advokats for the common needs of the chamber of advokats and grants and philanthropic assistance (donations) received from juridical and natural persons in the procedure established by legislation of the Russian Federation. A chamber of advokats shall be the owner of the particular property.*
2. *To expenditures for common needs of a chamber of advokats shall be relegated expenses for the remuneration of advokats working in organs of the chamber of advocates, contributory compensation to these advokats of expenses connected with their work in the said organs, expenses for earnings of workers of the apparatus of the chamber of advokats, material provision for the activity of the chamber of advokats, and by decision of the council of the chamber of advokats – expenses for the payment of labor of advokats rendering legal assistance to citizens of the Russian Federation free of charge, and other expenses provided for by the estimate of the chamber of advokats [as amended by Federal Law of 20 December 2004].*

1. Point one addresses the revenue dimension of a chamber of advokats and the legal capacity of the chamber to be the owner of property received or acquired as revenue.

The deductions levied by a chamber of advokats upon its member advokats are determined each year at the assembly or conference of the chamber. In Moscow Region for the calendar year 2010 advokats were required to pay 540 rubles per month by automatic bank transfer towards the common needs of the chamber. The amounts were adjusted to take account of a month in which an advokat acquired, renewed, suspended, or otherwise changed his status of advokat. Failure to comply is grounds for a disciplinary proceeding against the advokat. In addition, advokats upon whom the status of advokat was conferred after 27 January 2010 in Moscow Region were required to make a one-off payment of 5,000 rubles to be directed towards the expenditures of the Moscow Region Chamber on professional training. Certain members of the chamber were exempted from the compulsory deductions (World War II veterans, women on pregnancy or birth leave, advokats with more than 40 years experience in the Advokatura, certain categories of disabled persons, and others).

In the St. Petersburg Chamber of Advokats 21 members were deprived of their status of advokat in 2009 for their failure to pay the monthly deductions towards common needs of the chamber.

Some chambers of advokats had introduced during the 1990s and later the practice of entry fees payable before sitting the qualifications examination. In an Explanation issued on 22 April 2004, the Federal Chamber of Advokats declared this practice to be "inadmissible". However, chambers of advokats, in the view of the Federal Cham ber, might levy one-off or special-purpose deductions on newly-admitted members of a chamber – a right which flowed from the "organizational-legal form" of a chamber of advokats as "a non-State noncommercial organization" provided that these deductions were "within reasonable limits".

The fees imposed for sitting the qualifications examination are regarded as a contribution towards expenses of the chamber of advokats in providing premises, computers, lecturers for the preparatory sessions, and similar overheads, on condition that these fees are "insignificant in amount" and not an obstacle to applicants acquiring the status of advokat.

From time to time individual colleges of advokats in the Russian Federation have received grants from Russian and foreign foundations or other sources in connection with law reform assistance programs.

The special legal capacity of a chamber of advokats is reinforced by the stipulation that the chamber of advokats is the owner of property received by it in the form of deductions from member advokats or philanthropic sources. Insofar as grants and donations originate in organizations founded for scientific and educational purposes, they may qualify for tax relief under the Tax Code of the Russian Federation.

Other revenues consistent with the charter purposes of a chamber of advokats and not contrary to federal legislation on noncommercial organizations may be legitimately received by a chamber of advokats. Property may be transferred to the chamber in kind (equipment, premises, rights of use, and so on) or in the form of money. If a chamber of advokats is liquidated, the property of the chamber would not be distributed among the members of the chamber. Advokat members have no property interest in the property of the chamber, including in the amounts of their monthly deductions. Any disposition of property must be made by organs of the chamber of advokats on the basis of the estimate confirmed annually by the assembly or conference of advokats.

The revenues of legal consultation offices created by a chamber of advokats are not part of the chamber revenues. These offices are juridical persons having their own revenues and expenditures.

2. The expense dimension of a chamber of advokats is itemized in advance for each year in the "estimate" approved by the assembly or conference of the chamber of advokats. The word "estimate" should be understood in English as a "budget", although that term is not used in Russian for this purpose. An estimate is confirmed for both the revenue and the expenditure aspects of chamber activities.

The assembly or conference of a chamber of advokats confirms the revenue and expenditure portions of the estimate as a whole and, for certain line items, individually.

In Moscow Region, for example, the 2010 estimate required special confirmation for allocating advokat deductions to professional training expenses and a special appropriation to remunerate advokats additionally for work performed free of charge or under assignment from courts and investigative agencies. Authorization to acquire a land plot also required a special decision.

Article 35 Federal Chamber of Advokats of Russian Federation

1. *The Federal Chamber of Advokats of the Russian Federation shall be an all-Russian non-State noncommercial organization uniting the chambers of advokats of subjects of the Russian Federation on the basis of obligatory membership [as amended by Federal Law of 20 December 2004].*
2. *The Federal Chamber of Advokats as an organ of advokat self-government in the Russian Federation shall be created for the purpose of representation and defense of the interests of advokats in agencies of State power and agencies of local self-government, coordination of the activity of chambers of advokats, and ensuring a high level of legal assistance rendered by advokats.*
   The Federal Chamber of Advokats shall be an organization empowered to represent the interests of advokats and chambers of advokats of subjects of the Russian Federation in relations with federal agencies of State power when deciding questions affecting the interests of the advokat community, including questions connected with the allocation of means of the federal budget for the payment of labor of advokats participating in a criminal proceeding as defenders upon the assignment of agencies of inquiry, agencies of preliminary investigation, or court [added by Federal Law of 20 December 2004, as amended by Federal Law of 24 July 2007].
3. *The Federal Chamber of Advokats shall be a juridical person, have an estimate, settlement and other accounts in banks in accordance with legislation of the Russian Federation, seal, stamps, and letterheads with its own name.*
4. *The Federal Chamber of Advokats shall be formed by the All-Russian Congress of Advokats. The formation of other organizations and agencies with functions and powers analogous to the functions and powers of the Federal Chamber of Advokats shall not be permitted.*
5. *The Charter of the Federal Chamber of Advokats shall be adopted by the All-Russian Congress of Advokats.*
6. *The Federal Chamber of Advokats shall be subject to State registration in the procedure established by the Federal Law on the State Registration of Juridical Persons.*

6^1. *The Federal Chamber of Advokats shall not be subject to reorganization. The liquidation of the Federal Chamber of Advokats may be effectuated only on the basis of a federal law [added by Federal Law of 20 December 2004].*

7. *Decisions of the Federal Chamber of Advokats and its organs adopted within the limits of their competence shall be binding upon all chambers of advokats and advokats.*

1. The Federal Chamber of Advokats is the first professional organization in the history of the Russian Advokatura to combine all advokats throughout the country into a single organization at the federal level. All chambers of advokats are required to be members of the Federal Chamber, which is in essence an association of chambers of advokats created to advance the collective interests of advokats.

Once the present Law was enacted, the chambers of advokats of the subjects of the Russian Federation were created, one chamber in each subject. Delegates to the I All-Russian Congress of Advokats were elected by each chamber.

The legal status of the Federal Chamber of Advokats is regulated by the present Article. The concept of "all-Russian" means here that the Federal Chamber is the sole agency of federal significance on the territory of the Russian Federation which operates in this field of activity. Non-State here means that the Federal Chamber is independent from the State, has no financial support from the State, and presumably is not subject to influence or pressure from the State. Noncommercial refers to the status of the Federal Chamber pursuant to the Civil Code of the Russian Federation (Article 50) and the Federal Law on Noncommercial Organizations of 12 January 1996, as amended.

Individual advokats as natural persons are not members of the Federal Chamber. They contribute each month towards the expenses of the Federal Chamber through sums paid into the accounts of the chambers of advokats. Consequently, the Federal Chamber may be said to represent the interests of individual advokats indirectly through the chambers of advokats to which each natural person having the status of advokat belongs.

2. This point emphasizes two principal functions of the Federal Chamber of Advokats: representation of advokat interests through the chamber of advokats of the subjects of the Federation and the defense of advokat interests in agencies of State power and local self-government. The representation function is formal and informal. The Federal Chamber of Advokats engages extensively in lobbying on behalf of advokats in governmental and legislative corridors and on occasion has issued formal documents intended to influence the behavior of law enforcement agencies and courts. The Federal Chamber comments on draft legislation, submits its own preferred versions of draft enactments for discussion, and has negotiated with central and regional authorities to encourage the prompt payment of arrears in fees own to advokats for the provision of legal services on assignment.

On 25 August 2003 the Council of the Federal Chamber confirmed the Statute of the Representative of the Council – Deputy President of the Federation Chamber of Advokats of the Russian Federation in a Federal District. Such representatives are directly subordinate and accountable to the Council and to the President of the Federal Chamber. The principal tasks of the Representative include: (1) representation of the Council of the Federal Chamber in the respective federal district; (2) organizing interaction with territorial justice agencies, agencies of State power of subjects of the Federation, agencies of local self-government, social associations, and other organizations; (3) organizing work to implement decisions of the Federal Chamber, All-Russian Congresses of Advokats, , chambers of advokats, and advokat formations in the respective federal district; (4) coordinating the activities of chambers of advokats in the federal district on the basis of decisions taken by the Council and President of the Federal Chamber; and helping chambers of advokats comply with their duty to send monthly deductions for the maintenance of the Federal Chamber.

The Representative has office accommodation in the center of the federal district in which he serves. Under certain circumstances he may have an aide to assist in performing his duties.

The subject-matter of the activity of the Federal Chamber is elaborated in its Charter (Article 21) and includes: (1) uniting advokats in a professional organization and coordinating the activities of chambers of advokats; (2) promoting the recognition, compliance with, and defense of human rights and freedoms; (3) interacting with legislative and executive agencies and the Ministry of Justice of the Russian Federation; (4) participating in the expert examination of draft federal laws and laws of subject of the Federation relating to advokat activity and the Advokatura; (5) maintaining an information data base for members of the Federal Chamber; (6) promoting continuing legal education for advokats, apprentices, and aides; (7) establishing uniform norms for the professional ethics of advokats; (8) forming unified principles and criteria for the work of qualifications commissions; (9) establishing the procedure for admittance to the qualifications examination and assessing the knowledge of applicants; (10) taking measures to eliminate unfair competition in advokat activity; (11) analyzing normative acts and making proposals for their improvement; (12) establishing and developing links with international and foreign organizations of attorneys; (13) participating in the work of various international organizations; (14) representing the interests of advokats and advokat chambers in relations with the Government of the Russian Federation with regard to remuneration for legal services; and (15) performing other tasks provided by the Charter and not contrary to Russian legislation.

3. The Charter of the Federal Chamber reiterates point 3 of the present Law but adds that bank accounts may be opened abroad as well as in Russia. The Federal Chamber was registered as a juridical person in accordance with the 2001 Federal Law "On the State Registration of Juridical Persons".

4. The decision to form the Federal Chamber was taken by the I All-Russian Congress of Advokats held on 31 January 2003. The full legal name of the Federal Chamber is

the "All-Russian Non-State Noncommercial Organization 'Federal Chamber of Advokats of the Russian Federation'". The Federal Chamber is located in the City of Moscow and was created for an indefinite period.

The Federal Chamber enjoys a monopoly position with respect to its role and membership. The present Law expressly prohibits the formation of other organizations and agencies to perform similar functions.

5. The Charter of the Federal Chamber was adopted by the I All-Russian Congress of Advokats on 31 January 2003. Changes were made to the Charter on 8 April 2005 and 5 April 2007.

6. The Federal Chamber was duly registered pursuant to the 2001 Federal Law "On the State Registration of Juridical Persons".

6[1]. The prohibition against a reorganization of the Federal Chamber represents an exception from the Federal Law on Noncommercial Organizations. In effect, it means that if the Federal Chamber wishes to undergo reorganization, it would need first to seek a change in the present Law before doing so. A liquidation would need to proceed in accordance with the 2002 Federal Law on Bankruptcy (or Insolvency)[51] and the Charter of the Federal Chamber (Article 53). If the Federal Chamber were to be liquidated, under its Charter any property remaining after the demands of creditors had been satisfied would be directed, unless established otherwise by a federal law, to the interests for which it was created and/or for philanthropic purposes.

The remaining property would not be distributed among the chambers of advokats or among the advokats.

7. Since membership of all chambers of advokats in the Federal Chamber is compulsory and dictated by the present Law, it follows that decisions of the Federal Chamber or its organs are binding upon the members of the Federal Chamber provided that such decisions adopted are within the competence of the Federal Chamber. Issues of competence may be appealed to a court.

Article 36 All-Russian Congress of Advokats

1. *The highest organ of the Federal Chamber of Advokats shall be the All-Russian Congress of Advokats. The Congress shall be convoked not less than once in two years. The Congress shall be considered to be empowered if representatives of not less*

51 СЗ РФ (2002), no. 43, item 4190, as amended; transl. in W. E. Butler, *Russian Commercial and Company Law* (2003), pp. 366-543.

than two-thirds of chambers of advokats of subjects of the Russian Federation take part in its work [as amended by Federal Law of 20 December 2004].

Chambers of advokats shall have equal rights and equal representation in the Congress. Each chamber of advokats shall irrespective of the number of its representatives have one vote when adopting decisions [added by Federal Law of 20 December 2004].

2. *The All-Russian Congress of Advokats shall:*
   (1) *adopt the Charter of the Federal Chamber of Advokats and confirm the making of changes in and additions thereto [as amended by Federal Law of 20 December 2004] ;*
   (2) *adopt the Code of Professional Ethics of an Advokat; confirm the making of changes in and additions thereto [as amended by Federal Law of 20 December 2004];*
   (3) *form the composition of the Council of the Federal Chamber of Advokats, including elect new members and terminate powers of members of the Council subject to replacement in accordance with the procedure of renewal (or rotation) of the Council provided for by Article 37(2) of the present Federal Law, adopt decisions concerning the termination of powers before time of members of the Council, and also confirm decisions of the Council concerning the termination before time of powers of members of the Council whose status of advokat was terminated or suspended [as amended by Federal Law of 20 December 2004];*
   (4) *determine the amount of deductions from chambers of advokats for common needs of the Federal Chamber of Advokats by proceeding from the number of chambers of advokats;*
   (5) *confirm the estimate of expenses for the maintenance of the Federal Chamber of Advokats;*
   (6) *confirm reports of the Council of the Federal Chamber of Advokats, including execution of the estimate of expenses for maintenance of the Federal Chamber of Advokats;*
   (7) *elect the members of the internal audit commission of the Federal Chamber of Advokats for a term of two years and confirm its report concerning the results of financial-economic activity of the Council of the Federal Chamber of Advokats [as amended and renumbered by Federal Law of 20 December 2004];*
   (8) *confirm the reglament of the Congress [as amended by Federal Law of 20 December 2004];*
   (9) *determine the location of the Council of the Federal Chamber of Advokats;*
   (10) *effectuate other functions provided for by the Charter of the Federal Chamber of Advokats.*

1. The existence of the Federal Chamber of Advokats represents the culmination of a campaign conducted for decades by some Russian advokats who resisted the decentralized nature of the Advokatura. To be sure, that campaign was conducted within the USSR, and not merely the Russian Federation. But those who favored a national

organization for advokats believed this would be helpful in consolidating the identity of the profession and in promoting professional standards.

Such a body never did exist in the former Soviet Union. In 1950 and again in 1986 an All-Union Meeting of Advokatura Leaders was convoked by the USSR Ministry of Justice to explore possibilities (without success), and later the Association of Soviet Jurists pursued the issue on a less formal level, likewise without success. The latter Association encompassed during its short existence the entire legal profession, not merely advokats, and existed specially to encourage further contacts with legal personnel abroad.

The Federal Chamber has under its Charter three organs of self-government: the All-Russian Congress of Advokats; the Council of the Federal Chamber; and the internal audit commission (Article 27). Of these, the Congress is the highest organ. It has met at two-year intervals commencing in January 2003; there have been so far no extraordinary meetings.

Although voting in the Congress is by chambers of advokats, of which there are presently 83 in the Russian Federation, the quorum for a Congress is two-thirds of the representatives of the 83 chambers of advokats are present, that is, 55 chambers of advokats.

2. The specific functions of the All-Russian Congress are prescribed in the present Article and in the Charter of the Federal Chamber. These in effect form the agenda of each Congress.

(1). The Charter was adopted by the I All-Russian Congress of Advokats on 31 January 2003 and operates as amended at the II and III congresses.

(2) The Code of Professional Ethics of an Advokat was adopted by the I All-Russian Congress of Advokats on 31 January 2003 and amended at the II All-Russian Congress on 8 April 2005 and at the III All-Russian Congress on 5 April 2007. The final text was based upon a study of the numerous codes of ethics previously adopted by colleges of advokats in Russia under the 1980 legislation, other CIS countries, and several foreign jurisdictions.

(3) To "form the composition" means to nominate and elect the individual members of the Council of the Federal Chamber and to replace or terminate the powers of members whose terms have expired or who otherwise can no longer serve on the Council of the Federal Chamber. The rotation procedures are set out in Article 37(2) of the present Law and Article 29 of the Charter of the Federal Chamber. The Charter of the Federal Chamber (Article 31) requires that not less than one-third of the Council of the Federal Chamber be renewed every two years.

(4) Each advokat in the Russian Federation pays the sum of 120 rubles per month for the common needs of the Federal Chamber by crediting this sum to the account of the chamber of advokats of a subject of the Federation to which they belong. This sum does not vary depending upon what date of the month an advokat becomes eligible to pay.

In an Explanation adopted by the Federal Chamber of Advokats on 10 December 2003, it was decided that an advokat whose status of advokat was suspended does not fall into the category of those for whom deductions must be made for the common needs of the Federal Chamber. The reasoning is that a decision to suspend the status of advokat taken by a chamber of advokats simultaneously entails the suspension of advokat activity. This deprives the person suspended from the possibility to receive remuneration and to pay the deductions from these revenues. Accordingly, the suspension of status of advokat also results in the suspension of membership in the chamber of advokats. When making payments to the Federal Chamber, the chambers of advokats should exclude from persons required to contribute to the common needs of the chamber of advokats any advokats whose status has been suspended.

(5) Because the All-Russian Congress meets at two-year intervals, the estimate must be confirmed for a similar period. The III All-Russian Congress (2007) confirmed an estimate for the calendar years 2007 and 2008 which on the revenue side amounted to 113,280,000 rubles. Arrears on monthly obligatory deductions from advokats amounted to 3,374,261 rubles, a deficit which was covered in part by the sale of a motor vehicle, bank interest, and other unplanned revenues. The ultimate deficit was 2,127,814 rubles.

On the expenditure side the amounts appropriated were under spent by 2,929,838 rubles, economies being made by curtailing scientific research and legislative drafting work, training seminars, and certain overheads. Unforeseen expenses were substantial for a move to a new premise, founding of the Federal Chamber newspaper, and the acquisition of furnishings.

(6) The Congress routinely hears and discusses the reports of the Council of the Federal Chamber concerning the estimate. Both the present Law and the Charter of the Federal Chamber fail to address the issue of what transpires if the Congress refuses to confirm the report.

(7) Although the present Law does not establish how many persons should be elected to the internal audit commission, neither does the Charter of the Federal Chamber. The annual reports of the Council of the Federal Chamber make no reference to an internal audit commission; the website of the Federal Chamber does not include this commission among the numerous commissions listed on the website; and there is otherwise no indication that such a commission exists or has ever existed within the Federal Chamber. The list of organs of the Federal Chamber makes no mention of an internal audit commission.

(8) The reglament of the Congress is a procedural document confirmed by the I All-Russian Congress and followed at subsequent congresses, subject to minor adjustments. An All-Russian Congress is considered to be quorate if not less than two-thirds of the Congress delegates are present. In addition to the delegates, representatives may be invited to the Congress from the executive, legislative, and judicial branches and leading law enforcement organizations and the mass media. All

decisions in the Congress are taken by a simple majority vote of the delegates. A protocol is kept of the meeting.

The registration of delegates to a Congress commences before the Congress opens in order to verify that the necessary minimum of delegates have been chosen. An additional registration occurs at the Congress itself based upon the confirmed list of expected delegates and the submission of identity documents by each delegate. The delegate certifies the information recorded about him and, under signature, receives the prepared ballots for agenda items together with a packet of prepared materials and a temporary identity document for the Congress. The registration group draws up a protocol concerning the registration results which must be signed by all members of the group.

The Congress is opened by the most senior delegate in age present at the Congress. The presence of a quorum is confirmed by the number of signatures of registered delegates. In the absence of a quorum, the organizers must fix a new date for the Congress. Once the quorum is determined, the Congress elects a presidium and a secretariat, the numerical size of which is determined by the Congress. The senior presiding advokat suggests who should be on the presidium. Once formed, the presidium elects the person(s) presiding from among their number.

The secretariat of the Congress comprises three elected advokat-delegates, who in turn choose their chairman. The secretariat is responsible for preparing the protocol of the Congress and supervises the technical personnel who undertake this task.

Once the presidium is formed, the reglament of the Congress is confirmed by the delegates and the credentials, counting, financial, and editorial commissions are formed. The presidium then organizes how the Congress proceeds and assists the person(s) presiding in performing their duties.

The Congress has imposed strict time limits on speeches and reports. Up to 10 minutes for the report on the agenda, oral comments up to 3 minutes; candidates for elective office up to 3 minutes; discussion of candidacies up to 1 minute, and replies to discussions, up to 1 minute. The Congress reserves the right to lengthen or reduce the time periods allotted.

Delegates have the right to speak and make proposals on issues being discussed, nominate themselves or others for working organs of the Congress and the Federal Chamber, recuse themselves if elected to working organs; speak on the same agenda issue not more than twice.

(9) The Council of the Federal Chamber is located in the City of Moscow, pursuant to the Charter of the Federal Chamber (Article 11).

(10) The Charter of the Federal Chamber imposes on the All-Russian Congress the duty to confirm the reglament of the Council of the Federal Chamber. The Congress did confirm the Reglament of the Council of the Federal Chamber of Advokats of the Russian Federation on 31 January 2003. There have been no changes, additions, or amendments to this Reglament.

Article 37 Council of Federal Chamber of Advokats

1. *The Council of the Federal Chamber of Advokats shall be the collegial executive organ of the Federal Chamber of Advokats.*
2. *The Council of the Federal Chamber of Advokats shall be elected by the All-Russian Congress of Advokats by secret ballot in a quantity of not more than 30 persons and shall be subject to renewal (or rotation) once every two years by one-third [as amended by Federal Law of 20 December 2004].*
   In the event of a regular rotation the president of the Federal Chamber of Advokats shall submit for consideration of the Council of the Federal Chamber of Advokats candidacies for members of the council for withdrawal, and also candidacies of advocates for filling vacant offices of members of the Council of the Federal Chamber of Advokats. After confirmation by the Council of the Federal Chamber of Advokats candidacies submitted by the president shall be submitted for consideration of the Congress for confirmation [added by Federal Law of 20 December 2004].
3. *The Council of the Federal Chamber of Advokats shall:*
   (1) elect from its composition the president of the Federal Chamber of Advokats for a term of four years and upon his recommendation one or several vice-presidents of the Federal Chamber of Advokats for a term of two years and determine the powers of the president and vice-presidents. In so doing the same person may not occupy the office of President of the Federal Chamber of Advokats more than two terms in succession [as amended by Federal Law of 20 December 2004];
   (2) in the interval between congresses adopt decisions concerning the termination before time of powers of members of the council, the status of an advokat of which has been terminated or suspended. The said decisions shall be submitted for confirmation of the next Congress [added by Federal Law of 20 December 2004];
   (3) represent the Federal Chamber of Advokats in agencies of State power, agencies of local self-government, social associations, and other Russian organizations and beyond the limits of the Russian Federation [as amended by Federal Law of 20 December 2004];
   (4) coordinate the activity of chambers of advokats;
   (5) promote the raising of the professional standard of advokats, work out a single method of professional training and retraining of advokats, aides of advokats, and trainees of advokats;
   (6) defend the social and professional rights of advokats;
   (7) participate in conducting an expert evaluation of draft federal laws with regard to questions relegated to advocate activity;
   (8) organize the informational provision of advokats;
   (9) summarize disciplinary practice existing in chambers of advokats and work out necessary recommendations in connection therewith [as amended by Federal Law of 20 December 2004];
   (10) effectuate methods activity [as amended by Federal Law of 20 December 2004];

(11) *convoke not less than once in two years the All-Russian Congress of Advokats and form the agenda thereof;*
(12) *dispose of property of the Federal Chamber of Advokats in accordance with the estimate and with the designation of the property;*
(13) *confirm the norm of representation from chambers of advokats to the Congress [added by Federal Law of 20 December 2004];*
(14) *confirm the reglament of the council of the Federal Chamber of Advokats and personnel establishment of the apparatus of the Federal Chamber of Advokats [as amended by Federal Law of 20 December 2004];*
(15) *determine the amount of remuneration of the president and vice-presidents and other members of the council of the Federal Chamber of Advokats, members of the internal audit commission of the Federal Chamber of Advokats within the limits of the estimate of expenses confirmed by the Congress for the maintenance of the Federal Chamber of Advokats [as amended by Federal Law of 20 December 2004];*
(16) *effectuate other functions provided for by the Charter of the Federal Chamber of Advokats [point three renumbered as amended by Federal Law of 20 December 2004].*

4. *In the event of the failure by the council of the Federal Chamber of Advokats to perform the requirements of the present Federal Law, the powers of the council of the Federal Chamber of Advokats may be terminated before time at an All-Russian Congress of Advokats. An Extraordinary All-Russian Congress of Advokats shall be convoked by the council of the Federal Chamber of Advokats upon the demand of one-third of the chambers of advokats of subjects of the Russian Federation.*
5. *Sessions of the council of the Federal Chamber of Advokats shall be convoked by the president of the Federal Chamber of Advokats as necessary, but not less than once in three months. A session shall be considered to be empowered if not less than two-thirds of the members of the council of the Federal Chamber of Advokats are present at it [as amended by Federal Law of 20 December 2004].*
6. *Decisions of the council of the Federal Chamber of Advokats shall be adopted by a simple majority of votes of members of the council of the Federal Chamber of Advokats participating it its session.*
7. *The president of the Federal Chamber of Advokats shall represent the Federal Chamber of Advokats in relations with agencies of State power, agencies of local self-government, social associations, and other organizations, and also with natural persons, act in the name of the Federal Chamber of Advokats without a power of attorney, issue powers of attorney and conclude transactions in the name of the Federal Chamber of Advokats, dispose of property of the Federal Chamber of Advokats by decision of the council of the Federal Chamber of Advokats in accordance with the estimate and with the designation of the property, effectuate hiring and dismissal from work of workers of the apparatus of the Federal Chamber of Advokats, convoke sessions of the council of the Federal Chamber of Advokats, and ensure the execution*

of decisions of the council of the Federal Chamber of Advokats and decisions of the All-Russian Congress of Advokats.

8. *The president and vice-presidents, and also other members of the council of the Federal Chamber of Advokats, may combine work in the council of the Federal Chamber of Advokats with advocate activity, receiving in so doing remuneration for work in the council of the Federal Chamber of Advokats in the amount determined by the council of the Federal Chamber of Advokats [as amended by Federal Law of 20 December 2004].*
9. *The council of the Federal Chamber of Advokats shall not have the right to effectuate advokat activity in its own name, nor to engage in entrepreneurial activity.*

1. This formulation is reproduced verbatim in the Charter of the Federal Chamber (Article 31). The Council operates on a permanent basis in the interval between All-Russian Congresses and has a number of administrative, organizational, and dispositive powers.

2. The present Law provides for a Council not exceeding 30 persons. The procedure for renewal and rotation of membership of the Council consists of several stages. First, the president of the Federal Chamber submits to the Council the names of members who are candidates for rotation. Second, the president suggests the names of members who should be rotated out of membership at each Congress. Third, these proposals are subject to confirmation by the Council, which may offer other nominations. Fourth, the slate of nominations is submitted for consideration of the Congress. If the Congress does not confirm the candidacies proposed, the president submits new names by going through the entire process once again.

3. The competence of the Council is addressed for the most part in this point of the present Article.

(1) The president of the Federal Chamber is effectively elected for two Congresses, and his vice president(s), for a term of one Congress. The vice presidential nominations are in the discretion of the president. The president is limited to two terms of office in succession and then must stand down for at least one term.

(2) If the status of advokat of a member of the Council has been suspended or terminated, the Council is to adopt a decision to terminate the powers of this person as a member of the Council, subject to confirmation of this decision at the next All-Russian Congress. Presumably, the confirmation is a formality if the individual whose powers were terminated as a member of the Council no longer took part in Council sessions. What would be the consequences if the Congress refused to confirm the termination is not addressed by the present Law or by the Federal Charter.

(3) In exercising the representation function set out in this sub-point the Council acts in the name of the Federal Chamber. The Council reports in detail to the All-Russian Congresses upon specific representation measures undertaken. In 2008-2009,

for example, the Council collaborated with financial agencies to ensure that advokat secrecy would be protected satisfactorily when measures were taken against money-laundering;[52] increased payments for advokats working in criminal matters on holidays, days off, and at night were obtained through discussions with the relevant agencies; the Ministry of Economic Development and Trade was persuaded to revoke a departmental regulation that would have introduced a competition procedure for advokats to receive work by assignment from law enforcement agencies; the Council lobbied successfully against changes to the Federal Law on Noncommercial Organizations that would have affected advokats adversely, and others.

(4) Coordination takes various forms. In 2007 and 2008 the Council of the Federal Chamber concentrated upon developing legal assistance free of charge to indigent persons, supervision over compliance with decisions of organs of the chambers of advokats; forming unified principles and criteria for the operation of qualifications commissions and their disciplinary practice; and considering the complaints, appeals, and other recourses against advokat activities.[53] Staff from the Federal Chamber conducted meetings with chambers of advokats, visited local sites, organized conferences, forums, round tables, and other measures on current topics, and sent staff to consult with chambers of advokats on organizational and methods recommendations.

(5) Conferences, symposia, workshops, and the like are a primary means of promoting continuing legal education among advokats. The Council of the Federal Chamber organizes some of these on a federal or regional basis and encourages the chambers of advokats to do the same for their own constituencies. Each year the Federal Chamber organizes an All-Russian Scientific-Practical Conference "The Advokatura. State. Society", the papers presented at which are published in monograph form.

(6) Each advokat formation is required to keep a record and submit annual reports concerning violations of the professional rights of their members. In June 2008 the Council devoted a special session to this issue. For the calendar years 2007 and 2008 together, 442 violations of professional rights of advokats were recorded, including 146 involving advokat secrecy and 231 instances of interference in advokat activity. These were sub-classified as follows: illegal interrogations of advokats: 87; illegal searches of advokat premises and dwellings: 26; illegal operational-search measures with respect to advokats: 35.

52 On 27 September 2007 the Council of the Federal Chamber confirmed "Recommendations for Organizing the Performance by Advokats of Requirements of Legislation on Counteracting the Legalization (or Laundering) of Revenues Received by Criminal Means and Financial Terrorism".

53 On 6 June 2006 the Council of the Federal Chamber confirmed "The Procedure for the Consideration and Settlement of Recourses to Advokat Formations and Chambers of Advokats of Subjects of the Russian Federation".

Advokats and chambers of advokats filed 446 complaints for the calendar years 2007 and 2008 against the illegal actions of law enforcement agencies, including 243 with the procuracy and 203 with the courts. The procuracy satisfied 74 complaints, and the courts, 100.

The social and professional rights of advokats to receive prompt compensation for legal services rendered by assignment of courts, the procuracy, or agencies of inquiry and investigation received special attention in 2007 and 2008. The total indebtedness of ministries and departments to advokats in 2007 reached 475,500,000 rubles; through strenuous representations made by the Federal Chamber and the chambers of advokats, by 1 January 2009 these arrears had been reduced to 224,400,000 rubles, or less than half.

In October 2008 the Council of the Federal Chamber divided its Commission for the Defense of Professional and Social Rights of Advokats into two, separating the professional rights and social rights. Many chambers of advokats followed this example. Advokats whose respective rights are violated may have recourse directly to the relevant commission for assistance.

(7) Draft legislation is routinely referred to the Council of the Federal Chamber for expert evaluation. Among those reviewed were the Draft Federal Law on rendering qualified legal assistance in the Russian Federation and a draft law containing proposed amendments to the present Law.

(8) Information provision takes several forms at the level of the Federal Chamber. The Chamber has its own press service to encourage relations with all the media. A monthly newspaper, Новая адвокатская газета [New Advokat Newspaper], commenced publication in April 2007. The monthly journal Российский адвокат became an organ of the Federal Chamber commencing in 2004. Official documents of the Federal Chamber, together with others, appear in Вестник Федеральной палаты адвокатов Российской Федерации [Herald of the Federal Chamber of Advokats of the Russian Federation].

(9) The Federal Chamber is not itself directly involved in disciplinary proceedings. The statutory duty here provided requires the Federal Chamber to summarize reports submitted by the individual chambers of advokats and provide a general report on these, which occurs at the All-Russian Congresses.

For the calendar years 2007 and 2008, 9,051 disciplinary proceedings were considered and opinions given by the qualifications commissions in the individual chambers of advokats. In 4,911 cases the advokat concerned was deemed to have acted in violation of legislation regulating advokat activity or the Code of Professional Ethics. Proceedings were terminated in 4,140 cases. The status of advokat was terminated for 440 advokats in 2007 and 498 advokats in 2008; of these, 26 were terminated in 2007 and 11 in 2008 at the request of justice agencies. The advokats concerned appealed against disciplinary sanctions to a court in 170 instances, and the courts found in favor of the appealing advokats in 20 cases. Justice agencies in 2007 and 2008 sent five requests directly to the courts concerning the termination of the status of advokat; of these, three requests were satisfied.

On 6 June 2006 the Council of the Federal Chamber confirmed the "Procedure for the Consideration and Settlement of Recourses to Advokat Formations and Chambers of Advokats of Subjects of the Russian Federation" in pursuance of the present point.

(10) "Methods activity" takes many forms, but one in particular that will be novel to foreign jurists is the formal confirmation of "Methods Recommendations", or "Methods Instructions", or analogous documents intended to assist advokats or chambers of advokats conduct their affairs. An example is the Methods Recommendations on Conducting an Advokat Proceeding, confirmed by the Council of the Federal Chamber on 21 June 2010. Basically, an "advokat proceeding" is the case or matter file relating to an individual client. The Methods Recommendation was issued because the present Law does not contain an express requirement that such files be kept.

(11) The Council of the Federal Chamber convokes the All-Russian Congress of Advokats. Such congresses have been held at two-year intervals since 2003, April being the preferred date for all except the first.

(12) This provision is an indication of the special legal capacity of the Federal Chamber of Advokats. Property of the Federal Chamber must be used for its purpose and may not be disposed of except in compliance with the estimate and the purposes of the organization. Under the Charter of the Federal Chamber (Article 44), the balance sheet of the Federal Chamber should record all types of immoveable property, including land plots, buildings, installations, and premises, basic and intangible assets, cash in rubles and foreign currency, securities, and other property.

The Federal Chamber is expressly authorized in its Charter to receive dividends and revenues from stocks and other securities belonging to the Chamber.

The president of the Federal Chamber is empowered under the Charter (Article 47) to dispose of property within the limits of the estimate and ceilings for expenditures set out therein or in other decisions of the All-Russian Congress of Advokats.

(13) The norms of representation are confirmed in advance of each Congress and circulated to the chambers of advokats for implementation.

(14) The Reglament of the Council of the Federal Chamber of Advokats was confirmed by the I All-Russian Congress of Advokats on 31 January 2003. The personnel establishment is confirmed as part of the estimate at each Congress.

(15) The levels of remuneration of these officers of the Council of the Federal Chamber are not disclosed (as is routinely the case for the chambers of advokats of the subjects of the Federation) in the publicly available documentation on the Federal Chamber.

(16) Among other functions the Charter of the Federal Chamber provides additionally that the Council issue an information bulletin, create commissions of the

Federal Chamber, and confirm statutes on commissions and forms of representation in federal districts.

The Federal Chamber has formed ten commissions and four working groups and an arbitration court. The commissions are: (1) Commission for Legal Observation; (2) Commission for Draft Law Work; (3) Commission for Defense of the Professional Rights of Advokats; (4) Commission for the Social Defense of Advokats; (5) Commission for Interaction with Agencies of State Administration with Regard to Taxation and Financing Payment for Labor of Advokats; (6) Commission for Disciplinary Practice and Application of Code of Professional Ethics of Advokat; (7) Expert-Methods Commission; (8) Commission for Awards; (9) Commission for Professional Training; (10) and the Commission for the Development of the Sport Movement among Advokats.

The working groups are: (1) Working Group for Ensuring Accessibility of Legal Assistance to Citizens of Russian Federation; (2) Working Group for Preparation of Draft Law on Insurance of Risk of Professional Property Responsibility of Advokat; (3) Working Group for Study and Popularization of History of Russian Advokatura; and (4) Working Group for Preparation of Proposals to Improve Pension Security of Advokats.

The arbitration court is in the formative stages. Its mandate extends to disputes within the jurisdiction of arbitration courts arising from civil law relations in the effectuation of entrepreneurial and other economic activity, including the turnover of property rights, goods, work, services and information; securities transactions or operations, including bills of exchange, deposit certificates, bills of lading, warehouse certificates, and others; transactions with moveable and immoveable property; recognition of the right of ownership (excluding immoveable property); contracts of cession and others; responsibility for a violation of obligations; and independent-work contracts.

4. If the council fails to perform its functions, this point makes provision for an Extraordinary All-Russian Congress and the re-election of a council. This provision has never been used in practice.

5. The present Law contemplates at least quarterly sessions of the Council of the Federal Chamber. During the calendar years 2007 and 2008, the Council met six times per year. This frequency of meetings is consistent with the Charter of the Federal Chamber (Article 34), which unlike the present Law, requires meetings not less than once every two months.

6. The Charter of the Federal Chamber requires a quorum of two-thirds of Council members. If a quorum is present, decisions are taken by simple majority vote of those present.

7. The present Law determines powers of the president of the Council of the Federal Chamber of Advokats but must be read against the Charter of the Federal Chamber, which contains somewhat different formulations of these powers (Article 38). In particular, the Charter gives the president broader authority to issue powers of attorney, grants him the power to issue orders and give instructions which are binding upon the members of the apparatus of the Federal Chamber, among others.

8. Although the president and vice presidents of the Federal Chamber are remunerated (the amounts are not disclosed) for their services, they are also permitted to engage in and receive revenues from their advokat activity.

9. The Federal Chamber is prohibited from itself engaging in advokat activity, a limitation it shares with all of its constituent chambers of advokats, nor may the Federal Chamber engage in entrepreneurial activity.

ARTICLE 38 PROPERTY OF FEDERAL CHAMBER OF ADVOKATS

1. *Property of the Federal Chamber of Advokats shall be formed at the expense of deductions effectuated by chambers of advokats, grants, and philanthropic assistance (or donations) received from juridical and natural persons in the procedure established by legislation of the Russian Federation. The Federal Chamber of Advokats shall be the owner of the said property.*
2. *To expenditures for the general needs of the Federal Chamber of Advokats shall be relegated expenses for remuneration of advokats working in organs of the Federal Chamber of Advokats, contributory compensation to the said advokats of expenses connected with their work in the said organs, expenses for earnings of workers of the apparatus of the Federal Chamber of Advokats, material provision of the activity of the Federal Chamber of Advokats, and other expenses provided for by the estimate of the Federal Chamber of Advokat [as amended by Federal Law of 20 December 2004].*

1. The formulation of sources from which the Federal Chamber of Advokats forms its property is exhaustive in nature. Nonetheless, some commentators believe that in the absence of express prohibitions in the present Law against property being derived by using other sources, this is permissible.[54] The Federal Chamber of Advokats does engage in publishing activity, from which revenues are received, as part of its duties to coordinate the activity of chambers of advokats and to ensure that the legal

54 Grinenko (ed.), Комментарий к Федеральному закону «Об адвокатской деятельности и адвокатуре в Российской Федерации (постатейный) [Commentary to Federal Law "On Advokat Activity and the Advokatura in the Russian Federation" (Article-by-Article)] (2003), p. 240.

assistance rendered by advokats is of a high standard. Publications are required to perform those duties, monographs, bulletins, serials, and the like.

The reference to a "grant" is unusual in Russian legislation. The term is a direct calque from the English, and is defined by the commentators as a "... type of subsidy granted by an organization or private person to another organization or private person in order to effectuate specific projects in the domain of science, culture, and education".[55] See. Article 34 and Commentary thereto.

Point 1 makes clear that the Federal Chamber of Advokats has the legal capacity to be the owner of its property, although the language is sufficiently categorical to raise the question whether the Federal Chamber has sufficient legal capacity to conclude lease contracts or obtain property by right of economic jurisdiction.

2. The types of expenditure by the Federal Chamber of Advokats enumerated in point 2 are exemplary and not exhaustive. The estimate confirmed by the general meeting or conference of advokats may include other expenditures, including for publishing activities.

Although the right of the Federal Chamber of Advokats to redistribute grants or donations may depend upon the conditions thereof, the Methods Recommendations regarding the application of Chapter 25 of the Tax Code of the Russian Federation concerning the profit tax provide with respect to Article 251(2)(9) that the "redistribution of special-purpose receipts and grants between noncommercial organizations and territorial organizations within the structure thereof created in accordance with legislation on noncommercial organizations shall not be taken into account when determining the tax base".[56] In each instance such receipts and grants must be for special purposes connected with the charter activity of the respective recipients.

Article 39 Social Associations of Advokats

Advokats shall have the right to create social associations of advokats and/or be members (or participants) of social associations of advokats in accordance with legislation of the Russian Federation. Social associations of advokats shall not have the right to effectuate functions of advokat formations provided for by the present Federal Law, as well as functions of chambers of advokats of subjects of the Russian Federation or Federal Chamber of Advokats or organs thereof.

55 Grinenko (ed.), Комментарий к Федеральному закону «Об адвокатской деятельности и адвокатуре в Российской Федерации (постатейный) [Commentary to Federal Law "On Advokat Activity and the Advokatura in the Russian Federation" (Article-by-Article)] (2003), p. 240.

56 See the Order of the Ministry of the Russian Federation for Taxes and Charges of 26 February 2002, No. БГ-3-02/98.

1. All citizens of the Russian Federation enjoy the constitutional right of association, guaranteed by the 1993 Constitution of the Russian Federation, by human rights treaties to which the Russian Federation is a party, and by the Federal Law of 19 May 1995 "On Social Associations", as amended.[57] The Federal Law on Social Associations extends to all social associations created at the initiative of citizens, excluding religious organizations, commercial organizations, and noncommercial unions or associations created by the last.

2. A social association is a voluntary, autonomous, noncommercial formation created by individuals who have combined in the common interests in order to realize certain common aims set out in the charter of the association. The right to associate is both direct (natural persons joining together) and derivative (juridical persons which are social associations joining together to form a social association). A social association must take one of six forms: social organization; social movement, social foundation; social institution; agency of social activity; political party.

Although under legislation of the Soviet period the Advokatura was a social organization, it did not exist as such at the all-union level even though they were regulated by USSR legislation. They nonetheless felt the need, when the Soviet Union disappeared, to have an organization at the federal level for a variety of reasons, including to lobby for legislation in the interests of the profession, to represent their views on level of remuneration for services performed, to avoid infringements upon the rights of advokats generally by way of unfavorable legislation. Accordingly, a number of large social organizations of advokats were founded, amongst them the Association of Advokats of Russia, the Federal Union of Advokats of Russia, the International Union (or Commonwealth) of Advokats, and the Guild of Russian Advokats. All are based in Moscow, except the Association of Advokats of Russia, which is headquartered in Saratov. All in their own way have represented the interests of advokats on particular issues; the Guild of Russian Advokats and the Federal Union of Advokats pursued an action in the Constitutional Court of the Russian Federation on behalf of the profession to seek equity in Pension Fund contributions, whereas the Association of Advokats of Russia was vocal during the drafting of the 2001 Code of Criminal Procedure in defense of Advokatura interests.

57 СЗ РФ (1995), № 21, item 1930; (2002), No. 30, item 3029.

Chapter 5 Concluding and Transitional Provisions

Article 40 Preservation of Status of Advokat

1. *Advokats who are members of colleges of advokats formed in accordance with legislation of the USSR and RSFSR and operating on the territory of the Russian Federation at the moment of entry of the present Federal Law into force (hereinafter – colleges of advokats formed before the entry of the present Federal Law into force) and meeting the requirements of Article 9(1) and (2) of the present Federal Law, shall preserve the status of advokat after the entry of the present Federal Law into force without taking a qualifications examination and the adoption by qualifications commissions of decisions concerning the conferment of the status of advokat.*
2. *A college of advokats formed before the entry of the present Federal Law into force shall within a month's period from the day of entry of the present Federal Law into force send to the territorial justice agency a list of its members which is signed by the executive of the particular college of advokats and certified by the seal thereof. The said list shall be sent to the territorial justice agency of that subject of the Russian Federation where members of the college of advokats are registered at a tax agency as taxpayers of the single social tax. The Moscow Region College of Advokats and the Leningrad Region College of Advokats shall send the lists of their members respectively to the territorial justice agency for Moscow Region and territorial justice agency for Leningrad Region irrespective of where the members of the said colleges of advokats are registered at tax agencies as taxpayers of the single social tax.*
3. *The list sent to a territorial justice agency must contain the surname, forename, and patronymic of advokats, information concerning whom shall be submitted for entry into the respective regional register. To the list shall be appended the following documents:*
   - *(1) personal applications of advokats concerning the submission of information concerning them in the respective regional register;*
   - *(2) copies of documents certifying the identity of advokats;*
   - *(3) questionnaires containing biographical information concerning advokats;*
   - *(4) copies of labor books or other documents confirming work experience in the legal specialization;*

(5) *copies of documents confirming higher legal education or the presence of a learned degree in the legal specialization;*
(6) *copies of decisions concerning admission to a college of advokats formed before the entry of the present Federal Law into force.*

4. *The territorial justice agency shall organize the verification of the reliability of the submitted documents and information. In so doing the territorial justice agency shall have the right to have recourse, when necessary, to respective agencies and organizations.*
5. *After confirmation of the reliability of the said documents and information, the territorial justice agency within a three-month period from the day of entry of the present Federal Law into force shall submit information concerning advokats specified in point 1 of the present Article to a regional register and publish the said lists in alphabetical order in the regional mass media. The failure to submit information concerning an advokat in a regional register may be appealed to a court. Until the issuance to advokats of identity cards provided for by Article 15 of the present Federal Law the identity cards issued to advokats before the entry of the present Federal Law into force shall operate.*
6. *Colleges of advokats formed before the entry of the present Federal Law into force shall terminate the admission of new members of colleges of advokats not later than 1 July 2002. From the day of entry of the present Federal Law until the day of creation in the respective subject of the Russian Federation of a qualifications commission the conferment of the status of advokat shall be suspended.*

1. Advokats were required to meet two criteria in order to maintain their status as such after the present Law entered into force on 1 July 2002: (1) they must have been members of colleges of advokats formed in the procedure established by law; and (2) they must have met the requirements laid down by Article 9(1) and (2) of the present Law. See Article 9 of the present Law above, and Commentary thereto.

This provision "grandfathered" advokats who were members of colleges of advokats before 1 July 2002 and precluded their having to take a qualifications examination or the qualifications commissions having to adopt a decision with respect to them conferring the status of advokat.[1] The legal succession between the "old" and the "new" Advokatura was ensured in this manner both with respect to individual advokats and the colleges of advokats in existence. This approach had the further consequence of eliminating the distinctions between the traditional colleges of advokats and the so-called "alternative" or "parallel" advokat formations.

1 According to Huskey, some 10% of pre-existing advokats were denied re-registration and others experienced difficulties with re-registration. Given some of the criticisms publicly made of the Advokatura in the 1990s, this is perhaps not surprising. See E. Huskey, "The Bar's Triumph or Shame? The Founding of Chambers of Advocates in Putin's Russia", in F. J. M. Feldbrugge and R. Sharlet (eds.), *Public Policy and Law in Russia: In Search of a Unified Legal Space* (2005).

2. The reference to colleges of advokats formed in accordance with legislation of the USSR and the RSFSR has in view, first, the Law of the USSR "On the Advokatura in the USSR" of 30 November 1979[2] and the Statute on the Advokatura of the RSFSR, confirmed by a Law of the RSFSR of 20 November 1980.[3]

3. The regional registers of advokats continue to record the data submitted by advokats and advokat formations that existed prior to the entry of the present Law into force. In particular, the date of entry of an advokat into a college of advokats prior to 2002 is recorded in column 3 of the register pursuant to the Administrative Reglament of 5 February 2008, confirmed by Order of the Ministry of Justice of the Russian Federation.

ARTICLE 41 CONDUCTING CONSTITUTIVE MEETINGS (OR CONFERENCES) OF ADVOKATS

1. *Territorial justice agencies, jointly with presidiums of colleges of advokats formed before the entry of the present Federal Law into force, shall organize the conducting of constitutive meetings (or conferences) of advokats in subjects of the Russian Federation within five months from the day of entry of the present Federal Law into force.*
   The composition of a constitutive meeting (or conferences) of advokats shall be formed of advokats included in the regional register in accordance with Article 40 of the present Federal Law and who are members of colleges of advokats formed before the entry of the present Federal Law into force on 1 July 2001.
2. *Colleges of advokats formed before the entry of the present Federal Law into force shall elect at their general meetings of delegates for the constitutive conference advokats according to the norm of representation determined by the territorial justice agency jointly with the presidiums of the said colleges of advokats.*
3. *If advokats are on the register as taxpayers of the single social tax at tax agencies of one subject of the Russian Federation but are members of a college of advokats formed before the entry of the present Federal Law into force in another subject of the Russian Federation, the territorial justice agency at the place of registration of advokats as taxpayers shall organize the conducting of a general meeting of such advokats at which they shall elect delegates to a constitutive conference of advokats. The norm of representation for such advokats shall be determined by the organizers of the constitutive conference of advokats of the respective subject of the Russian Federation.*

---

2 Ведомости Верховного Совета СССР (1979), № 49, item 846.

3 Ведомости Верховного Совета РСФСР (1980), № 48, item 1596, as amended.

4. *Constitutive meetings (or conferences) of advokats shall be considered to be empowered if not less than two-thirds of the advokats (or delegates of the conference) take part in their work. A constitutive meeting (or conference) of advokats shall elect three delegates each to the First All-Russian Congress of Advokats.*
5. *The opening of the constitutive meeting (or conference) of advokats shall be charged to the eldest advokat participating in the particular meeting (or conference). The advokats participating in the meeting (or delegates of the conference) shall elect a presidium in order to conduct the session.*
6. *Decisions of a constitutive meeting (or conference) of advokats shall be adopted by a simple majority of votes of advokats participating in the particular meeting (or delegates of the conference). The organizers of the constitutive meetings (or conferences) of advokats shall have the right to establish the procedure for the nomination of candidates to organs of the chamber of advokats, taking into account the need for representation to an executive organ of the chamber of advokats from various colleges of advokats formed before the entry of the present Federal Law into force proportional to the number of their members.*
7. *Advokats who are not participants of the constitutive meeting (or conference) of advokats may be elected to the composition of organs of a chamber of advokats of a subject of the Russian Federation.*

On the procedure for conducting meetings or conferences of advokats, see Article 30 of the present Law and the Commentary thereto.

Article 42 Conducting First All-Russian Congress of Advokats

1. *The federal justice agency jointly with chambers of advokats shall organize the conducting of the First All-Russian Congress of Advokats within seven months from the day of entry of the present Federal Law into force.*
2. *The First All-Russian Congress of Advokats shall be considered to be empowered if not less than two-thirds of the delegates of the Congress take part in its work.*
3. *The opening of the First All-Russian Congress of Advokats shall be charged to the eldest advokat participating in the Congress. The delegates of the Congress shall elect a presidium to conduct sessions.*
4. *Decisions of the First All-Russian Congress of Advokats shall be adopted by a simple majority of votes of delegates of the Congress.*
5. *Advokats who are not delegates of the First All-Russian Congress may be elected to the composition of organs of the chamber of advokats of a subject of the Russian Federation and Federal Chamber of Advokats.*

1. An Organization Committee was formed by the Ministry of Justice of the Russian Federation jointly with the chambers of advokats of the subjects of the Federation to hold the I All-Russian Congress of Advokats. The I All-Russian Congress of Advokats

was held at Moscow on 31 January 2003. E. V. Semeniako (St. Petersburg) was elected the President of the Federal Chamber of Advokats and A. P. Galoganov (Moscow), V. V. Kalitvin (Voronezh), and Iu. G. Sorokin (Moscow) were chosen as Vice Presidents. Delegates from 78 chambers of advokats of subjects of the Russian Federation were present and voting at the I Congress.

The I Congress adopted the Charter of the All-Russian Non-State Noncommercial Organization "Federal Chamber of Advokats of the Russian Federation", elaborating the provisions of Articles 35 to 38 of the present Law and consisting of eleven chapters and 56 articles. The Congress also adopted the Code of Professional Ethics in its first version and a Reglament to govern the operational procedures of the Congress.

On the procedure for conducting the All-Russian Congress of Advokats, see Article 36 of the present Law and the Commentary thereto.

ARTICLE 43 BRINGING ORGANIZATIONAL-LEGAL FORMS OF COLLEGES OF ADVOKATS FORMED BEFORE ENTRY OF PRESENT FEDERAL LAW INTO FORCE INTO CONFORMITY WITH PRESENT FEDERAL LAW

1. *Bringing the organizational-legal forms of colleges of advokats formed before the entry of the present Federal Law into force into conformity with the present Federal Law shall be effectuated in the procedure established by the present Article.*
2. *After the registration of a chamber of advocates of a subject of the Russian Federation, colleges of advocates and other advocate formations formed before the entry of the present Federal Law into force shall not have the right to effectuate the functions of a chamber of advocates of a subject of the Russian Federation, Federal Chamber of Advocates, or organs thereof provided for by the present Federal Law, except for functions provided for by Article 44 of the present Federal Law.*
3. *Within six months from the day of registration of a chamber of advocates of a subject of the Russian Federation, colleges of advocates and other advocate formations formed before the entry of the present Federal Law into force shall be obliged to bring their organizational-legal forms into conformity with the present Federal Law.*
4. *Bringing the organizational-legal forms of colleges of advocates and other advocate formations formed before the entry of the present Federal Law into force based on membership and meeting the indicia of a noncommercial organization into conformity with the present Federal Law shall be effectuated by decision of the general meeting of the respective advocate formation by means of the reorganization (division, separation, transformation) into one or several advocate formations of the organizational-legal forms provided for by the present Federal Law.*
5. *Control over compliance with legislation when conducting the reorganization of colleges of advocates and other advocate formations formed before the entry of the present Federal Law into force shall be effectuated by territorial justice agencies.*
6. *The right of advocates working in a legal consultation office to demand the division thereof from a college of advocates formed before the entry of the present Federal*

Law into force, with the transformation of the said legal consultation office into a noncommercial organization as one of the organizational-legal forms provided for by the present Federal Law shall be recognized by the present Federal Law. The decision concerning division of a legal consultation office with transformation thereof into a college of advocates shall be adopted by a simple majority of the listed advocates working in the respective legal consultation office on the day of registration of the chamber of advocates. In so doing the right to become founders (or members) of the newly arisen college of advocates shall belong to all advocates working in the respective consultation office on the day of registration of the chamber of advocates, including those who did not participate in putting forward the demand concerning division.

The decision concerning separation of a legal consultation office with transformation thereof into an advocate bureau shall be adopted by two-thirds of the listed advocates working in the respective legal consultation office on the day of registration of the chamber of advocates. In so doing only advocates who have concluded the partnership contract become founders (or members) of the newly arisen advocate bureau.

7. *The decision of advocates of a legal consultation office concerning the separation from the college of advocates formed before the entry of the present Federal Law into force must be sent within a two-month period from the day of registration of the chamber of advocates by registered letter to the presidium of the college of advocates formed before the entry of the present Federal Law into force, and also to the respective territorial justice agency. The decision received shall be considered by the general meeting of the college of advocates formed before the entry of the present Federal Law into force within a four-month period from the day of registration of the chamber of advocates.*
8. *The rights and duties of the college of advocates being reorganized formed before the entry of the present Federal Law into force shall pass to the newly arisen juridical person in accordance with the separation balance sheet. In so doing to the newly arisen juridical person shall be transferred property in kind and property rights which were previously in the use of the respective legal consultation office.*
9. *The right of advocates working in an advocate bureau which is an institution of a college of advocates formed before the entry into force of the present Federal Law to the transfer to them of the right of ownership to property of the said institution, with subsequent bringing of the organizational-legal form of the said institution into conformity with the present Federal Law shall be recognized by the present Federal Law. The decision concerning the presentation of a demand concerning the transfer of the right of ownership shall be adopted by two-thirds of the listed advocated working in the respective advocate office on the day of registration of the chamber of advocates.*
10. *A demand concerning the transfer of the right of ownership must be sent within a two-month period from the day of registration of the chamber of advocates by registered letter to the presidium of the college of advocates formed before the entry*

of the present Federal Law into force, and also to the respective territorial justice agency. The demand received must be considered by the general meeting of the college of advocates formed before the entry of the present Federal Law into force within a five-month period from the day of registration of the chamber of advocates.

11. *As a result of satisfaction of the demands provided for by points 6 and 9 of the present Article, the college of advocates formed before the entry of the present Federal Law into force shall transfer in accordance with the act of transfer the right of ownership to the property of the advocate bureau or property of the legal consultation office to the advocates working in the respective bureau or consultation office in equal participatory shares on condition of the forming from these participatory shares of an indivisible fund of the newly arisen college of advocates or advocate bureau.*
12. *Advocates who have remained within the college of advocates formed before the entry of the present Federal Law into force shall after satisfaction of the demands provided for by point 6 and 9 of the present Article, have the right to adopt a decision concerning the transformation (or separation) of the college of advocates formed before the entry of the present Federal Law into force into one or several advocate formations of the organizational-legal forms provided for by the present Federal Law.*
13. *The separation of a college of advocates formed before the entry of the present Federal Law into force into two or more advocate formations shall be effectuated upon the demand of not less than half of the advocates who are members of the college of advocates being reorganized and who remain in the composition of the college of advocates after satisfaction of the demands provided for by points 6 and 9 of the present Article. The rights and duties of the reorganizing college of advocates shall pass to the juridical persons newly arisen as a result of the separation in accordance with the separation balance sheet. The distribution of rights and duties of the reorganizing college of advocated formed before the entry of the present Federal Law into force between the newly arisen juridical persons shall be effectuated proportionally to the number of advocates who are participants of the juridical persons newly arisen. Juridical persons which arose as a result of the separation of a college of advocates formed before the entry of the present Federal Law into force shall not have the right to use the name and symbol of the reorganized college of advocates.*
14. *A demand concerning the separation of a college of advocates formed before the entry of the present Federal Law into force into two or more advocate formations must be sent within a five-month period from the day of registration of the chamber of advocates by registered letter to the presidium of the college of advocates formed before the entry of the present Federal Law into force, and also to the respective territorial justice agency. The demand received must be considered by the general meeting of the college of advocates formed before the entry of the present Federal Law into force within a six-month period from the day of registration of the chamber of advocates.*
15. *The transformation of a college of advocates or other advocate formation formed before the entry of the present Federal Law into force into one of the organizational-*

legal forms provided for by the present Federal Law shall be effectuated by decision of the general meeting adopted by a majority of votes of members of the respective advocate formation. In so doing the rights and duties of the reorganizing colleges of advocates or other advocate formation shall pass to the newly arisen college of advocates or advocate bureau in accordance with the act of transfer.

16. *Colleges of advocates and an advocate bureau newly arisen in the course of a reorganization shall be the legal successors of colleges of advocates and other advocate formations formed before the entry of the present Federal Law into force in accordance with the separation balance sheet or act of transfer.*
17. *From the day of entry of the present Federal Law into force colleges of advocates and other advocate formations formed before the entry of the present Federal Law into force shall not have the right to effectuate the transfer of their members and transfer of property between legal consultation offices, advocate bureaus, and likewise to alienate property of a college of advocates formed before the entry of the present Federal Law into force other than in the procedure established by the present Article.*
18. *If within three months from the day of receipt of the demands provided for by points 6, 9, and 13 of the present Article the general meeting of the college of advocates formed before the entry of the present Federal Law into force does not confirm the separation balance sheet or act of transfer, and also in the event of the failure to submit by the said college of advocates within a 45-day period from the day of the present Federal Law into force of lists of advocates who are members thereof, appending the necessary documents specified in Article 40 of the present Federal Law to the territorial justice agency, an arbitrazh court upon the suit of the respective territorial justice agency shall appoint an external administrator of the said college of advocates and charge him to effectuate the reorganization thereof.*
19. *From the day of appointment of the external administrator to him shall pass all powers with regard to management of the college of advocates formed before the entry of the present Federal Law into force subject to reorganization.*
20. *An external administrator shall act in the name of the college of advocates being reorganized in court, draw up the separation balance sheet or act of transfer, and transfer it for consideration of the court together with the constitutive documents of juridical persons arising as a result of the reorganization. Confirmation by an arbitrazh court of the said documents shall be grounds for State registration of the newly arisen juridical persons.*
21. *State registration of juridical persons which arose as a result of bringing colleges of advokats and other advokat formations formed before the entry of the present Federal Law into force into conformity with the present Federal Law shall be effectuated in the procedure established by the federal law on the State registration of juridical persons.*
22. *To agencies effectuating the State registration of juridical persons shall be submitted notarially certified copies of the following documents:*
    (1) decision concerning reorganization;
    (2) separation balance sheet or act of transfer;

(3) constitutive documents of newly arising juridical persons;
(4) documents confirming the fact of entry of information concerning the founder-advokats in the regional register.

23. *The rules concerning the reorganization of juridical persons established by the Civil Code of the Russian Federation and by the Federal Law "On Noncommercial Organizations", unless they are contrary to the present Article, shall apply to the reorganization of colleges of advokats and other advokat formations formed before the entry of the present Federal Law into force.*

This Article is fundamentally a transition provision setting out the procedures and time limits for reorganizing the Advokatura as a whole. The forms of advokat formations are set out in Articles 20-24 of the present Law.

Worthy of enduring notice is the requirement that new advokat formations must meet the criteria laid down in legislation for a noncommercial organization. This is understood to constitute a prohibition against any advokat formation rendering legal services in the procedure established for commercial organizations. On the distinction between advokat activity and entrepreneurial activity, see the Commentary to Article 1(2) above.

It will be observed that all key documents and stages in the reorganization must be notified to territorial justice agencies of the Ministry of Justice of the Russian Federation. Although the State therefore is involved in ensuring compliance with Russian legislation with respect to advokat reorganizations, this has been understood by the Commentators to mean that the State may not interfere in any way with the freedom of advokats to choose a particular organizational-form or type of advokat formation.[4]

The provision of point 16 regarding legal succession is without qualification. It must accordingly follow that legal succession exists with respect to all rights, obligations, and duties of the respective advokat formations, including any liabilities for professional behavior of advokats.

Article 44 Ensuring the Rendering of Legal Assistance Free of Charge to Citizens of Russian Federation and also Legal Assistance by Assignment

1. *All chambers of advokats shall be obliged within a 20-day period from the day of their registration to adopt a decision connected with the procedure for the rendering legal assistance free of charge to citizens of the Russian Federation, and also with the*

4 Grinenko (ed.), Комментарий к Федеральному закону «Об адвокатской деятельности и адвокатуре в Российской Федерации (постатейный) [Commentary to Federal Law "On Advokat Activity and the Advokatura in the Russian Federation" (Article-by-Article)] (2003), p. 250.

procedure for the participation of advokats as defenders in a criminal proceeding by assignment of agencies of inquiry, agencies of preliminary investigation, or court [as amended by Federal Law of 24 July 2007].

2. *Until the adoption of the said decisions by chambers of advokats, colleges of advokats formed before the entry into force of the present Federal Law shall bear responsibility for the rendering of legal assistance free of charge to citizens of the Russian Federation, and also for the participation as defenders in a criminal proceeding by assignment of agencies of inquiry, agencies of preliminary investigation, or court [as amended by Federal Law of 24 July 2007].*

1. This Article reflects, as noted above, one of the major points of distinction between the Advokatura in Russia and the legal profession in the United Kingdom or the United States. What in the Common Law world would be characterized as *pro bono* work is treated in Russia as an integral, compulsory part of the professional duties of all advokats.

Point 1 underscores that duty and establishes a firm period within which a registered chamber of advokats must establish its internal procedures for making advokats available to accept assignments to provide free legal assistance. It is essentially a transitional requirement that all chambers were obliged to comply with.

2. Point 2 also operated during the transitional period and placed responsibility for the period that elapsed until the chambers of advokats did determine the internal procedures required for rendering legal assistance free of charge. It would continue to be relevant to any newly-formed chamber of advokats out of a pre-existing one. On the procedure for registering a chamber of advokats of a subject of the Russian Federation, see Article 29 above.

Article 45 Entry into Force of Present Federal Law

1. *The present Federal Law shall enter into force from 1 July 2002, except for Article 7(1), subpoint (6), of the present Federal Law, which shall enter into force from 1 January 2007.*
2. *From the day of entry into force of the present Federal Law:*
   (1) to deem not operating on the territory of the Russian Federation the Law of the USSR of 30 November 1979, No. 1165-X "On the Advokatura in the USSR" (Ведомости Верховного Совета СССР (1979), No. 49, item 846);
   (2) To deem to have lost force:
   Law of the RSFSR of 20 November 1980 "On Confirmation of the Statute on the Advokatura of the RSFSR" (Ведомости Верховного Совета РСФСР (1980), no. 48, item 1596);
   Decree of the Presidium of the Supreme Soviet of the RSFSR of 8 July 1991, No. 1560-I "On Measures With Regard to the Social Defense of Citizens Engaging

in Advokat Practice in Colleges of Advokats of the RSFSR in Conditions of Transition to an Economic of Market Relations" (Ведомости Съезда народных депутатов РСФСР и Верховного Совета РСФСР) (1991), no. 28, item 977;

3. *Until the entry into force of Article 7(1), subpoint (6), of the present Federal Law, an advokat shall have the right to effectuate voluntary insurance of the risk of his professional property responsibility. In so doing the insurance contributions to be paid by the advokat to the insurer under a contract of insurance shall be relegated to means to be deducted by an advokat in accordance with Article 25(7) of the present Federal Law.*
4. *Until the forming of the council of the Federal Chamber of Advokats, the councils of chambers of advokats of subjects of the Russian Federation shall effectuate the following powers of the council of the Federal Chamber of Advokats:*
   (1) *the working out and confirmation of a provisional statute on the procedure for taking the qualifications examination and evaluation of the knowledge of candidates, and also lists of questions to be offered to candidates;*
   (2) *the confirmation of forms of ballots for voting provided for by Article 33(6) and (7) of the present Federal Law.*
5. *To propose to the President of the Russian Federation and to charge the Government of the Russian Federation to bring their normative legal acts into conformity with the present Federal Law.*

1. The legislative practice of stipulating that individual provisions of a law may enter into force at different times is not uncommon in Russian law. Deferral of the entry into force of Article 7(1), subpoint 6, (see Commentary to Articles 7 and 19 above) on professional risk insurance is attributed to the lack of a proper legislative base for underwriting this type of insurance. In a market economy one would expect the insurance industry to take the lead in developing insurance of this nature, or the Advokatura itself, not least because advokats are at liberty to insure themselves voluntarily. In fact, it has proved necessary to defer the entry into force of this provision indefinitely.

2. More than a decade elapsed after the disappearance of the former Soviet Union before legislation of the Soviet era regulating the advokatura was no longer relevant. The formula contained in point 2 of this Article is instructive. The 1979 Law of the USSR on the Advokatura was deemed "not to operate" on the territory of Russia, rather than repealed or said to "have lost force", because the USSR Law continues to be in force in certain other member countries of the Commonwealth of Independent States and it is not within the powers of Russia to repeal that Law generally throughout the spatial expanse of the former Soviet Union.

The RSFSR enactments, however, are confined exclusively to the territory of Russia and are therefore deemed to have lost force as from 1 July 2002.

3. There is no information as to the extent to which advokats voluntarily insure themselves against professional risks pursuant to this point of Article 45. The deductibility of insurance premiums is provided for to remove any doubt on this matter with respect to the tax authorities. Article 25(7) of the present Law mentions the deductibility of insurance premiums but could have been construed to apply only to compulsory premiums once such become mandatory. The Article is so drafted that, literally interpreted, advokats may deduct only professional risk insurance and not other insurance expenditures.

4. Point 4 is a transitional provision intended to cover the gap which existed before the Federal Chamber of Advokats was fully operational.

5. Although point 5 is a routine provision in Russian legislation, it raises questions about the status of normative legal acts adopted in pursuance of USSR and RSFSR legislation and not yet changed or repealed to reflect the present Law. The general position is that by virtue of its stature in the hierarchy of Russian legislation, the present Law overrode from 1 July 2002 any inconsistent provisions of subordinate normative legal acts predating the Law. The majority of Russian jurists thus consider that such inconsistent provisions lost force as from 1 July 2002 and bringing them into conformity with the Law is merely a housekeeping exercise.

In practice, however, it happens that there are differences of opinion as to whether a subordinate normative act is consistent or not with the present Law, and until adjustments are formally made (which may take many months or even years), there is no official position on the matter. The enactment of the present Law also may occasion changes in or additions to other laws of the Russian Federation that can only be made by the Russian parliament. No such changes or additions were introduced in the present Law (as sometimes happens in legislative practice), nor has there been a general law adopted to introduce blanket changes in other laws as a consequence of the adoption of the present Law. Accordingly, in the event of inconsistencies between the present Law and earlier laws, the principle that the "law latest in time governs" would be applicable.

An exception arises when a particular federal law makes provision for its priority over other federal laws adopted later in time. Article 7 of the 2001 Code of Criminal Procedure, for example, provides: "A court, procurator, investigator, agency of inquiry, and inquiry official shall not have the right to apply a federal law which is contrary to the present Code. A court, having established in the course of a proceeding with regard to a criminal case the failure of a federal law or other normative legal act to conform to the present Code, shall adopt a decision in accordance with the present Code".[5] Although Article 7 attempts to endow the Code of Criminal Procedure in

5 Butler, *Russian Criminal Law and Procedure* (2011), pp. 250-251.

its capacity as a federal law with a stature higher than other federal laws, formally there is no barrier to the Russian parliament determining otherwise explicitly or indirectly. Article 7 does not sit comfortably beside the principle that the law latest in time governs.

Such an exception would not extend to an enactment having a stature higher than a federal law; for example, a federal constitutional law or an international treaty of the Russian Federation. If the Constitutional Court of the Russian Federation were to find any provision of the present Law to be unconstitutional, then those provisions would lose force at once.

The Jurisconsult in Russia

A thorough study of the jurisconsult in pre-revolutionary Russia has yet to be undertaken. It is evident that the term and position of jurisconsult existed in nineteenth century Russia and that the term itself dates back to at least Petrine Russia to refer more generally to a jurist or lawyer. Prior to the judicial reforms of 1864 in Russia, the term "jurisconsult" was ordinarily reserved for individuals who engaged in private practice in the capacity of what later came to be known as an "advokat". The term was used, nonetheless, also to designate jurists who held an official position in State service or at an enterprise.

It has been suggested that prior to 1917 the person closest to the jurisconsult by nature of occupation was the "prikazchik" [приказчик], a term used in various meanings from at least the sixteenth century and understood to refer, *inter alia*, to a person who entered into legal relations with third persons as an empowered representative of his principal to perform an assignment on the basis of legislation and the customs of business turnover.[1]

Historical Origins

The Statute on the Post of Jurisconsult of Imperial Plants of 7 November 1858 established the post of jurisconsult "in order to guard the rights of ownership of Imperial plants in instances when they are the subject-matter of an investigative, police, or judicial proceeding". The duties of a jurisconsult included offering advice at the request of plant management on the claims of a plant department against other departments and persons or on claims filed against the employer, watching over cases arising in various State agencies with regard to suits by the plant department against outsiders and suits against the department itself, and defense of the rights of the imperial plants in the event of an investigation.

It was customary for a jurisconsult to hold other posts together with that in the department of imperial plants. The plant management determined the amount of his salary. The number of places where a jurisconsult might work simultaneously was not limited by legislation.

1 A. N. Chashin, Юридическая служба в Российской Федерации [Legal Service in the Russian Federation] (2005), p. 6. The prikazchik in some instances bore civil and criminal responsibility for the failure to perform the assignment properly.

Jurisconsults appeared at once in the Soviet people's commissariats and other State agencies after the October Revolution and survived in a few of the large enterprises, where despite the early expectations of an administered economy and society, their skills were provisionally required. In the categories of Soviet workers established in 1918 for wage scales, jurisconsults were included in category 1 of Group I, the highest classification.[2] By 1920 the need for legally-trained personnel had become desperate. On 11 May 1920 the Council of People's Commissars ordered all individuals with a higher legal education to register so that "proper use of [their] specialized knowledge" might be made.[3] One week later the same agency created "consultation subsections of justice" to be staffed by jurisconsults in the "people's commissariats and all central institutions of the RSFSR".[4] The Moscow College of Defenders in 1922 requested the Moscow City Soviet to authorize members of the college to jointly hold the post of jurisconsult and practice in the College, which was approved on 23 July 1922.[5]

The establishment of the Procuracy in 1922 led to a reorganization of the regulation of the jurisconsult. Supervision over the jurisconsult previously vested in the People's Commissariat of Justice in May 1920 was transferred to the Procuracy in 1923, which was to register the jurisconsults and to oversee their activities in justice agencies. Outside that commissariat, the regulation of jurisconsults became largely a matter for the organization employing them. In industry an all-union conference of jurisconsults was convoked at the initiative of the USSR Supreme Economic Council. On 7 June 1925 the Statute on Jurisconsults of State Enterprises Subordinate to the USSR Supreme Economic Council was confirmed by Order No. 955.[6]

The 1925 Statute outlined the principal duties of a jurisconsult. They included the consideration and, when necessary, participation in drawing up draft contracts and various other acts of a legal nature and correcting them from a legal standpoint; and giving explanations of legal provisions and administrative regulations at the requests of the executive organ of the enterprise or sections thereof; giving oral and written opinions on all legal matters put by the executives of the enterprise; participation to give opinions in sessions of executive organs of the enterprise or in commissions and meetings convened by the enterprise; drawing up opinions at the request of the executive organ concerning the indicia and classification of illegal actions of workers and employees; and conducting cases of the enterprise in judicial, administrative, and social institutions.

---

2 СУ РСФСР (1918), no. 48, item 567.

3 СУ РСФСР (1920), no. 47, item 211.

4 СУ РСФСР (1920), no. 51, item 221.

5 Yu. Luryi, "Jurisconsults in the Soviet Economy", in D. D. Barry, et al. (eds.), *Soviet Law After Stalin* (1979), II, pp. 170-171.

6 Бюллетень финансового и хозяйственного законодательства [Bulletin of Financial and Economic Legislation], no. 6 (1925), p. 18.

This document also prohibited placing on jurisconsults administrative functions and especially the combining of jurisconsult duties with administrative posts. The opinion of a jurisconsult had the significance of a view with regard to the application and interpretation of laws and was not binding upon the enterprise management. If management disagreed with an oral opinion given by a jurisconsult, the last was required to set out his view in writing. A jurisconsult advising on a transaction was responsible solely for the transaction conforming to legislation and bore no responsibility for the economic necessity or advisability of entering into the transaction, nor for the choice of contracting party.

On 30 March 1927 the RSFSR Council of People's Commissars enacted a Decree "On Jurisconsults of State Institutions and Enterprises and Cooperative Organizations and the Supervision of Their Activity".[7] The decree confirmed the supervisory role of the Procuracy over the jurisconsult, which was broadened by subsequent legislation. Throughout the late 1920s conferences of jurisconsults were held on an all-union or lesser scale to exchange work experience, hear reports, and even adopt resolutions about organizing and supervising the profession.

Unlike the advokats in Russia, however, jurisconsults during the pre-revolutionary and Soviet eras never formed a professional body that transcended ministerial or departmental lines. The transition from the NEP to the planned economy posed an initial threat to the jurisconsult insofar as law was expected to rapidly wither away and be supplanted by Plan. The 1927 legislation on jurisconsults had become obsolete; in most branches of industry the 1927 decree was superseded *de facto* by commissariat statutes on jurisconsults from 1932 to 1939. In many people's commissariats and State enterprises there were no legal sections or jurisconsults at all. When they were present, they were commonly incorporated into the chancellery of people's commissariats, where they visaed draft internal normative acts, or at enterprises were part of other sections, such as bookkeeping or sale, and basically occupied themselves with the work of those sections.

The supervisory role of the Procuracy diminished accordingly. The 1939 Statute on the Advokatura prohibited advokats from serving simultaneously as jurisconsults, but in 1941 enterprises which did not have the post of jurisconsult included in their personnel establishment were allowed to retain an advokat's services by agreement.

In 1957 N. S. Khrushchev initiated a major reorganization and decentralization of the administration of the national economy. These reforms were followed by local legislation on the jurisconsult endowing the post with widely varying duties and status. At the union republic level "model statutes" on the jurisconsult were enacted to aid enterprises and organizations in fashioning their own. The Ukrainian SSR

7 СУ РСФСР (1927), no. 36, item 238.

approved a model statute in 1959 and the RSFSR on 29 March 1963,[8] among others. Despite these reforms, the great mass of enterprises were subordinated to union ministries and departments and the model statutes did not extend to them.[9]

Contemporary Status and Regulation of the Jurisconsult

Although the transition to a market economy in Russia has enlarged the employment opportunities of the jurisconsult, his current status remains deeply indebted to the 1965 and 1987 economic reforms in the Soviet Union which gave State enterprises greater responsibility for their contractual relations with other enterprises and expanded the scope of economic accountability (still an element of post-Soviet Russian civil law). The enlarged discretion accorded to enterprise management required disciplining; law and contract were the chosen instruments and, in the Soviet era, State Arbitrazh was initially the principal forum.

A massive increase in legal personnel was required together with improvements in the law, both on a scale reminiscent of the reforms of Emperors Alexander I and Nicholas I. Several tentative measures were introduced, but the key document for the jurisconsult was the Decree of 23 December 1970 "On the Improvement of Legal Work in the National Economy". The Decree, *inter alia*, required the enactment of a General Statute on the jurisconsult, the formation or strengthening of legal departments in the central apparatus and at all levels of economic administration, local government, collective and State farms; the USSR Ministry of Justice was reinforced in its role of exercising methods direction over legal work in the national economy and improving the substance and systematization of Soviet legislation; admissions to law faculties were greatly increased and measures introduced to raise the qualifications of jurisconsults already in post.[10]

On 22 June 1972 the USSR Council of Ministers confirmed the General Statute on the Legal Section (or Office), Chief (or Senior) Jurisconsult, and Jurisconsult of a Ministry, Department, Executive Committee of a Soviet of People's Deputies, Enterprise, Organization, or Institution.[11] On the basis of this General Statute, ministries and departments drafted and confirmed their own statutes for their respective legal offices or legal personnel. Social organizations were recommended to use this General Statute as a model when establishing a procedure for carrying on legal work within

---

8 See the Model Statute on the Legal (or Contract-Law) Section, Chief (or Senior) Jurisconsult, and Jurisconsult of an Enterprise, Institution, and Organization, confirmed by Decree of the RSFSR Council of Ministers of 29 March 1963, No. 386. СП РСФСР (1963), no. 7, item 44.

9 See B. I. Puginskii and O. G. Neverov, Правовая работа [Legal Work] (2004), p. 26.

10 J. Giddings [Henderson], "The Jurisconsult in the USSR", *Review of Socialist Law*, I (1975), pp. 171-211. The number of jurists working in the national economy in 1970 was about 30,000, which increased by 1978 to 60,000, in 1981 to 64,000; and on 1 January 1992, to 75,000 jurists. Puginskii and Neverov, Правовая работа [Legal Work] (2004), p. 26.

11 Transl. in W. E. Butler, *The Soviet Legal System: Legislation and Documentation* (1978), pp. 311-318.

their organizations. Collective farms and inter-collective farm enterprises and organizations arranged their legal services on the basis of an Instruction confirmed jointly by the ministers of agriculture and justice on 3 January 1973.

The 1972 General Statute, although dating from the Soviet era, remains in force in the Russian Federation as amended on 4 December 1980, 1 December 1987, and 21 December 1990, subject to a decision of the Supreme Court of the Russian Federation of 27 December 2000, No. ГКПИ 2000-1409.[12]

Status of Jurisconsult

In the Russian market economy the jurisconsult remains, unlike the advokat, a salaried employee in the establishment where he works. This includes not only State institutions, enterprises, organizations, State farms, and collective farms, but also house counsel in private companies, banks, and foreign law firms operating in Russia.

The term "jurisconsult" has been criticized in post-Soviet Russia as being not very "appropriate", unable to escape associations of the past with "work of little interest in State enterprises".[13] In some instances the term itself has been corrupted and become "juristconsult" or "juristconsultant". Officially, however, the correct appellation is "jurisconsult" as confirmed by the Ministry of Labor of the Russian Federation in the "Unified Nomenclature for Posts of Employees".

Numerically, jurisconsults are beyond doubt the largest component of the Russian legal profession, even though, in the absence of an all-inclusive professional organization or of any collective registration requirements, it is impossible to say how many there are. Certainly, there are several hundred thousand.[14] On 8 May 2001 the President of the Russian Federation adopted an Edict on Certain Measures to Strengthen

---

12 СП СССР (1972), no. 13, item 70. Entered into force 22 June 1972. Point 4, paragraph 4, of the General Statute provided that the head of a legal section or the jurisconsult of an enterprise, organization, or institution is appointed to and relieved from office by the executive of the enterprise, organization, or institution with subsequent confirmation by a superior agency. This provision was originally intended to protect jurisconsults against arbitrariness, pressure, and reprisal from the enterprise director. It was declared to be contrary to subsequent legislation, namely, Part One of the Civil Code of the Russian Federation. The Civil Code provides that the rights of a juridical person may be limited only by a law, whereas the General Statute is a subordinate normative act. The Supreme Court also noted that the General Statute continued *de facto* to be applied. Consultant Plus records the General Statute as being in force. See Бюллетень Верховного Суда Российской Федерации [Bulletin of the Supreme Court of the Russian Federation], no. 10 (2001).

13 A. E. Zhilinskii, Профессиональная деятельность юриста: Введение в специальность [Professional Activity of the Jurist: Introduction to the Specialty] (1997), p. 142.

14 Aizin and Tikhomirov observed that the profession of jurisconsult has become a "mass profession" because of the new legal space opened to enterprises as a result of the transition to a market economy and reforms in legal education that enabled technical and other nonspecialist educational institutions to produce graduates in the field of law. See S. M. Aizin and M. Iu. Tikhomirov, Юридическая служба на предериятии: Настольная книга юрисконсульта [Legal Service at the Enterprise: Manual for the Jurisconsult] (2001), p. 3.

the Legal Services of State Agencies.[15] In addition to introducing substantial increases in salaries and benefits for jurisconsults, the Edict directed the Government of the Russian Federation to confirm a "Model Statute on the Legal Service of a Federal Agency of Executive Power", duly confirmed by Decree of 2 April 2002.[16] Under the Model Statute, a legal service is to be organized as an autonomous structural subdivision of the central apparatus of the federal agency of executive power and to be headed by an executive who is appointed to and relieved from office by the head of the federal agency. The Model Statute applied, of course, only to State agencies, although it is widely used as a model in the Russian private sector.

Functions of Jurisconsult

The duties of a jurisconsult vary depending upon whether the jurisconsult is employed by a ministry, State enterprise, private company, local soviet, agricultural organization or large farm, or a Russian or foreign law firm. Within the State sector and even for Russian companies, the jurisconsult has responsibility for verifying and certifying personally that draft legal enactments confirm to legislation in force. The jurisconsult supervises the conformity to law of similar enactments in structural subdivisions of his employer and prepares amendments for enactments. When necessary, the jurisconsult may be involved in helping to draft collective labor contracts or other measures to strengthen labor discipline. As a rule he will be extensively involved in drafting, evaluating, or even "visaing" contracts and other transactions. He will represent the employer in litigation, including arbitration and the arbitrazh courts and courts of ordinary jurisdiction. He may be involved, and in State enterprises will assuredly be involved, in the procedures for accepting goods and products. He will supervise claims procedures and prepare materials relating to wastage, thefts, and shortages for transfer to investigative agencies or the courts.

The jurisconsult may be called upon to advise other organizations within the employer, including the local trade union committee. His office will most probably operate as the control center for receiving and filing all internal normative and non-normative acts issued by the employer, informing others about them, and in general drawing the attention of fellow personnel to new relevant legislation.

Within the State administrative sector there have not been dramatic changes in the role of the jurisconsult. The ministerial jurisconsult has less responsibility for direct economic operations and more involving legislation, administration, and supervision of inferior structural subdivision or enterprises. In some ministries the jurisconsult may be heavily engaged in issues of foreign law or of public and private international law. The ministries dealing with foreign trade, fisheries, civil aviation, shipping, and foreign relations are examples. The jurisconsult of a local soviet deals

15 СЗ РФ (2001), no. 20, item 2000.
16 СЗ РФ (2002), no. 14, item 1307.

extensively with the legality of draft normative materials and gives legal advice not only to the local soviet and its executive committee, but even to the permanent commissions or individual deputies of the local soviet.

The career structure and remuneration of a jurisconsult in the State sector will depend upon what level he achieves within the personnel establishment. The following categories exist, as set out in Decree No. 37 of 21 August 1998, as amended, which confirmed the Qualifications Manual of Posts of Executives, Specialists, and Other Employees:[17]

(1) jurisconsult: higher legal education but without work experience – Tier 6;
(2) jurisconsult of II category: higher legal education and work experience as a jurisconsult of not less than three years – Tiers 7 and 8;
(3) jurisconsult of I category: higher legal education and work experience as a II category jurisconsult of not less than three years – Tiers 8 and 9;
(4) leading jurisconsult: higher legal education and work experience in post of jurisconsult for not less than three years – 10 and 11 Tiers;
(5) jurisconsult of II or I categories or leading: head of legal administration, section, or bureau – higher legal education and work experience in specialty of not less than five years – 8 to 12 Tiers, depending upon to which group for payment of labor the executives have relegated the particular organization.

Many Russian commercial organizations also follow this pattern, although it is accepted that the nomenclature may vary from one company to another and entries in the labor books of the jurisconsults accordingly. One encounters appellations such as "general director for legal questions", or "director of the legal directorate", and others.[18]

Russian jurists employed by foreign law firms are advised in monographs published specially for them to expect a probation period and, if they are hired, a different life style. "Law firms with foreign participation", as they are sometimes styled, advise many "solid" clients who are foreign corporations that sell products or goods in Russia or invest in various projects in Russia. The work in law firms with foreign participation is "highly paid", being "much higher than the average level of earnings of practicing jurists" and is prestigious and interesting. Transnational "legal companies" systematically rotate personnel with their consent and allow Russians to undergo training in other offices of the law firm. But, there is another side to the experience: the foreign firms are "demanding"; there is "constant competition with other personnel of the firm, a tense work rhythm dictated by the client workload, and

17 Available on Consultant Plus.
18 See K. K. Lebedev, Правовое обслуживание бизнеса (корпоративный юрист) [Legal Servicing of Business (Corporate Jurist)] (2001), p. 17.

the “administration of the firm is far from always guided by norms of labor legislation concerning work time and leisure time”.[19]

Methods Assistance
During the Soviet era, the USSR and union republic ministries of justice issued methods recommendations to jurisconsults. These related to major policy matters, such as the procedures for drafting normative acts of ministries or departments, for using legal means to ensure the issuance of high quality products, or for registering and keeping normative acts. The last function has nearly disappeared with the development of commercial legal data bases, but would continue to be vital for internal, or local, normative acts which may or may not find their way into external data bases. Insofar as departmental jurisconsults continue to be involved in drafting or evaluating interdepartmental normative legal acts, such methods guidance would be useful.

State Legal Bureaus

On 25 August 2005 the Government of the Russian Federation adopted Decree No. 534 “On Conducting an Experiment with Regard to the Creation of the State System of Rendering Legal Assistance Free of Charge to Indigent Citizens”.[20] The stated aim of the experiment was to develop an optimal mechanism for the realization of State policy in the domain of rendering legal assistance free of charge to indigent citizens. The experiment was to be conducted for the calendar year 2006 (later extended to encompass 2007) in ten subjects of the Russian Federation (Republics Karelia and Chechnia, and the Volgograd, Irkutsk, Magadan, Moscow, Samara, Sverdlovsk, Tomsk, and Ulianovsk Regions). Each State legal bureau was created in the form of a federal State institution; each was allotted a personnel establishment of 15 jurists.

The agency responsible for organizing the experiment and setting up the State legal bureaus was the Federal Registration Service. Organizing the experiment included confirmation of the charters of the State legal bureaus, the internal structure and personnel establishment thereof, and ensuring the State registration of the charters.

On 25 December 2008 by Decree No. 1029 “On State Legal Bureaus” the Government of Russia extended the life of the legal bureaus and expanded the categories of citizens who might qualify for legal assistance free of charge.[21] The existing State legal bureaus were moved to the jurisdiction of the Ministry of Justice of the Russian Federation. A new Statute on Rendering Legal Assistance Free of Charge by State Legal Bureaus was confirmed by Decree No. 1029 to replace the Statute of 2005. By Decree

19 Lebedev, Правовое обслуживание бизнеса (корпоративный юрист) [Legal Servicing of Business (Corporate Jurist)] (2001), pp. 47-48.

20 СЗ РФ (2005), no. 35, item 3612, as amended. The Decree also confirmed the Statute on Rendering Legal Assistance Free of Charge to Indigent Citizens.

21 СЗ РФ (2009), no. 2, item 229.

No. 991 of 3 December 2009,[22] the Government of the Russian Federation extended the scheme to calendar year 2010.

Although the State legal bureaus have been characterized by some as an "alternative Advokatura",[23] they are in fact staffed by jurisconsults, a characterization confirmed by the personnel establishment of each legal bureau. The State legal bureaus provide legal assistance to two categories of persons: (1) those considered to be indigent under Russian legislation; and (2) designated categories of disabled persons, World War II veterans, and unemployed pensioners receiving an old-age pension.

The State legal bureaus give three types of legal assistance: (1) consultations in oral or written form; (2) drawing up applications, appeals, petitions, and other documents of a legal character; and (3) representation of the interests of citizens in a civil proceeding, execution proceeding relating to civil cases, and in agencies of local self-government, social associations, and other organizations. Because legal assistance is rendered free of charge to low-income and needy persons, evidence of their income or lack thereof must be submitted in accordance with legislation of the subject of the Federation where the legal bureau is located. Except for oral consultations, legal advice is rendered under an agreement between the State legal bureau and the client according to a form confirmed by the Ministry of Justice.

Advokats may become involved in the advice rendered by a State legal bureau if they conclude a contract with the bureau providing that such advice will be rendered free of charge to citizens on a permanent basis or to a specific citizen. A citizen who applies for legal advice free of charge has the right to receive such advice unless he fails to submit the requisite documents, or his income does not fall within the range provided, or he seeks legal advice on matters not provided for by the relevant legislation. A refusal by the State legal bureau to provide advice may be appealed by the citizen concerned to the territorial agency of the Ministry of Justice in the subject of the Russian Federation; such appeals must be considered within 10 working days. If the refusal is supported by the territorial agency, the citizen concerned may appeal to a court.

The head of each State legal bureau is appointed to and relieved from office by Order of the Ministry of Justice of the Russian Federation. Other workers of the bureau who give legal assistance are appointed and/or relieved by the head of the State legal bureau.

Legal personnel of a State legal bureau are required to have a higher legal education from a State-accredited educational institution, no conflict of interests with the interests of the citizen who has applied for legal advice, not participated as a judge, arbitrator, mediator, procurator, investigator, inquiry official, expert, specialist, or

22 СЗ РФ (2009), no. 50, item 6099.
23 Kucherena, Адвокатура в условиях судебно-правовой реформы в России [Advokatura in Conditions of Judicial and Legal Reform in Russia] (2009), p. 184.

interpreter in considering or deciding a matter related to that brought in by the citizen, not have been an official within whose competence was the adoption of decisions in the interests of this citizen, or not have rendered legal assistance to another person whose interests are contrary to the interests of the citizen who applied for legal assistance. The said personnel also may not divulge information communicated by the citizen in connection with rendering legal assistance unless the citizen consents to such divulgence.

The system of State legal bureaus was adapted from that existing in Finland. Initially strongly resisted by the Federal Chamber of Advokats, the experiment was modified to meet the major objections of the advokats. The objections were various. Some observed that under Article 48(2) of the 1993 Russian Constitution, legal assistance might be rendered free of charge in instances provided by a law. The decrees of the Government establishing the experiment of State legal bureaus are subordinate normative acts, not laws – and arguably unconstitutional. Moreover, although the recipient of legal assistance might not pay, the labor of advokats in supplying such assistance should be paid for by the State. The financial duty to pay advokats for giving legal assistance free of charge has been placed on the subjects of the Federation, many of whom made no such financial provision. Others who did make budgetary appropriations for this purpose massively underfunded the need for such services. Now the federal budget was stepping in to finance the State legal bureaus and bypassing the advokats in so doing.

The State legal bureaus, it was argued, represented the State seeking to defend people against itself. Those jurisconsults who staffed the State legal bureaus were civil servants, bureaucrats, whereas the essence of the Advokatura was acting in a civil society as an institution independent of the State. Many doubted the qualifications and experience of the jurisconsults to be hired in the State legal bureaus. It was also felt that the bureaus would be inundated with work – about 20% of the Russian population qualified as indigent. And the program ignored the role of nongovernmental legal defense organizations which already gave legal assistance to Russian citizens free of charge within the scope of their interests and specializations.[24]

The State legal bureaus must be seen as a realization on the part of the State that the Advokatura was unlikely to be able to meet the demand for legal assistance to indigent Russian citizens. Perhaps some of the difficulties were inherent in the Russian federative system, which delegated these matters primarily to the jurisdiction of the subjects of the Federation. Most subjects of the Federation did little to meet the massive latent needs for legal advice among the low-income segments of the Russian population. Those that made efforts in this direction offered derisory financial

24 These concerns and others are summarized in Kucherena, Адвокатура в условиях судебно-правовой реформы в России [Advokatura in Conditions of Judicial and Legal Reform in Russia] (2009), pp. 173-203.

support. Remarkable is the fact that the advokats were bypassed in the initiative. The State legal bureaus are a prime example of "advokat activity" being directly and expressly performed by jurisconsults.

❖

The jurisconsult survived throughout the entire Soviet era, albeit in unorganized form. The renaissance of the jurisconsult in 1970 represented at the time a concern for legality within a less centralized system of economic management of the national economy. Compliance with Soviet economic legislation was supposed to produce economic dividends measured by improved efficiency and "profit" as defined by the Planned Economy. State enterprises and collective farms were given a variety of incentives to employ jurisconsults, including through media campaigns which emphasized the role of the jurisconsult in reducing fines and penalties or enforcing claims successfully in court.

The role of the jurisconsult has assuredly survived the dissolution of the Soviet Union; indeed, that role has expanded as the private sector in the Russian Federation has created a greater demand for legal services from in-house counsel. Legal training and experience have in the rising generation been useful to those seeking careers in State service at the highest levels. Three of the last four Presidents of the USSR and Russian Federation have a higher legal education and experience as jurisconsults (Presidents M. S. Gorbachev, V. V. Putin, and D. A. Medvedev).

The Foreign Legal Practitioner in Russia

Law firms having an extensive international and foreign practice with offices in countries other than that where they were founded is primarily a twentieth-century phenomenon. Individual lawyers retained to represent foreign governments or clients within their own jurisdiction or country date back far into history. In the United States, for example, Peter Stephen Du Ponceau (1760-1844) developed a lucrative and flourishing practice in Philadelphia by acting in prize and other international law cases before state and federal courts and in a variety of personal transactions represented foreign, especially French, interests throughout the United States, including the Government of France.[1]

Historical Background

Foreigners were prohibited from being members of the Advokatura in the Russian Empire. They were not prohibited from holding positions in State service, however, and many did, including legal posts.

During the Soviet era, foreign citizens were prohibited from being advokats in the USSR. That prohibition was not removed until the present Law on the Advokatura entered into legal force, as from 1 July 2003. There was no explicit prohibition with respect to jurisconsults.

Foreign citizens received legal advice on matters of Soviet law through special legal consultation offices maintained by several colleges of advokats. These legal consultation offices chiefly handled civil cases for foreign citizens or organizations or represented Soviet citizens and organizations in foreign legal matters. The best-known legal consultation office was "Iniurkollegia", attached to the Moscow City College of Advokats. Iuiurkollegia specialized in inheritance, property, insurance, patent, trademark, and related matters. That organization would bring suit in the USSR or abroad on behalf of its clients. The fee schedule approximated the fees charged by leading Anglo-American law firms.

Foreigners could apply on the same basis as Soviet citizens to any legal consultation office for advice. The advantage of Iniurkollegia was special expertise not readily available elsewhere insofar as foreign law matters were involved.

1 W. E. Butler, *Peter Stephen Du Ponceau: Legal Bibliophile* (2010) (Tarlton Law Library. Legal History Series No. 12).

Foreign Advokats in Russia

The numbers of foreign citizens and stateless persons who have acquired the status of advokat in Russia is not known. The figure is believed to be a low one, and most probably comprises principally individuals who are citizens of other countries of the CIS.

On 22 April 2004 the Council of the Federal Chamber of Advokats issued an "Explanation" which took the view that:

> ... advokats of foreign States may effectuate advokat activity only with regard to questions of the law of the State of which they are a citizen with obligatory registration in a special register. Acquisition of the status of advokat of the Russian Federation by a person who simultaneously is an advokat of a foreign State is not provided for by prevailing legislation.
>
> Foreign citizens and stateless persons have the right to acquire the status of advokat in the established procedure if they in so doing are not advokats of other States.

The difficulties raised by the phrase "advokat of a foreign State" have been discussed above (see Commentary to Articles 2 and 9). The Explanation issued by the Federal Chamber would, but for the confusion inherent in the terminology of the legislation, preclude foreign "advokats", whatever that may mean, from acquiring the status of advokat in Russia or, to put it otherwise, multiple professional qualifications. There would be no reason for the legislator to address the issue of whether an "advokat of a foreign State" may become a Russian advokat; if that is not prohibited, it is permitted.

This construction of Russian legislation by the Federal Chamber is profoundly anti-competitive and not consistent with the legal status of foreign citizens and stateless persons under Russian law.[2]

Foreign jurists who do not wish to become members of the Russian Advokatura and acquire the status of advokat may engage in advokat activity on the territory of the Russian Federation by registering with the Ministry of Justice of the Russian Federation. Without such registration, engaging in advokat activity is prohibited in Russia. However, although a close reading of the Decree requiring registration suggests that registration is not an authorization or a license to practice, the Decree read against Article 6(2) of the present Law suggests that the fact of registration and the issuance of a certificate confirming registration amount to a special authorization for

2 The most thoughtful analysis by a Russian advokat of the issues involved is A. I. Muranov, Российское регулирование отношений с иностранными элементами: некоторые аспекты правового статуса и деятельности иностранных адвокатов [Russian Regulation of Relations with Foreign Elements: Certain Aspects of the Legal Status and Activity of Foreign Advocates] (2006), pp. 50-52. On 25 March 2011 the Federal Chamber withdrew this "Explanation".

advokats of a foreign State to carry on advokat activity in Russia.[3] The registration is a confirmation that the individual concerned has been included in the Register of advokats of foreign States.

The 2003 Statute on Keeping the Register of Foreign States Effectuating Activity on the Territory of the Russian Federation (reproduced as Annex 2 below) provides that the following documents must be submitted by an advokat of a foreign State for the purposes of registration: (a) completion of an application and questionnaire in the Russian language; (b) a document confirming the status of advokat of a foreign State, which must be legalized unless provided otherwise by international treaties of the Russian Federation; (c) an identity document; (d) documents confirming the legality of sojourn on the territory of the Russian Federation and copies of these documents certified by a notary; and (e) two photographs of the prescribed dimensions.

These documents must be submitted in the original and copies translated into the Russian language, and any translations must be notarially certified or the genuineness of the translation attested if the notary does not have a command of the relevant foreign language. The failure to submit the necessary documents or the submission of unreliable information is grounds for refusing registration.

The Ministry of Justice of the Russian Federation has three months in which to verify the reliability of the documents submitted, including recourse to law enforcement and other State agencies with a request to assist in the verification. These agencies are required to report the results of the verification or confirm their reliability within a month from the day of receiving the request from the Ministry of Justice. If reliability is confirmed, the Ministry issues a regulation to register the advokat of the foreign State.

On the basis of that registration, the advokat of a foreign State is issued a numbered certificate of registration. The registration number may not be conferred on any other person, even if the certificate were later to be annulled (although a duplicate certificate would be issued if the original were lost). An issued certificate is subject to annulment by the Ministry of Justice in the event of: (a) establishing the unreliability of documents submitted for registration; (b) deportation of the advokat from Russia in the established procedure; or (c) entry into legal force of the judgment of a court deeming the advokat to be guilty of the commission of a crime. If a certificate is annulled, the advokat concerned must return it to the Ministry.

Information contained in the register held by the Ministry of Justice may be provided to others upon the payment of an established fee, except for agencies of State power and agencies of local self-government, who may obtain the information free of charge. Such information is provided in the form of extracts relating to individual jurists under the Order on Confirmation of the Form and Procedure for the Provision of an Extract from the Register of Advokats of Foreign States Effectuating Advokat

3 Ibid., p. 80.

Activity on the Territory of the Russian Federation, issued on 12 January 2004, No. 2, as amended by Orders of 1 March 2006, No. 32, and 30 September 2008. No. 218.[4]

What are the risks for a foreign jurist who fails to register? Possibilities include administrative responsibility under an expansive interpretation of the CAdV (Article 19.20(2)), failure to pay which could lead to difficulties for the foreign jurist concerned in entering or leaving the Russian Federation. Another risk is that the contract for legal services entered into by the foreign jurist may be deemed to be invalid or void under the Russian Civil Code.[5] No Russian administrative or judicial practice is known in this connection.

Foreign Jurists in Russia

Foreign jurists in the Russian Federation are regulated under the general regime for the legal status of foreigners and stateless persons.[6] If they have the language skills and take the qualifications examination, they may qualify for the status of advokat. They may be appointed to academic positions in Russian law schools, obtain a diploma in law, magister degree, or the kandidat or doctor of legal sciences, or serve on the International Court of Commercial Arbitration attached to the Chamber of Commerce and Industry of the Russian Federation, or on other arbitration tribunals in Russia.

Most commonly they are employed as partners or associates in foreign law firms (and exceptionally, Russian law firms), where they are regarded as jurisconsults. A very few have founded their own law firms as Russian juridical persons which are not related to a foreign legal entity. Whether they actually advise on Russian law turns upon their language abilities and the extent to which they are prepared to assume the professional risks concerned. Some foreign jurists find positions with auditing companies in tax and legal sections or as house counsel for large corporations which have a Russian presence. It is estimated that upwards of 100 foreign law firms have a presence in Russia, principally in Moscow, secondarily in St. Petersburg, and less commonly in other Russian cities.

4 Available on Consultant Plus.

5 Muranov, Российское регулирование отношений с иностранными элементами: некоторые аспекты правового статуса и деятельности иностранных адвокатов [Russian Regulation of Relations with Foreign Elements: Certain Aspects of the Legal Status and Activity of Foreign Advocates] (2006), pp. 77-82.

6 See W. E. Butler, *Russian Foreign Relations and Investment Law* (2006).

Code of Professional Ethics of an Advokat

[Adopted by the First All-Russian Congress
of Advokats, 31 January 2003, as amended by II All-Russian
Congress of Advokats, 8 April 2005, and III All-Russian Congress
of Advokats, 5 April 2007.
Российская юстиция, no. 10 (2003), pp. 69-76]

Advokats of the Russian Federation, in accordance with the requirements provided for by the Federal Law "On Advokat Activity and the Advokatura in the Russian Federation", for the purposes of maintaining professional honor, development of the traditions of the Russian (sworn) advokatura, and being aware of a moral responsibility to society, adopt the present Code of Professional Ethics of an Advokat.

The existence and activity of the advokat community is impossible without compliance with corporative discipline and professional ethics, concern of advokats for their honor and dignity, and also the authority of the Advokatura.

Section One
Principles and Norms of Professional Conduct of Advokat

Article 1.

The Code of Professional Ethics of an Advokat establishes the rules of conduct binding upon each advokat when effectuating advocate activity based on moral criteria and the traditions of the Advokatura, and also on international standards and rules of the profession of advokat.

Advokats shall have the right in their activity to be guided by norms and rules of the Code of Conduct for Lawyers in the European Union insofar as these rules are not contrary to legislation on advokat activity and the Advokatura and the provisions of the present Code.

Article 2.

1. The present Code augments the rules established by legislation on advokat activity and the Advokatura.

2. No provision of the present Code should be interpreted as prescribing or permitting the commission of acts which are contrary to the requirements of legislation on advokat activity and the Advokatura.

ARTICLE 3.

1. The operation of the present Code shall extend to advokats.
2. Advokats (or executives of advokat formations or subdivisions) shall be obliged to familiarize aides of advokats, apprentice advokats, and other personnel with the present Code and ensure compliance by them with the norms thereof in the part corresponding to their labor duties.

ARTICLE 4.

1. Advokats under all circumstances must preserve the honor and dignity inherent in their profession.
2. The need to comply with the rules of the advokat profession arises from the fact of conferment of the status of advokat.
3. In those instances when questions of professional ethics of an advokat are not regulated by legislation on advokat activity and the Advokatura or by the present Code, an advokat is obliged to comply with the customs and traditions which have formed in the Advokatura corresponding to the general principles of morality in society.
4. If an advokat is not sure how to act in a complex ethical situation, he has the right to have recourse to the Council of the respective chamber of advokats of a subject of the Russian Federation (hereinafter – Council) for an explanation, which may not be refused to him.

ARTICLE 5.

1. The professional independence of an advokat is a necessary condition of trust in him.
2. An advokat must avoid actions directed against undermining trust.
3. Abuse of trust is incompatible with the title of advokat.

ARTICLE 6.

1. Trust in an advokat cannot be without confidence in the preservation of professional secrecy. Professional secrecy of an advokat ensures the immunity of the principal provided to the last by the Constitution of the Russian Federation.
2. Compliance with professional secrecy is an absolute priority of the activity of an advokat. The period of keeping secrecy is not limited in time.

3. An advokat may not be exempted from the duty to keep professional secrecy by anyone except the principal.
4. Without the consent of the principal an advokat has the right to use information communicated to him by the principal in the amount which the advokat considers reasonably necessary in order to substantiate his position when a civil case is considered between him and the principal or for his defense with regard to a disciplinary proceeding or criminal case instituted against him.
5. The rules for the preservation of professional secrecy extend to:
- the fact of recourse to an advokat, including the names of the principals;
- all evidence and documents collected by the advokat in the course of preparation for the case;
- information received by the advokat from the principal;
- information concerning the principal which became known to the advokat in the process of rendering legal assistance;
- the content of legal advice given directly to the principal or intended for him;
- all advokat proceedings with regard to a case;
- the conditions of the agreement concerning the rendering of legal assistance, including monetary settlements between the advokat and the principal;
- any other information connected with rendering legal assistance by the advokat.

6. An advokat does not have the right to give witness testimony concerning circumstances which became known to him in connection with the performance of professional duties.
7. An advokat may not assign a right of monetary demand against the principal with regard to the agreement concluded between them to anyone whatsoever.
8. Advokats effectuating professional activity jointly on the basis of a partner contract must when rendering legal assistance be guided by the rules concerning the dissemination of a secret to all partners.
9. For the purposes of the preservation of professional secrecy an advokat must keep clerical correspondence separately from materials and documents belonging to the principal. Materials which are part of an advokat proceeding with regard to a case, and also correspondence of the advokat with the principal, must be clearly and unambiguously marked as belonging to or emanating from the advokat.
10. The rules for the preservation of professional secrecy extend to aides and apprentices of the advokat, and also other personnel of advokat formations.

Note. For the purposes of the present Article a principal is understood to be:
- a person who has concluded an agreement with the advokat concerning the rendering of legal assistance;
- a person to whom legal assistance is rendered by an advokat on the basis of the agreement on rendering legal assistance concluded with another person;
- a person to whom legal assistance is rendered by an advokat free of charge or by appointment of an agency of inquiry, agency of preliminary investigation, or court.

Article 7.

1. An advokat shall accept a commission to conduct a case when he has doubts of a legal character not precluding the possibility of reasonably and in good faith supporting and vindicating it.
2. The prevention of judicial disputes is an integral part of legal assistance rendered by an advokat, and therefore an advokat concerns himself with eliminating all that would obstruct an amicable agreement.

Article 8.

When effectuating professional activity an advokat:
(1) honorably, reasonably, performs duties in good faith, skillfully, in principle, and in good time, actively defends rights, freedoms, and interests of the principals by all the means not prohibited by legislation, being guided by the Constitution of the Russian Federation, law, and the present Code;
(2) respects the rights, honor, and dignity of persons who have had recourse to him for the rendering of legal assistance, principals, colleagues, and other persons and adheres to a business-like manner of conduct and business-like style of dress.

Article 9.

1. An advokat shall not have the right to:
(1) act contrary to the legal interests of the principal, render legal assistance to him by being guided by considerations of own advantage, amoral interests, or under the impact of pressure from outside;
(2) take a position with regard to a case and act contrary to the will of the principal, except for instances when the advokat-defender is convinced of the existence of self-incrimination of the person under defense;
(3) make public statements concerning the evidence of the guilt of the principal if he denies it;
(4) divulge without the consent of the principal information communicated to the advokat by the principal in connection with rendering legal assistance to him;
(5) accept commissions to render legal assistance known to be more than the advokat is in a state to fulfill;
(6) thrust his assistance upon persons who need legal assistance and attract them as principals by means of the use of personal links with the workers of judicial and law enforcement agencies, the promise of a favorable resolution of the case, and other unworthy means;

(7) while participating in the trial of an examination of a case, permit utterances demeaning the honor and dignity of other participants of the examination, even in the event of their tactless conduct;
(8) acquire by any means property and property rights in personal interests which are the subject of a dispute in which the advokat takes part as a person rendering legal assistance.

2. An advokat has the right to combine advokat activity with work as the executive of an advokat formation and with work in elective posts in organs of a chamber of advokats of a subject of the Russian Federation or Federal Chamber of Advokats.

The performance by an advokat of powers placed on him in connection with election to office in a chamber of advokats of a subject of the Russian Federation or Federal Chamber of Advokats, and also the performance by an advokat of powers of an executive of an advokat formation (or subdivision), shall be his professional duty.

In so doing remuneration to be paid to an advokat for work in a chamber of advokats of a subject of the Russian Federation or Federal Chamber of Advokats in connection with the performance of the said powers shall bear the character of contributory compensatory payment on the part of the respective chamber for the enforced impossibility of effectuating advokat activity in full measure.

3. An advokat also shall not have the right to:

- engage in other paid activity in the form of direct (or personal) participation in the process of the realization of goods, fulfillment of work, or rendering of services;
- outside the framework of advokat activity render legal services or participate in organizations rendering legal services;
- accept a commission for the fulfillment of functions of management organs of the principal who is a juridical person with regard to the disposition of property and rights of the last. The imposition of the said functions on workers of advokat formations also shall not be permitted.

4. The fulfillment of professional duties with regard to accepted commissions should have for an advokat priority significance over other activity.

The effectuation by an advokat of other activity should not shame the honor and dignity of an advokat or caused harm to the authority of the Advokatura.

Article 10.

1. A law and morality are higher than the will of a principal in the profession of advokat. No wishes, requests, or instructions of a principal directed towards noncompliance with a law or a violation of the rules provided for by the present Code may be performed by an advokat.

2. An advokat shall not have the right to give to a person who had recourse for the rendering of legal assistance or to a principal the promise of a positive result with respect to the fulfillment of a commission which may directly or indirectly testify to

the fact that the advokat in order to achieve this purpose intends to take advantage of other means besides the good-faith fulfillment of his duties.
3. An advokat must not accept a commission if the performance thereof will obstruct the performance of another commission previously accepted.
4. An advokat must not place himself in dependence of indebtedness on the principal.
5. An advokat must not permit familiar relations with principals.
6. In the event of the revocation of a commission an advokat must immediately return to the principal all original documents received from the last with regard to the case and the power of attorney.
7. When performing a commission an advokat proceeds in his actions from the presumption of reliability of documents and information submitted by the principal and does not conduct an additional verification thereof.
8. Duties of an advokat established by legislation on advokat activity and the Advokatura do not differ when rendering legal assistance free of charge in instances provided for by this legislation or by appointment of an agency of inquiry, agency of preliminary investigation, or court from the duties when rendering legal assistance for a fee.
9. If after the acceptance of a commission, except a commission for defense with regard to a criminal case at a preliminary investigation or in a court of first instance circumstances are elicited under which the advokat did not have the right to accept the commission, he must dissolve the agreement. In adopting a decision concerning the impossibility of the fulfillment of a commission and dissolution of an agreement, an advokat must whenever possible notify the principal in good time so that the last may have recourse to another advokat.

Article 11.

1. An advokat does not have the right to be an advisor, defender, or representative of several parties in a single case whose interests are contrary to one another, but may only facilitate the reconciliation of the parties.
2. If as a result of specific circumstances the need arises for the rendering of legal assistance to persons with various interests, and likewise in the event of the potential possibility of a conflict of interests, advokats rendering legal assistance jointly on the basis of a partner contract shall be obliged to receive the consent of all the parties to the conflictual relation to continue performance of the commission and ensure equality possibilities of the legal defense of these interests.

Article 12.

In participating or being present at a court proceeding and proceedings with regard to cases concerning administrative violations, an advokat must comply with norms of respective procedural legislation, display respect to the court and other participants of the proceeding, watch over compliance with the law with respect to a principal, and in the event of violations of the rights of the last, petition concerning the elimination thereof.

In objecting to actions of judges and other participants of a proceeding, an advokat must make such in correct form and in accordance with a law.

Article 13.

1. Besides instances provided for by legislation on advokat activity and the Advokatura, an advokat does not have the right to accept a commission for the effectuation of defense with regard to a criminal case of two or more persons if:
(1) the interests of one of them are contrary to the interests of another;
(2) the interests of one, although not contrary to the interests of another, but these persons adhere to various positions with regard to the same episodes of the case;
(3) it is necessary to effectuate the defense of persons who have attained and who have not attained majority.

2. An advokat who has accepted by way of appointment or by agreement a commission for the effectuation of defense with regard to a criminal case does not have the right to refuse the defense, except for instances specified in a law, and must fulfill the duties of defender, including, when necessary, the preparation and filing of a cassational appeal against the judgment of the court with regard to the case of the person under defense.

An advokat who has accepted a commission for defense at the stage of preliminary investigation by way of appointment or by agreement does not have the right to refuse without important reasons the defense in a court of first instance.

3. An advokat-defender must not without necessity worsen the position of other persons on trial. Any actions of an advokat against other persons on trial whose interests are contrary to the interests of the person under defense are justified only when without this the defense of his principal cannot be effectuated in full measure.

4. An advokat-defender shall be obliged to appeal against a judgment:
(1) at the request of the person under defense;
(2) when there are grounds for a reversal or change of the judgment for reasons favorable to the person under defense;
(3) as a rule, with respect to a minor if the court did not share the position of the advokat-defender and assigned a graver punishment or punishment for a graver crime than the advokat requested.

Article 14.

1. In the event of the impossibility for important reasons to arrive at the assigned time in order to participate in a judicial session or investigative action, and also of an intention to petition concerning the assignment of another time, an advokat must

inform the court or investigator thereof in good time, and also notify the other advokats thereof participating in the proceeding and agree with them a time for the performance of procedural actions.
2. An advokat shall have the right to converse with the procedural opponent of his principal who another advokat represents only with the consent or in the presence of the last.

Article 15.

1. An advokat shall structure his relations with other advokats on the basis of mutual respect and compliance with their professional rights.
2. An advokat shall refrain from:
(1) the use of expressions diminishing the honor, dignity, or business reputation of another advokat when drawing up documents and utterances when effectuating advokat activity;
(2) the use in conversations with persons having recourse for the rendering of legal assistance and with principals of expressions defaming another advokat, and also criticism of the correctness of actions and advice of another advokat previously rendering legal assistance to these persons;
(3) the discussion with persons who have had recourse for the rendering of legal assistance and with principals of the well-foundedness of the fee recovered by other advokats.
3. An advokat shall not have the right to incline a person who has come to an advokat formation towards the conclusion of an agreement concerning the provision of legal assistance between himself and his person.
4. An advokat shall be obliged to inform the Council about the acceptance of a commission to conduct a case against another advokat in connection with the professional activity of the last.

If an advokat accepts a commission to represent a principal in a dispute with another advokat, he must notify the college thereof and in compliance with the interests of the principal offer to end the dispute peacefully.
5. Relations between advokats must not influence the defense of the interests of the parties participating in the case. An advokate does not have the right to waive the interests of the principal either in the name of the partnership or in the name of other relations.
6. An advokat is obliged to fulfill decisions of organs of the chamber of advokats and organs of the Federal Chamber of Advokats adopted within the limits of their competence.
7. An advokat is obliged to participate personally or materially in rendering legal assistance free of charge in instances provided for by legislation on advokat activity and the Advokatura, or by assignment of agencies of inquiry, agencies of preliminary

investigation, or court in the procedure determined by the chamber of advokats of a subject of the Russian Federation.
8. An advokat who is an executive of an advokat formation (or subdivision) shall be obliged to take measures for the proper fulfillment by advokats of professional duties with regard to participation in the rendering of legal assistance free of charge and assistance by assignment, and also the effectuation of deductions for the common needs of a chamber of advokats and the fulfillment of other decisions of organs of a chamber of advokats and the Federal Chamber of Advokats adopted within the limits of their competence.

ARTICLE 16.

1. An advokat has the right to receive remuneration (or fee) due to him for work performed, and also compensation for costs and expenses incurred by him.
2. The fee of an advokat is determined by agreement of the parties and may take into account the amount and complexity of work, duration of time necessary to fulfill it, experience and skills of the advokat, periods and degree of urgency for fulfillment of the work and other circumstances.
3. An advokat should refrain from the inclusion in an agreement of conditions in accordance with which the payment of remuneration depends upon the result of the case.

This rule does not extend to property disputes under which remuneration may be determined proportionally to the value of the suit in the event of the successful completion of the case.
4. An advokat is prohibited from sharing a fee, in particular under the guise of a division of duties with persons who are not advocates.
5. An advokat is prohibited from accepting from a principal any property to secure an agreement concerning a fee, except for monetary amounts paid in to the cashier of an advokat formation (or subdivision) as an advance payment.
6. If in the process of rendering legal assistance advokats accept a commission with regard to the disposition of monetary means belonging to the principal (hereinafter: 'means of the principal'), the following rules shall be binding upon advokats:

- means of the principal always must be in an account in a bank or other organization (including with professional participants of the securities market) enabling control to be effectuated on the part of agencies of power over operations to be conducted, except for instances of the existence of an express or intermediary instruction of the principal relative to the use of the means otherwise;
- in the documents accompanying each operation with means of the principal there must be an indication of the particular operation being performed by the advokat on behalf of the principal;

- payments to any person from means of the principal effectuated in his name and in his interests may be made only when there is a respective direct or intermediated commission of the principal expressed in written form;
- an advokat by way of advokat clerical correspondence is obliged to record financial documents relative to the fulfillment of commissions with regard to conducting operation with means of the principal, which must be provided to the principal upon his demand.

Article 17.

1. Information concerning an advokat and advokat formation is permissible if it does not contain:
(1) evaluative characteristics of an advokat;
(2) assessments by other persons concerning the work of the advokat;
(3) comparisons with other advokats and criticism of other advokats;
(4) statements, allusions, ambiguities, which may delude potential principals or give rise to unfounded hopes.
2. If an advokat (or advokat formation) has become aware of the dissemination without its knowledge of an advertisement concerning its activity which does not meet the present requirements, it is obliged to notify the Council thereof.

Article 18.

1. A violation by an advokat of the requirements of legislation on advokat activity and the Advokatura and the present Code committed intentionally or through gross negligence entails the application of measures of disciplinary responsibility provided for by the legislation on advokat activity and the Advokatura and the present Code.
2. An action (or failure to act) of an advokat which formally contains the indicia of a violation of the requirements of legislation on advokat activity and the Advokatura and the present Code provided for by point 1 of the present Article (hereinafter – violation) but by virtue of insignificance does not defame the honor and dignity of an advokat, nor diminish the authority of the Advokatura, nor cause material harm to a principal or chamber of advokats may not entail the application of measures of disciplinary responsibility
3. An advokat who has acted in accordance with explanations of the Council relative to the application of provisions of the present Code may not be brought to disciplinary responsibility.
4. Measures of disciplinary responsibility apply only within the framework of a disciplinary proceeding in accordance with the procedures provided for by Section 2 of the present Code.

When determining the measure of disciplinary responsibility the gravity must be taken into account of the offense committed, the circumstances under which it was

committed, the form of guilt, and also other circumstances which have been deemed by the Council to be material and taken into account when rendering a decision.
5. Measures of disciplinary responsibility may be applied to an advokat not later than six months from the day of discovery of the offense, not counting the time of illness of an advokat or being on leave.

Measures of disciplinary responsibility may be applied to an advokat if from the moment of the commission of a violation by him not more than one year has lapsed.
6. There may be measures of disciplinary responsibility:
(1) reprimand;
(2) warning;
(3) termination of status of advokat.

Section Two
Procedural Foundations of Disciplinary Proceeding

Article 19.

1. The procedure for the consideration and settlement of appeals, submissions, and communications with respect to advokats (including executives of advokat formations and subdivisions) shall be established by the present Section of the Code.
2. The offense of an advokat which defames his honor and dignity, diminishes the authority of the Advokatura; the failure to perform or improper performance by an advokat of his professional duties to a principal, and also the failure to perform decisions of organs of a chamber of advokats, must become the subject of a consideration by the respective qualifications commission and Council conducted in accordance with the procedures of a disciplinary proceeding provided for by the present Code.

When there is a disciplinary proceeding with respect to an advokat, his statement concerning termination of the status or change of membership in a chamber of advokats shall be considered at the end of the disciplinary proceeding.
3. A disciplinary proceeding must ensure the timely, objective, and just consideration of complaints, submissions, and communications against actions (or failure to act) of an advokat and the settlement thereof in accordance with legislation on advokat activity and the Advokatura and the present Code, and also execution of the decision adopted.
4. When effectuating a disciplinary proceeding, measures shall be taken for the protection of information comprising a secret of the personal life of persons who have had recourse with an appeal, commercial and advokat secrecy, and also measures to achieve reconciliation between the advokat and the applicant.
5. A disciplinary proceeding is effectuated only by a qualifications commission and the Council of a chamber of advokats, of which the advokat at the moment of instituting such proceeding is a member.

6. After instituting a disciplinary proceeding, the persons, officials and organizations which have had recourse with a complaint, submission, or communication, the advokat with respect to whom a disciplinary proceeding has been instituted, and also the representatives of the enumerated persons, agencies, and organizations, shall be participants of the disciplinary proceeding.
7. The retraction of an appeal, submission, or communication or reconciliation of the advokat with the person who filed a complaint expressed in written form is possible until the adoption of a decision by the Council and entails termination of the disciplinary proceeding. A second instituting of a disciplinary proceeding with regard to the said subject and grounds is not permitted.

ARTICLE 20.

1. The occasions for the commencement of a disciplinary proceeding are:
(1) a complaint filed at the Council by another advokat, principal of the advokat, or legal representative thereof, and likewise the complaint of a person who had recourse for the rendering of legal assistance in the procedure of Article 26 of the Federal Law "On Advokat Activity and the Advokatura in the Russian Federation" in the event of the refusal of the advokat to accept the commission without sufficient grounds;
(2) a submission made to the chamber of advokats by the vice-president of the chamber of advokats or person replacing him;
(3) submission made to the chamber of advokats by an agency of State power empowered in the domain of the Advokatura;
(4) communication of a court (or judge) addressed to a chamber of advokats.
2. A complaint, submission, or communication shall be deemed to be permissible occasions for instituting a disciplinary proceeding if they were filed in written form and there has been specified therein:
(1) the name of a chamber of advokats to which the complaint is filed or submission or communication is made;
(2) surname, forename, and patronymic of the advokat who filed a complaint against another advokat, affiliation to the chamber of advokats, and advokat formation;
(3) surname, forename, and patronymic of the principal of an advokat, place of residence thereof or name of the person if the institution or organization if they filed a complaint, location thereof, and also the surname, forename, and patronymic (or name) of the representative and address thereof if the application is filed by a representative;
(4) name and location of the agency of State power, and also the surname, forename, and patronymic of the official who sent the submission or communication;
(5) surname, forename, patronymic, and also affiliation to the respective advokat formation of the advokat with respect to whom the question is raised concerning

the instituting of a disciplinary proceeding, requisites of the agreement concerning the rendering of legal assistance (if it was concluded) and/or order;

(6) the specific actions (or failure to act) of the advokat in which the violation by him of professional duties was expressed;

(7) circumstances on which the person who filed the complaint, submission, or communication bases his demands and the evidence confirming these circumstances;

(8) list of documents appended to the complaint, submission, or communication.

3. Each participant of a disciplinary proceeding shall have the right to propose in oral or written form means for settling the disciplinary case. The person demanding the bringing of an advokat to disciplinary responsibility must specify the specific actions (or failure to act) of the advokat in which the violation by him of his professional duties is expressed.

4. Complaints, recourses, and submissions of persons not specified in point 1 of the present Article may not be a permissible occasion for instituting a disciplinary proceeding, and likewise complaints, communications, and submissions specified in the present Article of persons based on the actions (or failure to act) of an advokat (including the executive of an advokat formation or subdivision) not connected with the performance by them of professional duties.

5. Complaints and recourses of other advokats or organs of advokat formations which arose from relations with regard to the creation and functioning of these formations may not be a permissible occasion for instituting a disciplinary proceeding.

6. Anonymous complaints and communications against the actions (or failure to act) of advokats shall not be considered.

Article 21.

1. The president of a chamber of advokats of a subject of the Russian Federation, upon the receipt of documents provided for by Article 20(1) of the present Code, institutes a disciplinary proceeding within not later than 10 days from the day of their receipt. The participants of the disciplinary proceeding shall be notified in good time about the place and time of consideration of the disciplinary case by a qualifications commission, and the possibility shall be granted to them of familiarization with all the materials of the disciplinary proceeding.

2. In the event of receiving complaints and recourses which cannot be deemed a permissible occasion in order to institute a disciplinary proceeding, and likewise received from persons not having the right to put the question concerning the instituting of a disciplinary proceeding, or, having discovered circumstances excluding the possibility of instituting a disciplinary proceeding, the president of the chamber refuses to institute it, returns these documents to the applicant, indicating in a written reply the reasons for the decision adopted, and if the applicant is a natural person, explains to the last the procedure for appeal against the decision adopted.

3. The circumstances excluding the possibility of a disciplinary proceeding are:
(1) the decision of a Council previously constituted with regard to a disciplinary proceeding with the same participants and with regard to the same subject-matter and grounds;
(2) the decision of a Council previously constituted concerning the termination of a disciplinary proceeding on the grounds provided for by Article 25(1) of the present Code;
(3) the expiry of the periods for the application of measures of disciplinary responsibility.

Article 22.

A disciplinary proceeding includes the following stages:
(1) examination in a qualifications commission of the chamber of advokats of a subject of the Russian Federation;
(2) examination in a council of a chamber of advokats of a subject of the Russian Federation.

Article 23.

1. A disciplinary case which has been received at a qualifications commission of a chamber of advokats of a subject of the Russian Federation must be considered within not later than two months, not counting the time of postponement of the disciplinary case for reasons deemed to the qualifications commission to be important.

An examination in a qualifications commission of a chamber of advokats of a subject of the Russian Federation is effectuated orally on the basis of the principles of adversariality and equality of the participants of the disciplinary proceeding.

Before the commencement of the examination, all members of the qualifications commission shall be warned about the inadmissibility of divulgence and protection of information which became known to them in the course of the examination comprising a secret of personal life or the participants of the disciplinary proceeding, and also a commercial, advokat, or other secret.

2. A qualifications commission must give an opinion with regard to an instituted disciplinary proceeding in that session at which the examination took place with regard to the substance on the basis of a direct investigation of evidence submitted by the participants of the proceeding before the commencement of the examination and also of their oral explanations.

Copies of written evidence or documents which the participants intend to submit to the commission must be transferred to the secretary thereof not later than two days before the moment of commencement of the session. The qualifications commission may accept from participants of a disciplinary proceeding for consideration additional materials directly in the process of the examination if they could not be

submitted beforehand. In this event the commission, at the petition of the participants of a disciplinary proceeding, may postpone the examination to familiarize themselves with the newly submitted materials.
3. The failure of any of the participants of a disciplinary proceeding to appear is not grounds for postponement of the examination. In this event the qualifications commission considers the case with regard to substance according to the available materials and hears those participants of the proceeding who appeared at the session of the commission.
4. An examination in the commission is effectuated within the limits of those demands and those grounds which have been set out in the complaint, submission, or communication. A change of the subject-matter and/or grounds of a complaint, submission, or communication is not permitted.
5. The participants of a disciplinary proceeding have the right from the moment of the instituting thereof to:
(1) familiarize themselves with all the materials of a disciplinary proceeding, make extracts therefrom, take copies of them, including with the assistance of technical means;
(2) participate in the session of the commission personally and/or through a representative;
(3) give with regard to the essence of the examination oral and written explanations and submit evidence;
(4) familiarize themselves with the protocol of the session and the opinion of the commission;
(5) in the event of disagreement with the opinion of the commission, submit their explanations to the Council.
6. At the request of participants of a disciplinary proceeding, a commission has the right to request additional information and documents to which the participants refer in confirmation of their arguments.
7. The advokat with respect to whom a disciplinary proceeding is instituted has the right to take measures with regard to reconciliation with the person who filed the complaint before the decision of the Council. The advokat and his representative give explanations to the commission last.
8. A qualifications commission is obliged to render an opinion with regard to the substance if at the moment of instituting the disciplinary proceeding the periods provided for by Article 18 of the present Code have not expired.
9. With regard to the results of an examination a qualifications commission has the right to render the following opinions:
(1) concerning the existence in the actions (or failure to act) of the advokat of a violation of norms of legislation on advokat activity and the Advokatura and/or the present Code, or the failure to perform or improper performance by him of his duties to the principal; or the failure to execute decisions of organs of the chamber of advokats;

(2) concerning the need to terminate the disciplinary proceeding as a consequence of the absence in the action (or failure to act) of the advokat of a violation of norms of legislation on advokat activity or the Advokatura and/or the present Code or as a consequence of the proper performance by the advokat of his duties to the principal or chamber of advokats;
(3) concerning the necessity to terminate a disciplinary proceeding as a consequence of the opinion constituted earlier of a qualifications commission and decision of the Council of that or another chamber of advokats with regard to a proceeding with the same participants with regard to the same subject and grounds;
(4) concerning the necessity to terminate a disciplinary proceeding as a consequence of the retraction of the complaint, submission, or communication, or the reconciliation of the person who filed the complaint and the advokat;
(5) concerning the necessity to terminate the disciplinary proceeding as a consequence of the expiry of the periods for the application of measures of disciplinary responsibility;
(6) concerning the necessity to terminate the disciplinary proceeding as a consequence of the absence of an occasion, discovered in the course of the examination, for instituting a disciplinary proceeding.

10. An examination in all instances is effectuated in a closed session of the qualifications commission. The procedure for the examination is determined by the qualifications commission and brought to the information of the participants of the disciplinary proceeding. The session of the qualifications commission is conducted by its chairman (or deputy appointed by him from among the members of the commission), who ensures order in the course of its session. Violators of order may be removed from the session of the commission by the decision thereof. The participants of a disciplinary proceeding have the right to be present when the opinion of the commission is divulged.

11. A session of the qualifications commission is fixed by a protocol in which are reflected all material aspects of the examination, and also the formulation of the opinion. The protocol is signed by the chairman and secretary of the commission. In instances deemed to be necessary by the commission, a sound recording may be made, appended to the protocol.

12. With regard to the substance of the examination the commission adopts an opinion by means of voting by inscribed ballots, the form of which is confirmed by the Council. Formulations with regard to questions for voting are proposed by the chairman of the commission or deputy appointed by him. Inscribed ballots for voting of members of the commission are appended to the protocol and are an integral part thereof.

13. At the request of participants of a disciplinary proceeding an attested copy of the opinion of the commission is handed over to them or sent within a ten-day period.

14. The opinion of the commission must be reasoned and substantiated and consist of introductory, descriptive, reasoned, and resolutive parts.

In the introductory part of the opinion is indicated the time and place of rendering the opinion, name of the commission which rendered it, composition of the commission, participants of the disciplinary proceeding, and occasion for instituting the disciplinary proceeding.

The descriptive part of an opinion must contain an indication of the subject-matter of the complaint or submission (or communication) and the explanations of the advokat.

In the reasoned part of the opinion must be indicated the factual circumstances established by the commission, evidence on which its conclusions are based, and the arguments with regard to which the commission rejects particular evidence, and also the rules of the professional conduct of advokat provided for by legislation on advokat activity and the Advokatura and the present Code by which the commission was guided when rendering the opinion.

The resolutive part of an opinion must contain one of the formulations provided for by point 9 of the present Article.

Article 24.

1. A disciplinary case received at the Council of a chamber with the opinion of a qualifications commission must be considered not later than two months from the moment of rendering of the opinion, not counting the time of postponement of the disciplinary case for reasons deemed by the council to be important. The participants of the disciplinary proceeding shall be notified about the place and time of the session of the Council.
2. The Council shall consider complaints, submission, and communications in the procedure established by its reglament, taking into account the peculiarities determined by this Section of the present Code.
3. Participants of a disciplinary proceeding not later than ten days from the moment of rendering by the qualifications commission of an opinion have the right to submit through its secretary to the Council a written statement in which disagreement is expressed with this opinion or in support thereof.
4. The Council does not have the right during an examination to review the conclusions of the commission with respect to the factual circumstances established by it, consider to be established factual circumstances not established by it, and likewise exceed the limits of the complaint, submission, communication, and opinion of the commission. The submission of new evidence is not permitted.
5. An examination with regard to a disciplinary proceeding is effectuated in the Council in a closed session. The failure of any of the participants of a disciplinary proceeding to appear does not obstruct the examination and the adoption of a decision. Participants of a disciplinary proceeding are granted equal rights to set out their arguments in support of or against the opinion of the qualifications commission, and

also express in substance the measures of disciplinary responsibility proposed with respect to the advokat.

6. A decision of the Council must be reasoned and contain a specific reference to the rules of professional conduct of the advokat provided for by legislation on advokat activity and the Advokatura and the present Code in accordance with which the action (or failure to act) of the advokat was classified.

7. The Council, taking into account the specific circumstances of the case, must take measures to reconcile the advokat and the person who filed the complaint.

8. A decision with regard to an appeal, submission, or communication shall be adopted by the Council by voting. The resolutive part of the decision is disclosed to the participants of the disciplinary proceeding immediately at the end of the examination in the same session. At the request of a participant of the disciplinary proceeding, an attested copy of the decision adopted is issued (or sent) to him within a ten-day period.

In the event of the adoption of a decision concerning termination of the status of advokat a copy of the decision shall be issued (or sent) to the person with respect to whom the decision is adopted concerning termination of the status of advokat or to his representative irrespective of the presence of a request concerning this.

Article 25.

1. The Council has the right to adopt the following decision with regard to a disciplinary proceeding:

(1) concerning the existence in actions (or failure to act) of an advokat of a violation of norms of legislation on advokat activity and the Advokatura and/or the present Code, the failure to perform or improper performance by him of his duties to a principal or chamber of advokats and the application to the advokat of measures of disciplinary responsibility provided for by Article 18 of the present Code;

(2) concerning the termination of a disciplinary proceeding with respect to an advokat as a consequence of the absence in his actions (or failure to act) of a violation of norms of norms of legislation on advokat activity and the Advokatura and/or the present Code or as a consequence of the proper performance by him of his duties to a principal or chamber of advokats on the basis of the opinion of a commission or notwithstanding this if the actual circumstances were established by the commission properly but an error was made by it in the application or interpretation of a law and the present Code;

(3) concerning the termination of a disciplinary proceeding as a consequence of the opinion made earlier of a qualifications commission and decision of the Council or this or another chamber of advokats with regard to a proceeding with the same participants and the same subject-matter and grounds;

(4) concerning the termination of a disciplinary proceeding as a consequence of the retraction of the appeal, submission, or communication or reconciliation of the person who filed the appeal and the advokat;
(5) concerning the sending of a disciplinary proceeding of a qualifications commission for a new examination as a consequence of a material violation of procedure permitted by it during the examination;
(6) concerning the termination of the disciplinary proceeding as a consequence of the expiry of the periods for the application of measures of disciplinary responsibility discovered in the course of the examination by the Council or commission;
(7) concerning the termination of a disciplinary proceeding as a consequence of the insignificance of the offense committed by an advokat, indicating to the advokat the violation permitted;
(8) concerning the necessity of terminating the disciplinary proceeding as a consequence of the absence of a permissible occasion for instituting a disciplinary proceeding discovered in the course of examination by the Council or commission.

2. The decision of a council of a chamber of advokats with regard to a disciplinary proceeding may be appealed by the advokat brought to disciplinary responsibility within a three-month period from the day when it became known to him or he should have known about the decision.

ARTICLE 26.

1. If within a year from the day of imposition of a disciplinary sanction the advokat is not subjected to a new disciplinary sanction, he shall be considered to not have a disciplinary sanction. The Council has the right upon the expiry of a year to remove the disciplinary sanction at one initiative, upon the application of the advokat himself, or the petition of the advokat formation in which the advokat is.
2. The materials of a disciplinary proceeding are kept in the files of the Council for three years from the moment of rendering a decision. During the said period the participants of a disciplinary proceeding have the right to familiarize themselves with these materials and make necessary extracts from them.
3. Upon the expiry of the said period the materials of the disciplinary proceeding may be destroyed by decision of the Council.
4. The divulgence of materials of a disciplinary proceeding is not permitted.

ARTICLE 27.

The present Code, and also changes in and additions thereto, enter into force from the moment of adoption by the All-Russian Congress of Advokats.

Statute on Keeping the Register of Advokats of Foreign States Effectuating Advokat Activity on the Territory of the Russian Federation

[Confirmed by Decree of the Government of the Russian Federation, 19 September 2003, No. 584, as amended by Decrees of 30 December 2005, No. 847; and of 8 December 2008, No. 930. *СЗ РФ* (2003), no. 39, item 3768; (2005), no. 3, item 297; (2008), no. 50, item 5958]

1. The present Statute, worked out in accordance with the Federal Law "On Advokat Activity and the Advokatura in the Russian Federation", shall establish the procedure for keeping the register of advocates of foreign States effectuating advokat activity on the territory of the Russian Federation (hereinafter – register).

2. The Ministry of Justice of the Russian Federation shall register advokats of a foreign State effectuating advokat activity on the territory of the Russian Federation [as amended by Decrees No. 847, 30 December 2005, and No. 930, 8 December 2008].

3. The register shall be kept in the Russian language according to the form of Annex No. 1.

4. For registration in the register an advokat of a foreign State shall submit to the Ministry of Justice of the Russian Federation the following documents [as amended by Decrees No. 847, 30 December 2005, and No. 930, 8 December 2008]:
(a) an application in the Russian language according to the form of Annex No. 2;
(b) a questionnaire according to the form of Annex No. 3;
(c) a document confirming the status of advokat of a foreign State (the said document must be legalized unless provided otherwise by international treaties of the Russian Federation), a document certifying identity; and copies thereof translated into the Russian language.
The translation of the said documents must be certified by a notary if he possesses the respective foreign language, or the genuineness of the signature of the translator, if the notary does not possess such language;

(d) documents confirming the legality of sojourn on the territory of the Russian Federation in accordance with legislation of the Russian Federation regulating the legal status of foreign citizens in the Russian Federation, and also copies of these documents certified by a notary;
(e) 2 photographs (en face, without headgear, on a mat paper 4 x 5 cm. in dimension).

5. The submission of unreliable information or the failure to submit all documents specified in point 4 of the present Statute shall be grounds for a refusal of the registration of an advokat of a foreign State in the register.

6. The Ministry of Justice of the Russian Federation shall within 3 months after receipt of the documents specified in point 4 of the present Statute effectuate verification of the reliability thereof. In so doing the Ministry shall have the right to have recourse to law enforcement and other State agencies with a request concerning verification or confirmation of the reliability of the documents submitted. The said agencies shall be obliged to communicate the results of the verification of documents or confirm their reliability not later than one month from the day of receipt of the request [as amended by Decrees No. 847, 30 December 2005, and No. 930, 8 December 2008].

After confirmation of the reliability of the said documents, the Ministry of Justice of the Russian Federation shall issue a regulation concerning registration of the advokat of a foreign State in the register, on the basis of which a certificate shall be issued concerning the registration according to the form of Annex No. 4 (hereinafter – certificate concerning registration) [as amended by Decrees No. 847, 30 December 2005, and No. 930, 8 December 2008].

7. The number of the entry in the register shall be the registration number, consecutive numeration being effectuated without division into years in so doing.

A registration number may not be conferred on another person, including in the event of the annulment of the registration of an advokat of a foreign State in the register. The registration number shall be specified in the registration file of the advokat of a foreign State and on the certificate concerning registration.

8. The decision concerning a refusal of registration in the register may be appealed to a court in the procedure established by Russian legislation.

9. In the event of the loss of the certificate concerning registration of an advokat of a foreign State a duplicate shall be issued upon his application.

10. An application of an advokat of a foreign State concerning the registration thereof in the register, the regulation of the Ministry of Justice of the Russian Federation concerning registration of an advokat of a foreign State in the register, and other

documents having relation to the advokat of a foreign shall be formed as a register file [as amended by Decrees No. 847, 30 December 2005, and No. 930, 8 December 2008].

11. The annulment of a registration of an advokat of a foreign State in the register shall be upon the application of the advokat or the initiative of the Ministry of Justice of the Russian Federation [as amended by Decrees No. 847, 30 December 2005, and No. 930, 8 December 2008].

12. The Ministry of Justice of the Russian Federation shall annul the registration of an advokat of a foreign State in the register in the event of [as amended by Decrees No. 847, 30 December 2005, and No. 930, 8 December 2008]:

(a) the establishment of the unreliability of the documents submitted for registration;
(b) the deportation of an advokat from the Russian Federation in the established procedure;
(c) the entry into legal force of the judgment of a court concerning the deeming of an advokat to be guilty of the commission of a crime.

13. The Ministry of Justice of the Russian Federation shall issue a reasoned regulation concerning the annulment of registration of an advokat of a foreign State in the register [as amended by Decrees No. 847, 30 December 2005, and No. 930, 8 December 2008].

14. A decision concerning the annulment of registration in the register may be appealed to a court in the procedure established by legislation of the Russian Federation.

15. An advokat of a foreign State whose registration in the register has been annulled shall return the certificate concerning registration to the Ministry of Justice of the Russian Federation [as amended by Decrees No. 847, 30 December2005, and No. 930, 8 December 2008].

16. Information contained in the register shall be provided for payment in the amount of 300 rubles which are subject to transfer to the federal budget [as amended by Decrees No. 930, 8 December 2008].

The said information shall be provided free of charge to agencies of State power and agencies of local self-government.

Information shall be provided in the form of extracts concerning specific advokats.

The form of the extract, and also the procedure for the provision thereof, shall be established by the Ministry of Justice of the Russian Federation.

[Annex No. 1 is not reproduced -- WEB)

Annex No. 2
Ministry of Justice of the
Russian Federation

from ______________________________
(surname, forename, patronymic)
advokat ______________________________
(State in which status of advokat was acquired)
permanently residing at the address:
____
(address and telephone of permanent place of residence)
____
(address and telephone of sojourn in Russian Federation)

Application

In accordance with Article 2(6) of the Federal Law "On Advokat Activity and the Advokatura in the Russian Federation" I request that I be registered in the register of advokats of a foreign State effectuating advokat activity on the territory of the Russian Federation and issue a certificate confirming the possibility of my rendering legal assistance on the territory of the Russian Federation with regard to questions of law of ______________________________.
(Name of the State of which advokat is a citizen)

Advokat ______________________________
(surname, initials)

Date Signature

Annex No 3

QUESTIONNAIRE

Photograph

1. Surname ____________________

Forename ____________________ Patronymic____________________
(if surname, forename, or patronymic has changed, indicate this)
2. Sex ____________________
3. Day, month, and year of birth ____________________
4. Place of birth ____________________
5. Citizenship ____________________
6. Information on higher legal education ____________________
____
(when and which educational institutions graduated, number of diploma, specialization and qualification with regard to diploma)
7. Requisites of document confirming status of advokat in foreign state
Name of document ____________________ No. ____________________
Issued by ____________________
Date issued ____________________
8. Address of permanent place of residence ____________________
Telephone ____________________
9. Address of place of sojourn in Russia ____________________
____
Telephone ____________________
10. Requisites of document certifying identity
Name of document ____________________ No ____________________
Issued by ____________________

Date of issue ____________________
"_____" _______200 ____________________
(Date of completing questionnaire) (Signature)

Annex No. 4

CERTIFICATE

CONCERNING REGISTRATION IN REGISTER OF ADVOKATS OF FOREIGN STATES EFFECTUATING ADVOKAT ACTIVITY ON TERRITORY OF RUSSIAN FEDERATION

"____" ________ 200__

The registration is hereby confirmed of________________________________

____

(surname, forename, and patronymic of advokat)

in the register of advokats of foreign States effectuating advokat activity on the territory of the Russian Federation, "____" ________ 200 __ , No. ______ and the possibility to render legal assistance on the territory of the Russian Federation for questions of law of ______________________________________

(name of State and competent agency which issued document)

Deputy Minister of Justice
of the Russian Federation ____________________ (signature)

Seal ____________________ (date)

Bibliography (with annotations)

The present Bibliography contains works used in the preparation of this volume, nearly all from the author's own collection. A proper history of the Russian legal profession remains to be done that gives attention to the pre-1864 period based on archives and on the modern period when the archives become fully available. The recent bibliography by A. N. Kichikhin (see below) will transform the frontiers of research and documentary collections, such as those prepared by the Federal Chamber of Advokats (see Semeniako and Pilipenko, below), and greatly facilitate the task of the researcher.

Адвокатская палата г. Москва [Chamber of Advokats of the City of Moscow]. M., LeksEst, 2003. 352 p. 2000 pts. (vyp. 1)

Alphabetical list of advokats in the city of Moscow as of 1 February 2003, together with accompanying normative materials.

Aizin, S. M., Tikhomirov, M. Iu. Юридическая служба на предприятии: настольная книга юрисконсульта [Legal Service at the Enterprise: Manual for the Jurisconsult]. M., izd. G-na Tikhomirova M. Iu., 2001. 559 p. 10,000 ptd.

Anufriev, V. M., Gavrilov, S. N. (comp.). Организация и деятельность адвокатуры в России [Organization and Activity of the Advokatura in Russia]. M., Iurisprudentsiia, 2001. 574 p. 4000 ptd.

Aria, S. L. Мозаика: Записки адвоката: Речи [Mosaic: Notes of an Advokat; Speeches]. M., De Jure, 2000. 416 p. 5000 ptd.

Arsenev, K. K. (1837-1919) Заметки о русской адвокатуре [Notes on the Russian Advokatura]. Spb., Demakov, 1875. 2 vols.

Baburin, S. N., Gliskov, A. G., and Zabeivorota, A. I., Комментарий к закону «Об адвокатской деятельности и адвокатуре в Российской Федерации» [Commentary on the Law "On Advocate Activity and the Advokatura in the Russian Federation"]. 2d ed.; M., MTsFER, 2003. 384 p. 4000 ptd.

Baranov, D. P., Smolenskii, M. B. Адвокатское право [Advokat Law]. 3d ed.; M., Akadem Tsentr, 2009. 368 p. 2500 ptd.

Barry, D. D., Berman, H. J., "The Soviet Legal Profession", *Harvard Law Review*, LXXXII (1982), pp. 1-41.

Barshchevskii, M. Iu. Адвокат, Адвокатская фирма, Адвокатура: учебное пособие [Advokat, Advokat Firm, Advokatura: Instructional Manual]. M., Belye alvy, 1995. 144 p. 2000 ptd.

___. Организация и деятельность адвокатуры в России [Organization and Activity of the Advokatura in Russia]. M., Iurist, 1997. 320 p. 10,000 ptd.

Berman, H. J., Luryi, Yuri, "The Soviet Advokatura: The 1980 RSFSR Statute with Annotations", *Soviet Union*, XIV (1989).

Boikov, A. D. Роль защитника в предупреждении преступлений [Role of Defender in the Prevention of Crimes]. M., Iuridicheskaia literatura, 1971. 112 p. 10,000 ptd.

Boikov, A. D., Kapinus, N. I. Адвокатура России [The Advokatura of Russia]. M., Institut mezhdunarodnogo prava i ekonomiki imeni A. S. Griboedova, 2000. 376 p. 5000 ptd.

___, **Kapinus, N. I., Tarlo, E. G.** Адвокатура России [Advokatura of Russia]. 2d rev. ed.; M., IKF Omega-L; Institut mezhdunarodnogo prava i ekonomiki imeni A. S. Griboedova, 2002. 432 p. 5000 ptd.

___, **Kapinus, N. I., Tarlo, E. G.** Адвокатура России [Advokatura of Russia]. 3d rev. ed.; M., Izdatel'skii dom Kameron, 2005. 432 p. 5000 ptd.

Borodin, D. N. Исторический очерк русской адвокатуры [Historical Outline of the Russian Advokatura]. Petrograd., Petrogradskaia kommercheskaia tipo-lit., 1915. 101 p.

Commemorating the 50th anniversary of the Sworn Advokatura, 20 November 1864.

Brui, A. V. (ed.). Юристы Москвы 2000 [Jurists of Moscow 2000]. M., Zhurnal "Luchshie firmy Moskvy", 2000. 76 p. 100,000 ptd.

Burnham, William, Maggs, Peter B., Danilenko, G. M. *Law and Legal System of the Russian Federation* (3d ed.; Huntington, Juris Publishing, Inc., 2004). xvii, 681 p.

Burobin, V. N. (ed.). Адвокатская деятельность [Advokat Activity]. M., izd-vo MNEPU, 2001. 536 p. 5000 ptd.

___. Адвокатская деятельность [Advokat Activity]. 2d ed.; M., Ekmos, 2003. 624 p. 5000 ptd.

___. (ed.). Адвокатская деятельность [Advokat Activity]. 3d ed.; M., Statut, 2005. 604 p. 7000 ptd.

___. Адвокатская тайна [Advokat Secrecy]. M., Statut, 2006. 256 p. 3000 ptd.

Butler, W. E. *Russian Law.* 3d ed.; Oxford, Oxford University Press, 2009. lx, 923 p.

___. *Russian Public Law: The Foundations of a Rule-of-Law State: Legislation and Documentation.* 2d ed.; London, Wildy, Simmonds & Hill, Publishers, 2009. 1000 p.

Chashin, A. N. Адвокатура в России: учебник [The Advokatura in Russia: Textbook]. Moscow, Delo i servis, 2008. 432 p. 3000 ptd.

___. Юридическая служба в Российской Федерации [Legal Service in the Russian Federation]. M., ZAO IKTs "Dis", 2005. 176 p. 5000 ptd.

Cherkasova, N. V. Формирование и развитие адвокатуры в России: 60-80-е годы XIX в. [Formation and Development of Advokatura in Russia: 1860-80s]. M., Nauka, 1987. 142 p.

Chernenko, G. I. Настольная книга юриста [Manual of a Jurist]. M., Infra-M, 1994. 352 p. 22,000 ptd.

Collignon, Jean-Guy. *Les jurists en Union Soviétique.* Paris, Editions du Centre National de la Recherche Scientifique, 1977. v, 555 p.

Dekhanov, S. A. Западноевропейская модель организации адвокатуры [West European Model of Organization of the Advokatura]. M., Rossiiskii universitet druzhby, 2007. 200 p. 500 ptd.

Demidova, L. A., Sergeev, V. I. Адвокатура в России. Учебник [Advokatura in Russia. Textbook]. M., Iustitsinform, 2004. 576 p. 3000 ptd.

Devlikamov, A. A. На подпути от «Шемякина суда» (несвоевременные записки бизнес-адвоката) [Half Way from a "Shemiakin Court" (Untimely Notes of a Business Advokat]. M., ID "Forum", 2007. 176 p. 3000 ptd.

Fedotova, T. A. Роль адвоката по защите прав и законных интересов граждан в гражданском судопроизводстве [Role of the Advocate in Defense of the Rights and Legal Interests of Citizens in Civil Procedure]. Moscow, "Maska", 2007. 212 p. 1000 ptd.

Friedman, L. M., Zile, Z. L., "Soviet Legal Profession: Recent Developments in Law and Practice", *Wisconsin Law Review* (1964), pp. 32-77.

Galoganov, A. P. Российская адвокатура: история и современность [Russian Advokatura: History and Modern Day]. M., izd-vo Iurlitinform, 2003. 288 p. 5000 ptd.

Garmaev, Iu. P. Незаконнная деятельность адвокатов в уголовном судопроизводстве [Illegal Activity of Advokats in Criminal Procedure]. M., Ekzamen, 2005.

Gavrilov, S. N. Адвокат в уголовном процессе [Advokat in a Criminal Trial], ed. P. A. Lupinskaia. M., Iurist, 1996. 112 p. 7000 ptd.

Gessen, I. V. (1866-1943). История русской адвокатуры (1865-1914) [History of the Russian Advokatura (1864-1914)], comp. S. N. Gavrilov. M., Iurist, 1997. 376 p. 10,000 ptd.

Volume I of the classic three-volume work; apparently all published of this version. Some materials and all photographs, illustrations, and normative materials omitted.

Ginzburg, G. A., Poliak, A. G., Samsonov, V. A. Советский адвокат [Soviet Advokat]. M., Iuridicheskaia literature, 1968. 200 p. 20,000 ptd.

Goshuliak, V. V. Прокуратура, адвокатура, нотариат в конституционном праве России [Procuracy, Advokatura, Notariat in the Constitutional Law of Russia]. M., Alfa-M, 2005. 352 p. 1000 ptd.

Grinenko, A. V. Адвокатура в Российской Федерации [Advokatura in the Russian Federation]. 3d ed.; M., Prospekt, 2009. 224 p. 3000 ptd.

___. Комментарий к федеральному закону "Об адвокатской деятельности и адвокатуре в Российской Федерации". Постатейный [Commentary on Federal Law "On Advokat Activity and the Advokatura in the Russian Federation]. M., Prospekt, 2003. 296 стр.

Gruzenberg, O. O. *Yesterday: Memoirs of a Russian-Jewish Lawyer*, ed. Don C. Rawson. Berkeley, University of California Press, 1981. xxix, 235 p.

Guliaev, A. P., Rivkin, K. E., Saraikina, O. V., Iudushkin, S. M. Комментарий к федеральному закону "Об адвокатской деятельности и адвокатуре". С приложениями [Commentary to Federal Law "On Advokat Activity and the Advokatura"]. M., izd-vo "Ekzamen", 2004. 352 p. 5000 ptd.

Gutsenko, K. F., "New Legislation in the Union Republics with Respect to the Legal Profession", *Soviet Law and Government*, I, no. 2 (1962), pp. 57-62.

Harris, Richard (1833-1906). Школа адвокатуры: Руководство к ведению гражданских и уголовных дел [School of the Advokatura: Manual on Conducting Civil and Criminal Cases], transl. P. Sergeich. Tula, Avtograf, 2001. 352 p. 5000 ptd.

Probably translated from the 11th English edition (1897), the last during Harris' lifetime, although a posthumous edition appeared in London in 1911. "Sergeich" is the nom de plume of Petr Sergeevich Porokhovshchikov (1867-19?), a Russian jurist who wrote several books on advocacy skills himself.

Hazard, John N. (1909-1995). *Settling Disputes in Soviet Society.* New York, Columbia University Press, 1960. xiv, 534 p.

Huskey, Eugene. Российская адвокатура и советское государство [Russian Advokatura and the Soviet State], transl. T. Morshchakova. M., 1993. 184 p. 4000 ptd. (Institute of State and Law, Russian Academy of Sciences)

___. *Russian Lawyers and the Soviet State: The Origins and Development of the Soviet Bar, 1917-1939*. Princeton, New Jersey, Princeton University Press, 1986. xii, 248 p.

Iartykh, I. S., Адвокатура и власть [The Advokatura and the Authorities] M., izd-vo "Iurlitinform", 2003. 176 p. 5000 ptd.

Ivanov, V. Профессия -- юрист [Profession – Jurist]. M., Os-89, 1998. 208 p. 5000 ptd.

Jordan, Pamela. "The Russian Advokatura (Bar) and the State in the 1990s", *Europe-Asia Studies*, L (1998), pp. 765-791.

Kachalov, V. I., Kachalova, O. V. Юридическая помощь в Российской Федерации: схемы и комментарии [Legal Assistance in the Russian Federation: Diagrams and Commentary]. M., IKF "Ekmos", 2002. 208 p. 3000 ptd.

Kachalova, O. V., Kachalov, B. I. Адвокатура в Российской Федерации: схемы и комментарии [The Advokatura in the Russian Federation: Diagrams and Commentary]. M., Izdatel'stvo Prior, 2000. 96 p. 3000 ptd.

Kaminskaya, Dina. *Final Judgment: My Life as a Soviet Defense Attorney*, transl. Michael Glenny. New York, Simon and Schuster, 1982. 364 p.

___. Записки адвоката [Notes of an Advokat]. M., Novoe izdatel'stvo, 2009. 410 p.

Kichikhin, A. N. Адвокатура. Пять веков правозащиты. Библиография (1795-2008 гг.) [Advokatura. Five Centuries of Defense of Rights. Bibliography (1795-2008)]. M., Inform-Pravo, 2009. 528 p. 1000 ptd. (Federal Chamber of Advokats of Russian Federation)
Book One, organized in chronological order by years and covering the period 1795 to 2008. Entries do not indicate publishers of books nor pagination of journal references. Name index refers to years. Useful concluding article analyzes patterns of publication (pp. 472-523).

Klen, N. N. (ed.). Межреспубликанская коддегия адвокатов. 60 лет деятельности [Inter-Republic College of Advokats. 60 Years of Activity], Comp. I. M. Bashkevich, A. F. Zhdanovich, A. N. Permiakov. M., Izdatel'stvo OOO RITM, 2007. 368 p. 700 + 200 ptd.

Klevtsov, A. V. «Периодизация истории российской адвокатуры» [Periodization of the History of the Russian Advokatura], Адвокатская Палата [Advokat Chamber], no. 6 (2006), pp. 4-8.

Koblikov, A. S. Юридическая этика [Legal Ethics]. M., Norma, 2000. 168 p. 40,000 ptd.

Kogan, M. I., Исповедь строптивого адвоката [Confession of an Obstinate Advocate] M., Izografus, 2002. 432 p. + ill. 1000 ptd.

Konina, E. N. Функции юридической практики [Functions of Legal Practice]. Saratov: izd-vo GOU VPO "Saratovskaia gosudarstvennaia akademiia prava", 2006. 108 p. 300 ptd.

Kozak, D. N. (ed.). Научно-практический комментарий к Федеральному закону «Об адвокатской деятельности и адвокатуре в Российской Федерации» [Scientific-Practical Commentary to Federal Law "On Advokat Activity and the Advokatura in the Russian Federation"]. M., Statut, 2003. 236 p. 2000 ptd.

Kozhevnikov, M. V. Советская Адвокатура [Soviet Advokatura]. M., Iuridicheskoe izd-vo, 1939. 52 p.

Kratenko, M. V. Договор об оказании юридической помощи в современном гражданском законодательстве [Contract on Rendering Legal Assistance in Contemporary Civil Legislation]. M., Statut, 2006. 316 p. 1500 ptd.

Kravchenko, A. A. Записки адвоката [Notes of an Advokat]. Minsk, Amalfeia, 2000. 272 p. 5100 ptd.

Kruglov, A. A. (ed.). Советская адвокатура: задачи и деятельность [Soviet Advokatura: Tasks and Activity]. M., Iuridicheskaia literature, 1968. 144 p. 10,000 ptd.

Kucherena, A. G. Адвокатура: Учебник [Advokatura: Textbook]. M., Iurist, 2004. 351 p. 3000 ptd.

___. Адвокатура в условиях судебно-правовой реформы в России [Advokatura in Conditions of Judicial and Legal Reform in Russia]. M., izd-vo Iurkompani, 2009. 434 p. 1000 ptd.

Kucherov, S. A., *Courts, Lawyers, and Trial Under the Last Three Tsars.* New York, F. A. Praeger, 1953. ix, 339 p.

___. "The Legal Profession in Pre- and Post-Revolutionary Russia", *American Journal of Comparative Law,* V (1956), pp. 443-470.

Kudriavtsev, V. L. Реализация конституционно-правового института квалифицированной юридической помощи в деятельности адвоката (защитника) в уголовном судопроизводстве [Realization of Constitutional-Law Institute of Qualified Legal Assistance in Activity of Advokat (or Defender) in Criminal Proceeding]. M., izd-vo Iurlitinform, 2008. 440 p. 2000 ptd.

Lebedev, K. K. Правовое обслуживание биззнеса (корпоративный юрист) [Legal Servicing of Business (Corporate Jurist)]. M., Iurist, 2001. 475 p. 5000 ptd.

Lubshev, Iu. F. Адвокат в уголовном деле [Advokat in a Criminal Case], ed. I. B. Martinovich. M., Iurist, 1997. 408 p. 5000 ptd.

___. Адвокатура в России [Advokatura in Russia]. M., OOO "Profobrazovanie", 2001. 832 p. 3000 ptd.

___. Комментарий а Федеральному закону «Об адвокатской деятельности и адвокатуры в Российской Федерации (постатейный) [Commentary to Federal Law "On Advokat Activity and the Advokatura in the Russian Federation (Article-by-Article)] M., TON – Profobrazovanie, 2002. 192 p. 6000 ptd.

___. Курс адвокатского права [Cours of Advokat Law]. 2d ed.; M., OOO "Profobrazovanie", 2003. 424 p. 2000 ptd.

Lupinskaia, P. A. (ed.). Адвокат в уголовном процессе [Advokat in a Criminal Trial], comp. S. A. Gavrilov. M., Novyi iurist, 1997. 544 p. 5000 ptd.
Contains substantial extracts from classic works by M. Vinaver, I. Ia. Foinitskii, P. V. Makalinskii, R. Harris.

Makalinskii, P. V. С.-Петербургская присяжная адвокатура [St. Petersburg Sworn Advokatura]. Spb., n.p., 1889. viii, 560 p.

Martinovich, I. I. Адвокатура в БССР [Advokatura in the Belorussian SSR]. Minsk, izd-vo BGU im. V. I. Lenina, 1973. 176 p. 1800 ptd.

Masleev, A. G. (comp.). Кодексы профессиональной этики юриста: сборник [Codes of Professional Ethics of a Jurist: Collection]. Ekaterinburg, Izdatel'skii dom "Ural'skaia gosudarstvennaia iuridicheskaia akademiia", 2008. 100 p. 500 ptd.

Mirzoev, G. B., Eriashvili, N. D. (eds.). Адвокатура в России [Advokatura in Russia]. 4th ed.; M., Unity, 2011. 375 p. 10,000 ptd.

___, **Keizerov, N. M.** Правовая культура адвоката [Legal Culture of an Advokat]. M., Serial, 1996. 256 p. 3000 ptd.

Muranov, A. I. Российское валютное право: регулирование статуса и деятельность адвокатов [Russian Currency Law: Regulation of Status and Activity of Advokats]. M., Statut, 2006. 536 p. 1000 ptd.

___. Российское регулирование отношений с иностранными элементами: некоторые аспекты правового статуса и деятельности иностранных адвокатов [Russian Regulation of Relations with Foreign Elements: Certain Aspects of the Legal Status and Activity of Foreign Advocates]. Moscow: Gorodets, 2006. 144 p. 1000 ptd.

Norros, Merja. *Judicial Cooperation in Civil Matters with Russia and Methods of Evaluation*. [Helsinki], Kikimora Publications, 2010. 480 p.

«Об утверждении Положения об адвокатуре РСФСР» [On Confirmation of the Statute on the Advokatura of the RSFSR]. M., Bukvitsa, 1996. 32 p. 1000 ptd.

Contains five documents, including normative acts on payment for advokats and taxation of colleges of advokats, as well as United Nations material.

Pecherskii, V. V. Институт адвокатуры: теория основных понятий и принципов [Institute of the Advokatura: Theory of Basic Concepts and Principles]. Moscow, izd-vo Iurlitinform, 2008. 312 p. 2000 ptd.

Pechuro, E. E. (comp.). Заступница. Адвокат С. В. Каллистратова (1907-1989) [Protectress. Advokat S. V. Kallistratova (1907-1989)]. M., Zvenia, 1997. 352 p. 2000 ptd.

Petrukhin, I. L. (ed.). Проблемы Российской адвокатуры. Сборник статей [Problems of the Russian Advokatura: Collected Articles]. M., izd-vo Spark, 1997. 251 p. 2000 ptd.

Articles and institutional comments on draft reform legislation.

Pilipenko, G. L. (comp.). Адвокатура [Advokatura]. M., ZAO "Biznes-shkola 'Intel-Sintez'", 1998. 208 p. 3000 ptd.

Pitulko, K., Koriakovtsev, V. Постатейный Комментарий к федеральному закону Об Адвокатсктй деятельности и адвокатуре в Российской Федерации [Article-by-Article Commentary on Federal Law on Advokat Activity and the Advokatura in the Russian Federation]. Spb., Piter, 2002. 304 p. 5000 ptd.

Pitulko, K., Koriakovtsev, V. Постатейный Комментарий к федеральному закону Об Адвокатсктй деятельности и адвокатуре в Российской Федерации [Article-by-Article Commentary on Federal Law on Advokat Activity and the Advokatura in the Russian Federation]. Spb., Piter, 2003. 320 p. 5000 ptd.

In fact a revised edition of the 2002 version, but not designated as such.

Poliakov, A. V. (comp.). Адвокат-воин: Принципы и техника уголовной защиты [Advokat-Warrior: Principles and Technique of Criminal Defense]. M., Statut, 2007. 447 p. 1000 ptd.

Reissue of L. E. Vladimirov, Advocatus Miles: Пособие для уголовной защиты (1911).

Pospelov, O. V. Формы адвокатских образований в России [Forms of Advokat Formations in Russia]. M., Rossiiskaia Akademiia advokatury', 2008.

Postovalova, T. A. Адвокатское право [Advokat Law]. Minsk, Tesei, 2009. 604 p. 300 ptd.

Potapchuk, I. V. (comp.). С. А. Андреевский: Избранные труды и речи [S. A. Andreevskii: Selected Works and Speeches]. Tula, Izdatel'skii dom Avtograf, 2000. 424 p. 5000 ptd.

___. С. Л. Ария. Жизнь адвоката [Semen Lvovich Aria. Life of an Advokat]. 2d ed.; Tula, Izdatel'skii dom Avtograf, 2004. 464 p.

___. К. К. Арсеньев: Заметки о русской адвокатуре [K. K. Arsenev: Notes on the Russian Advokatura]. Tula, Izdatel'skii dom Avtograf, 2001. 560 p. 5000 ptd.

___. Н. П. Карабчевский: Около правосудия: Статьи, речи, очерки [N. P. Karabchevckii: About Justice: Articles, Speeches, Essays]. Tula, Izdatel'skii dom Avtograf, 2001. 672 p. 5000 ptd.

___. А. Ф. Кони: Избранные труды и речи [A. F. Koni: Selected Works and Speeches]. Tula, Izdatel'skii dom Avtograf, 2000. 640 p. 5000 ptd.

___. Ф. П. Плевако: Избранные речи [F. P. Plevako: Selected Speeches]. Tula, Izdatel'skii dom Avtograf, 2000. 368 p. 5000 ptd.

___. В. Д. Спасович: Избранные труды и речи [V. D. Spasovich: Selected Works and Speeches]. Tula, Izdatel'skii dom Avtograf, 2000. 496 p. 5000 ptd.

___. А. И. Урусов: Первосоздатель русской судебной защиты [A. I. Urusov: Creator of Russian Judicial Defense]. Tula, Izdatel'skii dom Avtograf, 2001. 352 p. 5000 ptd.

Potapenko, A. (ed.). Вся юридическая Москва: справочник [All Legal Moscow 2004/2005: Manual]. M., Prospekt, 2004. 344 p.

Puginskii, B. I., Neverov, O. G. Правовая работа [Legal Work]. M., Zertsalo-M, 2004. 168 p. 3000 ptd.

Radutnaia, N. V. (ed.). Защитник в суде присяжных [Defender before Jurors]. M., 1997. 152 p. 3000 ptd. (Russian Legal Academy)

Rozhkinov, L. (ed.). Вся юридическая Москва. 2010. Справочник [All of Legal Moscow. 2010. Manual]. M., Prospekt, 244 p. 10,000 ptd.

Issue 6 of this manual, which appears from time to time and consists almost entirely of advertisements of legal services and contact information. Organized by a myriad of subject categories. Information valid as of August 2010.

Semeniako, E. «Нравственные начала профессии» [Moral Principles of the Profession], *Российская юстиция* [Russian Justice], no. 10 (2003), pp. 69-76.

Appends the Code of Professional Ethics of an Advocate.

___, **Pilipenko, Iu. S.** (eds.). Адвокатская деятельность и адвокатура: Сборник нормативных актов и документов [Advokat Activity and the Advokatura: Collection of Normative Acts and Documents] 2d ed.; M., 2010. 648 p. 2000 ptd. (Federal Chamber of Advokats of Russian Federation)

Sergeev, V. I. *Адвокатура в России. Учебник* [The Advokatura in Russia: Textbook]. M. Iustitsinform, 2004. 576 p.

___. Комментарий к положению об адвокатуре [Commentary to the Statute on the Advokatura]. M., Iuridicheskii dom "Iustitsinform", 2001. 112 p. 1000 ptd.

Shablinskii, I. G. (ed. & comp.). Юридический бизнес в России [Legal Business in Russia]. M., Alpina Biznes Buks, 2006. 102 p. 2500 ptd.

Collected articles based on materials of First Legal Forum in Moscow, 20 April 2005.

Shalamov, M. P. История советской адвокатуры [History of the Soviet Advokatura]. M., Iurizdat, 1939.

Shamba, T. M., Kokin, V. N. Адвокатура в Российской Федерации [Advokatura in the Russian Federation] (3d ed.; M., izd-vo Norma, 2010). 480 p. 1500 ptd.

Shapiro, Isaac, "The Soviet Bar – Past and Present", *Russian Review*, XX (1961), pp. 143-150.

Shelley, Louise I. *Lawyers in Soviet Work Life.* New Brunswick, New Jersey, Rutgers University Press, 1984. xii, 175 p.

Sklovskii, K. I. Работа адвоката по обоснованию и оспариванию добросовестности в гражданских спорах [Work of Advokat With Regard to Substantiating and Contesting Good Faith in Civil Disputes]. 2d ed.; M., LeksEst, 2004. 64 p. 3000 ptd.

Smirnov, V. N., Smykalin, A. S. Адвокатура и адвокатская деятельность: учебное пособие [Advokatura and Advokat Activity: Instructional Manual]. M., Prospekt; Ekaterinburg: Izdatel'skii dom "Uralskaia gosudarstvennaia iuridicheskaia akademiia", 2010. 320 p. 700 ptd.

Smirnova, E. M. Адвокатура: учебное пособие [Advokatura: Instructional Manual]. Spb., izd-vo Mikhailova. V. A., 2002. 267 p. 5000 ptd.

Smolenskii, M. B. Адвокатская деятельность и адвокатура в Российской Федерации [Advokat Activity and the Advokatura in the Russian Federation]. Rostov-on-Don, "Feniks", 2002. 416 p. 5000 ptd.

___. Адвокатская деятельность в России [Advokat Activity in Russia]. M., IKTs "MarT"; Rostov on Don, Izdatel'skii tsentr "MarT", 2004. 448 p. 5000 ptd.

___. Адвокатура в Российской Федерации [The Advokatura in the Russian Federation]. Spb., Iuridicheskii tsentr, 2003. 446 p. 1550 ptd.

___. Адвокатура в Российской Федерации. 100 экзаменационных ответов [The Advokatura in the Russian Federation: 100 Examination Answers]. 2d ed.; M. -Rostov-on-Don, Izdatel'skii tsentr "MarT", 2003. 288 p. 5000 ptd.

___. (ed.). Адвокатура в России [The Advokatura in Russia]. M., Knorus, 2011. 312 p. 2000 ptd.

Sotov, P. V., Kamenetskii, R. A. Адвокатура и нотариат [Advokatura and the Notariat]. M., Prospekt, 1999. 400 p. 10,000 ptd.

Stetsovskii, Iu. I. Советская адвокатура [Soviet Advokatura]. M., Vysshaia shkola, 1989. 304 p. 50,000 ptd.

Stoianov, A. N. (1830-1907). История адвокатуры [History of the Advokatura]. Kharkov, 1869.

Sukharev, A. Ia. Роль и задачи советской адвокатуры [Role and Tasks of the Soviet Advokatura]. M., Iuridicheskaia literature, 1972. 220 p. 10,000 ptd.

Thorpe, K. M. "Further Control of Lawyer's Fees in Soviet Russia", *American Bar Association Journal*, XXII (1936), pp. 67-69.

___. "Remuneration of the Lawyer in Soviet Russia", *American Bar Association Journal*, XXI (1935), pp. 60-61.

Tikhonravov, Iu. V. (ed.). Правила адвокатской профессии в России: Опыт систематизации постановлений Советов присяжных поверенных по вопросам профессиальной этики [Rules of the Advokat Profession in Russia: Attempt to Systematize Decrees of Councils of Sworn Attorneys with Regard to Professional Ethics]. M., Statut, 2003. 384 p. 2000 ptd.

Reissue in modern Russian script of a work published by A. N. Markov in 1913 at Moscow.

Troitskii, N. A. Адвокатура в России и политические процессы 1866-1904 гг. [Advokatura in Russia and Political Trials, 1866-1904]. Tula, Avtograf, 2000. 456 p. 5000 ptd.

___. Корифеи Российской адвокатуры [Leading Lights of the Russian Advokatura]. M., Tsentropoligraf, 2006. 415 p. 3000 ptd.

Trunov. I. L. (ed.), Адвокатская деятельность и адвокатура в России [Advokat Activity and the Advokatura in Russia]. M., Eksmo Education, 2006. 560 p. 3000 ptd. (Part 1).

___. (ed.). Энциклопедия будущего адвоката [Encyclopedia of a Future Advokat]. M., Wolters Kluwer, 2006. 1344 p. 3000 ptd.

Reviewed: *Sudebnik*, XI (2006), pp. 151-152 (W. E. Butler).

___. (ed.), Комментарий к федеральному закону «Об адвокатской деятельности и адвокатуре в Российской Федерации» (с приложениями) [Commentary on Federal Law "On Advokat Activity and the Advokatura in the Russian Federation]. M., Iurist, 2003. 409 p. 3000 ptd.

___ (ed.). Комментарий к федеральному закону «Об адвокатской деятельности и адвокатуре в Российской Федерации» (с приложениями) [Commentary on Federal Law "On Advokat Activity and the Advokatura in the Russian Federation]. M., izd-vo Eksmo, 2005. 480 p. 3000 ptd.

___ (ed.). Настольная книга будущего адвоката: Пособие для подготовки к квалификационному экзамену на присвоение статуса адвоката [Manuel of a Future Advokat: Aid for Preparing for the Qualifications Examination for Conferment of the Status of Advokat]. M., ID Iurisprudentsiia, 2005. 576 p. 3000 ptd.

Tsukov, E. A. Философские аспекты правозащитной деятельности в истории государства Российского [Philosophical Aspects of Legal Defense Activity in the History of the Russian State]. M., Novaia iustitsiia, 2008. 288 p. 1000 ptd.

Vaskovskii, E. V. Будущее русской адвокатуры. К вопросу о предстоящей реформе [The Future of the Russian Advokatura: On the Question of the Forthcoming Reform]. M., 2000. 32 p. 1000 ptd. Reprint of an essay first published in 1893.

Vinaver, M. (1863-1926). Очерки об адвокатуре [Essays on the Advokatura]. Spb., n.p., 1902. 218 p.

Vlasov, A. A. Адвокат как субъект доказывания в гражданском и арбитражном процессе [Advokat as Subject of Proof in Civil and Arbitrazh Procedure]. M., izd-vo Iurlitinform, 2000. 240 p. 5000 ptd.

___. Дедятельность адвоката в суде по делам о защите чести, достоинства и деловой репутации [Activity of Advokat in Court with Regard to Cases on Defense of Honor, Dignity, and Business Reputation] M., Iurist, 2006. 207 p. 2000 ptd.

___., **Isaenkova, O. V.** (eds.). Адвокатура в России [Advokatura in Russia]. Moscow, Zakon i pravo, 2008. 303 p. 1000 ptd.

Volkomirskii, L. E. За советом к адвокату: Записки юриста [To an Advokat for Advice: Notes of a Jurist]. M., Delo, 1997. 208 p. 10,000 ptd.

Vorobev, A. V., Poliakov, A. V., Tikhonravov, Iu. V., Теория адвокатуры [Theory of the Advokatura]. M., Grant, 2002. 496 p.

Voskobitova, L. A., Lukianova, I. N., Mikhailova, L. P. (eds.). Адвокат: навыки профессионального мастерства [Advokat: Skills of Professional Mastery]. M., Wolters Kluwer, 2006. 592 p. 8000 ptd.

___, **Mikhailova, L. P., Shugrina** (eds.). Профессиональные навыки юриста: Опыт практического обучения [Professional Skills of a Jurist: Experience of Practical Training]. M., Delo, 2001. 416 p. 5000 ptd.

Wortman, R. S. (d. 2010) *The Development of a Russian Legal Consciousness.* Chicago, University of Chicago Press, 1976. xi, 345 p.

Zaitsev, Ia., Poltorak, A. *The Soviet Bar.* M., Foreign Languages Publishing House, 1959. 255 p.

Zhalinskii, A. E. Профессиональная деятельность юриста [Professional Activity of the Jurist: Introduction to a Specialty]. M., izd-vo BEK, 1997. 322, vi p. 10,000 ptd.

Zhilina, E. A. Юридическая служба предприятия: создание и управление [Legal Service of an Enterprise: Creation and Management]. M., Knorus, 2010. 168 p. 2000 ptd.

Index

A

Aizin, S. M. 255, 293
Aleksandrov, P. A. 36
Alekseev, G. 27
Aleksei Mikhailovich, Tsar 33
Alexander I, Emperor 26, 34, 254
Andreevskii, S. A. 36, 298
Anufriev, V. M. 50, 293
Aria, S. L. 293, 298
Arkhipov, V. V. 186
Arsenev, K. K. 36, 76, 293, 298

B

Baburin, S. N. 293
Balugianskii, M. A. 35
Baranov, D. P. 41, 114, 293
Barry, D. D. 47, 57, 252, 293
Barshchevskii, M. Iu. 37, 49, 106, 293
Bashkevich, I. M. 296
Belykh, A. P. 148, 166
Bentham, J. 34
Berman, H. J. 33, 47, 57, 293
Blackstone, W. 34
Bogatova, G. A. 28
Boikov, A. D. 294
Borodin, D. N. 294
Braginskii, M. I. 178
Brui, A. V. 294
Burnham, W. 76, 294
Burobin, V. N. 294
Burrage, M. 41
Butler, W. E. 33, 34, 53-55, 57, 59-61, 67, 68, 77, 81, 82, 84, 86, 87, 91, 92, 97, 98, 109, 116, 117, 119, 145, 147, 152, 158, 167, 179, 192, 221, 248, 254, 266, 294, 300

C

Catherine II, Empress of Russia, 30, 34
Chashin, A. N. 251, 294
Cherkasova, N. V. 36, 294
Chernenko, G. I. 294
Chistiakov, O. I. 27, 29
Collignon, Jean-Guy 294
Constantine, Emperor 26

D

Danilenko, G. M. 294
Dekhanov, S. A. 294
Demidova, L. A. 167, 294
Desnitskii, S. E. 29, 34
Devlikamov, A. A. 294
Dewey, H. W. 27
Dukes, P. 30

E

Eriashvili, N. D. 95, 192, 297

F

Fedotova, T. A. 295
Feldbrugge, F. J. M. 238
Fishman, L. 107
Foinitskii, I. Ia. 297
Friedman, L. M. 47, 295

G

Galoganov, A. P. 37, 50, 190, 241, 295
Garmaev, Iu. P. 295
Gavrilov, A. M. 109
Gavrilov, S. A. 297

Gavrilov, S. N. 50, 293, 295
Gernet, M. 36, 40
Gessen, I. V. 36, 295
Giddings, J. 254
Ginzburg, G. A. 295
Gliskov, A. G. 293
Gofshtein, M. 49
Goldman, A. L. 108
Goshuliak, V. V. 295
Griffiths, D. 30
Grinenko, A. V. 65, 68, 70, 76, 78, 80, 87, 166, 196, 233, 245, 295
Gruzenberg, O. O. 295
Gudavicius, E. 31
Guliaev, A. P. 295
Gutsenko, K. F. 47, 295

H

Harris, Richard 295, 297
Henderson, J.: see Giddings, J.
Hazard, J. N. 43, 295
Hellie, R. 26
Huskey, E. 36, 38, 39, 41, 43, 44, 238, 295

I

Iartykh, I. S. 48, 296
Isaenkova, O. V. 301
Iudushkin, S. M. 295
Ivanov, S. N. 118
Ivanov, V. 296

J

Jordan, Pamela 296

K

Kachalov, B. I. 296
Kachalov, V. I. 296
Kachalova, O. V. 296
Kaiser, D. H. 26
Kalitvin, V. V. 241
Kamenetskii, R. A. 300
Kaminskaya, Dina 296
Kapinus, N. I. 294
Karabchevskii, N. P. 36, 298
Keizerov, N. M. 297
Khrushchev, N. S. 47, 253
Kichikhin, A. N. 293, 296
Klen, N. N. 46, 296
Klevtsov, A. V. 25, 296
Koblikov, A. S. 296
Kogan, M. I. 296
Kokin, V. N. 25, 299
Koni, A. F. 36, 299
Konina, E. N. 296
Koriakovtsev, V. V. 137, 143, 298
Kostanov, A. 196
Kozak, D. N. 49, 74, 296
Kozhevnikov, M. V. 44, 296
Kratenko, M. V. 178, 296
Kravchenko, A. A. 296
Krompen, E. F. 29
Kruglov, A. A. 297
Krysko, V. B. 28
Kucherena, A. G. 28, 29, 31, 47, 258, 260, 297
Kucherov, S. A. 36, 297
Kudriavtsev, V. L. 297
Kuznetsov, N. 31

L

Lazutka, S. 31
Lebedev, K. K. 257, 297
Lenin, V. I. 41, 42
Loewe, Karl von 30
Lubshev, Iu. F. 50, 297
Lukianova, I. N. 301
Lupinskaia, P. A. 297
Luryi, Yu. 252, 293

M

Maggs, P. B. 294
Makalinskii, P. V. 297
Makarov, O. V. 76
Mankov, A. G. 29
Markov, A. N. 300
Martemianov, V. S. 147
Masleev, A. G. 139, 297
Maslov, V. I. 93
Mikhailova, L. P. 301
Millar, J. 34

Mirzoev, G. B. 95, 192, 297
Molotov, V. M. 43
Munro, G. E. 30
Muranov, A. I. 264, 266, 297

N

Napoleon, Emperor 34
Neverov, O. G. 254, 299
Nicholas I, Emperor 34, 254
Norros, Merja 74, 298

P

Palkhovskii, A. M. 76
Parshutkin, V. V. 108
Pashukanis, E. B. 44
Passover, A. I. 36
Pecherskii, V. V. 298
Pechuro, E. E. 298
Permiakov, A. N. 296
Peter the Great, Tsar 29, 30, 33
Petrukhin, I. L. 298
Phillipson, N. 34
Pilipenko, G. L. 90, 95, 96, 101, 102, 104-106, 111, 136, 164, 181, 185, 293, 298
Pilipenko, Iu. S. 299
Pitulko, K. V. 137, 143, 298
Plevako, F. N. 36, 299
Poe, M. T. 28
Poliak, A. G. 295
Poliakov, A. V. 29, 298, 301
Poltorak, A. 301
Porokhovshchikov, P. S. 295
Pospelov, O. V. 147, 298
Postovalova, T. A. 298
Potapchuk, I. V. 36, 298
Potapenko, A. 299
Pripuzova, A. Iu. 172
Prishliakov, A. D. 76
Puginskii, B. I. 254, 299
Pushkarev, S. G. 28

Q

Quigley, J. B. 47

R

Radutnaia, N. V. 299
Reshetnikova, I. V. 76
Rivkin, K. E. 295
Rozhnikov, L. 299

S

Samsonov, V. A. 295
Saraikina, O. V. 295
Savigny, F. C. von, 34
Semeniako, E. V. 55, 90, 95, 96, 101, 102, 104-106, 111, 136, 164, 181, 185, 241, 293, 299
Sergeev, V. I. 48, 167, 294, 299
Shablinskii, I. G. 299
Shalamov, M. P. 299
Shamba, T. M. 25, 299
Shapiro, Isaac 299
Sharlet, R. 238
Shelkoplias, V. A. 31
Shelley, L. I. 299
Shugrina 301
Sklovskii, K. I. 299
Smirnov, V. N. 300
Smirnova, E. M. 300
Smith, Adam 34
Smolenskii, M. B. 41, 293, 300
Smykalin, A. S. 300
Sorokin, Iu. G. 241
Sorokin, Iu. S. 28
Sotov, P. V. 300
Spasovich, V. D. 36, 299
Speranskii, M. I. 34, 35
Stalin, I. V. 44-46, 252
Stasov, D. V. 36
Stein, P. 29
Stetsovskii, I. Iu. 175, 300
Stoianov, A. N. 300
Sukharev, A. Ia. 300

T

Tarlo, E. G. 294
Terebilov, V. I. 47
Thorpe, K. M. 300
Tikhomirov, Iu. V. 29, 255
Tikhomirov, M. Iu. 255, 293

Tikhonravov, Iu. V. 25, 300, 301
Tomsinov, V. A. 29, 34
Totev, K. Iu. 148
Tretiakov, Ivan 34
Troitskii, N. A. 300
Tronchin, Th. 34
Truman, Harry S. 45
Trunov, I. L. 108, 114, 123, 148, 166, 190, 300
Tsukov, E. A. 301

U

Urusov, A. I. 36, 299

V

Valikonyte, I. 31
Vaskovskii, E. V. 36, 301
Vinaver, M. 297, 301
Vitrianskii, V. V. 178
Vladimirov, L. E. 298
Vladimirskii-Budanov, M. F. 27
Vlasov, A. A. 76, 301
Volkomirskii, L. E. 301
Voltaire, F. M. A. de 34
Vorobev, A. V. 25, 29, 301
Voskobitova, L. A. 301
Vyshinskii, A. Ia. 107

W

Wortman, R. S. 33-36, 301

Z

Zabeivorota, A. I. 293
Zaitsev, Ia. 301
Zhalinskii, A. E. 301
Zhdanovich, A. F. 296
Zhilina, E. A. 301
Zhilinskii, A. E. 255
Zile, Z. L. 47, 295